CW00373719

JOHN HARRISON.

From a mezzotint by Tassaert, published in 1768, after a painting by King. A copy of this painting is exhibited in the Science Museum, South Kensington. The machine behind Harrison is his No. 3 (drawn much too large), and that at his right hand No. 4.

THE MARINE CHRONOMETER

ITS HISTORY AND DEVELOPMENT.

LT.-COMMANDER RUPERT T. GOULD, R.N. (*retired*), F.R.G.S.,
Member of the British Horological Institute.

WITH A FOREWORD BY

SIR FRANK W. DYSON, LL.D., F.R.S.,
Astronomer Royal.

Antique Collectors' Club

© 1989 Antique Collectors' Club
World copyright reserved

ISBN 0 907462 05 7

All rights reserved. No part of this publication may be reproduced, stored in a retrieval system or transmitted in any form or by any means electronic, mechanical, photocopying, recording or otherwise, without the prior permission of the publisher.

British Library CIP Data
Gould, Rupert
1. Marine Chronometers
I. Title
681.1ª13

Front Cover: Thomas Mudge. Marine Timekeeper No. 1.

Printed in England by
the Antique Collectors' Club Ltd.
Woodbridge, Suffolk

To

Admiral of the Fleet

EARL BEATTY, G.C.B., O.M.,

under whom it was once my privilege to serve.

Publisher's Preface

To write a standard work of reference on a technical subject and make it readable is a considerable task achieved by only a handful of horological authors. Perhaps it was a happy mixture of skills which made this possible for Commander Gould spent part of his life at sea as a marine navigator and experienced the heavy responsibility that the job entails. He was too a skilled horologist who knew in detail how the delicate instruments worked and could repair them, but above all he was a great communicator with the gift of writing informal but exact English.

The result is therefore an excellent account of the prolonged struggle towards accurate timekeeping at sea and Commander Gould preserves a happy balance between the people and the object. No wonder that the sixty five years since the book was written nobody has attempted to better it.

We have augmented and improved the number of photographs where possible but nothing of the original has been disturbed.

FOREWORD

by

SIR FRANK WATSON DYSON, LL.D., F.R.S.

ASTRONOMER ROYAL.

Everybody who has made a sea voyage knows the interest taken by the passengers in the posting of the daily latitude and longitude of the vessel. They know that these are the results of some mysterious operations performed by the navigator, involving, probably, an " observation " of the Sun. If they are curious, they learn that he uses two small instruments, called a " sextant " and a " chronometer," and also a book entitled " The Nautical Almanac " : further, that with this apparently scanty equipment he is able, generally, to determine the position of his ship within a mile or two. But it is improbable, unless they have devoted their attention to the subject, that they realise what an amount of thought and skill has been spent, by many men and in many different ways, in devising and improving these three essential instruments of navigation.

In order to fix the position of a ship at sea, when out of sight of land, two problems of very unequal difficulty have to be solved—the determination of her latitude, and her longitude. The former is comparatively easy; the latter by no means so.

Both depend upon astronomical observations, and it follows that every navigator who fixes his ship's position is, in a sense, an astronomer, and in the direct line of descent from Ptolemy and Tycho Brahé. But the observations which can be made from a ship at sea are, necessarily, of quite a different standard of accuracy from those which can be made in observatories on shore, and so it comes about that the navigator afloat depends, for fundamental groundwork of his determination of position, upon tables motions of the Sun, and other heavenly bodies, which have been predicted as the result of observations and calculations made on shore.

There is thus a very direct and practical connection between the work of the various public observatories and the needs of navigation, and this connection has long been recognised. Greenwich Observatory was founded for the express purpose of furnishing the information needed by navigators, and principally (as the warrant appointing the first Astronomer Royal, John Flamsteed, puts it) " . . . to find out the so-much desired longitude . . . for perfecting the art of navigation."

A ship's latitude can readily be found by means of an observation taken with the sextant, an instrument for measuring angles which has the valuable property of being very little affected by an amount of motion which would render telescopic observations quite impracticable. All that is required is that positions of the Sun or stars should be tabulated beforehand, and compared with those obtained by observation. Such was the method employed in the time of Columbus, and such (with, of course, improvements in detail) is the method employed to-day.

But the determination of longitude is much more difficult, and, as explained by Lieut.-Commander Gould in his Introduction, its solution proved a hard and laborious task. Briefly, two methods ultimately emerged from the chaos of experiments and suggestions—that of lunar distances, and that of employing a chronometer.

Both are intimately connected with the history of Greenwich Observatory. As already related, it was founded (in 1675) to obtain data for the construction of tables predicting the motion of the heavenly bodies, especially the Moon, and it has continued at the task for nearly two hundred and fifty years. It has also conducted and supervised trials of chronometers for upwards of a century and a half.

The problem of making an Almanac of the Moon's position is most difficult, as may be seen from the fact that, in spite of the attention devoted to the Lunar Theory by some of the world's greatest mathematicians, it was not until 1767 that the "Nautical Almanac" was able to give predictions of the Moon's place in the heavens with sufficient accuracy for them to be of use for purposes of navigation. From that time to the present day, distinguished mathematicians of England, France, Germany, and America have given large portions of their lives to the Lunar Theory. More arithmetic and algebra have been devoted to it than to any other question of astronomy or mathematical physics. But, in the end, the problem has been solved so that observed positions agree very nearly with those predicted. Unfortunately, even with perfect tables, it is found that the most skilful navigator cannot obtain a very accurate position of his ship in this manner. With great pains and somewhat elaborate calculation he can be correct to within twenty miles.

The alternative solution requires the construction of a time-measuring instrument which, during a voyage of weeks or months, subject not only to rolling and pitching but also to considerable variations of temperature, can be relied upon to furnish Greenwich Time with the necessary precision. How this beautiful and very difficult mechanical problem was solved almost simultaneously by Harrison in England and Le Roy in France, and how the latter's solution was further developed by Berthoud, Arnold, Earnshaw, and other craftsmen of genius, is told by Lieut.-Commander Gould in the following pages. It is a story of genius and hope and patient industry.

The author has many qualifications for the task he has undertaken. Being a navigator, he appreciates to what a great extent the sailor is dependent upon the chronometer—although most navigators, very properly, are content to see that their timekeepers are carefully handled and regularly wound, and do not concern themselves very much with their construction. Lieut.-Commander Gould, however, delights to examine finely constructed mechanism. A thorough technical knowledge of the subject is combined with a real gift for handling the small parts of a delicate instrument. This he has demonstrated at Greenwich during the preparation of his book. Examination of Harrison's machines, which are preserved at the Observatory, led him voluntarily to undertake to clean the first and fourth machines, and re-assemble them in a condition worthy of works of such historical value. Moreover, he restored the fourth machine (the famous timekeeper which won the Government reward of £20,000, and whose mechanism had for some time past been deranged) to going order.

Lieut.-Commander Gould's practical skill is happily associated with the zeal of the antiquary. He has made an exhaustive search of all books and available documents bearing on the history and development of the chronometer, and the result is a book which, while of high technical value, is written in a very interesting manner, and contains an account of many incidents which help to form a true picture of the lives of the great artists and craftsmen whose inventions it chronicles.

F. W. DYSON.

Royal Observatory, Greenwich.

October, 1922.

PREFACE.

There is, I believe, an Arab saying, which runs—

> "Because I have been athirst, I have dug a well, that others may drink."

It is for a similar reason that I have ventured into print. Had there been any standard work of reference which I could have consulted in respect to various points in the chronometer's history, I am quite certain that this book would have remained unwritten.

As far as I am aware, it is the first of its kind. Shadwell's "Notes on the management of Chronometers," and Caspari's "Les Montres Marines," the latter out of print, deal chiefly with the determination of rates and the adjustment of their errors, not with the history of the machine and its makers; while Berthoud's various works on the subject, written long before, relate, like his nephew's similar treatise, exclusively to his own labours. Apart from these works, information is only to be found piecemeal, scattered amongst books on horology and the pages of technical journals.

Any book of the kind must of necessity be, to large extent, a compilation. I have, however, done my best to take no statement on trust that I could possibly verify, and to work, as far as possible, from original documents.

With regard to the latter, I have been most fortunate in receiving, through the very great kindness of the Astronomer-Royal, permission to refer constantly to the unpublished papers and minutes of the Board of Longitude, amounting in all to twenty-nine folio volumes, which contain an enormous amount of information relating to the early history of the modern chronometer. I have also been permitted to ransack the archives of the Observatory to my heart's content in search of material. Furthermore, Sir Frank Dyson has also given me access to documents of another kind—the timekeepers by Harrison, and other old makers, preserved in the Observatory. It is impossible for me to exaggerate the extent to which my study of Harrison's work, in particular, has been facilitated by being permitted to have his first and fourth timekeepers, temporarily, in my own hands for the purpose of cleaning and examining them.

I have tried to give references, in the footnotes, to at least the more important printed sources from which I have obtained information. But special mention should be made of one or two books which I have found particularly useful.

First amongst them I must place the late F. J. Britten's wonderful "Old Clocks and Watches and their Makers." It is, in a sense, the parent of this book, for my interest in marine timekeepers first awoke when I encountered a drawing of Mudge's remontoire while turning over the pages of my uncle's copy, some twenty years ago. Although the subject of the chronometer is only a side-issue in his book, which covers many other branches of horology, Britten gives, in about twenty pages, a rapid and remarkably accurate history of the machine and its makers, which serves admirably as a first introduction to the subject, while the miscellaneous information collected in his list of old makers is extremely varied and valuable.

Dr. Pearson's article " Chronometer " in Rees' " Cyclopædia," although it may be thought out of date, is still a masterpiece of its kind, and contains an enormous amount of information not readily found elsewhere. Together with Berthoud's " Histoire de la mesure de Temps," and M. Gros' learned and excellent treatise " Echappements d'Horloges et de Montres," it has rarely been far from my elbow.

As regards horological literature in general, I have done my best to make full use of the stores available in the Guildhall, Patent Office, Science Museum, and British Museum Libraries. I have also been fortunate in obtaining permission to consult the unique collection of horological works bequeathed by B. L. Vulliamy to the Institute of Civil Engineers, and in being granted the loan of various rare books and MSS. by Dr. George Williamson, Mr. A. E. Rutherford, Mr. Robert Gardner, and Mr. J. F. Hobson. To Dr. Williamson, in particular, I am indebted for permission to quote one or two items of information from his catalogue of the Pierpont Morgan collection of watches. I have also found much matter of interest in the files of the " Horological Journal," the " Journal Suisse d'Horlogerie," " L'Horloger," and the " Deutsche Uhrmachers Zeitung."

As originally planned, this book was to have contained a bibliography of its subject, but this was afterwards omitted as of insufficient general interest. It may find a place in a second edition, if one is ever required. I should be much obliged, in the meantime, by any information, sent c/o my publisher, which might be of use for a revised edition, and I can at least promise that it shall not be altogether wasted, since it will eventually be left, together with all my notes, MSS., etc., to the Library of the Clockmakers Company, so that those who come later may, if they wish, be spared the trouble of repeating my spade-work.

On the personal side, my thanks are due first and foremost to Admiral F. C. Learmonth, R.N., Hydrographer of the Navy, for the encouragement which he has given me during the three years which the writing of this book has occupied, and to Sir Frank Dyson, who has added to his other kindnesses that of contributing the Foreword. Secondly, to Mr. William Bowyer, head of the Time Department at Greenwich, who has, on all occasions, done everything in his power to assist me. Thirdly, to a whole host of other friends who have all, in one way or another, given me valuable help. I am especially indebted to Miss A. M. Britten, Lieut.-Commander A. C. Bell, R.N., Mons. L. Desoutter, Mons. P. Ditisheim, Capt. H. P. Douglas, R.N., Mons. A. L. Fraissard, Mr. A. F. G. Leveson-Gower, Mr. S. E. Litchfield, Mr. H. Otto, Mr. G. L. Overton, Admiral Sir J. F. Parry, R.N., Sir David Salomons, Mr. C. Welch, Mr. T. D. Wright, and to many others, who will, I hope, accept this general, but none the less grateful acknowledgment. Also to the following bodies: the Royal Society, Royal Geographical Society, Royal Astronomical Society, Royal United Services Institution, Institute of Civil Engineers, Clockmakers Company, and the Board of Education, who have all very kindly granted me facilities of various kinds.

In the course of compiling the book, I sent a circular to twenty-four chronometer makers, stating its aims, and enquiring whether they could see their way to assisting me by communicating any information from the private records of their firms. I was fortunate enough to receive acknowledgments from eleven, and useful information from eight—Messrs. Ditisheim, Frodsham, Gardner, Kullberg, Le Roy, Mercer, Nardin and Poole. To all of them, I wish to express my appreciation of their kindness and courtesy.

With regard to the illustrations, the Plates, with the exception of those specified below are from photographs taken by Miss Dorothy Cayley, of the Admiralty Photographic Section. Those from which Plates IV., V., XXI., XXII., XXIII., XXIV., and XXV. have been made were taken in Paris by M. Gabriel Gorce ; while Plates XI., XII., and XXXVI. are from photographs by M. Réné Desoutter. To all these artists I tender my most grateful thanks for the pains which they have taken in producing the best feature of the book. I am also indebted to the Council of the Royal Society for permission to reproduce Plate XXVII.; to Messrs. John Murray for similar permission with regard to Plate XV., which originally appeared in the late Arthur Kitson's " Life of Captain Cook " ; and to the Comptroller of H.M. Stationery Office for leave to reproduce figs. 83 and 84, which were originally drawn for the " Admiralty Manual of Navigation."

For these, and for the other figures, I am responsible, and perhaps I may be allowed to disarm criticism, to a certain extent, by pointing out that no attempt has been made to draw them with absolute accuracy, since they are designed to convey ideas, and not to enable a workman to construct the pieces of mechanism which they illustrate. On the other hand, I have tried to make them as correct as I could, and while they differ considerably, in some cases, from the representations given in other horological works, it will, I think, be found in most cases that the latter are inaccurate. For example, the generally-accepted drawing of Harrison's " grasshopper " escapement, which originally, I believe, appeared in Rees' " Cyclopædia " (1819), and has since done yeoman service, requires a pendulum-arc of about 25° to escape.

I owe a final word of acknowledgment to the Hon. Horace Woodhouse, who has very kindly read the whole of the revised proofs, and, last but not least, to my publisher, Mr. J. D. Potter, but for whose friendly enterprise this book, I am much afraid, would have remained unpublished.

As to my own part in it, perhaps the less said the better. This at least I can truthfully avow, that its writing has been a labour of love, and that I have never spent time more pleasantly. For the rest, I can only say, with Benserade :

" Pour moi, parmi des fautes innombrables,
Je n'en connais que deux considérables,
Et dont je fais ma déclaration.
C'est l'entreprise et l'exécution ;
A mon avis fautes irréparables
Dans ce volume."

RUPERT T. GOULD.

Epsom, December, 1922.

CONTENTS.

LIST OF PLATES.

LIST OF FIGURES.

LIST OF FIGURES—*continued.*

LIST OF FIGURES—*continued.*

INTRODUCTION.

THE PROBLEM OF FINDING LONGITUDE AT SEA.

Will the reader be good enough to imagine, for a few minutes, that he is Christopher Columbus?

It is the evening of Monday, February the 11th, 1493, and from the deck of the little "Nina" there is nothing to be seen but the "Pinta" labouring some distance astern, and the darkening rim of the sea horizon which surrounds them. Far behind them lies the new world of his discovery, and ahead is the old world, to which he is now returning. The ships are running bravely before a strong westerly breeze, and at intervals clouds of sea-birds sweep by, heralding the great gale that will burst upon him to-morrow.

As the sky fades and the stars come out, he turns his mind once more to the familiar and yet baffling task of determining the position of his little fleet. With his cross-staff he takes the altitude of the pole star, and, after some computation, obtains his latitude. Rough though this observation is, he can hope for no better, and it agrees tolerably well with his noon observation of the sun.

But in what longitude? Ah, that is beyond even his skill to determine—beyond the skill of any living man. He can do no more than guess at it, as he has guessed ever since they left Madeira some six months earlier, steering into the unknown West. True, he has been able to inspire his men with the belief that he can keep an exact reckoning of his ship's course and the distance she traverses, and also determine the amount to which these are affected by currents—but this belief is due to a pious fraud, prepared, like the falsified reckonings of the outward voyage, for their encouragement, and in sober truth he is as helpless as any of them. He knows his ship's course, roughly, and he can guess at her speed—so can they. And accordingly, as to their longitude, there is much difference of opinion. The admiral thinks that they are south of the Azores. Vincenti Pinzon, his second in command, and others of experience, consider that they have already passed these, and are approaching Madeira—600 miles further eastward! And meanwhile night has covered them, and the ships are running on blindly to meet their fate, not knowing whether the land is a hundred miles away or close at hand.

Next day comes the great storm, and all, even the Admiral himself, abandon hope. But his luck still holds, and after the pilgrimages and wax candles have been vowed, and the barrel with the tidings of the great discovery stealthily dropped overboard, the storm passes, and they find themselves in sight of—the Azores! Whether through luck or intuition, his guess is the correct one, and the event emphasises the fact that discoveries generally go to the men best fitted to make them; but it emphasises also the grave risks to which the navigators of his time were exposed by their utter inability to find their longitude when out of sight of land.

The case of Columbus is particularly striking, on account of the historical importance of his voyage, and the unusually long period, some six months, spent in total ignorance of his longitude*: but for many generations to come—in fact, until the close of the eighteenth century—navigators had practically no better method of finding their longitude than he had. All that they could do was to keep a reckoning, termed the "dead reckoning," of the courses they steered and the distances they ran, and to make such allowances as they thought fit for leeway, tide, current, variation of the compass, errors in estimating their speed, bad steering, and many other sources of error. When one considers the slow speed and comparatively enormous leeway of their clumsy vessels, the wonder is not that their dead reckoning was often absurdly wrong, but that it was ever anywhere near the truth. Practically their only advantage over Columbus was that they had a better means of estimating their speed—the hand log—than he had.

A few instances, taken almost at random during the period 1650-1750, will show the risks they ran.

In 1691 several warships were lost off Plymouth, having mistaken the Deadman for Berry Head.

Sir Cloudesley Shovel, returning from Gibraltar with his fleet in 1707, had cloudy weather during practically the whole passage, and, after some twelve days at sea, took the opinions of the navigators of all his ships as to his position. With one exception (which afterwards proved correct) their reckonings placed the fleet in a safe position some distance west of Ushant, and he accordingly stood on: but the same night, in fog, they ran on the Scillies. Four ships were lost, and nearly two thousand men, including the Admiral himself.†

Several transports were lost in 1711 near the entrance to the St. Lawrence River, having erred 45′ in their longitude in twenty-four hours.

Lord Belhaven was wrecked on the Lizard the same day that he sailed from Plymouth, November 17th, 1721.

The famous voyage of Commodore Anson, who took the Acapulco galleon in 1743 and came home round the world with over half a million in prize money, provides two particularly striking examples of the total inability of the navigators of his day to find their longitude when out of sight of land. In 1741 he spent over a month endeavouring to round Cape Horn to the westward, and having, by his reckoning, made

---

* Although the sighting of the Azores shows the *relative* accuracy of the reckonings kept on the outward and homeward voyages, yet Columbus' determinations of the *actual* longitude of his discoveries were marvellously erroneous. He firmly believed that Cuba was part of the mainland of Asia—nay, *he enacted that this was the case*, and compelled every member of his expedition, under heavy penalties, to make affidavit thereunto! Having thus abolished the Pacific Ocean by legislation, it is not surprising that he should remark to Queen Isabella "the earth is not so large as vulgar opinion makes it."

† A story was current, long afterwards, that a seaman of the flagship had kept his own reckoning, which showed that they were in a dangerous situation, and that on his making this known to his superiors he was hanged for mutiny, there and then. *Credat Judaeus Apella.*

good sufficient westing to place him 10° clear of the most western point of Tierra del Fuego, stood to the northward, only to sight land right ahead, and to find that owing to an unsuspected easterly current he was still on the eastern side of the Cape.

Again, after rounding the Horn and parting company with his squadron, scurvy broke out aboard his flagship, the "Centurion," and Anson, with his men dying like flies, ran to the northward, hoping to make the island of Juan Fernandez, where he could land his sick. In the ordinary way he would have steered to get into the latitude of the island a long way east or west of it, and then have run along that parallel until he sighted it—a plan still practiced by many Pacific traders. To save time and lives, and urged by the terrible fact that a few more days of the present death rate would leave the ship too short-handed to go about, he sailed straight northward for the island, with the result that he reached its latitude without sighting it, and was uncertain whether it lay to the eastward or the westward. He ran westward until (unknown to him) he was within a few hours' sail of it: then, concluding he was wrong, he sailed eastward until he made the coast of Chile, and had to turn and run back westward over the same track until he finally sighted the island. This uncertainty as to his longitude cost him the lives of some seventy or eighty of his men, who would probably have recovered if they could have been got ashore.*

Enough has been said to show that the problem of finding longitude at sea was no academic exercise, but a matter of the most urgent and vital importance, and one which no nation which used the ocean highways could afford to ignore. It overshadowed the life of every man afloat, and the safety of every ship and cargo. Yet, for nearly three centuries after the great voyages of Columbus, Cabot, and the Portuguese navigators had focussed attention upon it, it defied all attempts at solution—not only those of seamen, but of astronomers, mathematicians, geographers; in short, it baffled the best brains of the civilised world.

It was as a solution—and, until the introduction of W/T time-signals, the best solution—of this problem that the marine chronometer came into being. And before we can properly estimate its value to the navigator, it is necessary to form some idea of the difficulties which it overcame, and of the various other methods which are, theoretically, available for the finding of longitude at sea.

So long as a ship remains in sight of land whose position is accurately shown on her charts, and which she can identify, her own position can be readily obtained by direct observation. But when once she is out of sight of land, her position must be obtained by observations either (1) of some terrestrial phenomenon, or (2) of the heavenly bodies.

---

* To add to the pathos of this story, the "Centurion" was the ship which, some years earlier, carried Harrison's first timekeeper to Lisbon, and she was thus the first vessel to be provided, even temporarily, with a practical means of finding her longitude accurately. The machine itself was going, in Harrison's house in London, during the whole period of her voyage, and much later—from 1736 until 1766.

Of the first class, the method most often proposed and, to some extent, used (*e.g.*, by Columbus, Magellan and Tasman),* is the variation† of the compass. The compass needle points to the magnetic pole (whose position differs very considerably from that of the geographical pole), and, in consequence, it only points truly north and south when on the "line of no variation," which passes through both of these poles. In other places its indications differ from the true north by an amount varying (though not uniformly) with its distance from that line (and hence, roughly, with the ship's longitude). In theory, then, since the amount of the variation can be found on board ship by taking a bearing of the Pole Star, the ship's longitude can be found by comparing the value thus obtained with the tabulated variation at other places whose longitude is known.

This method was employed by Columbus in his later voyages across the Atlantic. In the course of his first voyage, the variation had changed from easterly to westerly, much to his crew's alarm, and it continued to change more or less uniformly as he advanced further westward.‡ Accordingly, in his later voyages, he was able to estimate his distance from either shore of the Atlantic by comparing the variation observed on board with that previously found ashore.

But although in favourable cases this method might give a rough idea of a ship's longitude, it was soon found to be of no general use. It pre-supposed an accurate knowledge of the amount of the variation in all parts of the world, an object not completely attained even now: moreover, the variation at any place changes from year to year: the isogonal lines in many parts of the world deviate very much from the north and south line: the changes to be observed are small, and require very accurate measurement: and that accuracy cannot be obtained under normal conditions. Even nowadays I doubt whether a ship could rely upon obtaining her longitude within 1° by variation, and therefore it is not surprising that although proposed by Bond in 1674§, Halley (who made the first variation chart), Whiston, and many others, this method never found favour afloat.‖

A second and totally inapplicable method¶ was proposed in 1714 by Whiston and Ditton—the former a dissenting clergyman, sometime Lucasian Professor of Mathematics, the latter a mathematician—

* Sebastian Cabot, on his death-bed, declared that he possessed, but might not reveal, a divinely-inspired method for finding longitude. It is believed to have been based upon variation.

† Also called "declination," but not by seamen.

‡ This was only the case as far as relates to the eastern half of the North Atlantic. After he crossed the meridian of approximately 30° W., the isogonal lines—the lines of equal variation—ran practically east and west, and accordingly no change of variation was observable.

§ A Commission was appointed by King Charles II. to investigate this project.

‖ A quarto pamphlet on this subject, published *circa* 1765 under the title of "An Account of an Attempt to ascertain the Longitude at Sea," by Zachariah Williams, is noteworthy as the work of no less a writer than Doctor Samuel Johnson. Williams was one of the Doctor's pensioners.

¶ "A New Method for discovering the Longitude," London, 1714. In 1721 Whiston also published an essay on finding longitude by variation, and latitude by the dipping needle, and in 1738 another on obtaining longitude by observing the eclipses of Jupiter's satellites.

both of them men of some note in their day, but now only remembered as the subject of a coarse poem by Swift.* They proposed that permanent floating lightships should be established at fixed points on the principal trade routes, firing at intervals star-shell arranged to explode at a height of 6,440 feet, thus affording ships an opportunity of determining their distance from the nearest lightship by timing the interval between the flash and the report. They added that this method would be of particular use in the North Atlantic, where, they calmly asseverated, no depth exceeded 300 fathoms.†

It is unnecessary to indicate where this plan fails. No attempt was ever made to put it into practice, but in very recent years a perfectly successful method has appeared which bears a faint resemblance to it. That is the method of wireless direction finding. A vessel within range of two D/F. stations can now determine her position as if by direct observation, even in the densest fog, a feat which not long ago would have been thought incredible. This method is not yet perfect, or of universal application, but it has already shown that it is one of the many achievements which will make our posterity speak of " Marconi " as we now speak of " Shakespeare " or " Newton."

But during the period when the problem of finding longitude was urgent and unsolved—1500 to 1760—the wonders of wireless were not dreamed of, and as no methods depending on terrestrial phenomena appeared sufficiently promising, attention was perforce directed to those involving observations of the heavenly bodies.

The position of any point on the earth's surface can be defined by the intersection of two lines—its parallel of latitude and its meridian of longitude, and the displacement consequent upon any change of position can always be completely expressed as the resultant of two alterations—a change in latitude and a change in longitude. In other words, if a ship start from a known position and sail any given distance in any given direction, we can consider her as having sailed so much north or south, and then so much east or west. It remains, then, to be considered what observable change, if any, is produced by either of these motions in the aspect of the heavenly bodies visible from the ship.

Consider a ship in north latitude sailing southward. As she advances, all the heavenly bodies southward of her original zenith will gradually become more elevated above her horizon. Stars which at first were below it will come into view, and all the Southern stars—those whose declination is southerly—will rise earlier, set later, and cross her meridian at an increased altitude. The Northern stars, on the other hand, will rise later and set earlier, and those to the northward of her original zenith—for example, the pole star—will gradually sink lower and lower. Thus, when she reaches the Equator, the pole star will no longer be visible.

---

* " Ode for Music, on the longitude." The curious will find it in any complete edition of Swift. I could not possibly quote it here.

† The average depth is about 2,000 fathoms, and the maximum 3,450.

Change of latitude, then, causes a corresponding change in the apparent altitude of the heavenly bodies, quite independent of their diurnal motion, and since the sextant* enables altitudes to be observed at sea with considerable accuracy, a ship's latitude can be easily found with the help of such observations in combination with tables, such as are given in the "Nautical Almanac," of the celestial position, at the time of observation, of the bodies observed. This, as we have seen, was the method used, in a rudimentary fashion, by the early navigators.

But when a ship sails eastward or westward, no change is produced by such motion in the apparent altitude of the heavenly bodies. The rotation of the earth will bring them across her meridian, for example, at exactly the same altitude as before, and the only alteration produced by her change of position will be that such transits will occur earlier if she has gone eastward, and later if she has gone westward. Thus, if she alter her longitude by 90° to the eastward, a star which previously crossed the meridian of her starting point at 11 p.m., local time, will cross that of her new position at 5 p.m., local time.

Now the local time at any place can be found in a number of ways, and the difference of longitude between any two places is simply the difference between their local times. Difference of longitude and difference of local time are, in fact, convertible expressions, and to say that one place is 90° eastward of another is the same thing as saying that it is six hours east of it.†

We have seen, then, that celestial observations taken by a ship in two different places will exhibit a relative change in altitude if she has gone northward or southward, and a relative change in local time if she has gone eastward or westward. Also, that by such observations she can obtain her latitude and her local time.

But, in order to know her change of longitude, she must not only know *her* local time, but also the local time of the place she sailed from: or, to know her actual longitude, which is more convenient, she must know the local time of some standard meridian. How is a knowledge of this time, which we may term "standard time," to be obtained?

There are several methods by which, theoretically, standard time can be obtained from celestial observations. The first was that proposed by Galileo, soon after his discovery of four of Jupiter's satellites‡ in the year 1610. These little bodies, as they circle round their huge primary, are frequently eclipsed. The times at which

* Invented by Hadley, *circa* 1730. Also, independently, by Newton, and by Thomas Godfrey, of Philadelphia.

† On some of the charts published by the Russian Government this is strikingly shown by the graduation for longitude, which is in degrees, minutes and seconds of arc along the bottom border, and in hours, minutes and seconds of time along the top. In this connection, one is tempted to recall a "Notice to Mariners" issued in 1916 by an Irish authority, in which a certain position is quoted as "lat. 54° 13 ft. 12 in. N., and long. 9° 5 ft. 50 in. W." It is to be presumed that the compositor was also a carpenter.

‡ Nine are at present known, but the other five are much smaller, and can only be seen with a powerful telescope. They were discovered during the period 1892-1914.

these eclipses occur can be predicted a long time in advance, and are unaffected by the location of the observer. Accordingly, if a mariner at sea observes an eclipse at 7h. 21m. 15s. local time, and finds from a table that it was due to occur at Greenwich at 9h. 51m. 15s. Greenwich time, he knows at once that he is

$$\frac{360° \times 2\frac{1}{2}\text{h.}}{24\text{h.}} = 37° 30' \text{ East of Greenwich.}$$

But, although admirable in theory, this plan is impracticable. First and foremost, the ship's motion, in any weather except a flat calm, prevents Jupiter and his satellites from being held in the field of the telescope long enough to observe an eclipse. Secondly, even if this could be got over, the eclipses are not instantaneous, and any alteration in the state of the atmosphere or in the power of the telescope affects the apparent time at which they occur. Lastly, Jupiter is often so near the Sun that the eclipses cannot be observed.

Galileo did his best to meet these objections. He proposed that the observer should be equipped with a helmet, something like a gas-mask, into which two telescopes, one for each eye, were rigidly fixed. Local time was to be found at about the same moment, and the time of the eclipse carried on for comparison with it by means of a pendulum or a sand-glass. He computed rough tables of the eclipses of all four satellites, and then, in 1616, offered his method successively to the Spanish, Tuscan, and Dutch Governments, the first and last of whom, as we shall see, had offered a reward for a solution of the problem. But the practical defects of his plan were, and are, unconquered, and his only reward was a gold medal and chain, the gift of the States-General.

No one since Galileo's time has succeeded in using Jupiter's satellites to find longitude at sea, although many attempts have been made, chiefly by persons who did not appreciate the practical difficulties involved.* And the same defect—the impossibility of making sufficiently accurate observations at sea—has been fatal to other methods, such as occultations of stars by the moon,† eclipses of the sun and moon, etc. The latter, moreover, could never, even if observable, be of more than very occasional use.

The moon, with her comparatively rapid motion in the heavens, has always been the sheet-anchor of those who wish to find standard

* Many inventors have attempted to provide a steady platform for an observer on shipboard, from which astronomical observations can be made. "Marine chairs" for this purpose were proposed by an anonymous author in 1719, Irwin (1762), Chevasse (1813), Dickinson (1816), Senhouse (1817), Lecount (1821-3), Leslie (1822), and Piazzi Smyth (1858). But no contrivance of this kind has yet been produced which can counteract the violent and unexpected motions of a ship at sea. That of Prof. Piazzi Smyth appears to have come nearest to success. He proposed a platform, large enough to accommodate an observer and his instruments, steadied by steam-driven gyroscopes. An apparatus of this kind was under contemplation for the ill-fated "Great Eastern," but lack of funds prevented its installation, although Brunel was strongly in favour of it.

† Occultations were successfully used for determining a ship's longitude by Shackleton in the Weddell Sea, 1915. In this case, however, the "Endurance" was jammed fast in the pack, and the observations were practically taken on land.

time by celestial observations. Her motion—some 12° in twenty-four hours—is quite obvious, and many plans have been proposed for making use of it.

The one most often proposed* is that of lunar transits—and theoretically it is quite sound. Unlike a star, which crosses every meridian at the same local time, the local time at which the moon crosses each meridian is affected by her motion round the earth, and if the time of her transit on any particular day be calculated, say, for Greenwich (as it can be), it will be found to get later and later for places further westward, and *vice versa*, by a regular amount, which is called her " retardation." Now if we could observe at sea the exact local time when the moon crossed the meridian, and compare it with the tabulated time of her crossing that of Greenwich, the difference between the two would give the retardation. And since this always bears a fixed relation to the difference of longitude between the standard meridian and the observer, the latter's longitude could readily be obtained.†

In practice, however, this method fails utterly, for the simple reason that there is no known means of determining, with anything like the accuracy required, when the moon, or any other heavenly body is on the meridian, whether by a direct transit observation or by the mean of sights taken on either side of the meridian. If it were not so, indeed, finding longitude would be a very simple matter.

But although this method of using the moon fails, there is another which is quite practicable, although no longer used—the method of " lunar distances." If the moon's motion be known with sufficient accuracy, tables can be drawn up forecasting her position in the heavens for a long time in advance, and also her angular distance, as observed on some standard meridian, from suitable fixed stars. These distances can also be observed, by means of the sextant, on board ship, and, by interpolation, the Greenwich time corresponding with that distance can be taken out of the tables. The local time of observing such " lunar distances " can be obtained by the ordinary observations, and the difference, of course, gives the longitude of the ship.

The possibilities of this method did not escape attention even at an early period in the history of the problem. It was proposed by Werner as early as 1514‡, by Morin in 1633, and by St. Pierre in 1674. But at that period, and much later, the theory of the moon's motion was far too rudimentary§ to allow of the accurate prediction of lunar distances. As Newton pointed out in 1713, it would allow of a ship's

* By Herne, in his " Longitude Unveiled," 1678, and many others since his time. In fact, the Board of Longitude were compelled, in 1802, to resolve that they would no longer consider any schemes involving either lunar altitudes or the variation of the compass.

† Throughout the foregoing passage, of course, the word " time " refers to sidereal time, not mean time.

‡ William Baffin attempted to use lunar distances in 1515. It is improbable that he knew of Werner's suggestion.

§ It cannot be said to be *complete* even now. The moon exhibits a progressive acceleration for which no adequate explanation is at present forthcoming.

place being found within two or three degrees, but not nearer—and such accuracy was little better than that of dead reckoning. St. Pierre's proposal, however, although its author was little more than a charlatan, had one good result—his advocacy of it to Charles II. brought about the establishment of Greenwich Observatory, "for rectifying the tables of the motion of the heavens, and the places of the fixed stars, so as to find out the so-much desired longitude of places for perfecting the art of navigation."*

It was a later Astronomer-Royal, Maskelyne, who brought the lunar method into general use. He published in 1763 the "British Mariners' Guide," which gave a general outline of its principles, and sufficient tabular information for their application (though by a very laborious method†), while four years later he instituted the "Nautical Almanac," in which he gave, for the first time in the history of navigation, lunar distances of the sun and seven selected stars computed for every three hours at Greenwich. The "Nautical Almanac" continued to publish such distances uninterruptedly, and several years in advance, until 1907, when they were discontinued, as no longer worth the trouble of computing.

But at no time during that period had they been an entirely satisfactory solution of the problem. In the hands of a good observer and computer they were excellent, but for general use they were unreliable. The reason was twofold. In the first place, the observations had to be extremely accurate—an error, such as the best observer could hardly make certain of avoiding, of only 1′ of arc produced, owing to the moon's comparatively slow motion, one of 30′ or so of longitude in the result. Secondly, the calculations were long and intricate, and although many efforts were made to simplify them, there remained many pitfalls and chances of committing some slight error which might easily pass unnoticed, and yet convert the result from a safeguard to a source of fearful danger. The combination of a good observer and a good computer was not very usual,‡ while even those expert in both branches could not guarantee, however favourable the observing conditions, that the mean results of several sets of distances would not exhibit considerable discrepancies.§

The method of lunar distances, as we have seen, was early suggested, but remained inapplicable till 1764 for lack of fundamental data,

---

* Quoted from the original warrant for the payment of Flamsteed's salary as first Astronomer-Royal.

† The nature of the necessary calculations may be inferred from a memorial in favour of this method signed by several officers of the Honourable East India Company, and read at a meeting of the Board of Longitude, February 9th, 1765, in which Mr. Charles Mears, of the H.E.I.C. ship "Egmont," states that "in the course of his last voyage the Observations taken in the method prescribed by Mr. Maskelyne were found very useful and not difficult, each observation not taking more than *four hours* time to find the result, which always, when near land whose longitude was correctly known, agreed within one degree."

‡ It is a matter of common knowledge that many a good seaman, in obtaining his "Extra Master" certificate, has correctly computed a lunar whose elements he was physically incapable of observing.

§ The mean of no less than 2500 lunar distances taken *on shore* at Winter I., 66° N., 83° W., by the Rev. G. Fisher in December, 1821, differed 14′ from that of an equal number taken at the same spot in the following March.

and no other method of obtaining a standard of time by celestial observations appeared feasible. It was natural, therefore, that enquiry should be directed towards finding some other means of obtaining such a standard.

The obvious method, of course, is to carry some clock or other timekeeper on board, which will give the standard time. The longitude can then be found very simply by comparing it with the local time found by observation.

This method was suggested by Gemma Frisius as early as 1530, but it lay dormant for two centuries, since no machine of the kind could be made to keep time with sufficient accuracy ashore, let alone at sea. As we have seen, a minute of time corresponds to fifteen minutes of longitude, so that if at the end of a six week's voyage we require to know our longitude within half a degree, the error of the timekeeper must not amount to more than two minutes in that period, or approximately *three seconds a day*.

Now, not only in 1530, but as late as 1700 or so, a clock which, even with the advantage of a steady base on shore, and the assistance of a pendulum,* kept time with such accuracy, was a thing unheard of; while the sand-glasses and clumsy portable watches which were the only timekeepers then available for ship use, could not be relied upon to within three minutes a day, much less three seconds. Thus, until an accurate marine timekeeper could be produced, this method, like that of lunar distances, remained merely a theoretical solution.

It is true that so long as a ship was inside the limit of visibility she could obtain a standard of time by observing such signals as those proposed by Whiston and Ditton, provided that these were made at stated times: but this would not be, in any sense of the word, a general method, and was as restricted in its application as their original plan, although not so chimerical.

But even Whiston and Ditton were left at the post by a scheme published anonymously in the year 1687,† which takes pride of place as the most bizarre plan ever proposed for finding longitude at sea. The inventor, who appears to have been quite serious, if scarcely sane, begins by citing a superstition, in which he formerly believed, that if a glass be filled to the brim with water, it will run over at the instant of full and new moon. Hence, as he acutely points out, a vessel's longitude may be found at least twice a month. But, finding the alleged phenomenon a fable, he turns to a better method. He appears to have been (in common, it must be admitted, with many of his contemporaries), a believer in the "powder of sympathy" invented by Sir Kenelm Digby—a nostrum which was supposed to cure wounds by being applied, not to the wound, but to the weapon which inflicted it. Digby claimed that on one occasion he made one

---

* First applied to clocks *circa* 1650.

† "Curious Enquiries," London, 1687.

of his patients start, when at a considerable distance from him, by putting into a basin of water a bandage taken from the wound, together with some of the miraculous powder! Acting on this hint, our author proposes that every ship, before leaving harbour, should be equipped with a wounded dog, and that a trusty person on shore, provided with a standard clock and a powdered bandage from the wound, should dip the latter into water at the stroke of each hour, thus causing the dog aboard ship to yelp at the same moment*!

To comment upon this scheme is difficult, but it is worth noting that the wireless time-signals now coming into general use really do perform the miracle falsely claimed for the "powder of sympathy," and that our grandfathers would doubtless have considered them no less absurd and impossible.

The methods briefly discussed in the foregoing summary can be tabulated as follows:—

TERRESTRIAL METHODS.

1. By the variation of the compass.
2. By sound signals.

CELESTIAL METHODS.

1. By the eclipses of Jupiter's satellites.
2. By occultations of stars by the moon.
3. By eclipses, and similar phenomena.
4. By meridian transits of the moon.
5. By lunar distances.
6. By a timekeeper.

The possibilities of all these methods had been attentively considered by the end of the sixteenth century, but, as we now know, only the last two were really applicable, and even these were not sufficiently developed to be of practical use until a century and a half later.

Many attempts were made, during the period 1500-1760, to encourage the discovery of some satisfactory method. These generally took the form of a large money prize offered by some Government or representative public body. Thus in 1598 Philip III. of Spain, possibly stimulated by memories of the Armada, offered a perpetual pension of 6,000 ducats, together with a life pension of 2,000 ducats and a gratuity of 1,000 more, to the "discoverer of the longitude." To stimulate those competing for this splendid prize, moreover, considerable encouragement was given to them by the payment of small sums on account, as it were, unaccompanied by any tiresome enquiries as to the practicability of their schemes. Indeed, it appears to have been the custom for any sharper, crank, or lunatic who made it officially known that he was investigating the problem of longitude† to have been at once importuned by the Escurial to give himself the fatigue of accepting a considerable sum of ready money. The following

* This is reminiscent of the standard timekeeper of the early Egyptians—the Cynocephalus, or sacred monkey.

† Then commonly called the problem of "the fixed point," or of "the East and West navigation."

instances* will demonstrate the liberality, if not the discrimination, of the Spanish Government at this period.

1607 Luis de Fonseca went to Seville, and ordered from D. Francisco Duarte the necessary articles to make the instruments he had offered for providing an invariable compass, to be supplied to the pilots of the fleet.

1610 A gratuity of 1,000 ducats was given to Luis de Fonseca.
To Dr. Arias de Loyola a gratuity of 400 ducats for his work on the invariable compass. (August 21st.)
To Luis de Fonseca 300 ducats to go to Lisbon for experiments with the compass. (September 18th.)
To Luis de Fonseca a gratuity of 600 ducats. (November 29th.)

1612 Dr. Arias de Loyola was promised 6,000 ducats of perpetual pension, and 2,000 ducats of life pension for his invariable compass, and in connection with this offer he is to enjoy henceforth 1,500 ducats per annum of the 8,000, which are to be invested. (October 3rd.)

1614 To Juan Mayllard, an allowance of from 40 escudos to 10 reals a month while at the Court studying the longitude.

1615 To Captain Lorenzo Ferrer Maldonado† an allowance of 40 escudos a month while afloat for observations on the longitude and the invariable compass, for which he was promised a perpetual pension of 5,000 ducats. (August 8th.)

1625 To Juan Mayllard, a Frenchman, 20 escudos and one man's rations in the Terra-Firma fleet‡, in which he had made certain experiments on longitude. (September 6th.)

1626 Lorenzo Ferrer Maldonado was given 200 ducats for making certain observing instruments.

It will be noted that the majority of these earnest workers considered that a compass without variation would be of great assistance in finding longitude (but why, is not obvious).

After many years of such payments, with no results to show for them, the Spanish authorities appear, not unnaturally, to have lost interest in the subject. Other nations, however, followed their example in endeavouring to stimulate inventors by the offer of a large reward. Considerable sums were offered at various dates by the Governments of Holland§, Venice, Great Britain and France,¶ and also by several private donors. Thus, the will of Thomas Axe, an Englishman who died in 1691, provided for a payment of £1,000 to the fortunate inventor,

---

* Quoted from Duro's "Disquisiciones Nauticas."

† The reputed discoverer of the "Strait of Anian," who is claimed to have made the North-West Passage in 1588.

‡ Presumably analogous to the Swiss navy.

§ Considerable obscurity surrounds the offer of this reward. Huyghens, who ought to have been well acquainted with the facts, speaks very definitely of the "long-promised reward" of the States of Holland, and it is referred to by many writers of the eighteenth century, the amount being put at from 1,000 to 30,000 guilders. Recent enquiries, however, very kindly made for me by Capt. Luymes, the Netherlands Hydrographer, have failed to find any trace of such an offer.

¶ 100,000 livres, in the year 1716.

coupled, however, with such an absurd number of stipulations as made it, whether intentionally or otherwise, practically impossible to win.* Again, a bequest from Councillor Rouillé de Meslay (a circle-squarer) enabled the Paris Academie des Sciences to give, in 1720 and succeeding years, a series of prizes for useful inventions in navigation.

But the largest and most famous reward was that offered by the British Government in 1714, and it has the additional distinction of being, I believe, the only one which was ever paid. Its history is somewhat curious.

When Whiston and Ditton had drafted their project, they published accounts of it in various periodicals,† and then, with the view of obtaining more publicity, engineered a petition submitted to Parliament on March 25th, 1714, by "several Captains of Her Majesty's Ships, Merchants of London, and Commanders of Merchantmen," setting forth the great importance of obtaining some method of finding longitude at sea, and praying that a public reward should be offered for such a method. This was referred to a Committee, who examined both the specific proposal of Whiston and Ditton, and also the general state of the question, and consulted a number of eminent scientific men, including Newton and Halley. Newton's evidence is extremely important, and as recorded in the report of the Committee it opened as follows:—

> "Sir *Isaac Newton*, attending the Committee, said, ‡ 'That, for determining the Longitude at Sea, there have been several Projects, true in the Theory, but difficult to execute:
>
> "'One is, by a Watch to keep time exactly: But, by reason of the Motion of a Ship, the Variation of Heat and Cold, Wet and Dry, and the Difference of Gravity in different Latitudes, such a Watch hath not yet been made.'"

He also mentioned and condemned the use of the eclipses of Jupiter's satellites and the "place of the Moon," while with regard to Whiston and Ditton's scheme, he merely remarked that it was rather a method of "keeping an Account of the Longitude at Sea, than for finding it, if at any time it should be lost."

As the result of the Committee's deliberations, a bill "for providing a publick reward for such person or persons as shall discover the Longitude," was introduced, and ultimately became law as 12 Anne., cap. 15. This famous Act offered, to any person who should invent a practicable method, the following scale of rewards:—

£10,000 for any method capable of determining a ship's longitude within one degree.

---

* It was only to be paid provided that (1) his wife and child died childless within ten years of his death, and also (2) that affidavits as to the merit of the invention were made before all the twelve Judges of England by the four Professors of Astronomy and Geography at Oxford and Cambridge, and by at least twenty experienced masters of ships.

† *E.g.*, the "Guardian" of July 14th, and the "Englishman" of December 19th, 1713. They also issued an anonymous broadside.

‡ Actually, he read a written statement. His verbal replies to the Committee's enquiries indicate that he was suffering from mental fatigue.

£15,000 if it determined it within 40′.
£20,000 if it dctermined it within half a degree.

The Bill also provided machinery for carrying its provisions into effect, in the shape of a permanent body of Commissioners, who were empowered to pay one half of any reward as soon as a majority of them were satisfied that the proposed method was practicable and useful, and gave security to ships when within 80 miles of the shore.* The other half was to be paid as soon as a vessel using the method should actually sail from the British Isles to a port in the West Indies without erring in her longitude more than the specified amount. They were also permitted to give a reduced reward for a less accurate method, and to spend a sum not exceeding £2,000 in experiments.

It might be thought that these enormous rewards, and the equally enormous margin of error permitted in winning them, would have so stimulated invention that the £10,000, at least, would have been won in a very few years. But, as has often been proved, inventions cannot be made to order, even if a fortune depend upon that being done. This method of offering bounties,† accordingly, has now been superseded in most countries by the far preferable plan of state-endowed research.

But if the Commissioners, who became known as the Board of Longitude, had to wait a long time for a practicable method, they were not left entirely idle. They became the immediate and accessible prey of every crank, enthusiast, fanatic, swindler and lunatic in or out of Bedlam. "The discovery of the longitude" added a fourth problem to the famous trinity—the quadrature of the circle, the trisection of the angle, and the duplication of the cube—which had so long been the staple amusement of this fraternity, and if to them we add the numerous and indefatigable army of perpetual-motion seekers, it will be readily understood that the Board, like their Spanish predecessors, found themselves officially compelled to winnow an intolerable deal of chaff in which they could be morally certain that they would find no wheat whatever.

It is probable that there has never been a period, during the last thousand years, at which there have not existed many worthy fools firmly possessed by the idea that they have successfully squared the circle or produced a perpetual motion, or both. And amongst them, by some esoteric process of reasoning, it appears to be a settled belief that both these feats have a direct and immediate application to the finding of longitude. So it comes about that, even

* This was obviously designed to benefit Whiston and Ditton, and was inspired by them, although nominally Newton's suggestion.

† A second reward of £20,000 for the discovery of the North-West Passage, was offered by the British Government in 1745, and one of 6,000 florins for an improved method of diamond cutting, by the Dutch Government, as recently as 1905. A prize of 100,000 marks is still, I believe, on offer for a general proof of Fermat's last theorem ($x^n+y^n=z^n$ is impossible if $n>2$), if given before A.D. 2007.

now, there are some who believe that the British Government has offered an enormous reward for an exact value of π, and this belief is entirely due to the reward it once really did offer for "the discovery of the longitude."

A few passages from the Board's minutes, although of a somewhat later date, will illustrate what they had to endure. It should be noted that many of their correspondents entirely ignored their official title, and sent in lucubrations upon all manner of subjects:—

(25.1.1772) "A person who calls himself John Baptist desiring to speak with the Board, he was called in and showed them some schemes and drawings of figures which he desired they would enable him to publish; He was informed that it was not in their power . . . He was then desired to withdraw."

(13.6.1772) "A Memorial from Mr. Owen Straton was read, proposing a method of finding out the Longitude by means of an Instrument of his invention, and the said Mr. Straton, who was attending, being called in, and it appearing that the instrument proposed is a Sun Dial, he was told it could not be of any service, and then withdrew."

(4.12.1790) "Mr. Robert Davidson hath invented a machine that keeps perpetually going, and may be completed to work the largest mills, or keep a clock constantly going."

(11.6.1791) "A Paper was read without a signature, but understood to have been written by Mons. De Lolme, respecting the fixing and moving a Ship's Rudder: and the preventing a boat from oversetting. But the Board not conceiving that these Contrivances tended in any shape to promote the discovery of the Longitude at Sea, declined entering into the consideration of them."

(1.12.1792) "A letter was read from Mons. T. Lowitz, chemist, of St. Petersburgh, containing a method of rendering putrid water drinkable, in which there did not appear to be anything new."

(11.6.1796) "A letter was read from Dr. Woemen, a native of Saxony, acquainting the Board that he can express π and the ratio of 1 to $\sqrt{2}$ in integrals, and that this comprehends the discovery of the Longitude. He was informed that the Board do not receive proposals of this nature."

(2.6.1808) "Mr. Benjamin Pacy can find time by the Steelyard, and start any machine in the Kingdom by a Perpetual Motion."

(3.6.1812) "M. Metiriet was informed that the Board declined any interference with the quadrature of the circle."

(1.4.1819) "Mr. Baines' Sea-Perambulator* was referred to the Committee on Instruments."

(5.6.1823) "Lieut. Couch's venticulean apparatus, his Debephora, his main topmast storm staysail, and his Theodolite were not judged likely to be of any utility."

It is unnecessary to give details of the Board's more serious transactions here, since a good deal must, of necessity, be said on this point later. But as no detailed account of their work has ever been published, the following short sketch may be useful.

The Board existed from 1713 until 1828, having been partially re-organised in 1818. From first to last they disbursed a large sum of public money—some £101,000. They met, as a rule, three times a year, at the Admiralty.

* This was a form of patent log.

They employed a paid secretary, but gave their own services gratuitously, although those members resident at the Universities received an allowance for their travelling expenses.* As originally constituted by the Act of 1712 they comprised, *ex officio*, the following dignitaries :—†

The Lord High Admiral or the First Lord of the Admiralty.
The Speaker of the House of Commons.
The First Commissioner of the Navy.
The First Commissioner of Trade.
The Admirals of the Red, White and Blue Squadrons.
The Master of the Trinity House.
The President of the Royal Society.
The Astronomer-Royal.
The Savilian, Lucasian, and Plumian Professors of Mathematics.

The chief alteration introduced in the re-organisation of 1818 was the appointment of three Resident Commissioners, to reside in London, and thus expedite the work of the Board.

A body of this character, meeting at long intervals, and comparatively irresponsible, was liable, of course, to such faults as delay, capriciousness, lack of proportion, and an undue sense of its own importance. It is due to the Board, however, to say that they appear to have taken a very commonsense view of their powers and responsibilities, and that they fulfilled to a large extent the object of their establishment—the reward and development of a better method or methods of finding the longitude at sea.

Generally speaking, their rule was to ask for *results*. They would assist no project without proof that it was likely to be of assistance to seamen. If they distrusted their own opinion, they took the best procurable. For wild-cat projects they had a set of stereotyped replies. On the other hand, they would, especially in their earlier days, give generous assistance to anyone whose scheme appeared to be new and practicable, provided that it had not been patented. On this latter point they were firm, as several otherwise deserving claimants found to their cost.‡ The worst fault that can be laid to their charge is that their procrastination and indecision were frequently worthy of the Circumlocution Office itself.

Such, then, was the unique§ body which was charged with the supervision of the attempts at winning the great reward, and whose existence served to remind the public at large of the existence of the

* This allowance was subsequently granted also to Maskelyne, when Astronomer-Royal, as compensation for the extra labour involved in acting as general scientific adviser to the Board.

† Any five of these constituted a quorum, and the average attendance did not often exceed six.

‡ *e.g.*, John Arnold, the chronometer maker, Ould and Syeds (1792), and many others.

§ The French "Bureau des Longitudes," which still exists, was not founded until 1795.

problem. The reward remained on offer for fifty years, during which time the phrase " the discovery of the longitude " passed into common English speech as expressing a thing of practical impossibility. Eighteenth century literature is full of such allusions. Swift makes it one of the great discoveries which, Captain Lemuel Gulliver suggests, will enrich the minds of the immortal Struldbugs: Goldsmith puts it into Marlow's mouth as a happy retort to one of Tony Lumpkin's sallies; magazines and newspapers use it as a stock satirical cliché.*

But, in spite of this popular verdict, the hour and the man were at hand, and in 1764 the great reward was won and the problem—that problem which had baffled Newton, Halley, Huyghens, Leibnitz, and a hundred others—definitely solved. And its solution proved to be a little ticking thing in a box, the unaided production of a Yorkshire carpenter, John Harrison.

It was thus that the chronometer came into existence, not as a scientific toy, but as a satisfactory solution of one of the gravest problems which have ever confronted the navigator. And accordingly it must be judged by the measure of the enormous benefits which its invention has conferred, both directly upon seamen, and indirectly upon the whole world. In its modern form it is not, actually, the invention of any one man, but for all practical purposes we may regard it as that of a little band of men, who converted it, in the short space of twenty-five years—1760 to 1785—from a mere possibility to a commercial reality. The object of the following chapters is to give, in Part 1, a short account of the lives and work of these men, and, in Part 2, an outline of the further mechanical development of the chronometer from the beginning of the last century until the present day.

---

* In the mad-house scene in the "Rake's Progress," Hogarth, as befitted the foremost satirist of his age, has, it will be noticed, had his typically British fling at the fanatical "projectors" who sought vainly for the longitude.

The following quotation, from "Idea Longitudinis" by E. Harrison, Lieut. R.N. (1696), is really too good to omit: "There was an Officer, in the Navy (as I was informed) who cursed and Damned the Man who should discover the Longitude; thou Old, Inveterate, Rusty, Musty, Filthy, Cankered, Carnal Devil, for cursing, down on thy Marrow bones (if thou hast any) and ask God Almighty's forgiveness for thy Sins, know that it is not in thy Power to Damn any man but thyself:".

PART I.

THE EARLY HISTORY OF THE CHRONOMETER

1530-1829.

PREFATORY NOTE.

Throughout the following pages the word "chronometer" has been used in its accepted English significance—that of a machine specifically designed for the purpose of keeping accurate time at sea, and fitted with the spring-detent, or "chronometer" escapement. On the Continent the word is used indifferently to describe machines fitted with either the chronometer or the lever escapement.

It is generally believed that it was first used in its modern sense by John Arnold in his pamphlet "An Account . . . of the going of a Pocket Chronometer," published in 1782. Actually, it was employed with precisely the same meaning by Jeremy Thacker, in the course of a description of his "machine for the longitude" published in 1714. It does not appear, however, to have been generally adopted in its present sense until Arnold's time. Accordingly, in the chapters dealing with previous inventors it has not been used, its place being taken either by the excellent and expressive word "timekeeper," which has now reverted to its more extended significance, or, particularly in the case of foreign inventors, by the terms "montre marine" and "horloge marine," or their English equivalents.

It has not been considered either practicable or desirable to avoid the use of technical horological expressions, and accordingly no attempt has been made to do so; but it will, I think, be generally found that such terms have, on their first appearance, been defined and explained, either in the text itself or in a footnote. A special index of these definitions is given at the end of the general index.

CHAPTER I.

THE "NUREMBERG EGG."

The first author who is known to have proposed the employment of a timekeeper for determining longitude at sea is Gemma Frisius, a Flemish astronomer and mathematician, in a work entitled "De Principiis Astronomiae et Cosmographiae," published at Antwerp in 1530. But the construction of such a timekeeper, as we have seen, was beyond the horological skill of his day, and accordingly there was no way of putting his proposal into practice. Still, it forms a landmark in the chronometer's history.

In his day, clocks were comparatively a new invention. The date at which they first came into general use cannot be accurately fixed, but it can hardly be earlier than the middle of the fourteenth century. At the time when he wrote, however, two distinct classes had already been evolved: non-portable clocks, driven by a falling weight, and portable timekeepers—table clocks and clumsy watches—driven by a coiled spring.* He suggested the use of the latter class for timekeeping at sea, the mariner being instructed to correct their errors by comparing them frequently with a sand clock or water clock.

This method of rating is not so absurd as it sounds.† These sand or water clocks, generally called clepsydrae, were in common use as timekeepers for many centuries, and, although crude timekeepers, it is quite possible that they would have been less affected by a ship's motion,‡ and by changes of temperature, than the clumsy watches, subsequently known, from their birthplace and shape, as "Nuremberg eggs," which were then coming into general use. But neither of these instruments was deserving of notice as an accurate timekeeper for determining longitude.

In 1530, as to-day, the standard of performance required from a marine timekeeper for finding longitude was that it should not vary, at most, more than two or three seconds a day, and this standard the "Nuremberg eggs," although better timekeepers over a long period than the clepsydrae, failed most signally to reach, for they could not

* The invention of the mainspring as a prime mover for portable timepieces is generally ascribed to Peter Hele, or Henlein, of Nuremberg, *circa* 1500.

† Instructions drawn up by the Royal Society in 1660 for the use of a party of observers, who were about to ascend the Peak of Teneriffe for scientific purposes, contain the proviso that the rate of going of a pendulum clock should be observed, by means of a sand-glass, at sea-level and at the summit, and any change noted.

‡ Clepsydrae, especially those using mercury in place of sand or water, have often been seriously suggested for use as marine timekeepers: for example, by Santa Cruz (*circa* 1570), an anonymous Dutch author (1737), Morgan and Short (sand-glass in vacuo, *circa* 1740), Brownlee (1768), Boorn (1771), Jaci (1785), Pattershall (1786), Adams (1810), and Rowland (1813). It may be noted that until 1839 H.M. ships were regularly supplied with hour and half-hour sand-glasses for deck use, and that half-minute glasses are still issued to them for use when heaving the hand-log.

be relied upon to within some fifteen minutes a day. Still, for more than a century after that date they remained *in statu quo*, and the arrangement of their escapement and balance continued to be the standard for clocks and watches of every description. And the world was no nearer obtaining a satisfactory marine timekeeper. It had to remain content with such windy promises as those of Alonso de Santa Cruz, who, in a manuscript work* dedicated to Philip II. of Spain stated :—

> " The longitude is now being sought for in Spain by means of clocks adjusted to register exactly twenty-four hours, and constructed in divers ways : some with wheels, chains, and weights of steel : some with chains of catgut and steel : others using sand, as in sandglasses : others with water in place of sand, and designed after many different fashions : others again with vases or large glasses filled with quicksilver : and, lastly, some, the most ingenious of all, driven by the force of the wind, which moves a weight and thereby the chain of the clock, or which are moved by the flame of a wick saturated with oil : and all of them adjusted to measure twenty-four hours exactly."

It may be as well to state here, briefly, the principles upon which the science of horology is founded.

The only practicable method of measuring a period of time is by measuring the amount of the motion, during that period, of something moving in a uniform, or approximately uniform, manner—whether that something be the water or sand of a clepsydra, the shadow of the gnomon on a sundial, or, as in all modern time-measurers, a rotating wheel. The degree of accuracy with which time can be measured therefore depends, obviously, upon the degree of uniformity of that motion. If it can be made absolutely uniform, a perfect standard of time is at once obtained, whatever the actual rate of that motion may be.

Now, even in the fourteenth century, it was generally recognised that neither clepsydrae nor sundials were accurate timekeepers, or likely to become so. The rate of flow of the sand or water, in the former, varied in different temperatures, and the total time of flow was never quite constant. The time shown by the latter was apparent time,† it was only correct for one latitude, and it could not be read with accuracy, upon a dial of ordinary size, within several minutes. Accordingly, recourse was had to the plan, still followed in every clock and watch, of causing a wheel to revolve as regularly as possible, and of recording its rotations.

To cause a wheel to revolve is easy ; to make its motion approximately regular‡ is not so easy: to make that motion *absolutely* regular

---

* This MSS is now lost. The extract is translated from a paraphrase given in Duro's " Disquisiciones Nauticas."

† It may be noted that a sundial showing the *mean* solar time of any required meridian was patented by Major-General J. R. Oliver, C.M.G., in 1892.

‡ It will be noticed that I use the word " regular," not " uniform." Strictly speaking, of course, a uniform motion is a continuous one, while the motion of the escape wheel—and, indeed, the whole train—of a timekeeper is intermittent, since it comes to rest at every beat. Indeed, in a chronometer the train only in motion for a total time of about half an hour in a day's running. Due to this intermittent motion, also, the time shown by the hands of any timekeeper can never be strictly correct for more than one instant of every beat. The motion of the escape wheel, however, may be regarded as regular, since the interval between each movement and the next is practically constant.

is still unaccomplished. But on this problem the whole success or failure of any timekeeper turns—on the degree of uniformity with which it can keep a certain wheel rotating. All the rest of its mechanism is subsidiary to that end, and, however complicated it may be, by that simple criterion its timekeeping must be judged.

Now if the motion of a wheel acted upon by some external force be unchecked, it will tend to accelerate, and to render it regular some check must be applied to the wheel. It might be thought that this could take the form of a frictional brake, or that the resistance of the air or of a fluid could be made to act upon a fan, or "fly," carried by the wheel.* But it has been found that the motion resulting from such checks as these is far from uniform, and at a very early period in the history of clock-making it was definitely recognised that the best method (the one used ever since) was to form teeth upon the rim of the wheel, and to control its motion by some contrivance which stood in the path of those teeth, and only allowed them to escape past it one by one, at intervals of time which, as far as possible, were all equal. From this method of operation, the wheel came to be known as the "escape wheel," while the contrivance itself was called the "escapement."

Now, with the introduction of the escapement, the problem assumes definite shape. If its action be uniform—if it allow the teeth of the escape wheel to escape at exactly equal intervals of time—the wheel will revolve regularly, and, as we have seen, a perfect timekeeper is obtained. Some controlling device, therefore, is needed for the escapement, which will operate it periodically at equal intervals of time.

The essential requirements, then, of any timekeeper employing these principles are an escape wheel, an escapement, and a controlling device to govern the latter. Subsidiary to these essentials are some means of conveying sufficient impetus to the escape wheel to keep it rotating, and some way of recording its rotations.

As we have seen, Gemma Frisius proposed to adopt the "Nuremberg egg" of his day as a portable timekeeper for use on shipboard. The mechanism of this, although rough and clumsy, embodied, in a rudimentary form, all the principles laid down above—*and, accordingly, all the principles of the modern chronometer.* Strange though it may seem, the difference between it and the modern machine is purely one of detail, and it is in very truth the egg from which the modern chronometer has been hatched. An explanation of its mechanism will, accordingly, serve as a starting point.

Figure 1 gives a general view of the mechanism of a "Nuremberg egg."

---

* A clock governed by flies, and designed to drive an equatorial telescope (for which an absolutely *continuous* motion is required) was made by the firm of Breguet for M. Villarceau in 1870, and seems to have given good results. But it is not probable that it was more accurate than an ordinary good-quality driving clock or a chronograph.

Taking first the essentials, C is the escape wheel. The escapement consists of the bar E, carrying the two projections *e*, *e′*, termed the "pallets." (The relative positions of these pallets and the teeth of the escape wheel can be more easily followed in fig. 2.) The controlling device is the bar *b*, carrying at either end the two weights BB′, and rigidly attached to the bar E so that they form a T, *b* being the cross and E the down-stroke. It is termed a "balance."

The subsidiary details are as follows. The escape wheel is kept in motion by the force of a spiral spring, termed the "mainspring," contained in the barrel A. This spring, when wound, tends to rotate A, and thus pulls the chain* *f*, which is wound round the pulley F, called the "fusee." Mounted on the same axis as F, and turning with it, is the toothed wheel 1, engaging in the smaller toothed wheel 2, termed a "pinion." This pinion is on the same axis as the wheel II, and they turn together. Similarly, the teeth of II engage with the pinion 3, and those of the wheel III, which turns with 3, with the pinion 4, which is mounted upon the same axis as that of the escape wheel.† Hence this assemblage of wheels and pinions, termed a "train,"‡ forms a direct connection between the barrel A and the escape wheel, and it is obvious that the spring works at a great mechanical disadvantage, so that the torque at the escape wheel is a very small proportion of that acting on A. On the other hand, for one revolution of A the escape wheel will revolve a large number of times, depending upon the respective numbers of teeth in the wheels and the pinions.§

Now consider the action of the escapement. The force of the mainspring is pressing a tooth of the escape wheel against the pallet *e*, and the balance will accordingly swing in the direction shown by the arrow. When it reaches the position XX′, the tooth will escape, slipping off the edge of the pallet, and the wheel will turn freely through a very minute arc, when a tooth on the opposite side of the wheel will drop on to the other pallet *e′*. The balance will be accordingly checked in its swing, brought to rest, and driven in the other direction past its original situation until, when it reaches the position YY′, this tooth will, in its turn escape, and another fall upon the pallet *e*.

Thus the teeth of the escape wheel are each, in turn, locked by the pallets, and before they can escape they must reverse the position in which they find the balance.

---

* In the early timekeepers, up to about 1600, a catgut line was used instead of a steel chain.

† It will be noticed that both the escape wheel, termed in this escapement the "crown wheel" (from its shape) and the wheel III., termed the "contrate wheel," have their teeth parallel with their axes, or "arbors." There is no actual necessity for the contrate wheel to be of this shape, but it was generally adopted for watches as allowing a more compact arrangement of the mechanism, or "movement."

‡ The wheels of the train run between two brass plates, kept at the correct distance apart by means of pillars. The pivots run in holes, termed "pivot holes," drilled in the plates. Although the latter are shown, for the purposes of the figure, as rectangular, they are actually circular (or, in the early "eggs," oval) and the planting of the wheels of the train is arranged round the centre wheel so as to conform with this shape.

§ Watches with this train generally went for some 15 hours only. Those from 1680 onwards had an additional wheel in the train to allow of their going 24 hours without increasing the number of turns of the mainspring.

See p. 26.

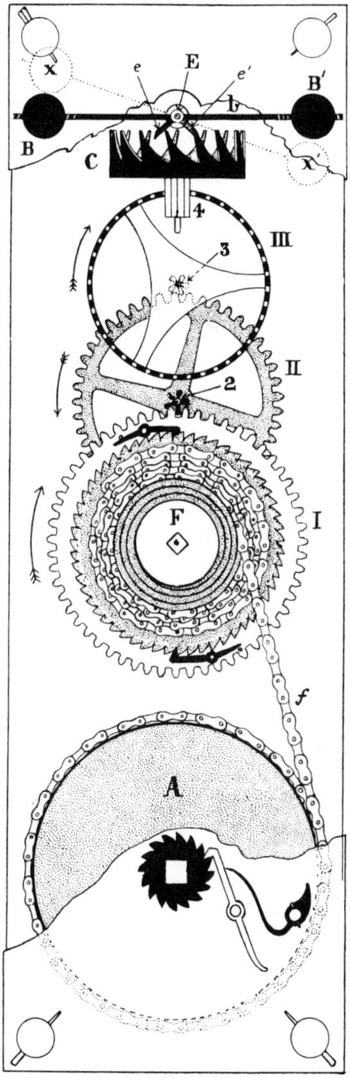

1. General arrangement of the mechanism of a "Nuremberg Egg."

The planting of the arbors in one straight line is purely conventional (see foot-note, p. 22.) The greater part of the top-plate is shown as cut away.

See p. 26.

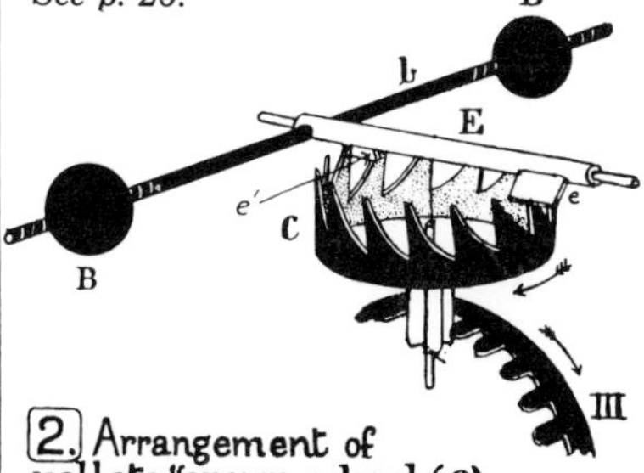

2. Arrangement of pallets, "crown wheel (C) and "contrate wheel" (III).

See p. 28

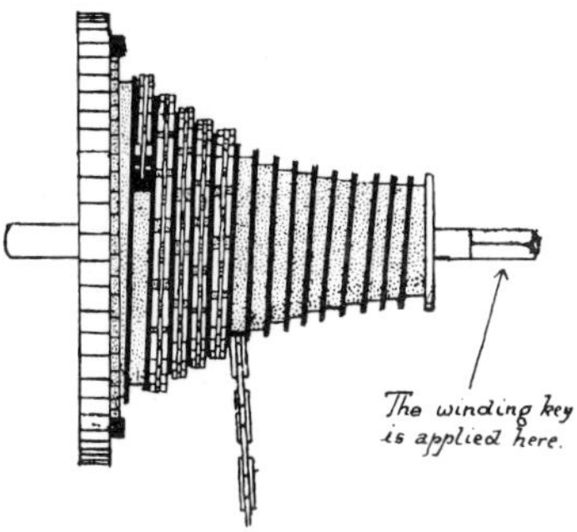

3. The fusee.

See p. 30.

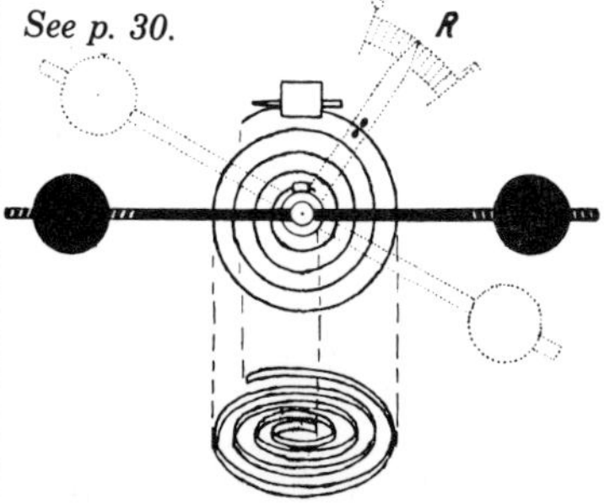

4. The balance spring. *(The device (R) in dotted line is the "regulator," for which see p. 26).*

It can readily be understood that this escapement, which is known as the "*verge*"* escapement, was not likely to perform with much accuracy. The time taken by any tooth to disengage itself depends (excluding friction) upon the force which it exerts on the pallet, on the inertia of the balance weights, and on the extent of the arc which they described; while for the interval between each release to be uniform it was necessary that all three of these factors should be invariable. And, since the arc and the force exerted by the teeth were, as a matter of fact, affected by the varying friction in the pivots and between every pair of teeth in a very roughly-cut train, it is not surprising that the intervals of release varied considerably, and that the going of the machine was erratic.

Incidentally, it was only the invention of the "stackfreed"† and, later, the "fusee" that made it worth while to construct spring-driven timekeepers on this plan at all. Large clocks using this escapement had been employed with more or less success for at least two hundred years, but these had the great advantage, denied to a portable clock, of being driven by a falling weight which exerted a constant torque, and so ensured that the force acting upon the first wheel of the train should be constant, however much that reaching the escape wheel might fluctuate through friction. But in a spring-driven clock the force exerted by the spring is proportional to the amount it is wound, and is far greater at the start than the finish. Without some equalising device, therefore, such a clock would have run through, say, five minutes in a minute just after winding, and a minute in five minutes when it had nearly run down.

The fusee removed this objection. Its arrangement is shown in fig. 3, from which it will be seen that the radius at which the pull of the chain acts gradually enlarges as the spring unwinds, so that the increase in leverage thus obtained compensates for the diminished strength of the pull. It is possible, in this manner, to make the power exerted on the first‡ wheel of the train practically the same at all states of the spring.

Such was the crude and erratic mechanism of the "Nuremberg egg," the first rough sketch, as it were, of that of the chronometer of to-day. Only one hand—an hour hand—was fitted, but even this *indicated* time more accurately than the machine could be relied upon to *measure* it.

The first effort to break up the general stagnation with regard to the development of portable timekeepers was made by an Englishman, Robert Hooke, and it resulted in the introduction of the greatest improvement ever applied to them—the balance spring.

* See also p. 219*f*.

† The stackfreed was an auxiliary spring, which opposed the action of the mainspring during the first half of its uncoiling, and assisted it in the latter half. It was superseded by the fusee from about 1540, although occasionally used at a later date. A patent granted to Frederick Kelhoff as late as 1764 (Pat. No. 819, Nov. 29th) includes the application of a stackfreed.

‡ Termed the "great" wheel. The second wheel is known as the "centre" wheel, since it is almost invariably planted in the centre of the movement. The third and fourth wheels have no special names.

HOOKE.

Hooke (1635-1703) was one of the outstanding figures of his age. His mind ranged over the entire scientific studies of his time, and there was hardly any branch of science which he did not consider, and to whose advancement he did not contribute. A mere catalogue of his inventions, suggestions, and experiments would more than fill this chapter. It must be admitted, however, that his attention was never steadily directed for any length of time to one subject, and that he seems to have considered that any hints he threw out as to the nature of his various incomplete inventions or calculations must secure to him all the credit of their actual completion in practical form. Add to this that he was jealous, vain, and quarrelsome, and it will readily be understood that his fellow scientific workers must have regarded him with very mixed feelings.

He seems to have turned his attention to the improvement of portable timekeepers about 1659. He gives an amusing account of the discouragement he received:—

> "All I could obtain was a Catalogue of Difficulties, *first*, in the doing of it, *secondly* in the bringing of it into publick use, *thirdly*, in making advantage of it. Difficulties were proposed from the alteration of *Climates*, *Airs*, *heats* and *colds*, temperature of *Springs*, the nature of *Vibrations*, the wearing of *Materials*, the motion of the *Ship*, and divers others. Next, it would be difficult to bring it to use, for Sea-men knew their way already to any Port, and Men would not be at the unnecessary charge of the *Apparatus*, and Observations of the Time could not be well made at Sea, and they would nowhere be of use but in East and West *India* voyages, which were so perfectly understood that every common Sea-man almost knew how to pilot a Ship thither. And as for making *benefits*, all People lost by such undertaking; much had been talked about the *Praemium* for the *Longitude*, but there was never any such thing, no King or State would ever give a farthing for it, and the like; all which I let pass . . . . ."

He read several of his Cutlerian lectures in 1664 upon applying springs to the balance of a watch in order to render its vibrations more uniform, explaining some 20 ways of applying them, and illustrating the same by models. He naively admits, however, that he kept the best methods secret, in order to use them for his own advantage. He appears to have negotiated with Lord Brouncker* and other eminent

---

* President of the Royal Society, 1662-1677. Best remembered by his expression of $\frac{\pi}{4}$ as a continued fraction.

§ The actual text of Hooke's anagram is c,e,i,i,i,n, o,s,s,s,t,t,u,v. This curious method of establishing a prior claim to a discovery without actually disclosing it was used by many eminent scientists of that age. Galileo, Newton, Wren and Huyghens, to name no others, frequently employed it, sometimes with amusing results, as when Kepler succeeded in torturing an anagram of Galileo's relating to Saturn into a statement, in extremely bad Latin, that Mars possessed two satellites (thus stumbling, as Swift and Voltaire did later, upon a truth not actually demonstrated until 1877).

An anagram by Wren, describing three instruments for the finding of longitude, is preserved in the archives of the Royal Society, and has, I believe, never been deciphered. Hooke published his secret method of controlling a marine timekeeper in the appendix to his "Description of Helioscopes," translated into Bishop Berkeley's "Universal Character," thus concealing it far more effectually, both from his own age and this, than if he had written it in Chinese. I believe the concluding portion of it to run " . . . by librating jugements moving contrary ways, and by friction."

men to form a syndicate to exploit his invention, but could not agree as to terms.

The principle of Hooke's balance spring was expressed by him in a Latin anagram, which can be resolved into "Ut tensio, sic vis" (as the tension is, so is the force).§ In other words, the force exerted by any spring is directly proportional to the extent to which it is tensioned.

Consider now the balance of the "Nuremberg egg," and imagine that its axis is encircled, as shown in fig. 4, by a spiral spring, the inner end of the spring being pinned to that axis, and the outer end to some fixed point. If the balance, considered for the moment as being at rest and entirely detached from the escapement, be displaced slightly by some external force into the position shown by the dotted lines, the spring will be tensioned, and will set the balance, when released, in motion towards its original position, termed the "dead point." The momentum of the weights will carry it past the dead point to a corresponding position on the opposite side of it, and the spring will now be in compression. The balance will then return under the influence of the spring, again swing across the dead point, and continue to go on vibrating in this manner—the arcs which it describes slowly diminishing in extent owing to friction.

Now here comes in the really valuable property of the balance spring—its isochronous effect. A balance moving with theoretically perfect freedom, under the influence of a theoretically perfect spring, would always perform one vibration in some constant interval of time, whether it described a large or a small arc. This follows directly from Hooke's law enunciated above. Accordingly, it would be just as accurate a time measurer as a perfect pendulum.

But a perfectly free balance has never been made, and in Hooke's time the balance-spring was never given a fair chance to show its powers. The friction at the pivots of the balance was considerable since their bearings were not jewelled*, and the springs were far from being perfectly homogeneous. Far more detrimental, however, was the effect of the escapement. As we have seen, the verge escapement never leaves the balance free for a moment, but is always pushing it either one way or the other, with varying force and a varying amount of friction. The utmost, then, that could be expected of the spring in such circumstances was that it should exert a steadying influence

§ See note at foot of preceding page.

* The use of jewelled pivot-holes, for the pivots of rotating arbors, greatly diminishes both the friction and the wear of such holes as compared with those of metal. The jewels employed are generally sapphire, ruby, or diamond, a hole being drilled in a flatted jewel for the reception of the pivot, while longitudinal motion is generally, but not invariably, prevented by means of a second (unpierced) jewel, termed the "end stone," covering the outer side of the hole. Jewelled holes are not necessary for slow-moving pivots, such as those of the fusee and centre wheels, but in chronometers those of the balance, escape wheel, and fourth wheel are invariably jewelled, and sometimes those of the third wheel also. The art of drilling jewel holes was invented about 1703 by Nicholas Facio, F.R.S., a Swiss resident in London, who attempted unsuccessfully to protect his invention by an Act of Parliament, having previously obtained a patent for it. Until about 1790 the art of jewelling was a jealously-guarded secret confined to a small coterie of English workmen, and was unknown on the Continent.

upon the motions of the balance, and upon the time of its vibrations. And this it did, with the result that in a very few years it became universally employed in portable timekeepers.

It was soon found, however, to have one marked defect: it was much affected by heat and cold. Heat makes a spring weaker, while cold has the reverse effect.* And as the actual time of vibration of a balance moving under the influence of a balance-spring depends upon the strength of the spring, it follows that such a balance would vibrate more quickly for a fall of temperature, and more slowly for a rise. It became, therefore, the practice to provide, in watches fitted with a balance-spring, a device called a "regulator," which enabled the user of the watch, (by altering the position of two small pins, called the "curb pins," which embraced the outer turn of the spring), to change its effective length and so compensate for the effects of temperature upon it, since a short spring is proportionally stronger than a long one of the same cross-section, and accordingly makes the balance vibrate more quickly. This method is still employed in common watches.

The balance spring, as we have said, is the most important single improvement ever applied to portable timekeepers,† and it is therefore doing bare justice to Hooke's memory to point out that there can be little doubt that it was his invention, although there have been several other claimants.‡

Hooke appears to have lost interest in the subject of longitude after his failure to form his syndicate. He suggested the construction of a marine watch fitted with two balances geared together, § his idea being that the effect of the ship's motion upon one would be neutralised by the corresponding effect on the other—a plan which, as we shall see, was adopted by several later inventors—and he made or caused to be made in 1669 a timekeeper whose balance was controlled by the attraction of a loadstone. It could be caused to go faster or slower at will by altering the distance between the loadstone and the balance, and Hooke appears to have thought well of it as a means of finding longitude. He died in 1703.

* Heat also increases the diameter, and hence the inertia, of the balance. The error this produces, however, while augmenting the retardation due to the weakening of the spring, is much smaller in amount than the latter.

† It has never been equalled or approached as a controller for the balance, although many other devices have been tried, including a vibrating tuning-fork (by Niaudet Breguet in 1866), and a magnet (by Hooke and others).

‡ Notably Huyghens and the Abbe Hautefeuille. The latter successfully opposed Huyghens' application for a French patent for his use of the balance spring, on the ground of his own work in the same field. But there is no reasonable doubt that Hooke had anticipated both of them.

§ A watch on this plan was made for him by Thomas Tompion, "the father of English watchmaking," in 1675, and became the property of King Charles II. It was inscribed "*Robt. Hooke, Inven*, 1658. *T. Tompion, fecit*, 1675" and had a form of "duplex" escapement.

The idea has often been revived. There is a watch in the Museum of the Clockmakers' Company, made by John Grant in 1800, with two balances and two balance springs, while two French watches on somewhat similar lines, one made by Berthoud, *circa* 1760, and the other in the present century, were described and illustrated in the "Horological Journal" for October, 1909.

The Horological Museum, Copenhagen, contains a watch, signed "Theodor Wiedeman, Vienna," and made about 1700, with *three* balances, all geared together.

See p. 33.

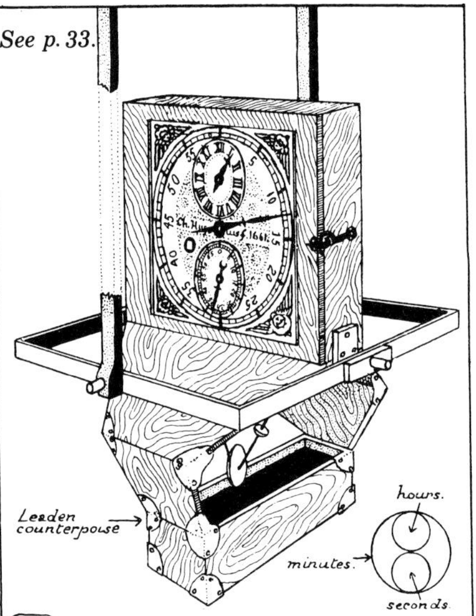

5 Huyghens' marine clock [1661].
The details of the dial are partly conjectural.

See p. 33.

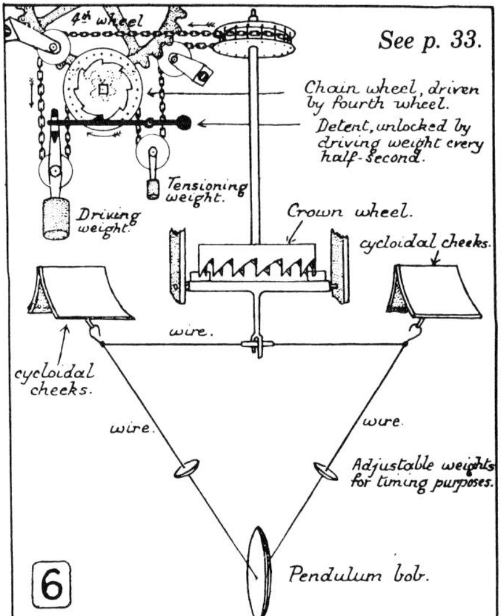

6 Escapement & pendulum of Huyghens' machine. [*Also a conjectural restoration of his remontoire.*]

See p. 37.

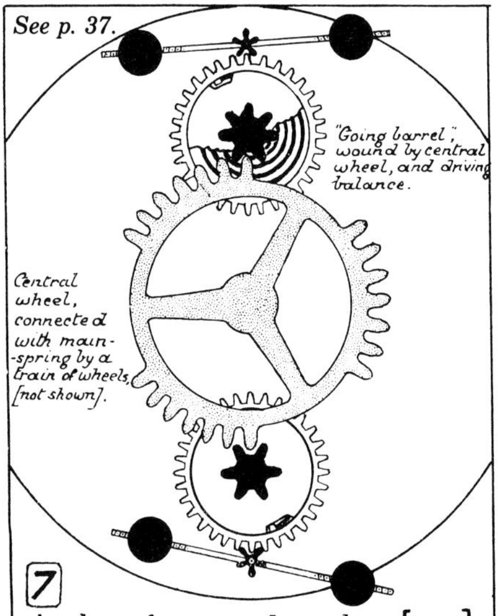

7 Leibnitz' proposed machine [1675].
From a very rough drawing published in the "Journal des Sçavans", 1675, p. 27.

See p. 42.

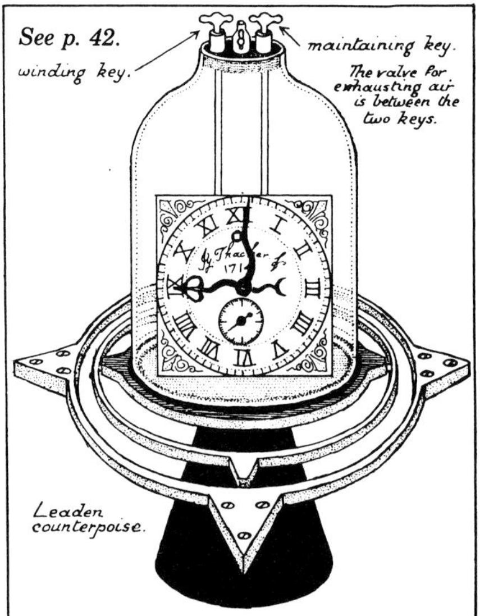

8 Thacker's machine [1714].

CHAPTER II.

EARLY EFFORTS TO CONSTRUCT A MARINE TIMEKEEPER, 1660—1760.

HUYGHENS. (*Plate I*).

The first timekeeper specifically intended for the purpose of finding longitude at sea was constructed in the year 1660. This machine, which it is much to be feared no longer exists, was designed by the famous Christian Huyghens, of Zulichem in Holland (1629-95). Huyghens' scientific abilities and achievements make him a worthy rival of Hooke. He was distinguished both as an astronomer (he discovered Saturn's rings and his largest satellite), an optician, a mathematician, and a horologist. He was one of the first who used a pendulum as the controlling agent of a clock, and was certainly the first to give the correct mathematical theory of its motion.* His first pendulum clock was completed in 1657, and about 1659 he turned his attention to the construction of a marine timekeeper.

Fig. 5 shows the general appearance of his machine, and fig. 6 gives details of his escapement and pendulum.

The machine was driven by a coiled spring, and had a verge escapement, but this latter was controlled by a pendulum, not a balance. In his pendulum clock, Huyghens had, in effect, taken the ordinary verge escapement with balance, as fitted in the "Nuremberg egg" amputated one arm of the balance, and lengthened the other. Then, finding that the weight of a pendulum ought to move, not in a circular arc, but in a cycloid, he had improved upon this by suspending his pendulum by a double thin cord which, as the pendulum swung, was bent around one of two curved wooden cheeks, thus altering the effective length of the pendulum, and causing the weight to take the correct cycloidal path.† In his marine timekeeper he fitted the same device, but here the pendulum was very short and shaped like a V, with the weight at the point. Its effective length was 9¾ inches, and accordingly it beat half seconds.‡ The crown wheel, it will be noticed, was set horizontally.

---

* In his "Horologium Oscillatorium," published at Amsterdam in 1673. The description of his timekeeper is mainly taken from this source.

† This method, although correct in principle, has long been abandoned for all classes of clocks. The error involved in the ordinary pendulum suspension, termed the "circular error," is very small when the arc described is short, and it can, moreover, be used to compensate another error which is always present in the ordinary "dead-beat" clock escapement.

‡ The time of vibration of a free pendulum varies as the square root of its effective length, and inversely as the force of gravity, but it is entirely independent of the mass of the pendulum.

I have said that the motive power was a coiled spring, but that is only partially correct. There appears in this machine the first published instance* of a contrivance which has been the *ignis fatuus* of many generations of clockmakers, and whose name, the "remontoire," includes some of the most ingenious, elaborate, beautiful and useless contrivances ever made by man. Let Huyghens describe his in his own words .

> "To the wheel, which has serrated teeth, and is nearest the pendulum, a small weight is hung by a thin and flexible chain. It is moved by this weight alone, and all the rest of the machine has nothing to do but to restore this small leaden weight to its original height every half-second."

The remontoires used by later inventors in marine timekeepers employed a spring, or springs, instead of a weight, but the principle involved was the same—that the force of the mainspring, instead of being transmitted to the balance, was made to wind up, periodically, an auxiliary source of power at the other end of the train, which, in its turn, drove the balance with practically constant force.

The machine had three dials, showing hours, minutes and seconds, and was suspended so as to be capable of moving about two axes at right angles. Thus, whatever the angle assumed by the ship, it would remain upright. This method of mounting an instrument is termed suspension in gimbals, and it was first used about 1530, for ships' lamps and compasses.†

Huyghens was assisted in his experiments by Alexander Bruce, second Earl of Kincardine,‡ who was a political refugee in Holland from 1658 to 1660. With his assistance, financial and otherwise, two of these machines were made and tested at sea.§ Hooke, in a paper read before the Royal Society in 1662, gives the following account of their early trials:

> "The Lord Kincardine did resolve to make some trial what might be done by carrying a pendulum clock to sea, for which end he contrived to make the watch to be moved by a spring instead of a weight, and then, making the case of the clock very heavy with lead, he suspended it underneath the deck of the ship by a ball and socket of brass, making the pendulum but short, namely, to vibrate half seconds; and that he might be the better enabled to judge of the effect of it, he caused two of the same kind of pendulum clocks to be made, and suspended them both pretty near the middle of the vessel underneath the decks. This done, having first adjusted them to go equal to one another, and pretty near to the true time, he caused them first to move parallel to one another, that is,

* Berthoud, in his "Histoire de la Mesure du Temps," mentions that the earliest known remontoire is one fitted to an old German astronomical clock, about 1600.

† Its invention is commonly ascribed to Girolamo Cardan (1501-1576), a mathematician, commemorated by the so-called "Cardan's formula" for the solution of a cubic equation, which he stole from Tartaglia. I have seen an old woodcut, however, of a much earlier date, illustrating a cart, for the conveyance of wounded men, fitted with this suspension.

‡ Huyghens afterwards fell out with Kincardine, and accused him of trying to steal his inventions.

§ Some notes on one of these trials, which lasted from April 29th to September 4th, 1663, during which time the ship visited Lisbon, are preserved in the British Museum (Sloan, 598). The machines were of different sizes, and while the larger went with fair regularity, the smaller frequently stopped, and had to be taken to pieces, cleaned and oiled during the voyage.

Plate I. CHRISTIAN HUYGHENS.
From the portrait prefixed to his "Opera Varia" (1724).
See p. 33.

to the plane of the length of the ship, and afterwards he turned one to move in a plane at right angles with the former; and in both cases it was found by trials made at sea (at which I was present) that they would vary from one another, though not very much."

It was probably due to Kincardine's influence, also, that when Major Holmes* sailed in 1664 with five ships to protect the English settlements on the Guinea coast from the encroachments of the Dutch, he took with him these two machines. An account of his experiences with them was published in the "Philosophical Transactions," Vol. I., from which I take the following:—

"The Major having left that coast (Guinea), and being come to the isle of St. Thomas under the Line, he adjusted his watches, put to sea, and sailed westward, seven or eight hundred leagues, without changing his course; after which, finding the wind favourable, he steered towards the coast of Africa, N.N.E., but having sailed upon that line about two or three hundred leagues, the masters of the other ships, under his conduct, apprehending that they should want water, before they could reach that coast, did propose to him to steer their course to the Barbadoes, to supply themselves with water there. The Major having called the master and pilots together, and caused them to produce their journals and calculations, it was found that those pilots differed from the Major in their reckonings, one of them eighty leagues, another about a hundred, and the third more; but the Major judging by his pendulum watches that they were only some thirty leagues distant from the isle of Fuego, which is one of the isles of Cape Verde, and that they might reach it next day, and having a great confidence in the said watches, they resolved to steer their course thither; and having given order so to do, they got the very next day about noon a sight of the said isle of Fuego . . ."

In a letter to a friend in Paris, written after Holmes' return, Huyghens remarks:—

"Major Holmes at his return has made a relation concerning the usefulness of pendulums, which surpasses my expectations. I did not imagine that the watches of this first structure would succeed so well, and I had reserved my main hopes for the new ones. But seeing that those have already served so successfully, and that the others are yet more just and exact, I have the more reason to believe that the finding of the longitude will be brought to perfection."

But his hopes were not destined to be realised. For a few years, indeed, his pendulum timekeepers were well thought of by the learned.† Thus in 1669 two members of the Royal Society revised and enlarged a set of instructions for the use of such timekeepers written by Huyghens, and published them‡ with a preface which began in the following remarkable manner:—

"*Whereas 'tis generally esteemed that there is no Practise for the* Finding of the Longitude *at Sea comparable to that of those Watches, which, instead of a* Ballance-Wheele, *are regulated by a* Pendulum . . ."

While the instructions themselves ended with a rather curious paragraph:—

"12. If all the watches should stop at sea, you must, as speedily as possible, set them going again, that you may know how much you

* Afterwards Admiral Sir Robert Holmes.

† They were tried in several ships of the French navy, with varying results, ascribed by Huyghens as much to the inexperience of those in charge of them as to the defects of the machines themselves. They were used with moderate success in the Duke of Beaufort's ill-fated expedition to relieve Candia, whose twenty years' siege by the Turks was drawing to its end.

‡ In the "Philosophical Transactions," May 10th, 1669.

advance from that place towards the east or west; which is of no small importance, since, for want of this knowledge, you are sometimes by the force of currents so carried away, that though you sail before the wind, yet you are driven a-stern, of which there are many instances."

But it soon became manifest that these timekeepers, though deserving of the utmost praise as a plucky effort, were hopelessly unsuited to sea use. In anything but a flat calm their going was most erratic; either they stopped altogether, till another roll set them going again, or they would go in jerks, their pendulums never swinging the same, or anything like the same, arc for two beats together. Moreover, even in a calm they were exposed to two sources of error for which no compensation was provided—the alteration of the pendulum's length through change of temperature, and the variation of gravity in different latitudes. Accordingly, we find that in 1674 Huyghens had abandoned this design, and proposed to control his marine timekeepers by a balance and balance spring.

His publication of this design caused an angry controversy with Hooke, who claimed that Huyghens had heard of his invention through Oldenburg, the Secretary of the Royal Society, and pirated it.

Whether there was any truth in this contention is doubtful, but at any rate Huyghens' method of applying the spring was original, for he geared up the balance so that instead of describing, like Hooke's, an arc of 120° or so, it revolved several turns at each beat.* He found himself, however, baffled by the effect of temperature on the strength of the spring, and such of his results as he cared to make public only appeared, in anagram form, shortly before his death in 1695.

LEIBNITZ.

Conjointly with Huyghens' account of his balance timekeeper,† there appeared a description of one proposed by Gottfried Wilhelm von Leibnitz, the great German mathematician. Leibnitz is now chiefly remembered by the violent controversy which once raged over his claim to be considered the inventor not only of the differential notation (which he undoubtedly was) but of the differential calculus itself, a controversy which was carried on with the utmost heat long after both Leibnitz and Newton were in their graves, and which had the effect of retarding English mathematical progress for a century.‡ But in his day he was best known as a metaphysician, and he carried metaphysics into the domains of physical science, particularly mechanics, with unfortunate results for his reputation. A sketch of his timekeeper is given in fig. 7. He proposed to use two balances and two spiral springs. Each spring was wound in turn by the train, and

* This device is termed a "pirouette." Huyghens used it in his pendulum clocks as well as in his marine timekeepers. It is theoretically objectionable on account of the friction in the gearing, and never came into general use.

† "Journal des Scavans," 1675, p. 130.

‡ English mathematicians, especially at Cambridge, Newton's *Alma Mater*, obstinately adhered to his obsolete "fluxional" notation until 1820, when they were at last converted by the efforts of three undergraduates, Babbage, Herschel and Peacock, who successfully opposed, as Babbage put it, "the principles of pure ***d***-ism to the ***dot***-age of the University."

then allowed to run down freely, controlled only by the inertia of the balance, the other spring being meanwhile wound. When the first spring had run down, it unlocked the second, which ran down in its turn, while the first was re-wound—and so on. He appears to have thought that the time taken by the springs to run down must of necessity be constant, and to have troubled very little about the inevitable errors involved in such a rough and ready method of time-keeping, merely remarking, airily:—

> " . . . all these defects, that proceed from the imperfection of the matter, may be surmounted by a general remedy, without examining them here in particular. And that is, that for executing it in great, we may make use of massy springs, as are those of cross-bows, we being masters of them, not wanting force or place in a ship to govern a great weight that may serve to bend them continually again . . . And it is easy to demonstrate, that by augmenting the size of the engine, and the force of the massy springs, we may make the error as small as we please . . .; which answer is so clear and so universal, that all those who have considered it have expressed their satisfaction therein."

His machine is really only of interest for two minor points: it illustrated his fatal propensity for writing upon subjects whose principles he had imperfectly mastered, and it very faintly foreshadowed the beautiful constant-force escapement used long afterwards by Mudge.

Leibnitz never went further with this design, although he appears to have had some correspondence with Ditton upon the improvement of marine timekeepers.

Another period of stagnation then supervened, and for fifty years very little was accomplished towards the construction of a marine timekeeper. Such attempts as were made seem mostly to have been of a trivial nature, and based upon an imperfect comprehension of the difficulties to be overcome.

HUTCHINSON.

Thus in 1712 John Hutchinson, a religious enthusiast of the Whiston type,* endeavoured to obtain an Act of Parliament for the better protection of his invention of an improved timepiece for the longitude. He was opposed tooth and nail by the Clockmakers Company, who expended in fees to this end the sum of £143 13s. 4½d., and finally carried the Committee to whom the Bill was referred by exhibiting a watch made *circa* 1698 by Charles Goode, which possessed most of the principal improvements claimed by Hutchinson. The Committee thereupon decided to proceed no further with the Bill.

Hutchinson published two broadsides putting forward his claim to the protection of an Act, instead of a patent, and these were answered by the Company, but even with the information these recriminations afford it is not easy to discover precisely where he conceived that the novelty of his invention resided. It seems, however, to have been well

* Like Whiston, who boasted with unconscious humour that Newton was afraid of him, Hutchinson was bitterly opposed, on religious grounds, to the great mathematician's theories, especially gravitation, and he published a work called "Moses' Principia" in which he supported the literal accuracy of the Book of Genesis by geological observations and reasonings. His sect survived its founder many years, and may not be quite extinct even now.

thought of by Newton. From Hutchinson's description, he appears to have eliminated the contrate-wheel, and to have used two escape wheels. He claimed that his watch would keep time accurately without a balance spring, and that he could prevent such a spring from "varying with the weather." He also used a dust-proof case, and "a contrivance to wind up this, or any other Movement without an aperture in the case through which anything can pass to foul the movement." He thus appears to be one of the first to make a keyless watch.*

He also studied the question of determining longitude by variation, and made a map for this purpose. After his death, two of his watches were found among his effects, one complete and the other in parts, but no notes or descriptions relating to them.

After the offer of the £20,000 reward in 1714, several methods employing timekeepers were put forward very confidently, on paper.

HALL, PLANK.

Thus William Hall, in that year, proposes simply to use "a good Watch," *tout court.*† Stephen Plank, at the same time, proposes to keep watches in a brass box over a stove with a continual fire in it, preserving a uniform heat by secret means. But his pamphlet does not succeed in conveying the impression that he understood why the rate of a watch's going varies with the temperature.‡

HOBBS.

Then William Hobbs,§ who describes himself as "Philo. Mathem.," proposes to use "a spring movement, accurate to a tenth of a minute," and fitted with two hands geared 100 to 1. The movement is apparently a perfect timekeeper, although we are given no details of its construction. There is more than a little of the second Marquis of Worcester's¶ style about the explanation of its use:—

> "Note that in this Movement, the Time is regulated or conformed to the Motion. Whereas in former Movements, the Motion is regulated or Conformed to the Time. And this ought to be well understood, before you can rightly comprehend what is herein contained."
>
> ". . . So that there is nothing wanting to complete this Discovery, but to put it into practice."
>
> ". . . If a common Minute Watch (by filing or loading the Ballance, or otherwise) be made to go, or already does go, any unknown quantity of time either too Fast or too Slow; by this device we may find the Hour and Minute of the day by such a Watch more exactly than can be done by the best timed common Watch whatever. And this even without touching it, other than by winding up the Spring as usual."

---

* An advertisement relating to a watch made by R. Bowen, which appeared in the "London Gazette" for January 10th—13th, 1686, described it as being wound up without a key.

† "A New and True way to find the Longitude," 1714.

‡ "An Introduction to the only Method for discovering the Longitude," 1714.

§ "A New discovery for finding the Longitude . .," London, 1714.

¶ Author of the famous "Century of Inventions," and reputed inventor of the steam-engine.

THE MOVEMENT OF ONE OF SULLY'S MARINE CLOCKS. The outcase is of wood, shaped like a mantel clock, with a handle at the top. (Clockmakers Company Museum).

There are two worthless plates in the pamphlet, showing the dial and the gearing of the hands. As far as can be gathered, Hobbs conceived that any watch movement, if let alone, would have a constant daily error, and that by combining such a movement with his two hands, he could at any time, by reading them, and then executing a sum in simple proportion, obtain the elapsed time since they were read last. Hence G.M.T., the longitude, fame, and fortune!

PALMER.

Slightly more sensible, but still unimportant, are the proposals of William Palmer.* His analysis of the causes of error in watches is correct and full, but, like Plank, he merely proposes to obviate the effects of temperature by keeping his timekeeper near a fire. He states that he has recently brought out a pocket watch without a contrate-wheel, and hopes that the Board of Longitude, if they approve of his notions, will communicate with him.

THACKER.

But one of these pamphleteers, Jeremy Thacker, of Beverley, was a man of vastly different mental calibre from the common run of them, and he deserves a better fate than the absolute oblivion into which his name has fallen. His pamphlet, published in 1714†, opens with a clever and satirical resumé of other contemporary efforts. He suggests, for instance, to " H - bbs " (Hobbs) that before he sends his machine to sea he should arrange for two consecutive Junes to be exactly equally hot. He assures a " Mr. Bill - - y," who appears to have tried a pendulum movement, that he has but one thing more to do—namely, to prove Newton's first law of motion false. Other projectors are criticised, " Mr. Br - - - e, the Corrector of the Moon's Motion,"‡ " Signor Al - - ri," who appears to be an Italian professor of mathematics, " Mr. J. H.," who uses a " portable barometer with spiral bason," and " Mr. Wa - - - n," who advertises a clock to make the Longitude known to those of the meanest capacity.

Then, becoming more serious, he describes his own work. He has verified experimentally the fact that springs lose strength in heat, and *vice versa*. (One of his figures shows a coiled spiral spring with a weight suspended at its outer end, whose rise or fall is measured on a scale.) Then he gives a description of his timekeeper, which is shown in fig. 8, re-drawn from a plate appearing in the pamphlet.

. The machine was suspended in gimbals, and, as far as can be gathered from his description, it embodied a spring movement of

* " A Great Improvement in Watchwork," York, 1715.

† " The / Longitudes / Examined, / beginning with a short epistle to the / Longitudinarians / and / ending with the description of a smart, pretty / Machine / of my Own / which I am (almost) sure will do for / the Longitude, and procure me / The / Twenty Thousand Pounds. By Jeremy Thacker, of Beverly in Yorkshire. ' . . . *quid non mortalia pectora cogis Auri sacra Fames* . . London. Printed for J. Roberts at the Oxford Arms in Warwick Lane, 1714. Price Sixpence."

‡ Robert Browne, author of " Method of finding the Longitude at Sea," London, 1714. He petitioned the Board of Longitude, unsuccessfully, for a reward in consideration of his work on the lunar theory.

ordinary construction. He gives no mechanical details, but emphasises that all the arbors were designed to be horizontal, in order to equalise the friction at the pivots. The main feature of interest, however, was that the whole of the mechanism worked *in vacuo*, a large glass, like the receiver of an air-pump, covering the movement, and a vacuum being maintained in it by means of an air-pump attached to a non-return valve fitted at its top. Close to the valve were also fitted two keys, communicating with the movement by means of rods passing through stuffing boxes. One of these was provided for the purpose of winding the mainspring, and the other brought into action an auxiliary spring which kept the machine going during the time of winding. The invention of this "maintaining power" is generally ascribed to Harrison, but Thacker antedates him by twenty years.*

The weak point of Thacker's machine was that he made no provision for the effects of heat and cold on his balance spring, but calibrated them: *i.e.*, he ascertained the machine's rate of going at various temperatures, and then kept a record of the temperatures to which it was exposed during any given period, obtaining its error in that period by calculation. This plan was also suggested, much later, by a far greater man, Pierre Le Roy, and to a limited extent, in comparatively recent times, by Hartnup;† but, although it is in accordance with the modern method of allowing for the errors of all delicate instruments, and not attempting to eliminate them entirely, yet the magnitude of the errors involved in using an uncompensated timekeeper, and the difficulty of keeping a sufficiently exact record of the duration and amount of the various changes of temperature, make its application in such cases impracticable.‡

Thacker states that he made one of these machines, and that its rate, obtained from star transits, never exceeded 6 seconds per day. I have not been able to find any record of his having made tests at sea. Probably they would have been disappointing. His work is valuable more for its promise, and the evidence it affords of his powers of invention and his grasp of the requisite essentials. He must certainly be regarded as the inventor of the system of keeping the mechanism of a timekeeper in vacuo, or at constant pressure, which is now looked upon as an essential requirement of any high-class astronomical clock,§ and he was also the first to provide a spring-driven timekeeper with maintaining power to keep it going while winding. Furthermore, he

* A maintaining device (for roasting jacks) was also patented in 1716 by Robert Evans, Pat. No. 407 of that year.

† Hartnup did not propose to use an uncompensated balance, but he suggested discarding all forms of auxiliary compensation, accepting the ordinary compensation balance (which is only correct at two particular temperatures) and tabulating its errors.

‡ It should be remembered, however, that the vacuum would greatly modify the effects of heat and cold upon the machine.

§ *e.g.*—The Riefler. It is customary to employ a constant and slightly reduced pressure inside the clock-case, rather than a pronounced vacuum. The rate of the clock is altered by varying the amount of rarefaction.

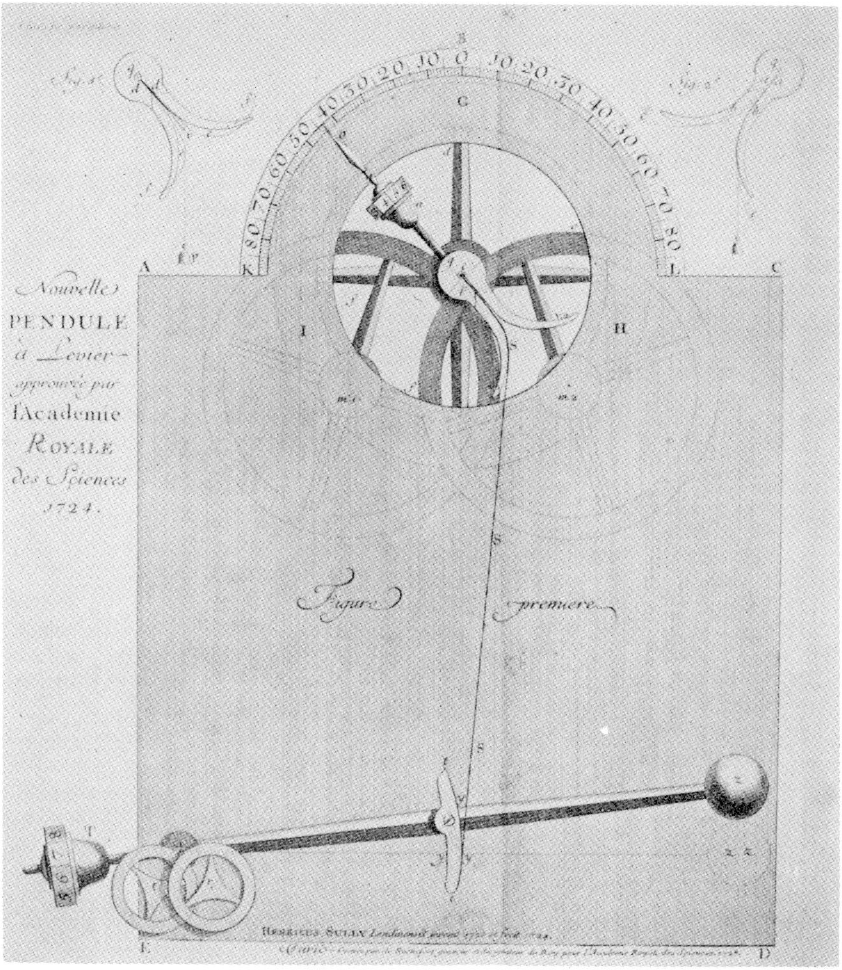

Plate III. CONTROLLING MECHANISM OF SULLY'S MARINE CLOCK. From an engraving in his " Description Abregée . . ."

See p. 46.

The Back of the Sully Marine Timepiece
For the Clockmakers' Company's Collection

was the first man to use the word "chronometer" to denote a marine timekeeper.* Here is the concluding passage of his pamphlet :—

> " . . . In a word, I am satisfied that my Reader begins to think that the *Phonometers*, *Pyrometers*, *Selenometers*, *Heliometers*, and all the *Meters* are not worthy to be compared with my *Chronometer*."

The next attempts at producing a marine timekeeper were made on the other side of the Channel.

HAUTEFEUILLE.

A machine of impracticable character was proposed by the Abbé Hautefeuille in 1719.† He was not a mere visionary, for he had previously done, as we have seen, a considerable amount of experimental work in connection with the balance spring, and he subsequently invented, in 1722, the rack-lever escapement. But the project in question, which involved a movement controlled by a pendulum dipping into a jar of sea-water, whose friction was intended to compensate for the effects both of change of temperature and of the ship's motion, does little credit to his ability.

SULLY.

The next attempt was made by the talented and unfortunate Henry Sully (1680-1723), who was by birth an Englishman, but spent practically the whole of his life in France. Sully was apprenticed to George Graham, the leading English horologist of his day, and first turned his attention to marine timekeepers in 1703, at the instance of Newton and Wren. But he was diverted from his investigations by the prospect of more remunerative employment, and spent many years in endeavouring, unsuccessfully, to establish watch factories at Versailles and St. Germain, being associated with Law, the notorious Scottish financier (who, for a time, controlled the whole revenues of France) and subsequently with the Duc de Noailles. During the financial stringency which followed Law's fall from power, Sully returned to England with his workmen, but found no greater measure of success in his native country. He made his way back to Paris, and fell into poor circumstances, being compelled to earn his living by repairing watches.

In 1720 the Paris Académie des Sciences offered one of the de Meslay prizes for the best memoir upon timekeeping at sea. This prize was won by Massy, a Dutch clockmaker, but he made no attempt to put his theories into practice.‡ This event may have served to re-awaken Sully's interest in the subject, for in 1721 he began the construction of a marine timekeeper upon a new principle, which, after prolonged tests, he presented to the Académie in 1724.

---

* Or, indeed, a time-measurer of any kind. The "New English Dictionary" quotes Derham (1735) as using the term "a pendulum chronometer," and, for the modern meaning of the word, a pamphlet by John Arnold (1780) entitled "A description of a pocket chronometer . . ." Thacker used it in precisely the same sense sixty-six years earlier.

† In the Paris "Mercure" for June of that year.

‡ The improvements which he proposed were comparatively trifling. He published an account of them in 1722.

Sully's machine appears in Plate II., which shows the dial of one of his early machines, and Plate III., which is taken from the description which he published in 1726. It represents the mechanism of one of his later models, which were slightly more elaborate in detail.

The actual machine shown in Plate II. was sent by Sully to Graham in 1724, together with a description and notes, for communication to the Royal Society. It is now preserved in the Museum of the Clockmakers' Company at the Guildhall,* where it forms the doyen of what is undoubtedly the world's largest and most representative collection of old chronometers and pocket chronometers.

Graham's comments on the machine were published by Sully in his very rare work " Description Abregée d'un Horloge D'un nouveau construction, pour le plus just mesure de temps en mer." Paris, 4-to, 1726.†

Its mechanism, although essentially unsound, was in the highest degree ingenious. As a controller, Sully employed, in both models, a weighted lever, which really constituted a horizontal pendulum. It was connected with the balance by means of a flexible cord playing between two curved cheeks,‡ so that any movement of the balance on either side of the dead point raised the weight. Theoretically, therefore, Sully considered that this design admitted of the motion of the balance being rendered as strictly isochronous as that of a pendulum moving in a cycloidal path, or as that of a balance vibrating under the influence of a perfect balance spring, while avoiding the ill effects produced by fluctuations of temperature upon the latter, and by the ship's motion upon the former.

Indeed, he went further. He claimed that his controller, unlike an ordinary pendulum, was unaffected by a change of latitude He was led to this conclusion, which is erroneous, by confounding the *mass* of his pendulum with its *weight*. He assumed, quite rightly, that its weight would vary as the force of gravity, but he overlooked the fact that its mass was constant in all latitudes, and that therefore if the force of gravity varied, as it does, in different places, the time of vibration would vary also. Had this been the only source of error, however, it would not have been difficult to allow for it.

But it was not. There was a far greater one—namely, the influence of the ship's motion. Any movement of the machine in a vertical plane, whether caused by pitching or rolling, caused the weight to lag

* The MS. description written by Sully is preserved in the adjoining Library.

† There is a perfect copy of this work in the Vulliamy Collection The British Museum copy only contains about a quarter of the complete work.

‡ Sully attached great importance to the precise form of these cheeks, which he described as a curve of his invention, previously unknown to geometers, and possessing the power of making the vibrations of lever and balance isochronous

See p. 48.

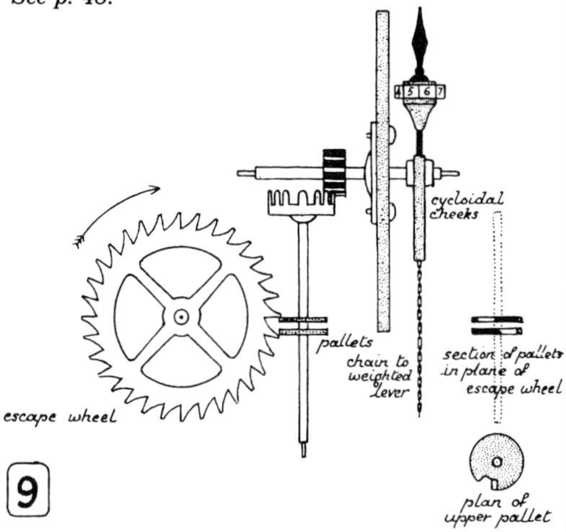

9

Escapement of Sully's marine clock.
[See also Plate III]

See p. 49.

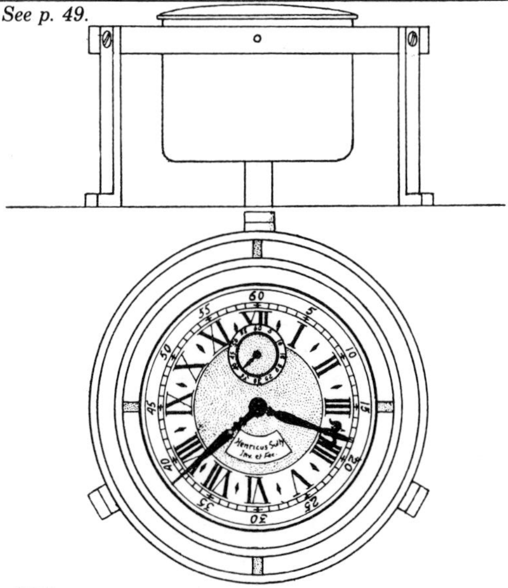

10 **Sully's marine watch.**

See p. 55.

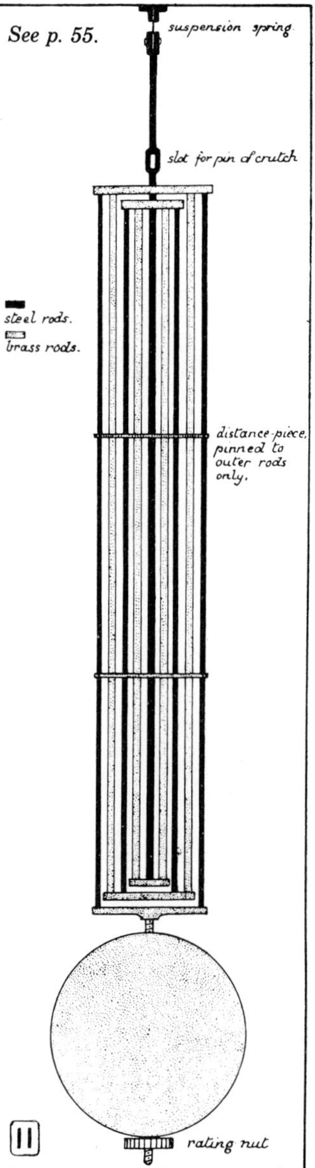

11

Harrison's "gridiron" pendulum.

behind, owing to its inertia, and so altered the pull on the cord, and, hence the force acting on the balance—and, consequently, the velocity of the latter.

Accordingly, as far as timekeeping in anything but the calmest weather was concerned, the machine was no advance upon Huyghens' "sea-watches."

Sully's escapement, which is shown in fig. 9, was based upon that invented by Debaufré, a well-known French clockmaker, *circa* 1700. Sully had seen this escapement in a watch made by its inventor for Sir Isaac Newton, and had been very favourably impressed by it. Its action will be understood on reference to the figure. The teeth of the escape wheel are normally locked upon one of two sector-shaped pallets mounted upon an arbor lying in the plane of the wheel. This arbor is geared, as in Huyghens' "pirouette," to the balance, and as the latter swings the teeth are enabled first to drop into the space between the two pallets, and next to escape altogether, giving impulse at each release by their action upon inclined planes formed on the edges of the pallets.

Unlike the verge, this escapement is "dead-beat": *i.e.*, there is no recoil of the escape wheel. The balance, however, is no more detached than in the verge, for it is always overcoming the friction between the escape wheel teeth and the surface of the sector. Still, its period is not so much affected by variations of the driving force as in the verge, and Sully took advantage of this fact to suppress the fusee in both his models, fitting in the earlier what is called a "going barrel," a barrel containing the mainspring and having teeth around its periphery. It forms the first, or "great" wheel of the train, and drives the latter with a force varying with the tension of the spring.* It is now in common use, but was very rarely employed until after the introduction of the lever escapement.

In his later model Sully abandoned the going barrel, and fitted a spring remontoire, wound by the force of the mainspring every 15 minutes: a period, however, which would allow of considerable fluctations becoming apparent in the force exerted by the remontoire spring.

In both models he made use of friction rollers to minimise the side-friction of the pivots. In the earlier one these were fitted to the balance staff only, but he subsequently used them also for the pivots of the weighted arm. He appears to have been the first, or one of the first,† to use these rollers, which were often employed later, notably by Harrison, Mudge, Le Roy and Berthoud.

* This variation is diminished, in modern practice, by using only a few of the turns of a long spring. The chief advantage of the going barrel is that it dispenses with both fusee and maintaining power.

† Graham, writing to Sully in 1724, mentions that he had seen an old watch, about twenty years before, in which the upper pivot of the balance ran between three friction rollers.

The cord connecting the weighted arm to the balance was, in the earlier model, a silk thread, but Sully subsequently used a fusee chain, the upper portion of which was made of gold in order to avoid friction against the cheeks as far as possible.

In addition to his marine clocks, Sully also designed at the same time a marine watch, with horizontal dial, slung in gimbals in a tripod stand (see fig. 10). It had the same escapement as that of the clock, but the weighted arm was replaced by two balance springs, one fitted to the balance itself, and the other to the arbor carrying the pallets, which was geared to the balance staff.*

Here it may be mentioned that the old marine watch shown in Plate IV. exactly resembles Sully's in external appearance, and it is possible that it may be one of his early efforts.† It is certainly not of the pattern described by him, for it has no balance spring, and but for the fact that the balance is not mounted integrally with the pallets, but driven from them indirectly, its mechanism is precisely the same, in essentials, as that of the "Nuremberg egg."

One of Sully's early models was tried in 1724 by a commission nominated by the Académie, who did not attempt, however, to test it at sea, but contented themselves with a number of not very definite experiments on shore. Having ascertained that it kept time with the Observatory clock within four or five seconds a day, they caused it to be driven about the Paris streets in a berline, whose vibrations produced a retardation of four seconds in an hour and a half. It was then swung at the end of a cord eighteen feet long, and made to describe arcs of from 40° to 50°, which caused it to accelerate several seconds in a short time. This, however, was hardly a fair test, since, unless it were stowed in the hold, such a motion was one to which it could scarcely be subjected on board ship.

In 1786 Sully took one of his improved clocks and one of the marine watches to Bordeaux, for actual trial at sea. The first two trials were made on the comparatively sheltered waters of the Garonne, and, from the report made by a commission appointed by the Académie Royale de Bordeaux, they seem to have been highly successful. In the first trial the clock, during eleven hours afloat, only altered its rate by 1 second per hour as compared with its going when on shore. The watch went 2½ seconds per hour slower.

In the second trial, conducted during a storm, the respective changes were half a second and 1 second per hour slower.

Sully was induced, however, by a naval officer named Radouay, to undertake a third trial in the open sea, and the results of this were so disappointing as to condemn the machines altogether. This was

* The arbor upon which the balance is mounted.

† It is described in the catalogue of the Conservatoire as being "earlier than 1700," and formerly in the possession of the Académie des Sciences. There is no clue to its maker. The appearance of Sully's watch is only known from a small representation of it which appears in one of the plates of his book, and another in "Machines Approuvées par l'Académie Royale des Sciences," Vol. III.

a great blow to Sully, as a number of the marine clocks were already under construction and paid for. Their failure involved him in considerable loss, which he was ill prepared to meet.

This most ingenious and unfortunate* man died in October, 1728. At the time of his death he was working on a new design of marine timekeeper, and if his life had been prolonged—he was only forty-eight when he died—it is quite probable that he would have triumphed over both his mechanical and financial difficulties. His clock, although impracticable, is evidence of his great abilities. It is to be regretted that he devoted so much of his time to improving it, and neglected his marine watch, which was far the more promising design of the two.

DUTERTRE.

In 1726 Jean Baptiste Dutertre, an eminent French clockmaker, constructed the curious and quite impracticable machine shown in Plate V.† It has a small spring movement suspended in gimbals, and is controlled by two pendulums geared together, and swinging $\frac{2}{3}$ seconds. The escapement is a form of the verge, the pallets being mounted on the arbors of the two pendulums, and engaging on opposite sides of the escape wheel. Dutertre was of opinion that this construction was well adapted for keeping time at sea, but a short trial must have soon undeceived him. The slightest motion of the ship would cause enormous friction in the gearing of the pendulums, and utterly destroy their time-measuring properties.

RIVAZ.

In 1749 Pierre Joseph de Rivaz, a Frenchman of some position who had interested himself in horology, is stated‡ to have made a marine timepiece, having a means of compensation in the balance. I have not been able to obtain any contemporary confirmation of this statement, and authorities which should have attested it are entirely silent. It is not intrinsically improbable, since Rivaz was a horologist of great ability, but there can be no doubt that the machine, if made, was unsuccessful, and attracted no attention.

JENKINS.

In a pamphlet§ published in 1760 by Henry Jenkins, a London maker, there appears a description of a "Marine Regulator" invented by him. It runs as follows :—

> ". . . . But as my machine has not yet had a trial, I shall only describe it as follows :—
>
> "It has a pendulum, and will go in any direction a ship may happen to be in at sea. And I believe it will keep regular time,

* Unfortunate both in his life and his death. Under the pious and benevolently paternal rule of Louis XV. he was compelled, on his death-bed, to abjure the Protestant faith in order to obtain Christian burial.

† This machine was presented to the Académie des Sciences, and is now preserved in the Conservatoire des Arts et Métiers in Paris. It is briefly described in Thiout's "Traite d'horlogerie, mechanique et pratique," 1741, vol. 1, p. 99.

‡ By Britten. I think the statement is founded on a misconception. See "Journal des Scavans," July, 1752.

§ "A Description of several Geographical and Astronomical Clocks . . . to which is added a Short Account of a Marine Regulator." London, 1760.

without suffering any disorder from heat or cold, or any disturbance it may be liable to. It shows the seconds, minutes, hours, day of the month, &c., and may have any other motion desired."

From the confident tone of the foregoing, it seems probable that the machine had not yet advanced further than the paper stage. If, as is most likely, it was never constructed, we can be certain that its designer was spared a good deal of disappointment.

And here the long catalogue of unsuccessful pioneer work comes to an end. In 1761 there took place the first public trial of Harrison's fourth timekeeper, the machine which demonstrated, *urbi et orbi*, that Man had made a fresh conquest, and that he was at last possessed of an accurate and reliable means of finding longitude at sea.

DUTERTRE'S MARINE CLOCK
Courtesy Conservatoire National des Arts et Métiers.

PORTRAIT OF JOHN HARRISON IN ENAMEL PASTE BY JAMES TASSIE
C.C. Library Guildhall Art Gallery Register (Bromley No. 1082).

CHAPTER III.

JOHN HARRISON.

PART I.

John Harrison, inventor of the first successful marine timekeeper and winner of the £20,000 reward, was born at Foulby, in the parish of Wragby, Yorkshire, in May, 1693. His father was a carpenter and joiner in the service of Sir Rowland Winn, of Nostell Priory, and John was the eldest of a numerous family.*

He was brought up to follow his father's trade, but even as a child he showed a fondness for mechanism. He had a severe attack of smallpox when he was six years old, and one of the amusements of his convalescence was to scrutinise the going of a watch laid on his pillow. A year later his father removed to Barrow on Humber, where his employer had another estate, and his son assisted him in the workshop. Harrison had thus little time or opportunity to acquire an education, but, like many another man of his fine type, he stole some hours from each night's rest, and became his own schoolmaster. A neighbouring clergyman also helped him in many ways, chiefly by lending him a copy of Saunderson's lectures on mechanics and physics. Of this book Harrison made a complete manuscript copy, diagrams and all, which still exists.† In this way he soon acquired enough knowledge of mathematics and the handling of instruments to be able to make a little money by land-surveying, and he also turned his attention to the repair and improvement of clocks.

By 1715 he had built his first grandfather clock, now preserved in the Museum of the Clockmakers' Company‡. It follows very closely the usual construction of the clocks of his day, except for the remarkable fact that with one exception—the escape wheel—all its wheels are of wood, turned out of oak, with the teeth let into a groove in the rim of the wheel. Soon after making this clock, however, he began to work out his own ideas as to the improvement of clocks in general.

His chief invention in this direction, and one which long enjoyed wide popularity, was the "gridiron" pendulum. The clocks of his day had simple pendulums, generally consisting of a metal rod and a leaden bob. Their length, accordingly, increased in hot weather and contracted in cold, with the result that the clock would go considerably faster in winter than in summer. This fact had not escaped notice—it was, indeed, quite obvious—and in 1725 Graham invented a pendulum with a bob composed of a jar of mercury, whose expansion upwards

* It is stated by Hatton ("Introduction to . . . Clock and Watchwork," 1773), that Harrison was assisted in his early experiments by his brother James. There is a grandfather clock by the latter in the Museum of the Clockmakers' Company.

† It was recently disposed of by Messrs. Sotheran.

‡ There is a very similar example in the Science Museum, South Kensington.

counteracted that of the rod downwards. He also experimented with another whose rod was composed of several different metals, and this was the idea which Harrison hit upon about the same time, and brought into extensive use.

Brass expands more than steel for a given rise of temperature, in the proportion of about three to two*. Accordingly, Harrison saw that if he took a steel rod nine feet long and a brass one six feet long, laid them side by side, and united their lower ends, their upper ends would be about three feet apart, and this distance would remain constant in any temperature, so that by fitting a suspension spring to the upper end, and a bob to the lower, he would have an invariable pendulum. But this arrangement would make a pendulum about nine feet long over all, while its effective length would only be three feet. A grandfather clock on this construction, beating seconds, would therefore have stood about eleven feet high. Accordingly he adopted the form shown in fig. 11, which is exactly the same in principle, but splits up the nine feet of steel rod and the six feet of brass into three-foot lengths, all of these (except the centre one), being duplicated to avoid distortion.†

As compared with the mercurial pendulum, this form called, from its appearance, the " gridiron," has the advantage that it responds immediately to a change in temperature, while the expansion or contraction of the mercury has a tendency to lag behind that of the rod from which it is suspended. But the disadvantage of the " gridiron " is that the weight of the rods is disproportionately large compared with that of the bob, and so, while it found favour for many years, especially abroad, it is now discarded in favour of either the mercurial pendulum, the zinc and iron compensation, which needs only two rods, or the modern form with an " invar "‡ rod, whose alteration is practically negligible.

Another of Harrison's inventions, which is even more ingenious, but whose delicacy prevented its general adoption, was the " grasshopper " escapement shown in fig. 12. A story is often told that Harrison was once summoned to repair a steeple-clock which had stopped, and that on his arrival he found the cause to be simply a lack of oil on the pallets of the escapement (it was the old-fashioned "recoil " escapement§). Accordingly, he set to work to devise an escapement that should not need oiling.

This may or may not be true,|| but my own opinion, founded both on Harrison's writings and on an inspection of the mechanism of a good many of his clocks and timekeepers, is that he had also a rooted objection, on principle, to any friction that could possibly be avoided,

* More accurately, as 100 to 62.

† In the clock shown behind Harrison's chair in the Frontispiece, it will be noted that the pendulum is composed of nine full-length and two half-length rods. The use of the latter is uncertain. I have never seen an actual clock so fitted, and it is possible that they only existed in the artist's imagination.

‡ An alloy of steel and nickel. See page 308.

§ See Fig. 47.

|| Contemporary accounts quote Harrison himself, in conversation, as their authority for this statement.

See p. 57.

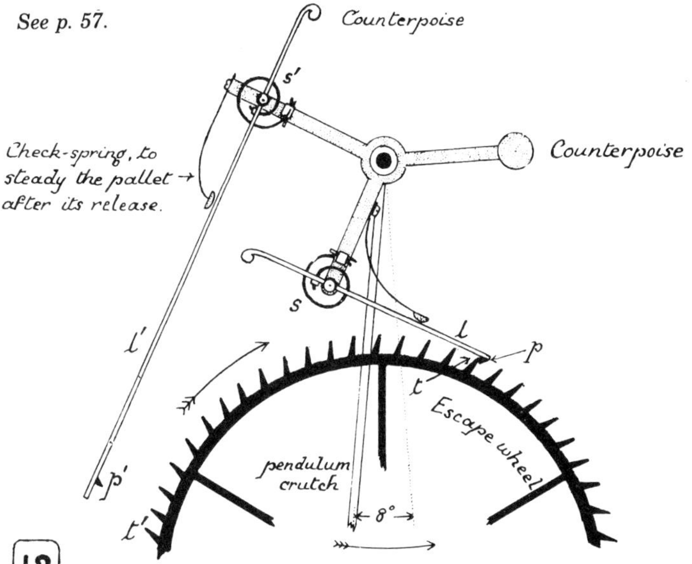

12

Harrison's "grasshopper" escapement.

See p. 62.

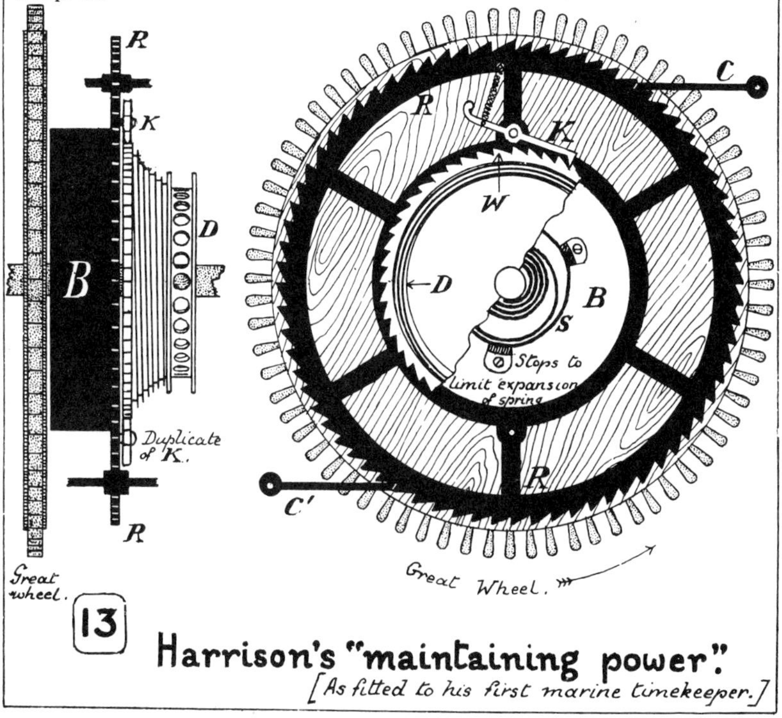

13

Harrison's "maintaining power".

[As fitted to his first marine timekeeper.]

and this explains both his invention of the "grasshopper" (so called from its resemblance to the hind legs of that insect) and the fact that he would never employ Graham's dead-beat escapement,* which is much simpler than his own, and gave equally good results.

The action of the "grasshopper" is as follows: The pallets *p*, *p'* are mounted on bell-crank levers *l*, *l'*, whose joints are normally kept at a right angle by the springs *s*, *s'*. Imagine, now, that a tooth *t* of the escape wheel is bearing upon the pallet *p*, and that the pendulum is swinging to your right. The escape wheel will turn slightly, giving impulse to the pendulum as it does so, and the pallet will tend to rise, but is prevented by the friction of the tooth on it. Instead, the spring *s* will be slightly torsioned. At the end of the pendulum's swing the pallet *p'*, which has been descending to meet the escape wheel, will engage on the tooth *t'*, and the wheel will recoil slightly. As it does so, the friction between *p* and *t* will cease, and the spring *s* will bring *l* back to its normal position. The pallet *p* will thus remain clear of the wheel during the return swing, until at its close it meets the tooth *t'*, when the wheel will again recoil slightly, and let *p'* disengage.

Thus it will be seen that the escape wheel alternately pulls *p* and pushes *p'*, and that its engagement with them is noiseless and practically frictionless—so much so, indeed, that in several of Harrison's clocks and timekeepers the pallets are of wood, since the wear on them is absolutely negligible.

This extremely ingenious escapement is open to the objection that it never leaves the pendulum at liberty, and that it needs very delicate adjustment, which is liable to be upset by dust or thick oil. Still, in Harrison's hands, and used in conjunction with a remontoire, it gave magnificent results. By 1726 he had completed two first-class regulators† embodying his pendulum and escapement, one of which, by his own account, did not vary a second a month during a period of fourteen years, while its total error never exceeded half a minute.

The great reward was offered in 1714, when Harrison was a lad of seventeen, and it is natural that it should have fired him with the ambition of constructing a timekeeper for finding longitude. It is

* In a MSS. description of his fourth timekeeper he remarks " . . . the Pendulum itself as according to Mr. Graham's way swings, or rather creeps."

† The term "regulator" is used to denote any high-class pendulum clock designed for use solely as an accurate time-measurer, without any additions such as striking mechanism, calendar work, &c. A splendid regulator by Harrison, with grasshopper escapement and a remontoire wound every half-minute is in the possession of the Royal Astronomical Society, through whose courtesy I was recently enabled to inspect it. There is a detailed description of it in the R.A.S. monthly notices for November, 1909, from the pen of Mr. E. T. Cottingham (reprinted in the "Horological Journal" for May, 1910). Amongst the evidences of Harrison's mechanical skill which it contains are roller bearings of quite modern pattern, the rollers pivoted into a revolving carriage. This device also appears in Harrison's second marine timekeeper. It is to be regretted that the clock's original gridiron pendulum has been replaced by one with a wooden rod. It swings, between cycloidal cheeks, through an arc of no less than 12°.

impossible to say exactly when he first turned his thoughts towards the subject to which he devoted the rest of a long life, but in 1728 he journeyed to London, taking with him examples of his pendulum and escapement, and the drawings of a marine clock which he proposed to build if he could obtain assistance from the Board of Longitude.

With this end in view, he called upon Halley, the Astronomer Royal, who was, *ex officio,* a member of the Board. Halley cautioned him against relying upon the Board's assistance, and suggested that he should consult George Graham, F.R.S., who was then generally regarded as England's leading horologist.

To Graham Harrison accordingly went, and in him he found a kindred spirit. On his first visit he arrived at 10 a.m., was invited to stay for dinner, and finally left at 8 p.m., having discussed horological topics with his host all the time. Graham supported Halley in advising Harrison to make his machine before applying to the Board for assistance; but he showed that his nickname of "Honest George Graham" was a general and well deserved tribute to a very noble character by lending him, out of his own pocket, the funds necessary for the work, and declining to exact either interest or security.*

Harrison returned to Barrow, and employed whatever time he could spare out of the next six years in building his timekeeper. This historical machine, which is preserved in the Royal Observatory, is shown in Plates VI. and VII.

Its mechanism, roughly speaking, is that of a large clock, but it is controlled by two huge balances instead of a pendulum. These balances, which weigh some 5 lbs. each, are connected together, as shown in Plate VIII.† by wires running over brass arcs, and in such a manner that their motions are always opposed. Accordingly, any effect produced by the ship's motion on one would be counteracted by the effect on the other.

The escapement was a modification of the "grasshopper," one pallet and lever being mounted on each balance staff, and engaging on opposite sides of the escape wheel. The pallets were of wood, and both were pulled by the teeth of the wheel. This was of brass, the remaining wheels being of oak, with the teeth, also of oak, let in in groups of four.

No remontoire was employed. There were two mainsprings, on separate drums, driving a central fusee.‡

* I believe the amount was £200, but I cannot lay my hand on the authority for this. Graham, by the way, although a Quaker, is buried, in the same grave as Tompion, in Westminster Abbey—the only two horologists who have ever been granted this honour.

† This Plate actually illustrates Harrison's second machine, but the interconnection of the balances and balance-springs is precisely the same as in No. 1.

‡ This statement is inferential, since the mainsprings of No. 1, and part of its winding mechanism, are missing, and no complete description exists of the machine in its perfect state. Harrison's three large machines were cleaned by Messrs. Arnold and Dent in 1835-41, and elaborate plans of them, compiled at the time, are preserved at Greenwich (see Plate VIII.). The drawings of No. 1, however, are fragmentary, and do not show the winding gear.

THE TOP PLATES OF H4 (TOP) & K1 (BOTTOM)
by permission of M.O.D. Hydrographer.

HARRISON'S NO.1.
The dials are arranged thus: seconds/minutes/hours/days. The small pillars supporting the movement are a recent addition. Royal Observatory, Greenwich.

Plate VII. THREE-QUARTER VIEW OF HARRISON'S No. 1.
The gridiron compensation is just visible between the two balances. Notice the wooden (second) wheel, and the friction-rollers behind the dial.

See p. 58. Royal Observatory, Greenwich.

In this fusee there was fitted Harrison's maintaining power, which is of particular interest as the only one of his inventions which has not been superseded. There can be little doubt that it was his own unaided invention, although, as we have seen, Thacker had used a maintaining power of some kind twenty-five years earlier.

The use of the maintaining power, of course, is to prevent a timekeeper fitted with fusee from stopping or going slow while it is being wound, during which period the fusee has to be turned backwards, and no power from the mainspring can reach the train. It was an absolute necessity in Harrison's machines, quite apart from the risk of their losing time during winding, since by reason of their design none of them could start themselves if once stopped.*

Fig. 13 shows its arrangement as fitted in his first machine. The fusee, instead of being rigidly mounted on the great wheel arbor, rides loosely on it, and beside it is the barrel B, containing a coiled spring, whose outer end is attached to the inside of the barrel, and its inner to the great wheel arbor. The barrel carries a ratchet wheel R, whose teeth engage with the fixed clicks C, C′, and a second ratchet wheel W, attached to the fusee, engages with the clicks K, K′. It will be noticed that the teeth of the two ratchets are cut in opposite directions.

The action of this mechanism is as follows. The mainsprings exert their pull, via the fusee chains, on the fusee, which turns and carries with it the barrel B by means of the click K. The great wheel is held by the train, and accordingly the spring S, which is adjusted so as to be rather weaker than the combined pull of the mainsprings, is wound a certain amount, limited by a stop (not shown). The fusee then continues to revolve slowly with the great wheel, as if rigidly fixed to it, and the teeth of the ratchet R pass one by one under the fixed click C.

To wind the machine, the fusee is revolved in the other direction by pulling a cord wound on the drum D. The click K, of course, trips while this is being done, and accordingly there is no force tending to keep the spring S wound. But the click C prevents it from rotating the barrel B backwards, and accordingly it is compelled to expend its force in continuing to revolve the great wheel forwards, which it does until the winding is completed, when it is re-wound by the pull of the fusee chains.

The balances were controlled by no less than four balance springs, as shown in Plate VIII. These were not of the ordinary spiral form, but helical, and acting in tension, being attached to the extremities of the balance arms by thin wires. Compensation for the effects of heat and cold was effected by varying their initial tension. To do this, Harrison

* Harrison is said to have made a special point, when petitioning Parliament, of the fact that No. 4, unlike an ordinary verge watch, could not start itself if once brought to rest—much to the bewilderment of the M.P.s, who could not at all understand the value of such a property.

Timekeepers fitted with Huyghens' "pirouette" w[illegible]y incapable of restarting themselves. The latter's "endless cord" [illegible]ing gear is often to be found in weight-driven clocks.

used his " gridiron " of brass and steel rods*, but reversed its action so that the distance between its extreme points, instead of remaining invariable, altered by the greatest possible amount. He thus obtained sufficient power from any change of temperature to be used, transmitted through a series of levers, in increasing or decreasing the tension of the balance springs by shifting the position of their inner (fixed) ends.

Perhaps the most remarkable feature of the machine was the extraordinary number and variety of the devices fitted to eliminate friction. Friction wheels were used wherever possible, the teeth of the pinions were lignum-vitæ rollers†, and the pivots of the balance staffs were supported by portions of friction wheels of 10 inches radius and upwards, mounted on the ends of long counterbalanced rods maintained in place by spiral springs.‡

The total weight of the machine was 72 lbs. It beat seconds, and showed seconds, minutes, hours and days, the day wheel being adjustable for the short months.

Crude though it may seem, it is hard to praise this machine too highly. In constructing it Harrison, working single-handed and self-taught, grappled successfully with several problems which had, as we have seen, defied all previous attempts at solution. Even if he had gone no further, this machine would have proved him a mechanical genius, and possessed of " an infinite capacity for taking pains." It may be noted that it is the first balance timekeeper to be fitted with any form of compensation for temperature.§

Harrison finished this machine, which will be referred to as No. 1, in 1735, and tried it successfully in a barge on the Humber, having mounted it in gimbals in a large wooden case suspended by spiral springs at its corners. He then repaired with it to London, and obtained a certificate, signed by five members of the Royal Society,|| to the effect that its principles promised a great and sufficient degree of accuracy. He next applied to the Board of Longitude for a trial

* Three small gridirons were employed, superimposed, and cumulative in their effect. The centre one, to which were attached the shorter arms of two levers whose fulcra were mounted on the outer pair, shortened with heat, while the others expanded, producing a considerable travel of the longer arms of the levers. Harrison, however, in a letter to Short, written in 1752, very candidly states that " still, it is a bad method."

† These pinions were an improved form of the ordinary " lantern pinion," in which the teeth are formed by a series of pins, or pillars, connecting two parallel discs.

‡ These arms, and their springs and counterbalances, will be noticed in Plates VI. and VII. Plates VIII. and IX. show the arrangement adopted for them in Harrison's second machine, which is very similar, except that instead of all the eight arms being in compression, four were in tension. The same plan was adopted in his third machine, as appears in Plate X.

§ Pierre le Roy saw this machine in London in 1738, and remarked that it was " d'un construction fort ingenieuse." At one time or another it was examined by most of the quidnuncs of London, and also by several other foreign makers, including Ferdinand Berthoud.

|| Halley, Smith, Bradley, Machin and Graham.

Plate VIII. HARRISON'S No. 2.

The inscription runs " John Harrison fecit. Made for His Majesty George the IInd, by order of a Committee held the 30th of June, 1737 " (*this refers to the Board of Longitude*). The long tail extending below the hour circle is used to let the remontoire off when starting the machine. The V-shaped side-frames are part of the gimbal suspension. (See also Plate IX.).

See p. 68. Royal Observatory, Greenwich.

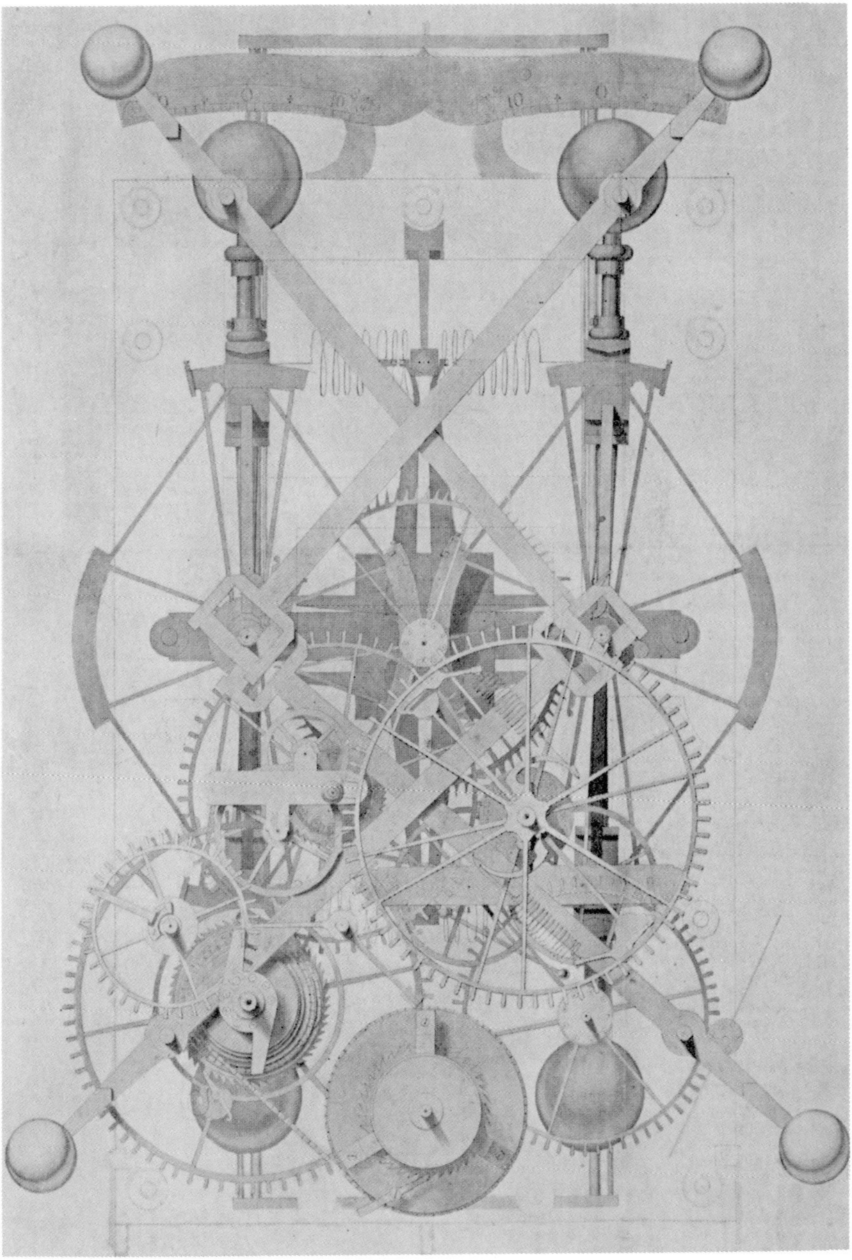

Plate IX. MECHANISM OF HARRISON'S No. 2.
One of a set of four very fine wash drawings of this machine, made by Thomas Bradley in 1840. (See also Plate VIII.).

See p. 68. Royal Observatory, Greenwich.

HARRISON NO.2 THREE-QUARTER VIEW
by permission of M.O.D. Hydrographs.

at sea, and was sent to Lisbon in H.M.S. "Centurion." The correspondence on this occasion between Sir Charles Wager, First Lord of the Admiralty, and Captain George Procter of the "Centurion," is interesting.

Wager to Procter.

"Admiralty, 14th May, 1736.

"The Instrument which is put on Board your Ship, has been approved by all the Mathematicians in Town that have seen it (and few have not) to be the Best that has been made for measuring Time: how it will succeed at Sea, you will partly be a Judge: I have written to Sir *John Norris*, to desire him to send Home the Instrument, and the Maker of it (whom I think you have with you) by the first Ship that comes . . . The Man is said by those who know him best to be a very ingenious and sober Man, and capable of finding out something more than he has already, if he can find Encouragement. I desire, therefore, that you will see the Man be used civilly, and that you will be as kind to him as you can."

Procter to Wager.

"'Centurion,' at Spithead, 17th May, 1736.

"I am very much honoured with yours of the 14th, in Relation to the Instrument I carried out, and its Maker: the Instrument is placed in my Cabbin, for giving the Man all the Advantage that is possible for making his Observations, and I find him to be a very sober, a very industrious, and withal a very modest Man, so that my good Wishes can't but attend him; but the Difficulty of measuring Time truly, where so many unequal Shocks, and Motions, stand in Oposition to it, gives me concern for the honest Man, and makes me feel he has attempted Impossibilities; but Sir, I will do him all the Good, and give him all the Help, that is in my Power, and acquaint him with your Concern for his Success, and your Care that he shall be well treated . . ."

There are no particulars in the "Centurion's" log or journals relating to Harrison, and if Captain Procter made a report on the subject it has been lost.* Harrison and No. 1, on arrival at Lisbon, were transferred to H.M.S. "Orford" for the voyage home, and in her log, under date of Sunday, May 30th, 1736, appears the following reference to him:

"(In Lisbon River) . . . At 6 a m our Signle On board ye 'Brittania' for a Lievt. at ½ past Recd. On board a Macheen invented for ye finding of Longtd: ye Maker wth. it pr. Ordr. of ye Admll . . ."

On this voyage the machine undoubtedly performed very well, as witness the following certificate given to Harrison by Roger Wills, master of the "Orford." †

"When we made the land, the said land, according to my reckoning (and others), ought to have been the Start; but, before we knew what land it was, John Harrison declared to me and the rest of the ship's company that, according to his observations with his machine, it ought to be the Lizard—the which, indeed, it was found to be, his observation showing the ship to be more west than my reckoning, above one degree and twenty-six miles."

The nature of this voyage, however, was not calculated to exhibit the advantages of a marine timekeeper in the best light, since its

---

* He died at Lisbon soon after the ship's arrival.

† Not captain of her, as generally stated. In those days, and long afterwards, the term "master" was used in the Navy to denote the officer responsible for the navigation of the ship. The "Orford," on this voyage, was commanded by Captain Robert Man.

direction was practically north and south, and accordingly there was comparatively little risk of the ship losing her longitude : although as we have seen, she made an error of 90 miles in her landfall. Nor could it be held to entitle Harrison to any reward under the Act of Queen Anne, since this specified a voyage to the West Indies. Still, it demonstrated clearly that he was working on sound lines.

On June 30th, 1737, the name of Harrison appears, for the first time (but by no means the last), in the official minutes of the Board of Longitude. We read:

> " Mr. John Harrison produced a new invented machine, in the nature of clockwork, whereby he proposes to keep time at sea with more exactness than by any other instrument or method hitherto contrived . . . and proposes to make another machine of smaller dimensions within the space of two years, whereby he will endeavour to correct some defects which he hath found in that already prepared, so as to render the same more perfect . . ."

The Board voted him £500 to assist him, one-half to be paid immediately, and the other as soon as he should put No. 2 into the hands of the captain of one of H.M. Ships.*

No. 1 was never tried again at sea. It continued to go in Harrison's house (he settled permanently in London after his return from Lisbon†) until May 23rd, 1766, when it was damaged during its removal to the Royal Observatory.‡ It was tried there, after repair, from September 1766 to May, 1777, and some particulars of its going will be found in the Appendix. I am doubtful whether its rate was ever consistent enough to win any of the rewards, but with a little luck it might have carried off the £10,000.

Harrison, on his return, set to work and built a second machine, shown in Plates VIII. and IX. This machine was practically a replica of No. 1, with some improvements in detail. Harrison fitted a remontoire, consisting of a pair of third wheels mounted side by side, one driven from the second wheel and the other driving the escape wheel, the pair being connected by two spiral springs in tension, these being rewound sixteen times an hour. The wooden wheels were replaced by brass ones, and the balance staffs were prevented by small axial wires from shifting longitudinally.

The gridiron compensation employed four large rods only. The machine weighed 103 lbs., and its case and gimbal suspension 62 lbs.

Harrison completed No. 2 in 1739, and in January, 1741, he wrote to the Board stating that he was engaged upon a third machine, which he expected would far surpass either No. 1 or No. 2. He received the sum of £500 to assist him in constructing it. No. 2 was

---

* Graham urged them strongly to increase this to £800 or £1,000, but unsuccessfully.

† First in Orange Street, off Red Lion Square, and afterwards in the Square itself.

‡ Maskelyne and one of his workmen dropped it on the stairs of Harrison's house. It was then conveyed to Greenwich, together with Nos. 2 and 3, in a springless cart.

Plate X. HARRISON'S No. 3.

The compensation curb is mounted in the centre of the fiddle-shaped frame above and to the left of the seconds' dial. There are four seconds' hands, which come into view successively, and two minute hands.

The cross-bar above the minute dial is part of a frame to which are normally attached metal cases, with glass windows, covering the upper and lower halves of the machine.

See p. 48. Royal Observatory, Greenwich.

never tested at sea, although Harrison states that it was repeatedly tested, with success, in conditions of "great heat and motion."* Like No. 1 (and also No. 3), it was tried at Greenwich in 1766, and some account of its going is given in the Appendix.

Now begins the most obscure period of Harrison's life. We have seen that it took him six years to build No. 1, and two years to make No. 2. Balancing the fact that he altered his design considerably against the consideration that he was now much better equipped with tools—which he had chiefly made himself—it would be a fair assumption that the construction of No. 3 would occupy another two, or at the outside three years. As a matter of fact, although begun in 1740 it was not completed until 1757—seventeen years later.

The cause of this extraordinary delay is not clear. It was not due to any lack of enthusiasm or application on Harrison's part. He did a certain amount of clockmaking and clock-designing to keep the wolf from the door, but in the main he seems to have been entirely engrossed in the construction of No. 3, and to have chiefly depended for support upon the sums advanced to him from time to time by the Board of Longitude.†

Plate X shows the general appearance of No. 3 (which also appears in the frontispiece). It differed from its predecessors in the form of the balances and the arrangements for compensation. The balances were circular, connected together by wires as those of Nos. 1 and 2 had been, and controlled by a single large spiral spring, with 1½ turns, fitted to the staff of the upper balance.

The compensation was effected by what Harrison termed his "thermometer kirb," a device better known later by the more generally-used name of "compensation curb." As we have seen in Chapter I, the watches of his time were regulated by adjusting the position of two curb pins which determined the effective length of the balance-spring. Harrison devised an automatic way of doing this, using for the purpose the dissimilar expansions of brass and steel, as before, but in a different manner. He rivetted together a strip of brass and one of steel so that they formed a compound strip, and mounted the curb pins at one end of it, which was left free to move, while the other end was fixed. Now, if at any particular temperature this strip, or "curb" were absolutely straight, it can easily be seen that a rise of temperature would cause it to become convex on the brass side, and concave on the steel side, and that the curb pins would thus be moved along the balance spring. By adjusting the length of the curb, it could be arranged that for a rise of temperature the amount of the movement should shorten the spring exactly enough to compensate for the retardation produced, by that rise, in the machine's going; and, conversely, that for a fall of temperature it should lengthen the spring

* The Board were disinclined to try it at sea at the time of its completion as we were then at war with Spain, and it might have been captured.

† Between 1746 and 1761 he received from the Board five sums of £500 each.

sufficiently to produce a similar result. The initial position of the curb pins could be adjusted, by moving the framework carrying the curb, so as to alter the machine's rate of going.

Like No. 2, No. 3 was fitted with a remontoire, in this case in the escape wheel, and wound every half-minute. It embodied much the same anti-friction devices as its predecessors, and, like them, beat seconds. It weighs 66 lbs., and its case and gimballing 35 lbs.

There is no doubt that Harrison's chief difficulties with this machine were due to a faulty method of calculating the "moment of inertia"* of its balances. In an appendix to an unpublished description of his fourth timekeeper, of which I possess a copy, he goes fully into this question. On January 16th, 1741, he stated that he could get it going by the 1st of August, and put it upon one of H.M. Ships two years after that date. But five years later (4, 6, 1746), we find him reporting:

> That it does not go as well, at present, as he expected it would, yet he plainly perceived the Cause of its present Imperfection to lye in a certain part†, which, being of a different form from the corresponding part in the other machines, had never been tried before.

He laid before the Board, at the same time, a testimonial to the value of his inventions, signed by twelve fellows of the Royal Society, including the President, Martin Folkes, and men of such standing as Bradley, Graham, Halley and Cavendish.

The interest taken by the Royal Society in his work was also strikingly shown three years later, when he was awarded the Copley medal—the highest honour it could bestow. Folkes made an eloquent, if slightly vague, speech on that occasion, in which he paid many compliments not only to Harrison's labours, but also to his modesty and perseverance. He mentioned, incidentally, that Harrison hoped to make No. 3 accurate to within 3 or 4 seconds a week. Some years later, Harrison was proffered the dignity of F.R.S., but he begged leave to decline it in favour of his son William. By 1757 No. 3 was sufficiently tractable for Harrison to report that he proposed shortly to apply for a trial at sea, and he suggested at the same time that he should make two smaller timekeepers, one of pocket size‡, and the other somewhat larger. This proposal was approved, and he accordingly constructed the very remarkable machine shown in Plates XI and XII, which, by reason alike of its beauty, its accuracy, and its historical interest, must take pride of place as the most famous chronometer that ever has been or ever will be made.

---

* If m be the mass of the balance's rim, and r the distance of its effective radius of gyration, Harrison considered that its moment of inertia would be proportional to mr (instead of mr^2, which is correct).

† The balances.

‡ The pocket sized timekeeper was never made. Harrison found that he could not conveniently reduce the size of his mechanism so much. A pocket watch, embodying some of his improvements, had been made for him in 1753 by John Jeffreys, of Holborn, who was allowed by Harrison to put his own name on it. It went almost as well as No. 4, and was successfully used in two voyages by Admiral Campbell.

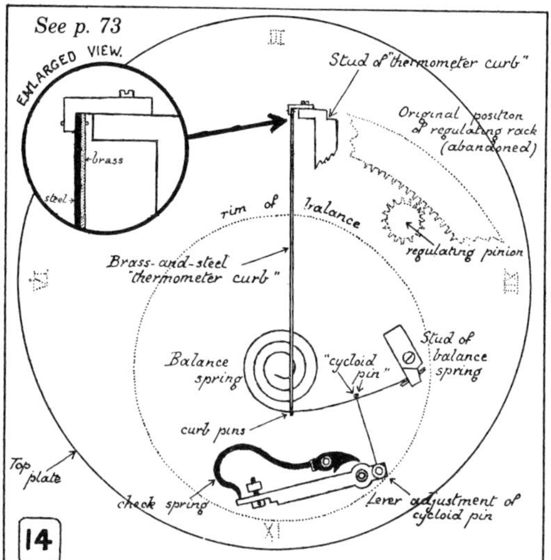

14

Compensation of no. 4.

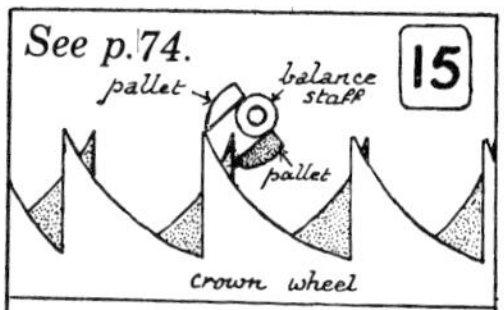

15

Escapement of no. 4.
[Enlarged about 5 times linear].

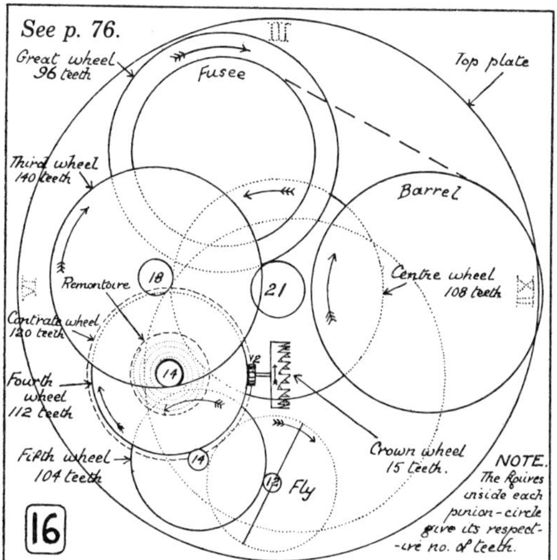

16

Arrangement of train in no. 4.

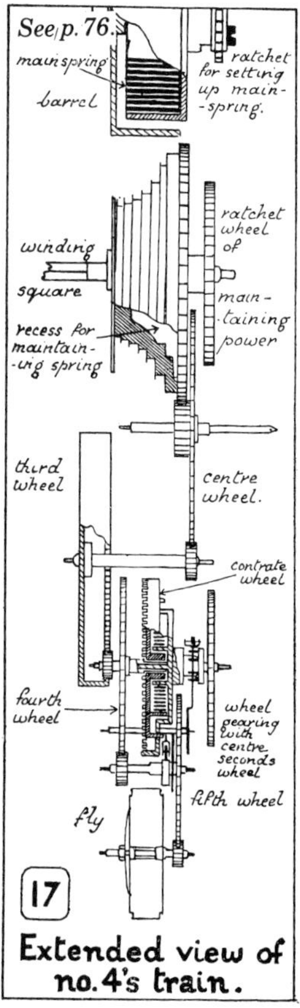

17

Extended view of no. 4's train.

Externally, it resembles an enormous silver pair-case* watch, about five inches in diameter. Indeed, it is an exact reproduction, on a larger scale, of the common pocket watches of the day, even to the fitting of a pendant, as if it were intended for daily wear in the pocket of some Brobdingnagian. The dial is of white enamel, with an ornamental design in black. The hour and minute hands are of blued steel, and there is also a polished centre seconds hand.† This hand rotates between the other two—*i.e.*, it passes above the hour hand and below the minute hand. The timekeeper is wound through a hole in the back of the inner case, normally kept covered by a revolving disc.

It is not suspended in gimbals. Although Harrison had used these for his first three machines, he subsequently conceived an aversion for them, and alleged that they caused more errors than they removed. No. 4 was merely laid on a soft cushion in its box, and had to be carefully tended, on its two voyages, by William Harrison, who adjusted its position, by means of an adjustable outer case and a divided arc, so as to suit the lie of the ship, keeping the pendant always slightly above the horizontal.‡

The movement can be swung out of the case, turning on a bolt and joint exactly as do those of the ordinary watches of the period. Its mechanism was practically a sealed book for over a century after its maker's death.§

Taking its parts in order of importance, the balance is a plain steel three armed one of large size, 2.2 inches in diameter, and weighing $28\frac{5}{8}$ grs. (Troy). The balance spring is of polished and tempered steel, and has slightly over three turns. A compensation curb, similar to that of No. 3, is employed (see fig. 14). Harrison originally made provision for shifting the fixed end of this curb by means of a curved rack and pinion, so as to adjust the watch for mean time, but this

* The watches of Harrison's time were always made with a "pair-case"—*i.e.*, an inner case to which the movement was attached with a hinge, enabling it to be swung out for inspection, and a separate and detachable outer case, fitting closely over the inner one. Occasionally, ornamental watches may be met with having three or even more cases, one inside the other.

† This is a very early example of the use of a centre seconds hand, but it is not the earliest. The watch made by Mudge for Queen Charlotte in 1757 (the first lever watch ever made) had a centre seconds hand, and Mr. H. Otto possesses an undated centre seconds watch, by Graham, which cannot be of later date than 1751, since Graham died in that year.

‡ It was not then adjusted to go equally in all positions. This was subsequently effected, in part, by altering the weight of various portions of the balance rim. Maskelyne, in "The Principles of Mr. Harrison's Timekeeper," asserts that Harrison considered the timekeeper ought to be firmly fixed to some part of the ship: but this was immediately and explicitly disavowed by William Harrison.

§ The first account of it was published by Mr. H. M. Frodsham in the "Horological Journal" for May, 1878. He also gave drawings of the escapement, train and remontoire, taken from Kendal's duplicate of No. 4. This was taken apart, cleaned, the drawings made, and the machine re-assembled, in six days—a very smart piece of work.

It should be added that this machine, which had not been subsequently cleaned or adjusted in any way, was set going on the occasion of the Annual Visitation of the Royal Observatory in 1922, and that its error on G.M.T. between 11 a.m. and 7 p.m. amounted to 0.4 seconds only.

was found to involve so much readjustment of the spring that he abandoned it, although he left the pinion and its indicator in position. Screws are provided for adjusting the position of the curb both laterally and longitudinally.

It was impossible to use the " grasshopper " in a machine of such small size, and the escapement is a modification of the " verge " fitted to the " Nuremberg egg " and to the common watches of Harrison's day. But the modifications are extensive. The pallets are very small, and have their faces set parallel, instead of at the usual angle of 95° or so. Moreover, instead of being steel, they are of diamond, and their backs are shaped to cycloidal curves, as shown in fig. 15.

The action of this escapement is quite different from that of the verge, which it appears to resemble. In that escapement, the teeth of the crown wheel act only upon the faces of the pallets. But in this, as will be seen from fig. 15, the points of the teeth rest, for a considerable portion of the supplementary arc*—from 90° to 145° (limit of banking)† past the dead point—upon the *backs* of the pallets, and tend to assist the balance towards the extreme of its swing and to retard its return.

This escapement is obviously a great improvement upon the verge, as the train has far less power over the motions of the balance. The latter is no longer checked in its swing by a force equal to that which originally impelled it, but by the balance spring, assisted only by the friction between the tooth and the back of the pallet.

The pallet-radius and crown wheel are both very small compared with the size of the balance, and this fact, also, causes the latter to be much less affected in its motion by the influence of the train.‡ But, not content with this, Harrison fitted between the fourth and crown wheels a most ingenious remontoire, whose action, at first sight, is almost uncanny. Its operation is shown in fig. 18, and its arrangement is briefly as follows.

The fourth wheel is mounted loosely upon the arbor of the contrate wheel, and the two are connected by a slender spiral spring. The fourth wheel engages with the pinion of a fifth wheel, which in its turn drives a fly. This fifth wheel has a stop projecting at right angles to its rim, and this is normally held by a pivoted detent of peculiar shape, with five arms. The whole train is thereby kept from moving, but the contrate wheel is free to turn and drive the crown wheel under the influence of the slender remontoire spring. Mounted on the contrate

* The " supplementary arc " of a balance or pendulum is that portion of its excursion away from the dead point which it describes after the impulse has been completed.

† The motion of a balance is said to be " banked " when it is prevented from exceeding a certain arc. The mechanism effecting this is generally referred to as the " banking." In No. 4 it was accomplished by means of a pin below the rim of the balance, which engaged, at 145° from the dead point, with one of two brass arms mounted on the third wheel cock.

‡ Harrison remarks: " . . . In this my Time-keeper, the Wheels have only about *One-eightieth* Part of the Power over the Balance that the Balance-spring has; and, it must be allowed, the less the Wheels have to do with the Balance the better."

18 Harrison's remontoire.

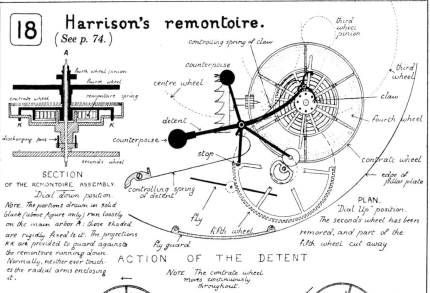

(See p. 74.)

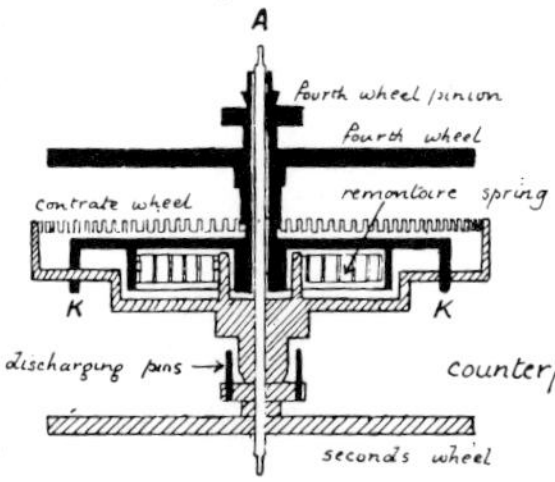

SECTION
OF THE REMONTOIRE ASSEMBLY.
"Dial down" position.

NOTE. The portions drawn in solid black (above figure only) run loosely on the main arbor A: those shaded are rigidly fixed to it. The projections KK are provided to guard against the remontoire running down. Normally, neither ever touches the radial arms enclosing it.

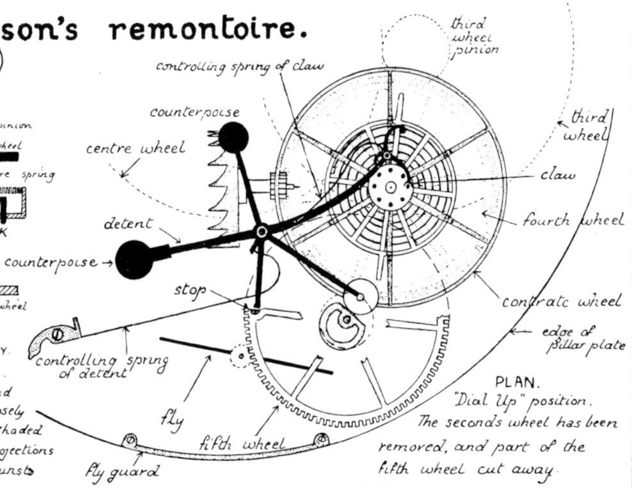

PLAN.
"Dial Up" position.
The seconds wheel has been removed, and part of the fifth wheel cut away.

ACTION OF THE DETENT

NOTE. The contrate wheel moves continuously throughout.

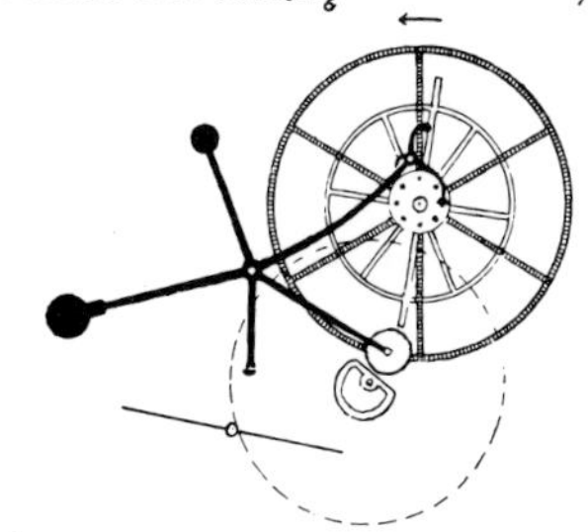

I. The contrate wheel is in motion, and the remainder of the mechanism locked, the stop on the fifth wheel being in contact with the short arm of the detent. A pin is just entering the claw.

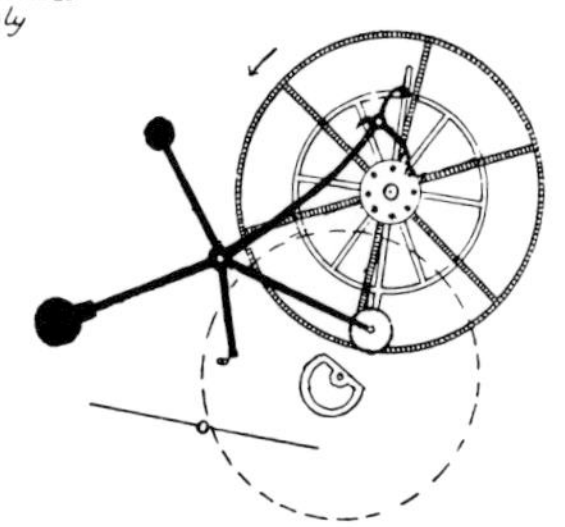

II. 7 seconds later. The detent has been turned slightly anti-clockwise by the pin, and the short arm is just about to clear the stop.

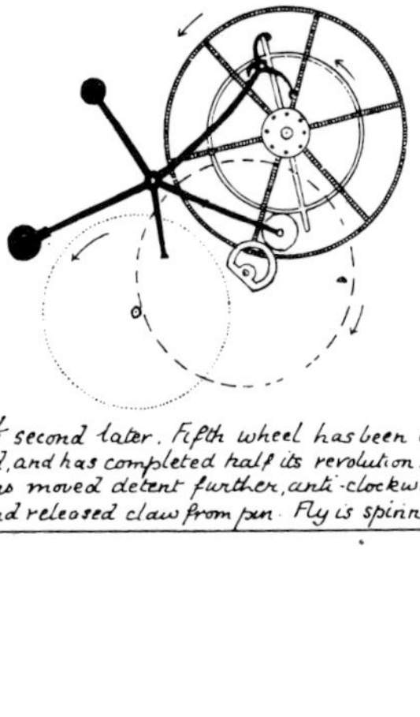

III. $\frac{1}{4}$ second later. Fifth wheel has been unlocked, and has completed half its revolution. Cam has moved detent further, anti-clockwise, and released claw from pin. Fly is spinning.

R.T. Gould 1922

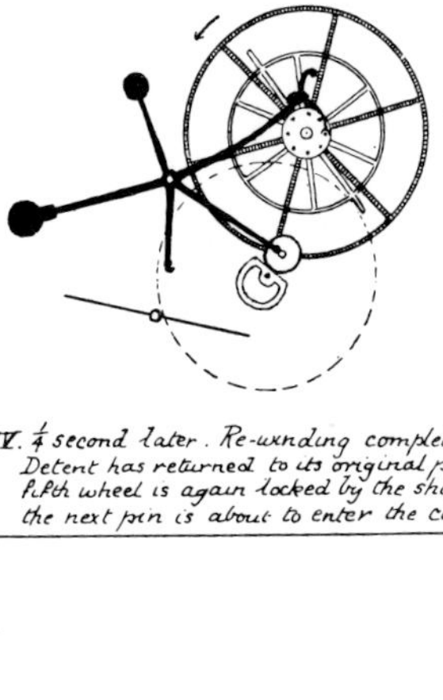

IV. $\frac{1}{4}$ second later. Re-winding completed. Detent has returned to its original position, fifth wheel is again locked by the short arm, & the next pin is about to enter the claw.

wheel arbor, which turns once in a minute, is a small lantern pinion of eight pins, and these pins, as the contrate wheel rotates, engage successively with a claw carried on one of the arms of the detent. Accordingly, every $7\frac{1}{2}$ seconds, they push the detent clear of the stop on the fifth wheel, and unlock the train. The fourth wheel is thus free to rotate and rewind the remontoire spring through the eighth of a turn which it has run down. While it does so, the fifth wheel makes a complete turn, and a cam on its arbor, taking on a roller mounted on another arm of the detent, disengages the claw from the pin. The claw is pivoted, and controlled by a tiny spring in the same manner as the pallet arm in the " grasshopper " escapement. This spring has been slightly tensioned during the unlocking, and returns the claw, as soon as it is disengaged from the pin, to its normal position ready to meet the next pin, while the detent, under the influence of a second spring which keeps the roller bearing on the cam, comes back to its place in time to meet the stop as it comes round again, and so re-lock the train. The fly prevents the re-winding being done too fast, but this can also be provided for, in great part, by adjusting the initial tension of the remontoire spring to be not much weaker than the torque exerted by the maintaining spring, via the train, upon the pinion of the fourth wheel.

This mechanism, in action, is most fascinating to watch. The mechanical intelligence with which the claw unerringly selects the right pin, disengages itself, and returns to meet the next is, as the Marquis of Worcester said of his perpetual motion, " A thing most incredible, if not seen."

This remontoire entirely cuts off the contrate wheel, and hence the balance, from any fluctuations of force caused by the friction of the train. The best mean tension for the remontoire spring is a turn and a half (corresponding to a weight of 43 grs. (Troy) hung on the rim of the contrate wheel), so that the torque at the contrate wheel actually varies, every $7\frac{1}{2}$ seconds, in the proportion of 13 to 11, and there is furthermore the (very slight) variation caused by the power absorbed in unlocking the detent. But these fluctuations are constant, and they recur at such short intervals that, practically speaking, the force impelling the balance during a long period may be regarded as uniform.

The remainder of the mechanism does not call for such detailed description. The arrangement of the train is shown in Figs. 16 and 17. The third wheel is remarkable for having internal teeth, so that the fourth wheel rotates in the same sense as the third. This was done in order that the seconds hand, whose motion work consists of two equal-sized wheels, one mounted on the arbor of the contrate wheel and the other riding loosely on the " cannon pinion,"* might rotate clockwise. Harrison, by the way, called the centre wheel the " second wheel," and the great wheel the " first wheel."

---

* The cannon pinion is a principal part of the " motion-work " of all timekeepers, which provides for the correct relative motion of the hour and minute hands. Its operation is explained on p. 352.

The fusee contains Harrison's maintaining power, fitted in a very similar manner to that employed by him in his previous machines. The maintaining spring is very large*, and will keep the machine going for eleven minutes, although the operation of winding only takes a few seconds.

Harrison's foresight is well exemplified by his fitting a frictional brake, acting upon the rim of the balance, as shown in Plate XII. Without this, the watch, if it were ever allowed to run down, would stop with the remontoire down too, and, after rewinding, it could not be restarted, however much motion were given to the balance, unless the detent of the remontoire train were first unlocked—a difficult and delicate operation for anyone but a skilled watchmaker. The brake gets over this difficulty. Operated by the last turn of the fusee chain as this unwinds from the fusee, it stops the timekeeper, *with the remontoire wound*, half an hour before the mainspring can run down.

The mainspring† is mounted in a " resting barrel "—that is to say, it does not directly rotate the barrel on which the fusee chain is wound, but fits inside a stationary barrel fixed to the plate nearest the dial, generally termed the " pillar-plate." The outer end of the spring is attached to this barrel, and the inner to an arbor upon which is mounted the barrel for the fusee chain. The resting barrel can be rotated to adjust the initial tension of the spring, and is held by a ratchet and click. This construction was imitated by Kendall and by Mudge‡, but its practical advantages are slight. However, it enables the barrel, being rigidly attached to a pivoted arbor, to be better supported and less affected by side strains than the ordinary construction, in which the arbor is fixed and passes through two holes in the barrel and its cover, constituting the bearings on which the pull of the chain is exerted.

The watch beats five to the second, a slight recoil being perceptible at each beat, and goes for thirty hours. The finish of the movement is very good, particularly for a man not trained as a watchmaker. The plates are of brass, polished, but not gilt. The pivot holes are jewelled as far as the third wheel—that is to say, those of the balance staff, detent, contrate wheel, fly, fifth, fourth, and third wheels. The jewels are rubies, and the end stones diamonds.

---

* It is not of the modern " split-ring " pattern, but a large spiral spring, considerably bigger than the mainspring of an ordinary watch.

† This spring, as well as those of the remontoire and maintainer, was made by Maberley, a famous London spring maker. The balance spring was made and tempered by Harrison himself.

When I cleaned No. 4 recently, I found the mainspring, which was lettered " I.M.—E.C." and dated " 2.13.(*sic*) 1760," broken. I was able, however, to obtain a duplicate, made for me by Messrs. Cotton, of Clerkenwell.

‡ It is interesting to note that there are many points of resemblance between Harrison's resting-barrel and that invented by Mr. Lewis Donne for going-barrel watches.

Some of the detail work of the watch is probably not Harrison's own. I imagine that the jewelling, the chasing of the top-plate* and balance cock†, and the enamelling of the dial, were done for him by workmen more expert in these technical branches than he could hope to be. On the top-plate is engraved " John Harrison and Son, 1759." The " Son " referred to is William Harrison, F.R.S., who had grown up to be his father's right-hand man, and who, as we shall see, played a leading part in the trials of No. 4.

But after making every allowance for his assistance, which was doubtless of great value to his father, now a man of nearly seventy, the full credit for the production of this marvellous piece of mechanism must go to the master spirit which planned and in great measure constructed it. To the making of No. 4, a masterpiece weighing less than the brain that conceived it, went fifty years of self-denial, unremitting toil, and ceaseless concentration : years filled with labour and thought—the patient labour of a pair of hands that were never idle, and the long reveries of a mind that never would admit defeat, but toiled onwards patiently, steadily, and indomitably towards a mechanical ideal generally regarded as unattainable. To the present age, No. 4 is but a beautiful and obsolete piece of intricate and over-complicated mechanism, but it must ever remain Harrison's chief and unquestioned title to immortality, for with it he showed, in the most practical manner possible, that a satisfactory marine timekeeper *could be* constructed, and by so doing he made the whole world his debtor.

No. 4 was finished in 1759, and Harrison, after comparing it with his regulator for some time, reported to the Board of Longitude in March, 1761, that its going equalled that of No. 3, and greatly exceeded his expectations. He asked for a trial of both machines at sea.

---

* Both in No. 4 and the modern chronometer, the train is contained between two brass plates, in which are the pivot-holes of the various arbors. The plate nearest the dial is termed the " pillar-plate," from the fact of the pillars which connect the plates being made fixtures in it. The other plate is termed the " top-plate."

† The " balance-cock " is a separate piece carrying one of the pivot-holes of the balance, and screwed to the top-plate. Any such piece, if outside the plates, is generally termed a " cock," and, if inside, a " potence."

CHAPTER IV.

JOHN HARRISON.

PART II.

The trial which Harrison requested was at once granted by the Board, and he received £250 to fit his son out for the voyage to the West Indies, since, at the age of sixty-seven, it was hardly to be expected that he should attend the trial in person. William Harrison, with No. 3, proceeded to Portsmouth in April, 1761, his father intending to follow with No. 4, but the vessel originally allotted for the trial* was ordered on other duty, and a substitute, H.M.S. "Deptford," was not obtained until October. It had originally been intended that the longitude of Jamaica, whither the "Deptford" was bound, should be determined *de novo* by means of observations of Jupiter's satellites, but owing to the lateness of the season it was decided that the present determination should be accepted, and that the local time there and at Portsmouth should be obtained by equal altitudes of the sun and compared with the time shown by the timekeepers—or, rather, timekeeper, for in October Harrison definitely determined to rest his claims upon the going of No. 4 only.

It was agreed that the timekeeper should be put in a case with four locks, whose keys were entrusted to William Harrison, Governor Lyttleton of Jamaica, who was taking passage in the "Deptford," Dudley Digges (her captain) and his first lieutenant. All four had therefore to attend before the case could be opened, even for winding.†

The "Deptford" sailed from Spithead with a convoy on November 18th, 1761, and after touching at Portland and Plymouth set sail for Madeira. On the ninth day after losing sight of land, the ship's longitude, by dead reckoning, was 13° 50′ west of Greenwich, but by No. 4 it was 15° 19′ W. Digges was inclined to prefer the dead reckoning, but William Harrison maintained very forcibly that the timekeeper was correct, and that if Madeira were correctly marked on the chart they would sight it the following day. Accordingly, although Digges offered to bet him five to one that he was wrong, he held on his course, and was rewarded by sighting Porto Santo, the N.E. island of the Madeira group, at 6 a.m. the next morning. This greatly relieved the ship's company, who were afraid of missing Madeira

* H.M.S. "Dorsetshire."

† This stipulation was not rigorously interpreted, but a certificate given by these three officials to William Harrison, at the conclusion of the trial, recounted that he had never had access to No. 4 except in the presence of one or more of them.

altogether, "the consequence of which," as a contemporary account put it, "would have been Inconvenient, as they were in Want of Beer."*

This practical demonstration of No. 4's worth greatly impressed the officers of the "Deptford,"† and William Harrison followed it up by predicting in the same manner the other islands, such as Deseada, with which they fell in during the passage, while on the ship's arrival at Jamaica the timekeeper was found, after allowing for its rate of going‡, to be five seconds slow, corresponding to an error in longitude, provided that the situation of Jamaica was correctly determined, of $1\frac{1}{4}'$ only. Accordingly, under the Act of Queen Anne, Harrison became entitled§, provided he could demonstrate to the satisfaction of the Board of Longitude that the use of his timekeeper constituted a "method generally practicable and useful," to the reward of £20,000.

Now, when a large sum of money, and especially of public money is in question, it is natural that difficulties and delays should arise in connection with its payment, and that the sterner and less pleasant side of human nature should be brought prominently forward. Accordingly, we find that the relations existing between Harrison and the Board of Longitude, which had hitherto been cordial and even amicable, soon became strained. There was a good deal to be said on both sides, and, as generally happens, neither could see the other's point of view. Harrison had spent a lifetime in complying with the Act of Queen Anne, which was still in force: he had at last done so, and he knew that the performance of his timekeeper was no fluke, but a feat that it was always capable of performing: he felt himself as justly entitled to the reward as he undoubtedly was legally, and he said so. Moreover, he was an old man, and he knew that his time was short.

The Board, on the other hand, were not fully satisfied that No. 4's good going was not accidental. They knew nothing of its mechanism,

---

* On December 7th, the "Deptford's" log records "Condemned by Survey 1057 Galls. Beer, 480 pds. cheese, which was thrown in the Sea," and the Master's journal, on the 9th, states "This day the Ship's Beer is all expended, the People obliged to drink water." But relief for these thirsty souls was close at hand. On arrival at Madeira we read "Received 3 Pipes of Wine for the Ship's Company," and again "Received 9 Butts of Wine and stowed it away."

† It led Digges to bespeak the first timekeeper that should be produced for sale. During the ship's stay at Madeira, No. 4's utility was further emphasised by the circumstance that H.M.S. "Beaver," which had sailed for that island ten days earlier than the "Deptford," arrived three days later, having over-run her reckoning in precisely the same manner as the "Deptford" did.

‡ William Harrison had determined this, at Portsmouth, to be $2\frac{2}{3}$ seconds per day losing, as the result of equal altitude observations extending over a period of nine days only. The observations were made with an "equal altitude instrument," like an equatorial telescope with its main axis vertical.

§ The official trial ended at Jamaica. William Harrison and No. 4 returned in the "Merlin" sloop, and experienced extremely rough weather. No. 4 had to be shifted to the poop, as the only dry place in the ship, and there experienced a number of violent shocks. Its total error, however, in the five months, was still only 1m. $53\frac{1}{2}$s. = $28\frac{1}{2}'$ of longitude.

for Harrison would not disclose its secrets,* and it was pointed out that if an adventurer were to take a gross of ordinary watches to the West Indies, and one of them happened to show correct time on its arrival, he would be just as much entitled to the reward, under the terms of the Act, as Harrison was. Accordingly, they refused (August 17th, 1762) to give him a certificate that he had complied with the requirements of the Act until after a further trial of the timekeeper, basing their decision upon the technical grounds that the longitude of Jamaica could not be regarded as determined with sufficient accuracy to afford an accurate standard of comparison with the time shown by No. 4, and that the method of obtaining the latter's rate at Portsmouth was untrustworthy. They agreed, however, since it had shown itself a useful invention, to give its inventor an interim reward of £2,500, to be deducted from any reward to which he might afterwards become entitled. It was resolved that a second trial should be made, and Harrison consented to let No. 4 be rated at Greenwich beforehand, provided he were first allowed four or five months to make some alterations to it.

These alterations related to the isochronism of the balance. Harrison had found, when No. 4 was first made, that the balance described a long arc of vibration in slightly less time than it took for a short one, and he had endeavoured to correct this by the form of the curve on the backs of the pallets. He now added another device for the same purpose. Between the curb pins and the fixed stud which secured the end of the balance spring to the top-plate, he fitted, as shown in fig. 14, a third curb pin, called the "cycloid-pin," inside the curve of the spring, and so placed as to touch it when at rest. When the balance had turned 45° in the direction which coiled the spring, the latter would leave the cycloid pin, and its effective length would become increased by the distance between this and the stud. As the spring left the pin for a longer time in the long arcs than the short ones, the motion of the balance was relatively accelerated in the latter case.†

It was the fitting of this device that caused Harrison finally to abandon his adjustment for mean time. He found that any movement of the fixed end of the curb upset the adjustment of the cycloid pin. In his last machine, No. 5, he reversed this procedure, retaining the mean time adjustment, and discarding the cycloid pin. The latter was never much more than a makeshift. It should be noted that if

* It must be borne in mind that although Harrison had exhibited No. 4, complete, to the Board, no clear idea of its mechanism could be obtained without taking it to pieces—for example, the thermometer curb, its most essential portion, is entirely concealed by the elaborate balance cock. And to take it to pieces is not easy: even the first step, the removal of the hands, is an operation requiring a considerable amount of time and patience.

† No. 3 contains an earlier device of Harrison's for accomplishing the same end, the "saddle piece"—an adjustable metal stirrup fitting over the lower balance-staff, and touched by a projection on it in the long arcs. Berthoud afterwards experimented with a similar device. It will be noted that Harrison's pallets were designed to correct the long arcs, and his cycloid pin the short.

It should be pointed out that a very similar device to Harrison's cycloid pin had been previously used by Gourdain, a French horologist, and described by him in the "Memoirs de l'Académie des Sciences," 1742.

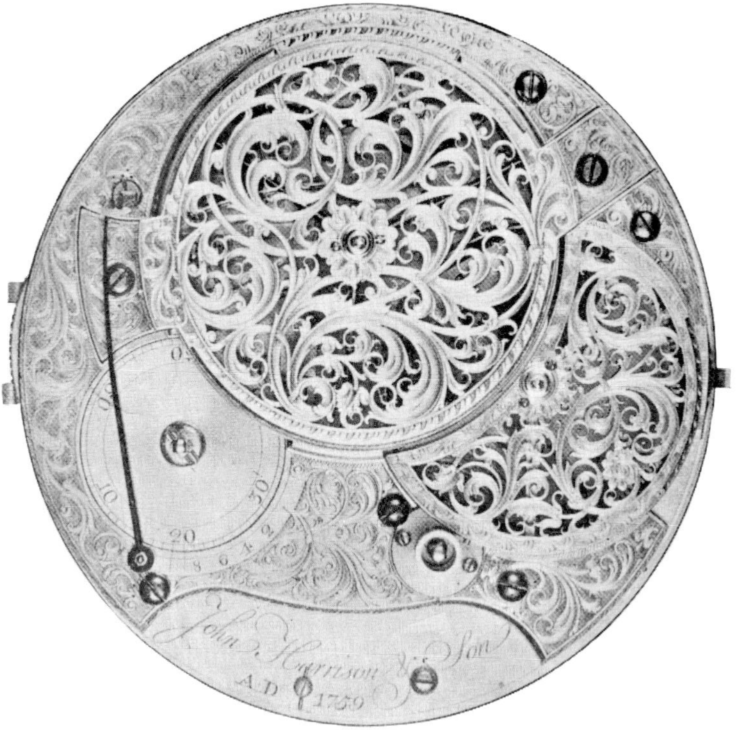

Plate XII. TOP-PLATE OF HARRISON'S No. 4.

The larger of the two pierced and engraved cocks covers the balance, and the smaller the third wheel. The arm crossing the indicator-dial of the regulator (discarded) is the automatic brake for stopping the balance.

See p. 73 et. seq. Royal Observatory, Greenwich.

Harrison had succeeded in equalising the time of the long and short arcs by means of his pallets only, he could have regulated his machine very easily by using a second set of curb pins traversing the arc between the stud and the thermometer curb pins.*

In February, 1763, Harrison, supported by the Board, obtained an Act of Parliament enabling him to receive £5,000 as soon as he disclosed the principles of his invention to certain Commissioners named in it, and the rest after a second trial or trials.† But this became a nullity, owing to the absurd construction put upon its terms by the Earl of Morton, P.R.S., Chairman of the Commissioners and Harrison's *bête noire*. This injustice was, very honestly, admitted by Lord Sandwich, then First Lord of the Admiralty, who declared that it was obviously not in Harrison's power to comply with the Commissioners requirements, and that therefore he should have a new trial when he pleased, and as soon as he pleased.

Arrangements for the second trial of No. 4 "dragged their slow length along." Harrison ultimately declined to allow No. 4 to be rated at Greenwich prior to sailing, as desired by the Board. He gave as his reason "that he did not chuse to part with it out of his hands till he shall have reaped some advantage from it." He eventually agreed that before the ship sailed he would send a sealed paper, containing the timekeeper's rate as determined by himself, to the Secretary of the Admiralty.

Elaborate arrangements were made relating to the instruments to be employed, and it was determined that the difference of longitude between Portsmouth [the point of departure] and Jamaica should be determined *de novo* by corresponding observations of Jupiter's satellites.

The observers selected to take the Jamaica observations‡ were Green, assistant to Bliss (the Astronomer-Royal), and Maskelyne, newly returned from his unsuccessful expedition to St. Helena in connection with the 1761 transit of Venus. Maskelyne, however, declined to go to Jamaica on account of the state of his health, and accordingly, with Harrison's consent, Barbados was selected instead.

Maskelyne and Green embarked in H.M.S. "Princess Louisa,"§ together with one Christopher Irwin,¶ the inventor of a marine chair

* An exactly contrary statement was made by Mr. H. D. Gardner in a lecture at the R.U.S. Institution in 1890, and repeated by Britten in his "Old Clocks and Watches." I have, however, satisfied myself of the practicability of regulating No. 4 in this manner by actual experiment with it. It must be remembered that the portion of the spring between the curb pins and the "stud" by which its fixed end is attached to the top-plate is very much longer than in ordinary watches, and the effect caused by its flexure therefore much more noticeable.

† The Board allowed Harrison £300 for his expenses in procuring the passing of this Act, and for his son's outfit in the second trial. As related in Chapter VI., the French Government were officially invited to send representatives to attend Harrison's expected disclosure (which Morton's conduct temporarily postponed) and Camus, Berthoud, and Lalande came over for this purpose.

‡ The Portsmouth observations were taken by Mr. Bradley, purser of H.M.S. Dorsetshire."

§ Maskelyne, being in holy orders, was appointed to her as chaplain, and Green as purser, fifth-rate.

¶ He was distantly related to Bradley, the late Astronomer-Royal.

which had been favourably reported on by Lord Howe. In consequence of this report, the Board granted its inventor £500 for further experiments, directing him to embark his invention for test by Maskelyne and Green. A short trial convinced the former that the invention was of no practical value.

William Harrison embarked with No. 4 in H.M.S. "Tartar," at the Nore, on February 14th, 1764*, having previously sent to the Secretary of the Admiralty, for transmission to the Board, the following declaration :—

> "My Lords and Gentlemen,
>
> "In obedience to your instructions, dated the 9th of August, 1763, I humbly certify that I do expect the rate of the going of the timekeeper will be as followeth ; viz.
>
> "When the thermometer is at 42°†, it will gain 3 seconds in every 24 hours.
>
> "When the thermometer is at 52°, it will gain 2 seconds in every 24 hours.
>
> "When the thermometer is at 62°, it will gain 1 second in every 24 hours.
>
> "When the thermometer is at 72°, it will neither gain nor lose.
>
> "When the thermometer is at 82°, it will lose 1 second in every 24 hours.
>
> "Since my last voyage, we have made some improvement in the timekeeper ; in consequence of which, the provision to counterbalance the effects of heat and cold, has been made anew ; and for the want of a little more time, we could not get it quite adjusted ; for which reason the above allowances are necessary. This is its present rate ; and as the inequalities are so small, I will abide by the rate of its gaining, on a mean, one second a day for the voyage. I would not be understood, that it will always require so long time to bring those machines to perfection ; for it is well known to be much harder to beat out a new road, than it is to follow that road when made. During the time of this experiment, the mean height of the thermometer shall be each day carefully noted down, and certified, which I will lay before the Board on my return.
>
> "I am, etc., WILLIAM HARRISON."

The "Tartar" proceeded to Portsmouth, where William Harrison checked the timekeeper's rate by comparison with a regulator‡ installed in a temporary observatory. The ship left Portsmouth on March 28th, 1764, and William Harrison was able, as he had done in the "Deptford," to predict with confidence, by means of the timekeeper, their falling in with the islands of Madeira and Barbados. The observations were made at the latter place from May 14th-17th, inclusive, although an unforeseen difficulty threatened at one time to delay them.

Maskelyne and Green had arrived earlier than the "Tartar," and had, very naturally, made the acquaintance of the local residents. Now Maskelyne had occupied his voyage to St. Helena and back with a series of experiments on the taking of lunar distances, and he had just published his "British Mariner's Guide," in which he strongly extolled their practical value for finding longitude at sea. The one topic of the hour at Barbados was, of course, the great reward and the problem of longitude, and Maskelyne seems to have made no secret of the fact that he considered his method superior to Harrison's.

* It is interesting to note that Erskine, who subsequently became Lord Chancellor, was serving aboard the "Tartar" as a midshipman. He became a lifelong friend and patron of the younger Harrison. † Fahrenheit.

‡ Lent for this purpose by the Duke of Richmond.

This got round to William Harrison's ears, and he promptly and naturally objected to Maskelyne as an observer, pointing out that by his own admission he was an interested party, and, indeed, a rival competitor. He was supported in this contention by Sir John Lindsay, Captain of the "Tartar." However, it was finally agreed that observations should be taken alternately by Maskelyne and Green, but for the first series the former was much discomposed, and could hardly observe.

The results of the observations, as compared with those taken at Portsmouth, gave for the mean value of the difference of longitude between Portsmouth and Jamaica 3h. 54m. 18.2s., while by the timekeeper it was 3h. 54m. 56.6s., an error of 38.4s. in seven weeks, corresponding to 9.6′ miles of longitude at the equator. Moreover, the machine's total error when again compared, after an elapsed period of 156 days, with the clock at Portsmouth, was a gain of only 54 seconds in 156 days* (after allowing for the rate of 1 second per day gaining), while if further allowance were made for the changes of rate in different temperatures declared by Harrison before sailing, this would be reduced to a loss of 15 seconds in five months, or an error of *less than a tenth of a second per day*. Harrison's pride in his masterpiece was fully justified.

Faced with this decisive proof, the Board passed a resolution on February 9th, 1765, to the effect that they were "unanimously of opinion that the said timekeeper has kept its time with sufficient correctness, without losing its longitude in the voyage from Portsmouth to Barbados beyond the nearest limit required by the Act 12th of Queen Anne, but even considerably within the same," but that Harrison had not yet explained the principles on which No. 4 was constructed. They accordingly resolved to give him half the reward as soon as he complied with this requirement, and the other half as soon as other timekeepers of his making should perform equally well. These resolutions were soon embodied in an Act of Parliament, 5 Geo. III., cap. 20.

Then began a long contest between the Board and the Harrisons. The capabilities of No. 4 were no longer disputed—but, as already explained, the Board were determined to make sure that it was not a mechanical phœnix, while Harrison was equally determined not to disclose its mechanism without payment to the last penny.

The Board decided (May 28th, 1765) that to obtain the first half of the reward he must :—

1. Give them, on oath, the drawings from which No. 4 was made, a written explanation, and the machine itself.
2. Give, also, to such persons as they should appoint, a further verbal explanation, take No. 4 to pieces in their presence, answer all questions about it, and demonstrate any obscure points in its making (such as the tempering of the springs) by experiment if necessary.
3. Make over to the Board his other three timekeepers.

*After William Harrison's return in the "New Elizabeth."

These conditions elicited a most righteously indignant letter from Harrison. After accepting the first condition, and part of the second, but declining to give any experimental demonstrations, or to part with the three early machines until after receiving his reward, he continues :

> " I cannot help thinking but I am extremely ill used by gentlemen who I might have expected a different treatment from ; for if the Act of the 12th of Queen Anne be deficient, why have I so long been encouraged under it, in order to bring my invention to perfection ? and, after the completion, why was my son sent twice to the West Indies ? Had it been said to my son, when he received the last instructions, there will, in case you succeed, be a new Act at your return, in order to lay you under new restrictions, which were not thought of in the Act of the 12th of Queen Anne ; I say, had this been the case, I might have expected some such treatment as I now meet with.
>
> " It must be owned that my case is very hard, but I hope I am the first, and, for my country's sake, shall be the last that suffers by pinning my faith on an English Act of Parliament.
>
> " Had I received my just reward, for certainly it may be so called after 40 years close application in the improvement of that talent which it has pleased God to give me, then my invention would have taken the course which all improvements in this world do, that is, I must have instructed workmen in its principles and execution, which I should have been glad to have had an opportunity of doing : but how widely this is different to what is now proposed, viz. for me to instruct people that I know nothing of ; and if I do not make them understand to their satisfaction, I may then have nothing ! Hard fate indeed to me, but harder still to the world, which may be deprived of this my invention, which must be the case, except by my open and free manner of describing all the principles of it to gentlemen and workmen, who almost, at all times, have had free recourse to see my instruments ; and if any of these workmen shall have been so ingenious as to have got my invention, how far you will please to reward them for their piracy must be left for you to determine ; and I must sit myself down in old age, and thank God I can be more easy in that I have made the conquest, and though I have no reward, than if I had come short of the matter, and by some delusion had the reward."

After reading this stinging reproof, the Board tried to tone down the severity of their conditions, especially that relating to the " experimental exhibitions." Whereupon Harrison " left the Board abruptly, swearing that he would never consent to it, so long as he had a drop of English blood in his body."

The Board accordingly resolved to deal no further with him, " until he alters his present sentiments." To clear themselves in the eyes of the public, they resolved on the publication of all of their minutes which related to Harrison and his inventions.*

On Harrison's side, his staunch friend and champion, James Short, F.R.S.,† also made an appeal to the public‡. He had already published, in 1763, an anonymous pamphlet recounting the attempts made, up to that time, to find the longitude‡, and he now issued a

---

* They were published by Billingsley, London, as a 4to pamphlet, price 6d.

† Celebrated as an optician and maker of reflecting telescopes.

‡ " An Account of the Proceedings in order to the discovery of the Longitude . . . . " London, 1763. This pamphlet contains a very useful appendix, in which are collected a number of documents relating to Harrison's early work.

second, which brought the story of Harrison's efforts up to date, and gave particulars of the trials of No. 4 and of the subsequent negotiations.*

At length, finding the Board as stubborn as himself, and too strong for him, Harrison bowed to the inevitable and accepted their conditions. On August 22nd, 1765, and subsequent days, he took his timekeeper to pieces at his house before a committee of six nominated by the Board—Rev. John Michell, Rev. William Ludlam, and Messrs. John Bird, Thomas Mudge, William Matthews and Larcum Kendall, the last-named three being practical watchmakers. He also gave, upon oath a full explanation of its mechanism and manufacture. This committee reported to the Board that they were satisfied that Harrison had given them all the information in his power, and accordingly on October 28th, 1765, having re-assembled No. 4 and delivered it up to the Board, undertaking at the same time to deliver up the other three timekeepers whenever called upon to do so, he received their certificate entitling him to £7,500, which, with the £2,500 he had received after the voyage to Jamaica, made up the first half of the £20,000.

Having made No. 4 their property, in trust for the public, the Board set about making its mechanism as widely known as possible, and proceeded to publish Harrison's drawings and explanation, together with the notes taken by the members of the committee.† This action was bitterly resented by Harrison‡, but its effect was absolutely nugatory, since the information thus given was, whether intentionally or otherwise, entirely insufficient to allow of anyone constructing a similar timekeeper by its aid. The drawings, although they may have been enough for Harrison to work from, are hopelessly obscure, and the description almost equally so. At the end of the latter, however, is one passage that may be quoted as showing Harrison's trust in his invention :—

> " My Time-keeper's Balance is more than three times the Weight of a large sized common Watch-balance, and three times its diameter ; and a common Watch-balance goes through about six Inches of Space in a Second, but mine goes through about twenty-four Inches in that Time : So that had my Time-keeper only these Advantages over a common Watch, a good Performance might be expected from it. But my Time-keeper is not affected by the different Degrees of Heat and Cold, nor Agitation of the Ship ; and the Force from the Wheels is applied to the Balance in such a Manner, together with the Shape of the Balance-spring, and (if I may be allowed the Term) an artificial Cycloid, which acts at this Spring ; so that from these Contrivances, let the Balance vibrate more or less, all its Vibrations are performed in the same Time ; and therefore, if it go at all, it must go *true*. So it is plain from this, that such a Time-keeper goes intirely from Principle, and not from Chance."

* " A Narrative of the Proceedings relative to the Discovery of the Longitude . . . . subsequent to those published in the year 1763." London, 1765.

† " The Principles of Mr. Harrison's Time-keeper, with Plates of the same." London, 1767, 4to, price 5s. In addition to the description and drawings, this pamphlet also contains some notes on the mechanism, contributed by the members of the committee, and a short preface by Maskelyne.

‡ In his remarks upon Maskelyne's account of the Greenwich trial of No. 4, he says : " . . . they have since published all my Drawings without giving me the last Moiety of the Reward, or even paying me and my Son for our Time at a rate as common Mechanicks ; an Instance of such Cruelty and Injustice as I believe never existed in a learned and civilised Nation before."

What he really thought of No. 4 can best be seen in the following passage from an unpublished description, of which I possess a copy :—

> " I think I may make bold to say, that there is neither any other Mechanical or Mathematical thing in the World that is more beautiful or curious in texture than this my watch or Time-keeper for the Longitude . . . and I heartily thank Almighty God that I have lived so long, as in some measure to complete it."

Another step taken by the Board galled Harrison even more. They sent No. 4, with much ceremony, to Greenwich, to undergo a prolonged trial in the hands of the man whom he regarded, rightly or wrongly, as his declared and bitter enemy—the Rev. Nevil Maskelyne, Astronomer-Royal.* It cannot be denied that Maskelyne executed this commission with a rigour which was at least sufficient to give ground for a suspicion that if No. 4 did badly he would not be inconsolable.

The results were not very good. Maskelyne first tried the watch in positions (XII, III, VI, and IX up, dial up, and dial down) in order to test its isochronism, and then through the same series when inclined at an angle of 20° to the horizontal, a position which, as he pointed out, it might often assume through its lack of gimbals. These tests occupied two months, and the watch was then kept going for ten months (July 6th, 1766, to May 6th, 1767) in a horizontal position, with face upwards. During the whole trial it gained 1h. 10m. 27.5s., giving an average rate of 14.2 seconds gaining, which, in the main, it adhered to pretty consistently: but it exhibited irregularities in its going in positions, and in the action of the compensation.

A full account of the trial was published by the Board,† with a preface by Maskelyne, in which he did not neglect to draw attention to the fact that the case of the timekeeper was always kept locked, and that he was unable to have access to it, even for winding, except in the presence of an officer detailed by the Governor of Greenwich Hospital to witness that operation‡: and he concluded by giving, as his considered opinion :—

> That Mr. Harrison's Watch cannot be depended upon to keep the Longitude within a Degree, in a West-India Voyage of six weeks, nor to keep the Longitude within Half a Degree for more than a Fortnight, and then it must be kept in a Place where the Thermometer is always some Degrees above freezing."

But this opinion, even if unbiassed, was far too harsh, and ridiculously at variance with the results of the sea-trials, while Harrison was not slow to point out§ a number of circumstances which put a very different complexion on the matter.

---

* Bradley died in 1762, and was succeeded by Bliss, who was already dying of consumption. He died two years later, and Maskelyne was appointed Astronomer-Royal in his stead. He held the position for no less than forty-seven years, a record only equalled, in later times, by Airy.

† " An Account of the going of Mr. John Harrison's Watch, . . . By the Rev. Nevil Maskelyne, Astronomer-Royal." London, 1767, 4to. Price 2s. 6d.

‡ These officers received five guineas apiece from the Board as compensation for their trouble and expenses (coach-hire, &c.) while executing this duty.

§ " Remarks on a Pamphlet lately published by the Rev. Mr. Maskelyne." London, 1767. Price 6d. Maskelyne planned, but did not publish, a reply.

In the first place, the Harrisons had been trying some experiments with No. 4 since its return from Barbados, and had not had time to re-adjust it fully before delivering it up to the Board. Its large gaining rate*, of which they had made no secret at the time, was due to this reason.

Secondly, the limits of heat and cold to which the thermometer curb was adjusted, and which were amply sufficient for use on shipboard, were 42° and 82° Fahr.† But the temperatures to which it was exposed during the trial ranged from freezing point to well over 100°. ‡ Personally, I am surprised that it did not stop altogether, as a very moderate increase in the travel of the curb would bring it in contact with the balance staff. In any case, the excessive alternations of temperature probably distorted the curb permanently, and so produced the irregularities noticed in its action.

The experiments in positions, also, proved nothing, in the face of Harrison's express declaration, made to the Board previously, that No. 4 was not adjusted to go truly in such positions, into which the motion of a ship could never put it. Its general performance, neglecting its antics in positions and extreme temperatures, was amply sufficient, on Maskelyne's own showing, to keep the longitude within half a degree in a six weeks' voyage, as called for by the Act of Queen Anne, whose conditions had, all along, governed its adjustment.

Harrison had other mortifications to face. The Board contracted with Larcum Kendall to make them a duplicate of the timekeeper, and, while they intimated to Harrison that he must construct two others for test before he could qualify for the other half of the reward, refused him the loan of No. 4, even for a short period (which would have been of great assistance to him), on the ground that Kendall required it to work from. He, on the other hand, had freely given Kendall all the advice and instruction he required.

Furthermore, the Board were full of plans for a more exhaustive trial of Nos. 5 and 6 than the simple West Indies voyage performed by No. 4. They spoke of sending them to Hudson's Bay, or of letting them roll for two months in the Downs. The facts that Harrison was now 77, that his sight was failing, and that it was uncertain whether he would ever complete even one more timekeeper, appear to have

* As previously related, there was no adjustment for mean time, and the effect of the compensation curb could only be modified by a tedious process of trial and error, its sides being rubbed down to increase its action, and the edges thickened by burnishing to reduce it. Harrison claimed, however, that it was, when once adjusted, permanent in its effect, and that if the watch were at any time taken to pieces and re-assembled, it would show its rate of going, accurately, in three hours' running.

† The average temperature while at Barbados, however, was 86°-87°.

‡ The room in which No. 4 was tried was not heated in any way during the winter. The machine's box had a glass top, and was screwed down to a window-seat in the full glare of the forenoon sun. The thermometer, whose daily readings were regarded as an accurate record of the temperatures to which the timekeeper was exposed, hung in another part of the room, *in the shade*.

worried them as little as any forebodings of their conduct being, possibly, stigmatised as callous to a degree—and, moreover, lacking in foresight.

For Harrison, however harmless they may have thought him, was not without friends, and he had at last found a very powerful and a very warm-hearted protector—no less a person than His Majesty King George the Third. The King's attention had been drawn to him by the published accounts of the "Tartar's" voyage, and he and his son had been granted an audience soon afterwards at Windsor. He now found another opportunity of access to His Majesty, and related the treatment he had received at the hands of the Board.

The proposal to send the new timekeepers to Hudson's Bay proved too much for "Farmer George's" patience. He was heard to remark, *sotto voce*, "These people have been cruelly wronged," and then, explosively, "By God, Harrison, I'll see you righted." And he kept his word.*

From 1767 to 1770 John and William Harrison had been occupied in making a fifth timekeeper,† an improved No. 4. This machine, which is now the property of the Clockmakers Company, is shown in Plates XIII. and XIV. In essentials, it differs very little from its prototype, but the dial and top plate are practically devoid of ornament. There are two glasses over the top of the inner case, an inner one covering the dial, and an outer one over the whole top of the case. In the centre of the inner glass is a brass star which can be rotated to set the hands without uncovering the dial, thus keeping the movement practically dust-tight. There is no cycloid pin, and the position of the compensation curb can be adjusted to bring the watch to mean time.‡

In 1771, Harrison, having finished the adjustment of No. 5, and hearing that the Board intended to send Kendall's duplicate of No. 4 out with Captain Cook (then preparing for his second voyage), appealed to them to send, instead, No. 4 and his new timekeeper, offering to rest his claim to the remainder of the reward upon their performance, or to submit "to any mode of trial, by men not already proved partial, which shall be definite in its nature, conclusive as to the reward in case

---

* This anecdote, and many of the other particulars relating to the struggle between Harrison and the Board, is taken from his grandson's book "Memoirs of a Trait in the character of George III.," published in 1835, which, although verbose and prejudiced, is a valuable store of information. It is based chiefly upon a MS. journal (never published) kept by the two Harrisons. See the note at the end of this chapter.

† The story is told, that while No. 5 was under construction a schoolboy found his way into the work-room, eating an apple whose juice he discharged liberally over the movement, covering the balance with spots of rust. The old man, however, dismissed him with a gentle reprimand.

‡ This was the last timekeeper completed in Harrison's lifetime. Four are said to have been ordered by the King of Sardinia, at £1,000 each, but these were never made. A sixth timekeeper, with considerably simpler mechanism, was, however, constructed by William Harrison after his father's death. This was never tried officially. I have not been able to ascertain whether it still exists.

Plate XIII. HARRISON'S No. 5.

The outer case, which is similar to that of No. 4, has been removed in order to show the arrangement of the pendant.

The small brass star in the centre of the dial can be used to set the hands.

See p. 90. Clockmakers Company Museum.

of success, and, in any degree, near the limitation of the Act of Queen Anne in point of duration and exactness." He was told, in reply, that the Board did not think it fit that No. 4 should be sent out of the Kingdom, and that they saw no reason to depart from the manner of trial which they had already laid down.

He then requested the King to permit him to have No. 5 tried at His Majesty's private observatory at Kew. This request was readily granted, and the trial was facilitated by the hearty co-operation of Dr. Demainbury (the resident astronomer), and of His Majesty himself. It was, however, retarded by two accidents. The going of the timekeeper for the first three days was amazingly erratic, after which a "powerful combination of loadstones" was found to have been accidentally left in a cupboard near it. Then, after three weeks comparisons had been taken, William Harrison injured his arm through a fall, and had to lie up. The trial was restarted on his recovery, and continued for ten weeks,* during which time the machine's *total error* on mean time was only 4½ seconds. King George took the utmost interest in its performance, and attended the daily comparisons.

Harrison communicated the circumstances and result of this trial to the Board in a memorial read at the meeting of November 28th, 1772, which produced a resolution of that body to the effect that they saw no reason to depart from the manner of trial they had proposed, and that no regard would be paid to the result of any trial made in any other manner.

Accordingly, Harrison washed his hands of the Board, and resolved to appeal to the House of Commons. Backed by the King's strong Parliamentary interest, he presented a petition in April, 1772, recounting the circumstances of his claim, and asking for relief. Owing to one or two slight mis-statements, he subsequently obtained leave to withdraw this petition and substitute an amended one, which was strongly supported by Fox, and heralded in the following significant manner:

> "The Lord *North*, by His Majesty's Command, acquainted the House that His Majesty, having been informed of the Contents of the said Petition, recommended it to the Consideration of the House.†" (*Journal of the House of Commons*, 6.5.1772.)

He also circulated a broadside, "The Case of Mr. John Harrison," which stated his claims to the second half of the reward.

This activity scared the Board, who were informed by the Speaker that consideration of the petition had been deferred until they could meet to revise their proceedings with relation to Harrison. They hastily resolved to print all their resolutions respecting him, and also summoned William Harrison, who underwent the following catechism:

> Q. Will you make two other timekeepers, and submit them to be tried

* By the King's express wish, it was extended to this length, instead of stopping at six weeks (the period laid down in the Act of Queen Anne), in order to leave no ground for cavil.

† His Majesty was willing, if necessary, to appear at the Bar of the House under an inferior title, and give his personal testimony in Harrison's favour.

according the mode fixt upon by this Board* of which you have already been informed ?

A. One timekeeper is already made, and my fathėr is not in a condition to make another. I fear he will not live many days.

Q. Are you willing that the Timekeeper should be tried according to the above mode ?

A. No, I am not.

Q. Supposing the Board should appoint two or more persons (to whom you have no objection) to make this trial, will you submit to it ?

A. No, I don't chuse to have anything further to do with it : not being willing to lose more time.

Q. Why do you refuse to submit to the trial ?

A. For the following reasons : viz.—

Loss of time.
Expense attending it.
Uncertainty of reward afterwards, and
I think I can employ my time better.

Q. Have you any other reason ?

A. No.

Seven Admiralty clerks were employed day and night, at two guineas each, copying out the Board's resolutions concerning Harrison, but these never appeared, for while they were in the press a money bill, drawn up in consequence of the petition, received the Royal assent. This granted Harrison a further sum of £8,750, which, with the assistance given him to construct his early timekeepers, made up the second £10,000.†

And so the humble Yorkshire mechanic, who had already shown himself a master horologist, proved also, at the age of eighty, more than a match for the Board, and for those powerful rivals who so pertinaciously advocated the method of lunar distances. He had fought his fight, and could now take his rest. In the three years of life which remained to him he produced no fresh inventions, although he left two unfinished at his death,‡ but he published, in 1775, an extraordinary pamphlet, which, unlike that previously issued in his name, was his own unaided work (Short had died in 1768). It contrasts very forcibly with it by reason of its extraordinarily turgid style, which, with its endless formalities and parentheses, might well be that of a partially intoxicated scrivener. Here is a portion of the opening sentence, which, in the original MSS.§ (the printer punctuated it to the best of his ability) extends over some 25 pages, and then breaks off abruptly, for no apparent reason :—

" As first, or rather as here at the first (viz, as without the taking any Notice of the great or chief Matter, viz, of what pertains to different

* The Board finally decided (11.4.1767) that, when the new machines were finished, they should be subjected to a trial of ten months at Greenwich and two months in the Downs. See p. 368.

† The total sum received by Harrison at various times, under the Act of Queen Anne, was £22,550. He also received assistance from Graham, as narrated, Martin Folkes, the East India Company (£200), and Charles Stanhope (four sums of £20).

‡ One was a regulator, which he expected to be accurate to within $\frac{1}{100}$ of a second per day, and which he had originally intended to present to Greenwich Observatory. The other was a marine timekeeper on a new plan, whose wheels and plates were of various different alloys, such as bell-metal and tutenage, while the arms of the balance were formed of hard wood, to minimise their expansion.

§ See Plate XV.

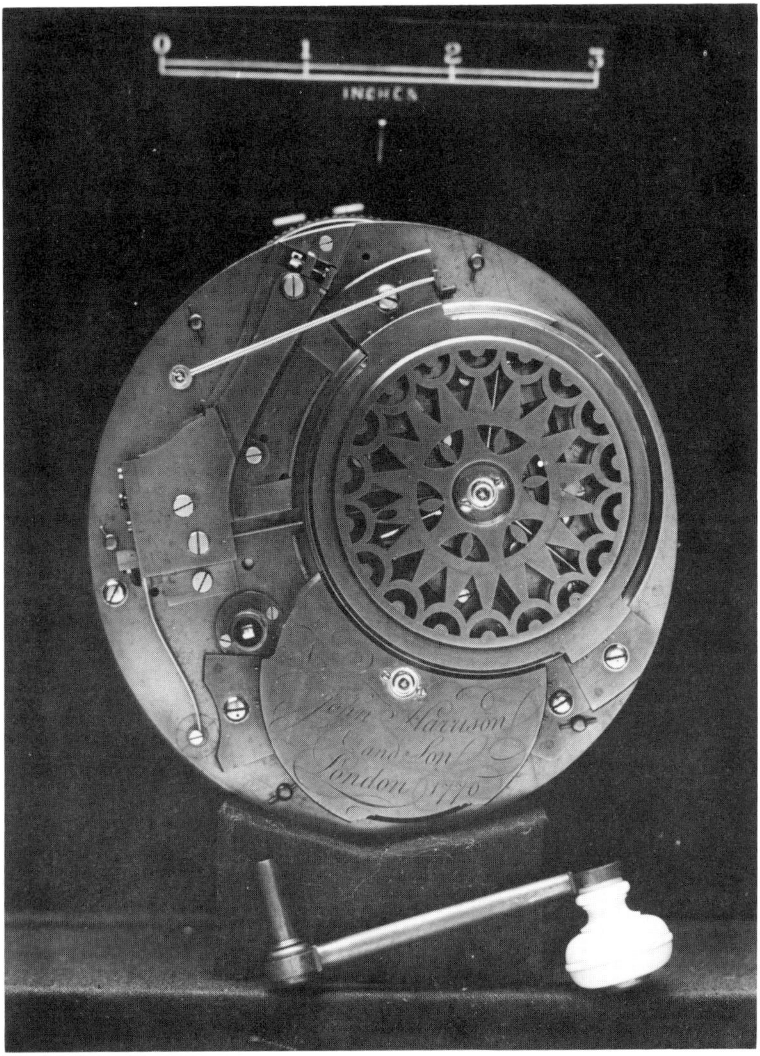

Plate XIV. TOP-PLATE OF HARRISON'S No. 5.
The capstan-headed screw above the automatic brake can be used to bring the machine to time by altering the position of the plate carrying the compensation curb.
Notice the winding key in the foreground.
See p. 90. Clockmakers Company Museum.

Vibrations, or rather, as more properly speaking, of what advantage pertains to, or accrues from the largeness of a Vibration), the bare length of a Pendulum can be no otherwise rightly considered or esteemed but only as to what it bears, or may (as according to the common application) bear in proportion to the length of the Pallats, and as together with such improper Powers of Circumstances thereunto belonging, or may, as farther thereunto belong; *i.e.*, in other words, (and as still in the first place) to the equivalent distance from its Centre of Motion, to where the Pallats, according to their Construction, and as may or will continually happen with their different states of the Oil, as in the common way touch or are applyed to the wheel; nay, sometimes, some men, as being quite ignorant in what I am here about to show or speak of, and as when they are about to do something very extraordinary as they imagine, do render the matter as still worse than so, yea even by far . . . "

Contrast this gibberish with the masterly explanation of longitude given in Short's pamphlet of 1765:—

" The Longitude of any Place is its Distance East or West from any other given Place; and what we want is a Method of finding out at Sea, how far we are got to the Eastward or Westward of the place we sailed from. The Application of a Time-Keeper to this Discovery is founded upon the following Principles: The Earth's Surface is divided into 360 equal Parts . . . which are called Degrees of Longitude; and its daily Revolution round its own Axis is performed in 24 Hours; consequently in that Period, each of those imaginary Lines or Degrees, becomes successively opposite to the Sun . . . ; and it must follow, that from the Time any one of those Lines passes the Sun, till the next passes, must be just four Minutes . . . ; so that for every Degree of Longitude we sail Westward, it will be Noon with us four Minutes the later, and for every Degree Eastward four Minutes the sooner . . . Now, the exact time of the Day at the Place where we are, can be ascertained by well Known and easy Observations of the Sun if visible for a few Minutes at any Time from his being ten Degrees high till within an Hour of Noon, or from an Hour after Noon till he is only 10 Degrees high in the Afternoon; if therefore, at any Time when such Observation is made, a Time-Keeper tells us at the same Moment what o'Clock it is at the Place we sailed from, our Longitude is clearly discovered. To do this, it is not necessary that a Watch should perform its Revolutions precisely in that Space of time which the Earth takes to perform hers: it is only required that it should invariably perform it in *some known Time*, and then the constant Difference between the Length of the one Revolution and the other, will appear as so much daily gained or lost by the Watch, which constant Gain or Loss, is called *the Rate of its going*, and which being added to or deducted from the Time shown by the Watch, will give the true Time, and consequently the Difference of Longitude."

It would not be easy to give a simpler or better explanation of the use of a chronometer, and the application of a " rate."

Still, with all its faults of style, Harrison's last pamphlet has some redeeming features, and anyone who survives its perusal will have obtained a considerable amount of information concerning its author's mechanical ideas, and, incidentally, his prejudices against all " professors," " Parsons," " Priests," and " men of theory." Such a passage as the following:—

" . . if it so please Almighty God, to continue my life and health a little longer, they the Professors (or Priests) shall not hinder me of my pleasure, as from my last drawing, viz. of bringing my watch to a second in a fortnight, I say I am resolved of this, though quite unsuitable to the usage I have had, or was ever to expect from them; and when as

> Dr. Bradley* once said to me (not but what I understood the same without his saying it) viz. that if timekeeping could be to 10 seconds in a week, it would, as with respect to the longitude, be much preferable to any other way or method. And so, as I do not now mind the money (as not having occasion so to do, and withal as being weary of that) the Devil may take the Priests . . ."

is certainly not destitute either of meaning or of vigour.

But the most interesting and important passage is the following :—

> " . . . and I can now boldly say, that if the Provision for Heat and Cold could properly be in the Ballance itself†, as it is in my Pendulum, the Watch (or my Longitude Time-Keeper) would then perform to a few seconds in a Year ; . . ." (See Plate XV.)

The book also contains an account of Harrison's musical theories. In his early life he led the village choir at Barrow, and made many experiments with a monochord of his own invention. He also tuned the bells of Hull Parish Church, which badly needed it. His experience led him to propose, in this book, a revolutionary method of tuning, in which the tone and the major third should be to the octave as $\frac{1}{\pi}$ and $\frac{1}{2\pi}$ are to 1.‡

In 1770 Harrison's health had begun to decline, and he was attacked, for the first time in his life, by gout. He only survived the publication of this pamphlet a few months—long enough to hear of the wonderful performances of Kendall's copy of No. 4 in the South Seas, although too early to read Cook's glowing tribute to it in the pages of his journal: " I must here take note that our longitudes can never be erroneous while we have so good a guide as Mr. Kendall's watch."§

" Longitude Harrison," as he was often called, died at his house in Red Lion Square on March 24th, 1776, in the eighty-third year of his age. His second wife, Elizabeth, survived him only a year, dying on March 5th, 1777, aet. 72. William Harrison died in 1815.

All three are buried in the cemetery of St. John's Church, Hampstead. The tomb is within a few feet of the South porch, and a long and garrulous epitaph||, in the bad taste of the period, records

* Bradley, in 1761, told him, in a moment of confidence, that " if it had not been for his plaguey watch, he and Meyer " (author of the first reliable lunar tables, for which his widow received £3,000 from the Board) " would have shared £10,000 between them."

† According to Mudge, Harrison tried, unsuccessfully, to accomplish this.

‡ He left, in MSS., a work entitled " A True and Full Account of the Foundation of Musick." Also another entitled " A Description of two Pallets, to be introduced into the middle of a great Log," dealing with a proposed improvement in the ordinary hand-log used for measuring a ship's speed.

§ This is quoted from the published (and edited) journal. Cook actually wrote " . . . indeed our error (in Longitude) can never be great, so long as we have . . ."

|| In 1879 this epitaph, being then almost illegible, was recut by the Clockmakers' Company as a tribute of respect to Harrison's memory (he was not a member of the Company). William Harrison's epitaph was found to have perished completely.
A ceremonial visit was paid to the grave in July, 1885, by a number of Positivists, in whose " Calendar of Great Men " Harrison is enrolled in company with Graham and Le Roy.

Composed in B.

periment; neither any notice of the most chief, viz. of the Difference there will be (in that Case) betwixt when the Pallats and Wheel are clean and new oil'd, to what there will be when foul.

To Page 112 at the bottom.

Proceedings: For, towards a Proof of which, let it be remembred, that I have said in this Book, that if it please God to continue my Life and Health a little longer, that then, from my last Improvement, I would bring my Watch or Time-Keeper so as to perform to a second in a Fortnight; and now, since the drawing up of that part of the Book, I have indeed put the Major part, but still, not the most nice Part thereof, viz. of my last Improvement in execution, not venturing, upon serious thought, to attempt the whole, lest I should not live to see it perfected, and I now find the Watch to perform as above express'db! but still no astonishing Matter, save only to them [or such Philosophers] who cannot be able to weigh its Construction, or the main Points of its Contrivancea: But indeed, had I continued under the Hands of the rude Commissioners, this Completion, or great Accomplishment, neither would nor could ever have been obtain'd; but however, Providence otherwise order'd the Matter, and I can now boldly say, that if the Provision for Heat and Cold could properly be in the Ballance it self, as it is in my Pendulum, the Watch [or my Longitude Time-

b nay even to nearer than so!

a and as wherein, hardly to be influenced whether any Oil or not:

122

Time-Keeper] would then perform to a few seconds in a Year; take farther to this on the following Page at a.

Plate XV. HANDWRITING OF JOHN HARRISON.

From the original MS. of his " Description of such Mechanism . . . . . "

The famous passage relating to the advantage of a compensation balance occurs towards the bottom.

See p. 96.

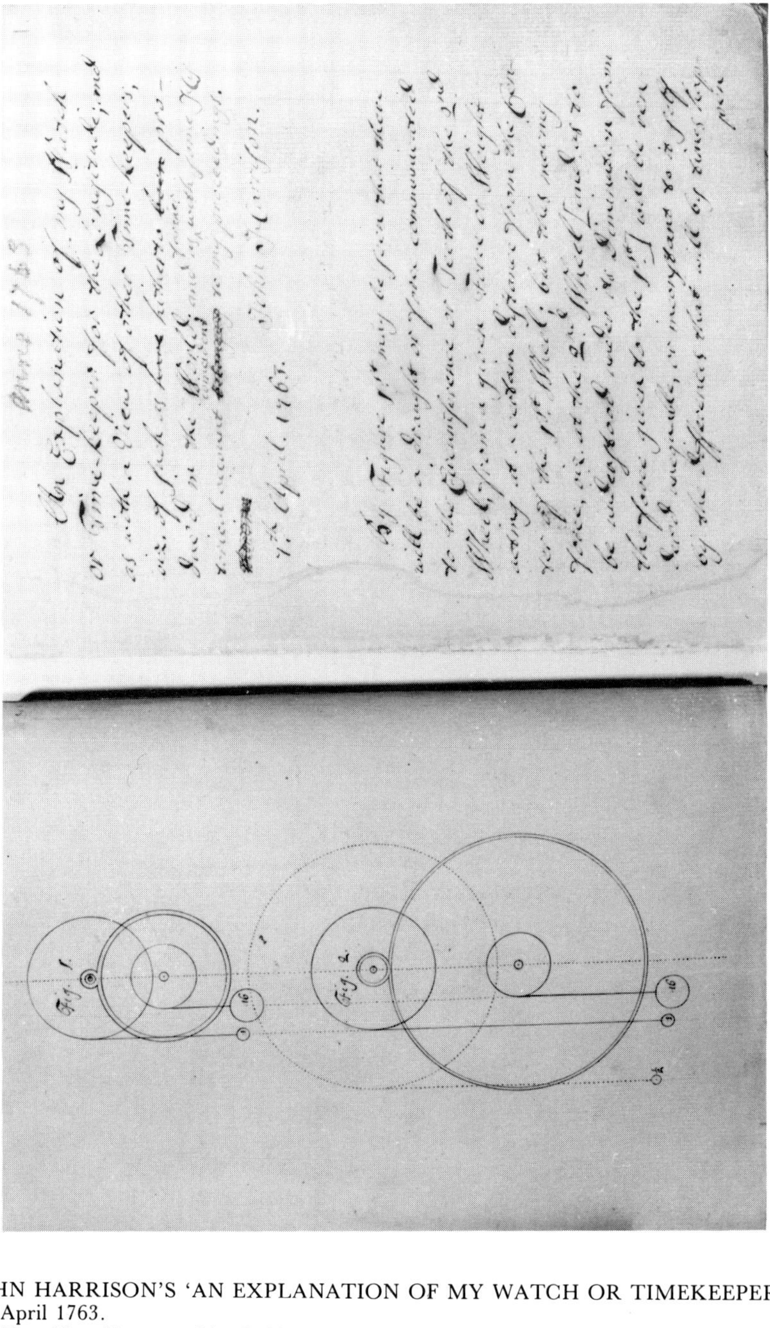

JOHN HARRISON'S 'AN EXPLANATION OF MY WATCH OR TIMEKEEPER'.
7th April 1763.
(Godfrey New Photographics Ltd.)
Courtesy of The Worshipful Co. of Clockmakers.

Harrison's achievements in horology. But his truest memorial is to be found in the hearts of those who know and appreciate at its full value the pioneer work of the man who lies there—

" . . . still loftier than the world suspects
Living and dying."

NOTE. Two very important manuscripts relating to John Harrison were sold recently by Messrs. Sotheran, one being a portfolio containing some 200 *sheets of biographical information, the other the original MSS.* (1,376 *pages*) *of his grandson's book "Memoirs of a Trait in the Character of George III."* (*published under the name of* JOHANN HORRINS (*anagram*).) *Only a small portion of the MSS. was published.*

Although Messrs. Sotheran have given me every assistance, I have not been able to trace the purchaser of these MSS. or to ascertain their present whereabouts. If this book should fall into the hands of anyone possessing such information, I should be much obliged if he would write to me, c/o my publisher, as I am very anxious to obtain their owner's permission to examine them. Should he be intending to write a biography of Harrison, I shall be glad to share with him any information I possess.

CHAPTER V.

KENDALL & MUDGE.

The two men whose names head this chapter were, in a sense, disciples of Harrison, and endeavoured to develop the chronometer along the lines which he had laid down, Kendall striving to eliminate some portions of his mechanism, and Mudge to obtain better timekeeping by additional complication and refinement of detail. There can be no question that the latter's work showed the greater mechanical ingenuity and all-round ability, but it is equally undeniable that the principle on which Kendall proceeded was the sounder of the two. The work of both men has a pathetic interest, since it was of no permanent value, and became obsolete almost as soon as it was produced.

KENDALL.

Larcum Kendall was born of Quaker stock* at Charlbury, Oxford, in 1721, and was apprenticed in 1735 to John Jeffreys, of Holborn (who, as we have seen, made a pocket watch for Harrison in 1753, embodying much of the mechanism of No. 4). When out of his time, he set up in business for himself, and by 1765 had obtained sufficient standing in his profession to be chosen one of the committee appointed to receive Harrison's explanation of the mechanism of his timekeeper. He subsequently contracted with the Board of Longitude to make a duplicate of No. 4 for the sum of £450, half down and the remainder on completion.† He stipulated, however, that he should only be required to execute an exact part-for-part copy, and should not be held responsible for its performance, since he considered that Harrison's method of adjusting the compensation was precarious.

He received personal instruction from Harrison, and No. 4 was placed in his hands in May, 1767, at the conclusion of its trial at Greenwich. Thus equipped, he set about his task, and completed it two years later. The duplicate, which it will be convenient to call K1, was exhibited to the Board in May, 1769, and, after further adjustment, Kendall finally delivered it to them in January, 1770.

* The certificate of the marriage of his father, Moses Kendall, to Ann Larcum (18th June, 1718) is preserved, amongst a number of similar Quaker documents, in the MSS. Room of the British Museum. Moses Kendall was a linendraper, of St. Clement Danes, Westminster.

† The contract, signed by Lord Howe, The Earl of Morton, and Maskelyne, *inter alia*, is preserved in the British Museum. Kendall had originally asked a considerably larger sum as the price of duplicating No. 4, but the Board, considering his proposal, and a similar one made by William Matthews, exorbitant, declined to consider either. On the completion of K1, however, Kendall received, in addition to the stipulated £450, a bonus of £50, in recognition of his having taken the two machines to pieces to facilitate their comparison.

Plate XVI. THE "BOUNTY'S" TIMEKEEPER (K2).
The inscription on the dial is "Larcum Kendall, London."
See p. 104. R.U.S. Institution.

LAREUM KENDALL POCKET WATCH, 1986.
Silver pair cases. Pivoted detent escapement. Clockmakers' Co's. Museum, Guildhall (Catalogue No. 422).

It is now at Greenwich, and forms a fine testimony to its maker's ability and thoroughness. The workmanship throughout is first-class, and William Harrison freely admitted that it surpassed that of its prototype. In appearance and mechanism K1 is a close copy of No. 4, the only noticeable differences being that the indicator plate of the regulator is omitted as useless,* and that the cocks are chased and pierced in a somewhat more elaborate manner. On the top-plate is engraved "Larcum Kendall, London, 1769."

K1 underwent a satisfactory trial at Greenwich, and was then sent to sea with Captain Cook in H.M.S. "Resolution." This was the second of Cook's three famous voyages—the one in which he circumnavigated the South polar regions and crossed the Antarctic Circle for the first time in history—and, with its alternations of dead calm and furious gales, tropical heat and extreme cold, it constituted as severe a test of the timekeeper as could well be imagined. Yet so well did K1 perform, and so accurate was its going throughout the three years' voyage, that Cook, the most exact and least enthusiastic of men, had nothing but praise for it,† and made a special point of taking it with him again, on loan from the Board, in his last voyage in 1776. Its only fault, if fault it can be called, was that its rate accelerated, slightly but steadily, throughout the whole of the voyage.

During Cook's third voyage it performed equally well until stopped by dirt lodging in the teeth of the seconds wheel, a defect temporarily remedied by Benjamin Lyon, one of the crew, who had formerly been apprenticed to a watchmaker.‡ It was also used by Vancouver, in his famous survey of the N.W. coast of North America.

---

* It will be remembered that Harrison abandoned the use of a regulator in No. 4, but left its indicator in place. There are one or two minor points of difference in Kendall's copy: *e.g.*, the dial plate is held on by two small screws, and the nib that holds the movement in the case is fitted under the dial, and not let into it. There is also no disc over the winding hole.

† In addition to the passage already quoted on p. 69, here is an extract from his MS. journal:

> "Cape of Good Hope, Oct., 1772.
>
> " . . . Mr. Kendall's watch had answered beyond all expectations, by pointing out the Longitude of this place to one minute of time to what it was observed by Messrs. Mason and Dixon in 1761."

"Elsewhere he speaks of 'Our trusty guide, the Watch,' and 'our never failing guide, the Watch,' and the concluding passage of the journal (the Admiralty copy stops at the Cape) runs as follows: "On our making the land of the Cape, the error of Mr. Kendall's watch was no more than 18′ of longitude . . . It would not be doing justice to Mr. Harrison and Mr. Kendall if I did not own that we have received very great assistance from this useful and valuable time piece as will more fully appear in the course of this journal."

‡ It stopped again a few days later, with a broken balance spring, and was not tampered with further. Its case is a good fit, and it is difficult to understand how the movement can have got so dirty, even assuming it to have been frequently opened up for inspection. Lyon subsequently made a new balance spring, but without much success. Still, his attempt, considering his almost entire lack of tools and materials, was perfectly heroic, and deserved a better fate. It is reminiscent of the feat of a Chinese workman in comparatively recent times, who, confronted with a chronometer whose balance spring had snapped in half, succeeded in soldering the broken portions together. The repaired spring is now exhibited in the Museum of the Clockmakers' Company.

After completing K1, Kendall was asked by the Board to train other workmen to make copies of it: but this he declined to undertake, alleging that unless Harrison's mechanism could be simplified many years must elapse before such machines could be made for even £200 each. The Board thereupon requested him to make a new timekeeper, omitting whatever portions of Harrison's mechanism he considered non-essential.

Accordingly, he made one of his own design, K2, completed in 1772, and subsequently a second, K3, completed in 1774. He received £200 for the former, and £100 for the latter.

K2, which appears in Plate XV, is practically a large watch of ordinary pattern, having a simple verge escapement with ruby pallets, and no remontoire. Harrison's maintaining power is fitted, and a compensation curb. This is an improvement upon Harrison's, although the same in principle, for the brass-and-steel strip is formed into a spiral, and moves a pivoted lever, carrying the curb pins, which is counterbalanced so that its position (and hence the rate of the machine's going) is unaffected by its weight.*

K3 is practically identical with K2, except in the escapement, which has two coaxial crown-wheels, whose teeth engage with a single ruby pallet placed between them.† It has three small dials showing hours, minutes and seconds.

A remarkable point about both of these machines is that Kendall, while very ill-advisedly eliminating Harrison's remontoire, yet retained the frictional brake he had provided for preventing his timekeeper from running down with the remontoire left unwound. Apparently Kendall considered that it was worth retaining so as to prevent possible injury to the pallets through the balance being allowed to swing idly after the machine had run down.

Neither K2 nor K3 equalled or approached the performances of K1. K2, however, had a most romantic history.

After trial at Greenwich, it was lent by the Board to Capt. Phipps for his North Polar expedition, and was afterwards used for several years on the North American station. In 1787 it was lent by the Board to Capt. Bligh, of the ill-fated "Bounty," and was carried off in that ship by the mutineers. It remained at Pitcairn Island until 1808, when it was bought by the captain of an American whaler. Stolen from the latter soon afterwards, it next made its appearance at Concepcion, in Chile, where it was bought for three doubloons by an old Spanish muleteer named Castillo. On his death, in 1840, it

* Harrison's curb was, of course, liable to bend slightly through its own weight, and hence to make the timekeeper go slightly faster with III up, and slower with IX up. Harrison's prejudice against gimbals must have been extremely strong to make him reject that simple means of nullifying this defect. K1 and K2 were never mounted in gimbals, being stowed in boxes between two cushions which completely filled the box. K3, which was originally designed for the same treatment, was given gimbals in 1802, after its maker's death, previous to being lent to Crosley, Flinders' astronomer. The gimbals were not made an integral part of the machine, but attached to a separate (wooden) outer case.

† A drawing of this escapement appears in Reid's "Treatise on Clock and Watch Making," 1826

THE BACK-PLATE OF LARUM KENDALL'S 'K3', LONDON, 1774.
Exhibited Courtesy of M.O.D. Hydrographic Dept., at the N.M.M.

Plate XVII. THOMAS MUDGE.

From the engraving by Schiavonetti (after the portrait by Dance) prefixed to " A Description . . . of the Time-keeper invented by the late Mr. Thomas Mudge."

The portrait is in the possession of the Clockmakers Company.

See p. 107.

was sold by Alex. Caldcleugh, of Valparaiso, for fifty guineas, to Capt. Thomas Herbert, R.N., who had it repaired there*, and brought it home in 1843. Strange to say, after nearly sixty years of neglect, it showed no signs of wear, except a deep notch worn in the lower pallet: and, after cleaning, it still kept a fairly close rate. It is now preserved in the museum of the Royal United Service Institution.

K3 was used on board H.M.S. " Discovery " in Cook's third voyage, and subsequently by both Vancouver and Flinders. It is now at Greenwich, minus its outer case and gimbals.

Whether Kendall was discouraged by his inability to rival Harrison, or by the fact that the Board's prices for his timekeepers appeared to be decreasing in geometrical retrogression, I cannot say, but he made no more of them, if we except a beautiful little pocket-chronometer, with his spiral curb and a pivoted-detent escapement, which was found in his workshop after his death, and presented by B. L. Vulliamy† to the Clockmakers Company. He died in 1795.

MUDGE.

(*Plate XVI*).

Thomas Mudge, born at Exeter in 1715, was the second son of Zachariah Mudge, a clergyman of that place, who removed soon afterwards to Bideford, and opened a school there. Young Mudge showed a natural bent for clockmaking, and was apprenticed to Graham, subsequently becoming one of his master's most trusted assistants. On Graham's death, in 1751 Mudge, who had taken one of his fellow apprentices, William Dutton, into partnership in the preceding year,‡ succeeded to his business.

Even as a workman he had established a considerable reputation as a sound horologist and a painstaking and fair-dealing tradesman. He made for the King of Spain a most elaborate clock-watch and minute repeater, which was mounted in the head of a walking cane, and showed both mean and apparent time, striking the hours and quarters according to the latter. He was honoured with a standing commission from his royal patron to construct and supply, *carte blanche*, any examples of his art that he chose, and, to Mudge's credit be it said, he consistently declined to ask an excessive price for such pieces of work, or to make more than a normal profit upon them.

About 1754 he invented an escapement which constituted the greatest single improvement, except the balance spring, ever applied to pocket watches, and which, in course of time, beat all its rivals—the

* By a watchmaker named Mouat.

† Master of the Clockmakers Company, and for many years the acknowledged head of his profession. He competed unsuccessfully for the making of the Westminster clock (" Big Ben "), and subsequently made a number of bitter and unfair attacks upon E. J. Dent, who secured the contract, and E. B. Denison (afterwards Lord Grimthorpe), who designed the clock.

‡ Dr. Johnson bought his first watch from them in 1768.

verge, cylinder, duplex and chronometer escapements—completely out of that field. This was the lever escapement*, now used in every pocket timekeeper from the Ingersoll and Roskopf up to the finest productions of Ditisheim or Kullberg. But it is curious to note that for many years after its inventor's death it was almost totally neglected, and had to make its way entirely by its own merits, since Mudge took practically no steps to claim its invention† or to make it widely known. He merely fitted it in two or three watches and small clocks for wealthy patrons, and made a large model of it which was shown to some others of his trade, such as Margetts and Emery, who used it in a certain number of their best watches. It must be confessed, however, that in his hands and theirs it was almost as delicate and expensive to construct as the present-day chronometer escapement—a very different thing from the brass stampings, costing a fraction of a penny, which constitute the quite satisfactory lever escapement of the modern cheap alarm-clock.

In 1765, as previously mentioned, he was chosen a member of the Committee appointed by the Board of Longitude to report upon the mechanism of Harrison's timekeeper‡, and in order to forestall any charge of plagiarism he deposited with the Royal Society, and afterwards published, a short tract containing suggestions for the improvement of marine timekeepers§. This contains the germ of his constant-force escapement||, but is not otherwise remarkable, except that it shows that some details of Harrison's mechanism must have leaked out, since he mentions that the latter used the different expansions of two metals to compensate for the effects of heat and cold on the balance spring.

His examination of No. 4 was the turning point of his life, and from that time onwards his attention was fixed upon the improvement of marine timekeepers. Two cogent reasons urged him to this. He was stimulated both by the belief—in which he was fully justified—that he could make a better timekeeper than Harrison's, and by the hope of gaining some such large reward as that inventor had obtained. Indeed, he seems to have persuaded himself that so long as the Act of Queen Anne remained unrepealed, the minor rewards—£10,000 and

* This escapement is described and illustrated in Chapter IX.

† In a letter to Count Bruhl about this escapement, he says . " . . . as to the honour of the invention, I must confess, I am not at all solicitous about it: whoever would rob me of it does me honour."

‡ He subsequently got into hot water with the Board, who happened to find out that he had given a good deal of information about No. 4 to Ferdinand Berthoud, who had come over from Paris to be present, if possible, at its dissection. On being taxed with this by the Board, he promptly admitted it, and added that he thought it was his duty, and the Board's intention, that he should do so. Apparently the Board's resolution—that no particulars relating to No. 4 should be published by any member of the Committee without their previous sanction—had never been communicated either to Mudge, or to Ludlam, who published some notes on the mechanism of No. 4 almost immediately.

§ "Thoughts on the Means of improving Watches, and more particularly those for the use of the Sea." London, 1765.

|| About the same time Mudge tried to embody this escapement in a pocket watch, but found it could not be successfully carried out on such a small scale.

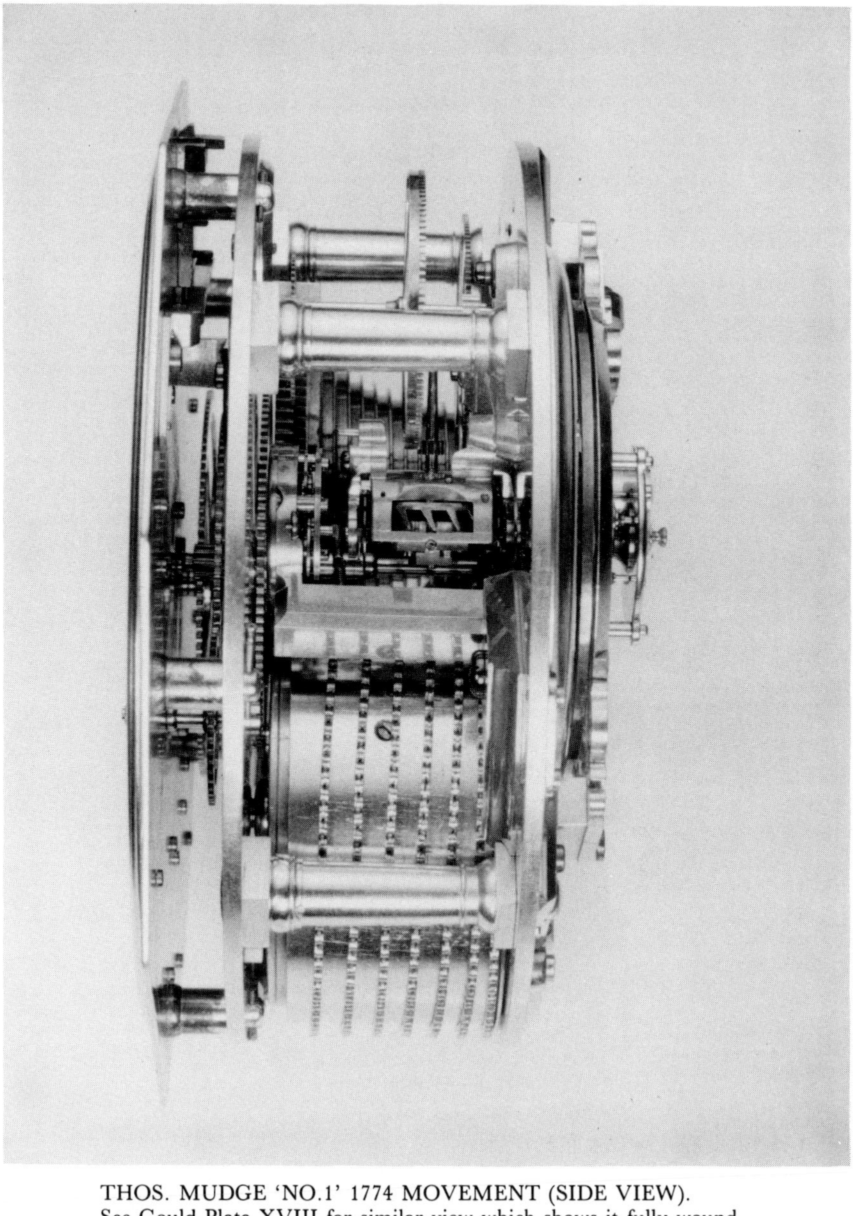

THOS. MUDGE 'NO.1' 1774 MOVEMENT (SIDE VIEW).
See Gould Plate XVIII for similar view which shows it fully wound.
Courtesy of the British Museum.

THOMAS MUDGE MARINE TIMEKEEPER NO. 1.
Courtesy of the British Museum.

THOMAS MUDGE BRACKET CLOCK WITH LEVER ESCAPEMENT.
Compare with Harrisons H-3 movement.
Courtesy B.M.

£15,000—which it offered were still open to competition, and might be won by any timekeeper which should, like No. 4, comply with its requirements.*

Accordingly, in 1771, he gave up the conduct of his business entirely to his partner, and removed to Plymouth, in order to have leisure for his experiments and also to be near his only brother,† who was in delicate health. His first timekeeper was completed in 1774, and in the same year he was disagreeably surprised by the passing, at the instance of the Board of Longitude, of an Act‡ which repealed the Act of Queen Anne, and, although it offered a further £10,000 for competition, did so under conditions which, for a timekeeper, were four times as onerous as those enacted previously.

The portion of this Act relating to timekeepers directed that payment of the reward should be made:

> "When and so soon as two or more Time-keepers of the same construction shall have been tried at the same time, for the space of twelve months, at the Royal Observatory at Greenwich; then in two voyages round the island of Great Britain in contrary directions, and in such other voyages to different climates as the said Commissioners shall think fit to direct and appoint; and after their return from such voyages, or any of them, for such longer time at the said Observatory, not exceeding twelve months, as the said Commissioners shall judge necessary; and also when and so soon as the said Commissioners, or two-thirds of them at the least, shall after such experiments and voyages have been made and performed as aforesaid, have declared and determined that such method is generally practicable and useful, and sufficiently exact to determine the Longitude at Sea, within the degrees or limits aforesaid§ in all voyages for the space of six months (impediments from cloudy and hazy weather excepted) and also when and so soon as the principles and practice of such method are fully discovered and explained to the satisfaction of the said Commissioners, or two-thirds of them at least; and such author or authors, discoverer or discoverers, shall have delivered up and assigned over to the said Commissioners, for the use of the Public, the absolute property of such Time-keepers as shall have been tried by such experiments and voyages as aforesaid; together with all places, descriptions, theories, and explanations belonging or relating to the same, and which shall contain the whole of such Discovery of the Longitude."

It will be conceded that the terms of this Act were not unduly favourable to the success of a timekeeper||, and that any inventor who might entertain the idea of complying with its provisions had little

* He was supported in this opinion by his elder son, Thomas Mudge, Jun., who was a lawyer, and should have known better.

† Dr. John Mudge, a well-known physician, and renowned as an amateur maker of reflecting telescopes.

‡ 14 George III., cap. 66.

§ To obtain the £10,000, the total error of the machines in four months was not to exceed half a degree: to obtain £7,500, 40′: and to obtain £5,000, half a degree.

|| The opinion expressed on this point by the author of an anonymous attack on Arnold, referred to on p. 180, is worth quoting: "It seems, at the time of enacting this Act, they (the Board) were so sensible of having been fairly bilked out of the first reward, that they were determined to reserve a power to themselves of bilking every future competitor for the second."

more than an outside chance of success.* Indeed, it was currently reported that Maskelyne, who had a considerable share in drafting it, remarked, privately, that he "had given the Mechanics a bone that would crack their teeth." Still, it is amusing to note that the Board of Longitude already possessed, in K1, a mechanism quite capable of complying with its requirements.

Mudge's first timekeeper is shown in Plate XVII.

It may be described as an over-developed No. 4. Harrison's watch went for a day, Mudge's for eight days: No. 4 had a single balance spring and compensation curb, Mudge fitted two of each: Harrison's remontoire was wound eight times a minute, Mudge's machine had two remontoires, each wound 150 times a minute: lastly, Harrison's workmanship was good, but Mudge's was exquisite.

It cannot be denied that Mudge was very greatly impressed by Harrison's work, and that he made full use of the opportunity afforded him in 1765 to make himself fully acquainted with it. Besides the resemblances, or rather exaggerations, already cited, both machines have the same type of resting barrel and maintaining gear†. In fact, the only strikingly original part of Mudge's design was the escapement, which is, theoretically, a very perfect one, but far too complicated for general use.‡

It is shown in fig. 19. Its basis is the ordinary verge escapement, but the crown wheel, instead of impelling the balance directly, winds a pair of small spiral springs to a given tension, and these latter in turn keep the balance in motion. *A* is the balance, and *B* its staff, cranked to clear the escapement, and counterpoised by the weight *W*. The cranked portion carries two pins p,p', which stand in the path of the two radial arms r,r' projecting horizontally from the two staffs S,S', which are pivoted, independently, in the axial line of the balance, and to which the inner ends of the remontoire springs are attached by collets, their outer ends terminating in fixed studs. The staffs S,S', also carry the two pallets P,P', terminating in small hooks, or nibs. The acting surfaces of these pallets were made of flint in the first machine, but rubies were subsequently employed. *C* is the crown wheel.

The action of the escapement is as follows. As drawn, a tooth of the crown wheel, acting on the pallet *P*, has wound the upper remontoire spring through an arc of 27° from its normal position§ (in which it rests against a stop, not shown) and is now locked on the nib. The balance must be imagined to be swinging in the direction shown by the arrow, and when it has swung 27° beyond the dead point the pin *p* meets the arm *r*, and carries it along, winding the remontoire spring further, and unlocking the tooth previously locked on the nib.

* This second reward was never won. The Act was repealed in 1828.

† Both, also, have left-handed crown wheels.

‡ Mudge also designed a very simple gravity escapement for clocks, in which the same basic idea—the nibbed pallets—again appears. Although decried by Grimthorpe, this plan has recently been revived in two very accurate patterns of astronomical clock—the Riefler and the Strasser.

§ The remontoire springs were given an initial tension, which could be adjusted as required.

See p. 113.

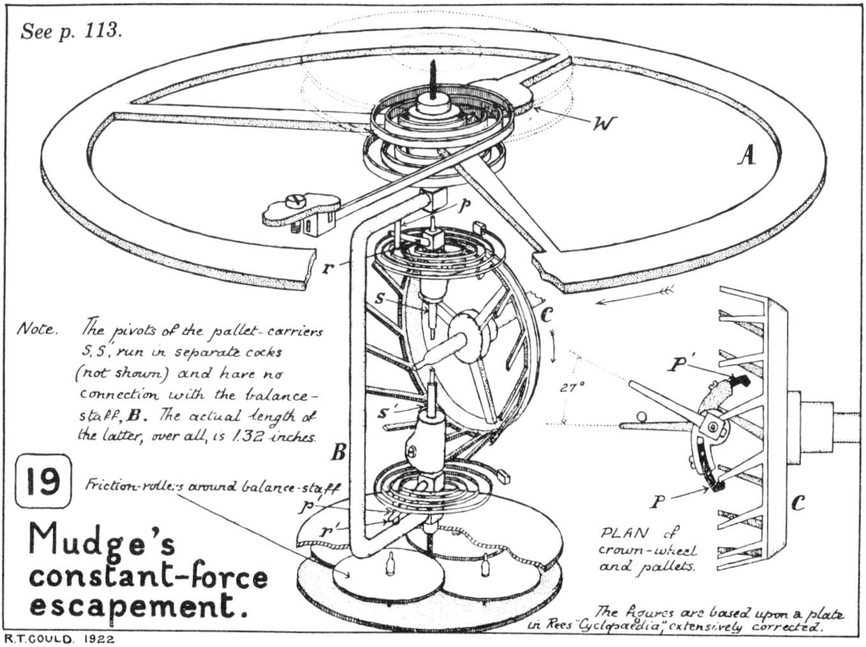

19

Mudge's constant-force escapement.

R.T. GOULD. 1922

See p. 116.

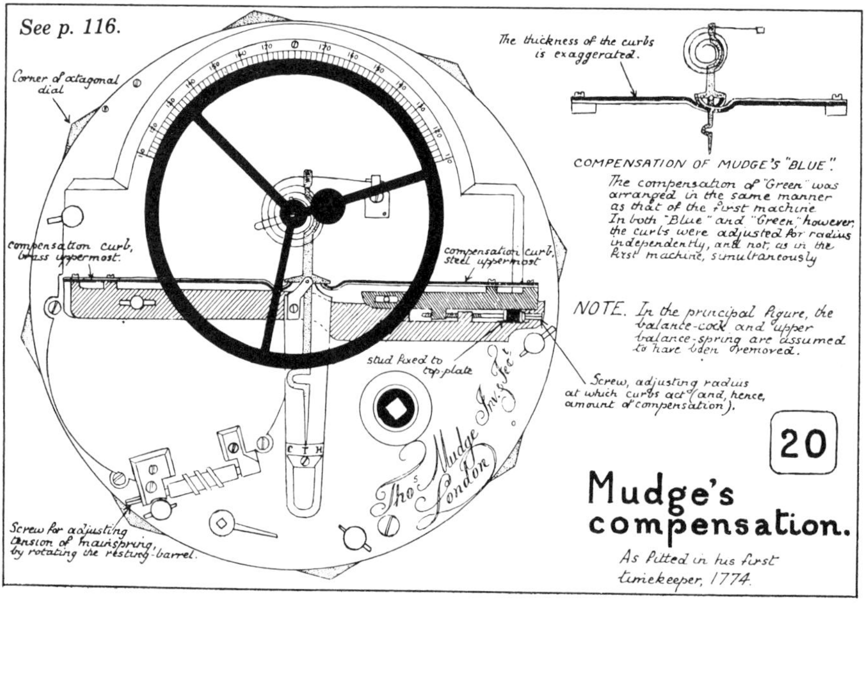

20

Mudge's compensation.

As fitted in his first timekeeper, 1774.

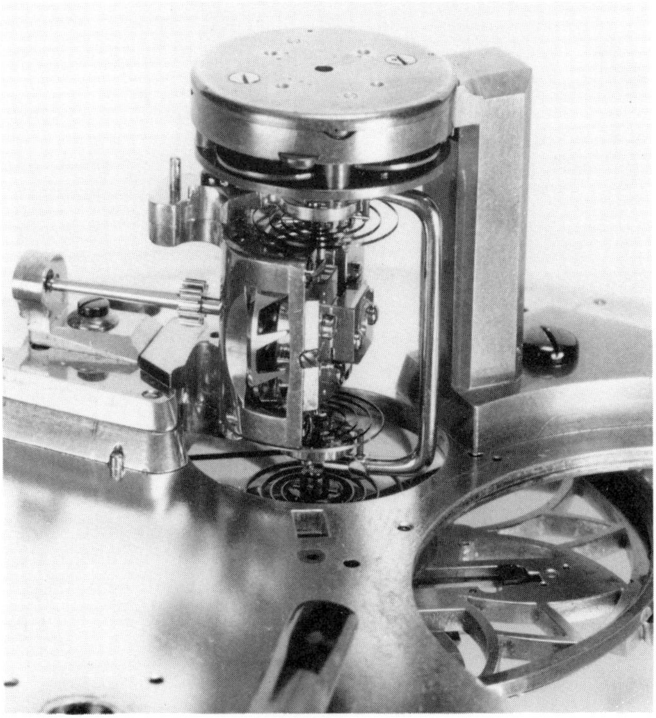

MUDGE 'NO.1' — 1774
Detail of the constant-force escapement. See figure 19, pp.113-120. Courtesy of the British Museum.

THOS. MUDGE 'NO.1' 1774 MOVEMENT. Courtesy of the British Museum.

The crown wheel, now being freed, rotates under the influence of the mainspring, transmitted through the train, and the tooth t', acting on the pallet P', winds the lower remontoire spring through 27° and locks on the nib. The balance, on its return, picks up the arm r' after swinging 27° beyond the dead point, and again unlocks the crown wheel, which rewinds the upper remontoire—and so on.

It will be seen from the foregoing that the balance is completely detached from the train, and that the impulse is given by the remontoire springs, which act with it for a slightly longer arc than they do against it.

This escapement differs from all others in giving impulse without any jerk, and Atwood, in the course of a mathematical investigation* of its properties, has shown that the remontoire springs can be so adjusted as to compensate for any want of isochronism in the balance springs themselves. But its construction and adjustment demand a very high degree of skill, and involve an expense entirely disproportionate to the advantage obtainable from its use.

Mudge's compensation, shown in fig. 20, was effected by two compensation curbs, acting on the ends of a T-shaped arm carrying the curb pins†. It will be noticed that two balance springs appear in fig. 19. The curb pins of the compensation acted on the lower one only, while a second set embraced the upper spring, and could be adjusted by hand to bring the machine to time.

A remarkable feature of the machine, which illustrates both Mudge's appreciation of correct principles and his innate conservatism, is the use of a "reversed" fusee‡: one, that is to say, in which the usual direction of its rotation is reversed, and the pull of the fusee chain is divided between the arbors of the centre wheel and the fusee arbors, greatly reducing the side friction of the latter in its pivots. Instead of planting his fusee on the opposite side of the barrel, however, Mudge retained it in its usual position, and accordingly, in order to get the seconds hand to rotate clockwise, he had to have recourse to the clumsy expedient of an additional idle wheel in the train. The motion of the hour and minute hands was similarly reversed by planting the cannon pinion out of the centre of the movement.

The detailed refinement of the machine is almost incredible—for instance, the upper and lower ends of the balance staff run between

* Published in the "Philosophical Transactions" for 1794. George Atwood was the inventor of the well-known "Atwood's machine" for determining the acceleration of falling bodies.

† Mudge fitted this compensation to his first lever watch—that made for Queen Charlotte in 1757. It was therefore not derived from Harrison's No. 4, but may have been suggested by No. 3.

‡ Britten, in his "Watch and Clockmaker's Handbook, . . .," is opposed to the use of either the term "reversed fusee" or "left-handed fusee" to describe this arrangement, "as the fusee is neither reversed nor left-handed." As, however, either the planting of the fusee (with respect to the barrel) or the direction of its rotation *must* be reversed, the term "reversed fusee" is quite applicable. The fusee is only "left-handed" in the latter case. See p. 331. The Schoof lever-chronometer at South Kensington is a good specimen of a correctly arranged movement with reversed fusee.

two sets of four tiny friction rollers, and one curb pin of the mean time adjustment is carried on a most complicated pivoted detent, controlled by two springs, so as to ensure that the pins traverse the spring without friction.

And no timekeeper ever made was more beautifully finished. The workmanship is a sheer joy to the eye, and it is enhanced by the mounting of the movement in an octagonal gilt case with glass panels. The spaces between the enamelled dials are filled in with silver filigree work.

Its tests, at first, promised well, and in December, 1774, Mudge, with the Board's permission, deposited it at Greenwich for trial. It was kept in the Great Room, and carried down to the Transit Room, situated on the other side of the courtyard, for daily comparisons. After three months of this treatment it stopped, probably through the fault of the person carrying it*, and after being started again by Dutton, stopped again a month later, with a broken mainspring. Mudge, after lodging a complaint against its treatment, deposited it for a second trial in November, 1776, during which it was kept in the Transit Room.

On March 1st, 1777, Maskelyne reported to the Board :—

> " . . . that the watch made by Mr. Mudge, which has been at the Royal Observatory for trial, . . . had gained in 109 days only 1' 19", and that it is greatly superior, in point of accuracy, to any timekeeper which hath come under his inspection."

Meanwhile, the Board, being informed that Mudge wished to make two others, and to compete for the reward, had advanced him £500 for that purpose. The trial of the first machine was continued, but its going accelerated very considerably,† while in February 1778 it again stopped with a broken mainspring.‡ These stoppages, and its acceleration, whose effect was exaggerated, by Maskelyne's method of calculating the rates, caused it to be regarded, quite unjustly (see Appendix 2) as a comparative failure.

---

* The arc allowed the balance was restricted by " banking pins " to about 160°, to prevent the cranked portion of the balance staff from hitting the crown-wheel cock. The normal arc described by the balance was 120°-130°, so it will be seen that any sudden turn while the machine was being carried would either stop it altogether (by bringing the balance to rest relatively to the arms of the remontoire staffs), or else make the balance hit the banking (which would accelerate its motions considerably).

Maskelyne's assistant, Hellins, strenuously denied that the stoppage could have been caused by any fault of his while carrying the machine. His remarks, in a letter to Francis Maseres, were privately printed and circulated at the time of Mudge's petition to Parliament.

† A *slight* acceleration generally occurs in most new chronometers, although the fact was not known in Mudge's time.

‡ After this Mudge put a stop on the fusee, which prevented the spring from being wound more than enough for two days' going. The machine subsequently performed extremely well in the hands of Count Bruhl, and in two voyages with Admiral Campbell. But Mudge never sent it to Greenwich again. He writes to Bruhl : " . . . I have not any idea of its ever answering to me any pecuniary purpose, there seeming to be a resolution that it never shall. However, as long as I am capable of amusing myself with it, it will serve for a hobby-horse, and when I can no longer do that, I will destroy it." It was bought by Bruhl, and is now on view in the Science Museum, South Kensington, having been lent by its owner, Mr. A. Mallock.

Plate XIX. DIAL OF MUDGE'S "BLUE."

See p. 120. Dresden-Math Phys Saloon.

BACK PLATE OF 'MUDGE'S BLUE'
Dresden — Math. Phys. Saloon.

MUDGE'S BLUE. SIDE VIEW
Dresden — Math. Phys. Saloon.

Meanwhile, Mudge had made the two others, exactly alike,* and similar to the first in their mechanism, except that they only went 36 hours, and had only two dials, one showing seconds, and the other hours and minutes (see Plate XVIII). It is a remarkable fact that although Mudge's eyesight was failing, to such an extent that a considerable portion of the work on them was done by touch only, his workmanship exhibits no falling off in delicacy and finish.

These machines, named "Blue" and "Green"† from the colour of their cases, were tried three times at Greenwich, in 1779-80, 1783-4, and 1789-90, but their going in all three trials showed progressive acceleration and irregularities, due, I think, to the defective design of the compensation.‡ Accordingly, Maskelyne reported, after each trial, that they had not gone within the limits of the Act, and after the third trial the Board's patience gave out, and they declined to try them further.

By this time, 1790, Mudge was suffering from senile decay, but his son, Thomas Mudge of Lincoln's Inn, took up the cudgels for his father, and after a fruitless application to the Board drafted a petition to Parliament, recounting his father's labours, and praying that they might be adequately rewarded. He followed this up by a pamphlet,§ in which he made a violent attack on Maskelyne, to which the latter wrote a long and dignified reply||, which elicited a further rejoinder.¶

It is not necessary to go into the controversy in detail. The main points in Mudge's attack were that the first machine had met with unfair usage, and that Maskelyne's method of calculating the rates

* Mudge himself stated that he was obliged to keep the parts intended for each machine separate, as he could not distinguish them. There is, however, one difference. In "Blue" the compensation curbs, instead of acting as shown in Fig. 20, which represents their arrangement in "Green," overlap, and act on the further ends of the T-piece. It is now (1922) in the hands of Messrs. W. E. Hurcomb, who very kindly showed it to me, and I was able to identify it by this circumstance. "Green" is believed to have been lost at sea.

† Similar fantastic names were given to certain later chronometers, notably to some of the productions of J. S. Eiffe, who gave to various of his machines the titles of "The Hydrographer," "The Arctic Circle," "The Off-She-Goes," "The North-West Passage," and (out of compliment to E. J. Dent) "The Fool of the Strand." The Admiralty, however, were by no means sympathetic to this innovation, and resolutely declined to receive the last-named chronometer except under a less controversial alias.

‡ After a rise in temperature, the curb pins did not return quite so far as they had advanced. Mudge tried to get over this by thinning the balance spring in the extremes of their travel, but without much success.

§ "A Narrative of Facts, relating to some Time-keepers constructed by Mr. Thomas Mudge . . . with some Observations upon the conduct of the Astronomer-Royal respecting them." London, 1792.

|| "An Answer to a pamphlet entitled 'A Narrative of facts,' lately published . . . ." London, 1792. This pamphlet is superior to Mudge's, both in matter and manner, but its style is occasionally very turgid. Two of the sentences contain respectively 150 and 302 words. The Board paid the expenses of its publication (£61 7s. 11d.).

¶ "A Reply to the Answer of the Rev. Dr. Maskelyne . . . ." Maskelyne's copy of this pamphlet, with copious pencil notes, is in my possession.

Plate XX. EIGHT-DAY TIMEKEEPER ON MUDGE'S PLAN.
This machine appears to be mounted in gimbals, but in reality these are only trunnions, allowing it to be reversed for winding.
This timekeeper was originally purchased, for £167 10s., by the Duke of Marlborough, and bears his arms.

See p. 124, f. Soane Museum.

of "Blue" and "Green" was bound to exaggerate their errors. Maskelyne's defence to the first charge was not very convincing, and to the second still less so, but it must be added, in fairness, that the alternative methods proposed by Mudge, junior, and by Count Bruhl,* his father's staunch friend and patron, were equally unsound.†

It is due to Maskelyne's memory, also, to point out that there was no justification for the bitter recriminations directed against him by Harrison and Mudge.‡ He was a man of honourable and upright character, with a strong sense of duty. But it cannot be denied that he strongly preferred the method of lunar distances: that he was not disposed to allow to the use of timekeepers more than a secondary importance in the finding of longitude: and that he showed himself a rigid and unsparing critic of their defects.

The House of Commons appointed a committee to consider Mudge's petition.§ Their report, which contains a great deal of very interesting evidence, was generally favourable to him, and accordingly he was awarded, in spite of the strong opposition of the Board, a further £2,500. In the main, the Board were undoubtedly right in saying that this action tended to encourage an inferior artist at the expense of a superior||, but in view of Mudge's labours, and (though this was not fully appreciated at the time) his invention of the lever escapement, it can hardly be doubted that the action of Parliament was substantially just.

Mudge died in 1794. Shortly before his death, his son endeavoured to set up a manufactory of his timekeepers, engaging Howells, Pennington, and other workmen to make them, and Mudge lived just long enough to see the first completed. But he was spared the mortification of finding that no one else could make a timekeeper of his design perform nearly so well as the original ones, a circumstance which, coupled with the younger Mudge's ignorance of the trade, led him to

---

* John Maurice, Count of Bruhl (1736-1809), diplomatist and astronomer. He was Envoy-Extraordinary from the Kingdom of Saxony at the Court of Great Britain from 1764 until his death. The first published account of Mudge's escapement appeared in his tract "A Register of one of Mr. Mudge's Timekeepers," 1794, and he contributed to the "Reply to the Answer" an appendix on the best method of obtaining a mean daily rate.

† This question is more fully discussed in the Appendix.

‡ Harrison accused him, in so many words, of falsifying, before the daily comparisons of No. 4, the time shown by the transit clock. (*P. 5 of his "Remarks . . . . , &c."* 1767.)

§ Pitt, Fox, Sir Gilbert Elliott, Sir George Shuckburgh, and Messrs. Ryder, Bragge, Gregor and Windham.

|| Evidence was given to show that two chronometers made by Arnold (Pocket chronometers Nos. 36 and 68) had gone much better than Mudge's. But it must be remembered that these were the pick of nearly a thousand, as against Mudge's total of three, and, further, that they were not entered in competition for the reward.

abandon the scheme a few years later, after losing heavily by it.* He performed a service to his father's memory by publishing a full account of his timekeeper†, containing also a series of letters written to Count Bruhl, which give a very delightful picture of old Mudge's character—gentle and affectionate, a patient and laborious workman, quietly and uncomplainingly accepting the downfall of his high hopes, and struggling to the last to rectify the errors of his machines and to render them worthy of the care he lavished on them—a man

". . . Who fortune's buffets and rewards
Has ta'en with equal thanks."

POSTSCRIPT. WILLIAM COOMBE.

During the first trial of "Blue" and "Green" at Greenwich, another English maker, William Coombe, of whom very little is known, also sent a machine there for test.

He first appears as the author of a MS. entitled "Researches on a measure of Time for determination of the Longitude at sea," which he laid before the Board in June, 1777, and which was referred to Dr. Hornsby (Plumian Professor, Oxford) for his opinion.

In November, 1778, Coombe transmitted to the Board an account of the going of a timekeeper made by him. It appeared reliable, and he was accordingly asked to send it to Greenwich for trial, which, at his leisure, he did. It was received at Greenwich on June 28th of the following year, "together with a paper of directions concerning it." At the end of four months, Maskelyne reported very favourably upon its going, and Coombe accordingly received £200 "to prosecute further improvements."

But after this promising début, his star appears to have set. We hear no more of his timekeeper, and on his petitioning the Board in November, 1783, for some further assistance, he is told that he "must first bring proof of his having made some improvement worthy the Board's notice." A renewed application two years later receives the same reply, and the only other passage in the minutes relating to him is dated February 3rd, 1787, when he was paid £13 1s. for repairing an astronomical clock on board H.M.S. "Sirius." He had evidently dropped out of the race.

* He lost about £1,700. Some twenty machines were made. One is shown in Plate XX.: three are at Greenwich, but have been converted to the ordinary chronometer escapement: one is in the Museum of the Clockmakers' Company, and there is a particularly fine specimen in the British Horological Institute. It is remarkable for having a single helical balance spring and a compensation balance of Arnold's pattern. It shows no sign of having been converted. The year of its manufacture, 1796, is that in which Arnold's patent expired. Mudge sold six timekeepers to the Admiralty at 150 guineas each, but was then torpedoed by the Board of Longitude, who pointed out that better machines could be obtained from Arnold and Earnshaw at half the price. He subsequently offered "Blue" and "Green" to the Admiralty at the enormous price of 250 guineas each.

† "A Description, with Plates, of the Time-keeper invented by the late Mr. Thomas Mudge." London, 1799. The book is well written and well printed, and the illustrations of the timekeeper's mechanism, from drawings by Robert Pennington, are excellent.

It is to be regretted that no details of his machine appear to have been preserved. He was evidently no charlatan*, and the recorded going of his timekeeper† in a considerable range of temperature is sufficient to prove that, whether he had copied Harrison or worked on original lines, he had produced a reasonably accurate machine. The actual duration, up to the time of Maskelyne's report, of the machine's trial at Greenwich was 20 weeks, or not much less than that of a modern trial (29 weeks), and during that time its greatest weekly rate was + 56.38 s., and its least – 20.24 s., while the greatest difference between any two consecutive weeks was 26.52 s., so that its "trial number"‡ to-day would be 129.66. Although actually far from good, this is relatively better than some which have been obtained in the Greenwich trials by quite modern machines. Unfortunately, although Coombe's machine showed itself a good timekeeper in moderate fluctuations of temperatures, as may be seen from the following week's work : —

	Daily rate.	Temperature.
Sept. 30, 1779	Gaining 3.88 s.	70°
Oct. 1, ,, ...	,, 4.30 s.	66°
Oct. 2, ,, ...	,, 3.85	70°
Oct. 3, ,, ...	,, 3.66	61°
Oct. 4, ,, ...	,, 3.04	60°
Oct. 5, ,, ...	,, 3.18	60°
Oct. 6, ,, ...	,, 3.18	58°

its compensation was unstable, and when the temperature fell to freezing point in December its timekeeping became most erratic. Its maker removed it from the Observatory on January 26th, 1780.

* Shortly before the trial of Coombe's timekeeper, one John George Thiells, of Bremen, attended the Board with a timekeeper, and asked that it might be tried. Maskelyne accordingly tried it for four days, at the end of which period he reported that it went no better than an ordinary watch, and that he had therefore returned it to its maker.

† The MS. register kept during this trial is preserved in the archives of the Royal Observatory.

‡ See Appendix I.

CHAPTER VI.

LE ROY AND BERTHOUD.

The true development of the chronometer, on modern lines, may be traced back to the work of Pierre Le Roy and Ferdinand Berthoud, both of Paris. The question of deciding upon their respective merits is a difficult one, but it may briefly be said that Berthoud was a man of extraordinary talent, who was quick to seize any hints from the work of others, or from his own mistakes, and who steadily groped his way through a long series of experiments until, by a process of trial and error, he had produced a satisfactory marine timekeeper—while Le Roy was a genius, who tackled the problem in a thoroughly scientific manner, and produced, with far less labour, a machine embodying all the essential features of the modern chronometer. It should be added that the two men were bitter rivals, and that neither was inclined to concede to the other his proper share of credit.

LE ROY.

Pierre Le Roy was born in 1717. His father, Julien Le Roy, was a celebrated clockmaker, inventor of a form of repeating mechanism much used in the French watches of his day, and of many other improvements in clocks and watches.* He held the appointment of "Horloger du Roi," with apartments in the palace, and on his death in 1754 his son succeeded to this situation.

In 1748, Le Roy communicated to the Académie des Sciences his invention of a "detached" escapement, which must be regarded as the first known example of that class. It is probable that similar devices had been made before his time—indeed, he himself admitted that Dutertre's son showed him an escapement of the kind which the elder Dutertre had made many years before,† while the germ of the invention may be found in the mechanism (one can hardly call it a clock) devised by Vicenzio Galilei in 1649 for maintaining the vibrations of a pendulum—but they had never come into general use, nor had much information been published relating to them.

For any form of timekeeper controlled by a balance, some form of detached escapement is practically a necessity if it is to preserve an accurate rate of going during a long period, and therefore some explanation of its properties is advisable.

The gist of the whole matter is contained in Harrison's remark, " . . . the less the Wheels have to do with the Balance, the better." The good going of any balance-timekeeper depends entirely

* Amongst them may be instanced the "all-or-nothing piece," which ensures that a repeater, so long as it strikes at all, shall strike the correct number of blows corresponding to the time shown by the hands.

† See also an escapement described in Thiout's treatise, p. 110, Vol. I. Like Le Roy's first design, it is only semi-detached.

upon the ability of the balance to perform its vibrations in some constant unit of time, and any external cause, such as friction, which checks it from swinging freely under the influence of the balance spring introduces a disturbing element which may greatly impair, or even entirely nullify, the property with which the latter normally endows (or may be made to endow) it—that of performing vibrations of any extent in some unchanging unit of time.

Now, it is obvious that in such escapements as the verge, previously described; the cylinder, in which the teeth of the escape wheel are locked upon the polished surfaces of a hollow cylinder mounted on the balance staff; or the duplex (once in great favour for high-class watches) in which they rest on a much smaller solid cylinder mounted in the same manner, the balance is never at liberty, and that its motions are, to some extent, either constrained, as in the verge, or impeded. The expression "detached," on the other hand, is applied to those escapements, such as the "chronometer" and "lever," in which, except at the instants of receiving impulse and actuating the escapement, the balance is left to swing with perfect freedom, the escape wheel being locked meanwhile upon a pallet entirely disconnected from the balance. In these escapements the motion of the balance approximates very closely to a perfectly free vibration, provided that the two disturbing elements—the giving of impulse and the work of unlocking the escapement—act upon it at or near the dead point, when their influence upon the time of its vibrations is practically negligible.

From the foregoing, it will be seen that the detached escapement exhibits, in principle, a very distinct advance upon all former ones. It must be remembered, however, that its competitors were not without advantages of their own. Thus the verge proved its vitality by remaining in constant use for over a century after Mudge had made his first detached lever:* the cylinder escapement, possessing in itself a rough form of compensation due to the varying consistency of the oil upon its surface, was tremendously popular until within the last generation: and the duplex was regarded for many years as surpassing the lever, and rivalling the chronometer escapement itself, although it never recovered from the death-blow dealt by its adoption in the original Waterbury watch. But for accurate timekeeping founded upon scientific principles none of these could presume to compete on equal terms with any form of detached escapement.

Le Roy's first escapement, although rather rudimentary, was of this kind. The escape wheel, after giving impulse to the balance, was locked upon a pivoted "detent,"† kept in the unlocking position

* Clerkenwell was making verge watches as recently as 1885.

† So called because it detains the teeth of the escape wheel. The detent, as will appear, may either be pivoted, like the wheels of the train, and controlled by a spring, or mounted upon a flat spring, which serves both as pivot and as controller. The detent, in either case, carries a pallet, generally jewelled, and termed the "locking pallet." In the lever escapement, described on p. 237, two such pallets are employed,

Le Roy's 'Montre Marine' on its later stand.

Pl. V.

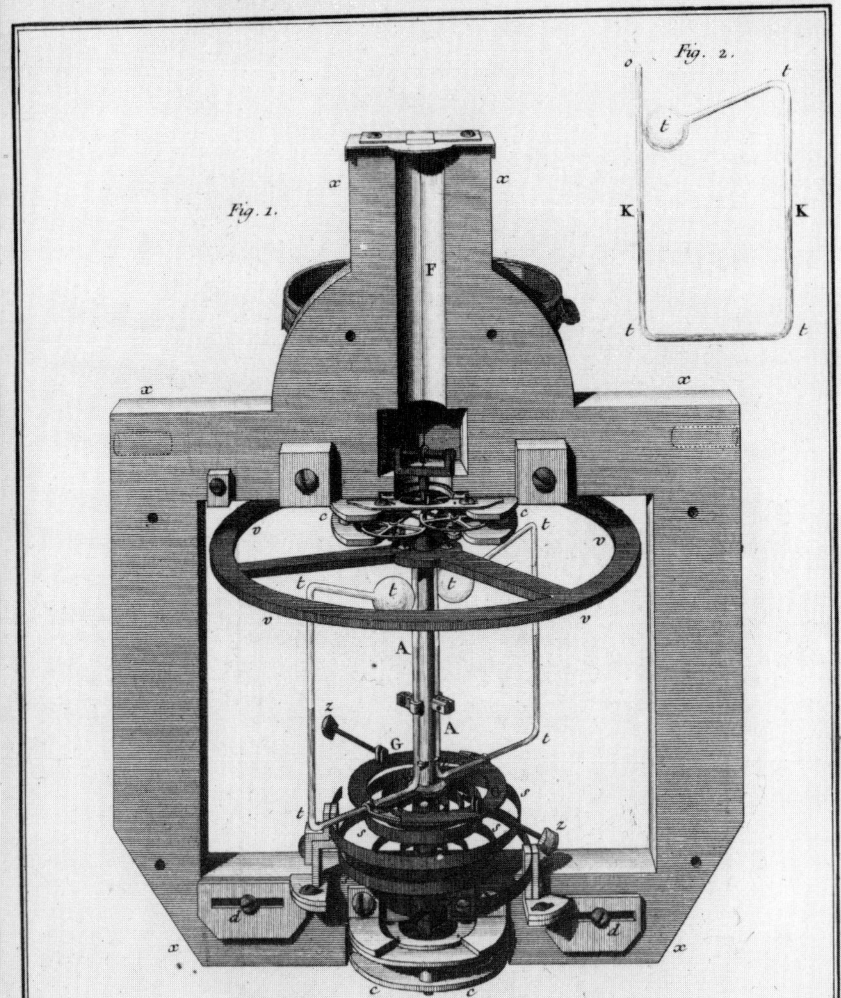

de la Gardette del. et Sculp.

Le Roy' Montre Marine.

LE ROY'S 'MONTRE MARINE'.
View showing the circular balance, and its mercury/alcohol compensation tubes.

The movement of Le Roy's Montre Marine seen from below.

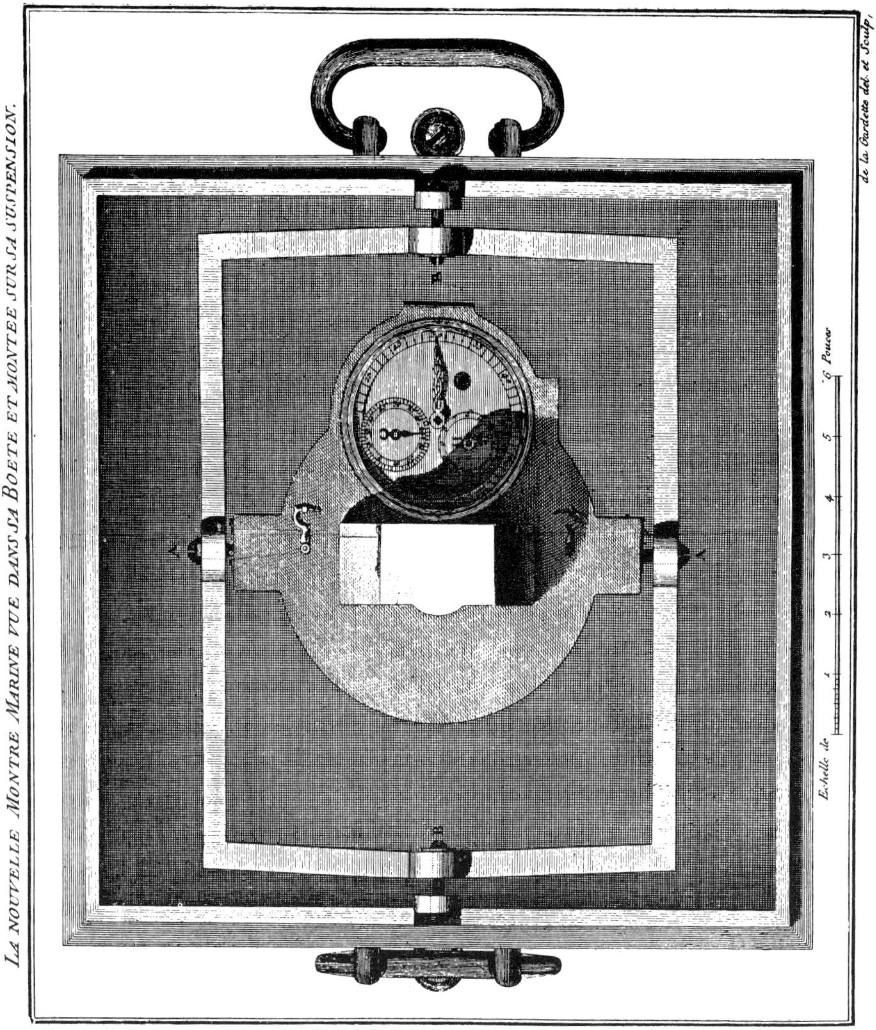
LA NOUVELLE MONTRE MARINE VUE DANS SA BOETE ET MONTEE SUR SA SUSPENSION.
de la Gardette del. et Sculp.
Echelle de 6 Pouces

Plate XXI. LE ROY'S "MONTRE MARINE."
From an engraving in his "Memoir sur la meilleure maniere de mesurer le tems en mer." (1770).
See p. 87.

by a spring, and moved at each beat into the path of the escape wheel by a cam mounted on the balance staff. Like the modern chronometer escapement, and unlike the verge or the cylinder, the impulse was only given in one direction, and at every beat instead of every half beat. The unlocking, however, was clumsy, involving a considerable recoil, and the detached arc of the balance—the portion of its swing in which it was entirely detached from the escapement—was not of great extent, amounting to a little less than half of a complete vibration. Le Roy does not seem to have made any further use of this escapement.

In 1754 he deposited with the Académie des Sciences a sealed paper, containing the description of a proposed marine timekeeper. It was afterwards published,* and although the machine itself was crude and inefficient, the following details of its design are interesting as showing to what conclusions Le Roy's experiments had led him at this period :—

It beat half seconds, and embodied a spiral-spring remontoire let off every two and a half seconds. Its regulator was a single spherical ball, some two or three pounds in weight, mounted upon a vertical axis transfixing its centre, and suspended by a straight spring five or six inches in length, the upper pivot of the axis being prolonged through the pivot hole to form the point of attachment of the spring. Le Roy believed the vibrations of a spring of this kind to be more nearly isochronous than those of a spiral spring, and he adjusted the machine for mean time by making the upper end pass through a slit with as little clearance as possible, so that by raising or lowering the spring he could alter its effective length. The lower pivot of the balance, like those of Sully's "montre marine," revolved between four friction rollers.

The machine was slung in gimbals, and for simplicity's sake Le Roy designed it to go only six hours, remarking naively :

> " . . . there are always people enough on board a ship, who have nothing to do ; 'tis their business to keep watch in the night : it cannot therefore be any inconvenience for my clock to go no longer than six hours ; this time I chose as preferable to any other, because a ship's officers relieve one another in their duty, every four hours, and so any of them can easily wind up the clock when they come upon duty . . ."

He shows himself fully acquainted with the effects of heat and cold upon the balance and balance spring, and proposes three alternative means of correcting them.

1. By means of a brass and steel gridiron, three feet in length, arranged to alter the effective length of the balance spring.
2. By keeping the machine at one uniform temperature through the use of lamps burning in its box, more or fewer being lit according to the readings of a thermometer kept in the box.

---

* As an appendix to his " Exposé Succinct."

3. By determining, once and for all, the going of the machine in various temperatures, and subsequently, when in use afloat, recording the temperature whenever the machine was wound, its gain or loss being then obtained by calculation.

Of these methods, Le Roy himself preferred the third, but it is open to the obvious objection that the errors of an uncompensated machine are large, and that to obtain a correction accurate enough for purposes of navigation it would be necessary to know not merely the change of temperature between one winding and the next, but the extent and duration of the several fluctuations of temperature to which the machine had been exposed during that interval.

The second method was impracticable at the time, and would not be particularly easy of execution on board ship even to-day. The first might have worked, but the machine, as a whole, could never have been anything but a failure, or, at best, a *succès d'estime*.

This was probably Le Roy's experience. He appears to have constructed a machine upon these lines almost immediately, for he prints in his " Précis des Recherches . . . " a letter from M. de Petitmont, testifying that Le Roy showed him in December 1756 a marine timekeeper, having a balance suspended by means of a wire, and a form of dead-beat (or, possibly, detached) escapement, with star-shaped escape-wheel. It would go for six hours, but ought to be wound every three.

Le Roy continued his investigations, and in 1763 presented to the Académie a marine clock, three feet high. The following year he produced another, of half the size, which was tested by Prof. le Monnier, on behalf of the Académie, for nearly a year. Finally, on August 5th, 1766, he had the honour of presenting to King Louis XV. the very remarkable timekeeper shown in Plates XIX. and XX., which stamps him for all time as one of the very greatest masters of horology who ever lived.

The exact genesis of many great inventions is hotly debated. Whether Heron, De Caus, the Marquess of Worcester, or Savery invented the steam engine: who first printed from moveable types: who invented the mariner's compass: and who first applied the pendulum to a clock, are questions as unresolved and as puzzling as those of " . . what song the Sirens sang, or what name Achilles assumed when he hid himself among women." But there can be no doubt at all that the inventor of the modern chronometer is Pierre Le Roy. Nothing can rob Harrison of the glory of having been the first man to make a satisfactory marine timekeeper, one, too, which was of permanent usefulness, and which could be duplicated as often as necessary. But No. 4, in spite of its fine performance and beautiful mechanism, cannot be compared, for efficiency and design, with Le Roy's wonderful machine. The Frenchman, who was but little indebted to his predecessors, and not at all to his contemporaries, evolved, by sheer force of genius, a timekeeper which contains all the essential mechanism of the modern chronometer.

PLATE XXII. LE ROY'S MONTRE MARINE.

MUDGE CONSTANT-FORCE ESCAPEMENT probably by Howell's & Penningtor
c.1795. Removed from a 'Mudge Copy' — perhaps No. 11 or No. 12.
Clockmakers' Company (C.C. Cat. 631).

And he went further. As Poe once wrote, " . . . It is the curse of a certain order of mind, that it can never rest satisfied with the consciousness of its ability to do a thing. Nor even is it content with doing it. It must both know and show how it was done." And this latter service Le Roy has performed very thoroughly. In a memoir published in 1770* he gives a full account of the investigations which led him to adopt the final form of his machine, and of the mechanical considerations which dictated the details of its mechanism. He writes with the utmost candour, with scientific accuracy and thoroughness, and with that perfect lucidity and precision of which few except French writers have ever succeeded in capturing the secret.

The true value of his work will become more apparent in the later portion of this book, but a mere catalogue of his inventions may be enough to show its extraordinary character. He was the inventor of the *compensation balance*†—both in its ordinary bi-metallic form and in one which is, theoretically, more perfect, the mercurial—and also of the *first detached chronometer escapement.* Moreover, he was the first to enunciate a method of obtaining an *isochronous balance spring.*

The general appearance of Le Roy's chronometer is shown in Plate XXI. Compared with the modern machine, its appearance conveys a suggestion of deformity—a deformity which a doctor might diagnose as unilateral hypertrophy. And this is actually the case, for although the mechanism is astonishingly akin to that of the modern machine, the balance is, from a modern point of view, enormously too large, and the remainder of the mechanism both relatively and absolutely dwarfed.

The movement is distinguished by extreme simplicity—a simplicity, however, which is in no way rudimentary, but results from a ruthless suppression of non-essentials, and a perfect adaptation of the means to the end.

The controlling device is a large circular steel balance, about five inches in diameter, weighing some five ounces, and swinging seconds. The pivots of the balance staff run between two sets of four friction rollers, as used by Sully in 1714, and the weight of the balance is taken, not by an end-stone, but by a very fine suspension wire. Two blued balance springs, of large size, are attached to collets near

* "Memoire sur la meilleure maniere de mesurer le tems en mer." The Académie des Sciences, at their session of April 5th, 1769, awarded the double prize to this memoir, and the timekeeper accompanying it, which had both been submitted by Le Roy under the motto of "*Labor improbus omnia vincit.*" It was published in the following year as an Appendix to Cassini's "Voyage fait par ordre du Roi en 1768, pour eprouver les montres marines inventées par M. le Roy."—Paris, 1770.

† As previously narrated in Chap. II., there is some evidence to show that, before Le Roy, experimental compensation balances had been tried by Harrison and by Rivaz. But since Harrison's, by his own confession, was unsuccessful, and that of Rivaz probably not less so, their work does not in any way affect Le Roy's claim to be the inventor of the compensation balance as we know it to-day.

the lower pivot, and above them is a metal ring carrying two radial screws, which can be screwed in or out as required to alter the inertia of the balance, and so adjust the machine for mean time.

Between this ring and the balance wheel is fitted the compensation. It will be remembered that Harrison, in his pamphlet of 1775, declared that the compensation ought to be in the balance. Had he read Le Roy's memoir, which appeared five years previously, he would have found that this was already a *fait accompli*. The Frenchman, working independently, had come to the same conclusion, and after trying and discarding a balance in which a central gridiron controlled, through a system of levers, two arms carrying the balance weights (this proved unreliable owing to the play in the joints), he hit upon the very happy idea of using thermometers as a means of compensation.

Accordingly, he fitted to the balance staff the two shown in Plate XXII. and Fig. 21, having their bulbs and the upper portions of their tubes filled with spirits of wine, and the lower portions with mercury. It can readily be seen that a rise of temperature would cause a certain portion of the mercury to approach the axis of the balance, thus diminishing the moment of inertia of the latter, and that the shape and proportions of the thermometers could be arranged so that the acceleration caused by this decrease of inertia should exactly balance the retardation caused by the own slight expansion of the balance and by the loss of strength of the balance springs.

It may be noticed that the arrangement of the thermometer tubes is particularly ingenious, since as long as the axes of the outer portions are parallel with that of the balance the compensation is unaffected by any accidental variations in the cross-sections of the tubes. The alcohol is, of course, used to obtain a greater motion of the mercury columns than would be possible if the bulbs contained mercury.

Le Roy subsequently devised a laminated brass and steel balance, practically as used to-day, but he preferred his thermometers, and, I think, justly. To his logical mind the mercurial form must undoubtedly have appealed strongly, as offering the theoretical possibility of obtaining absolutely perfect compensation, which was not the case with the bi-metallic balance.

Le Roy was led to use a compensation balance by his discovery of the fact that if the length of a balance spring be varied by the use of a regulator or a compensation curb, the relative duration of the long and short arcs of a balance controlled by that spring will vary also. This is how he enunciated his discovery:

> " . . . It is only lately that I have at last discovered, as I shall explain more particularly, a very important fact, which will henceforth serve as a basis for the theory of watches, and a guide for the workmen who construct them: it is, *that there is in every spring of sufficient extent, a certain length where all the vibrations, large or small, are isochronous; and that if, having found this length, you shorten the spring, the large vibrations will be quicker than the short ones; if, on the contrary, you lengthen the spring, the small arcs will be described in less time than the large ones.* It is upon this important property of the spring, unknown hitherto, that the good going of my marine watch principally depends . . . ."

See pp. 137-138

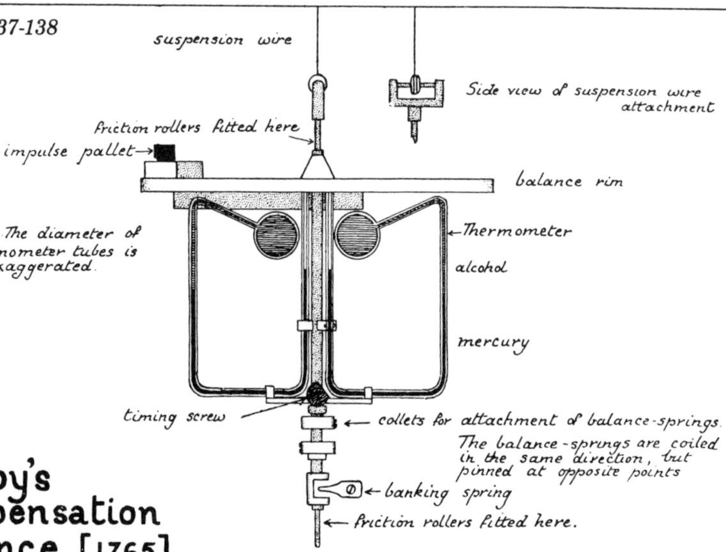

NOTE. The diameter of the thermometer tubes is slightly exaggerated.

21

Le Roy's compensation balance [1765]

See p. 140.

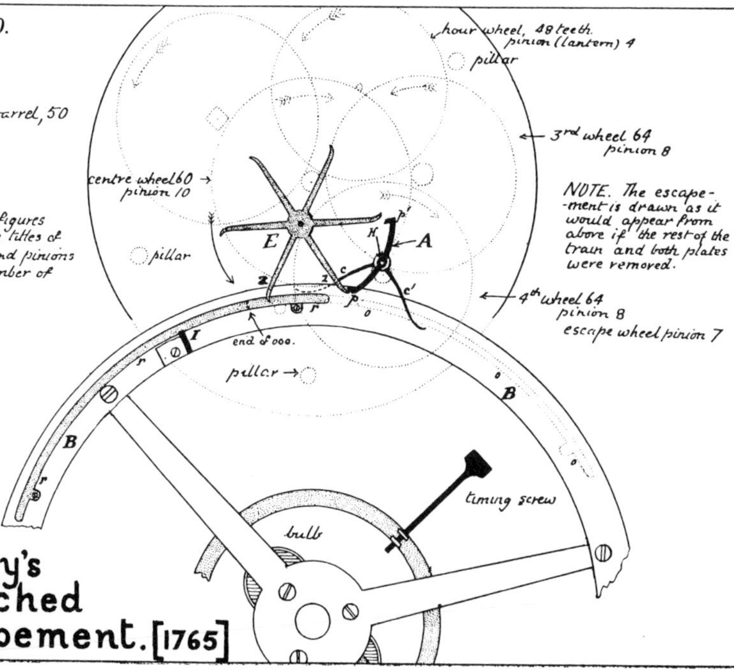

NOTE. The escapement is drawn as it would appear from above if the rest of the train and both plates were removed.

NOTE. The figures following the titles of the wheels and pinions give the number of their teeth

22

Le Roy's detached escapement. [1765]

To obtain isochronism is not quite so simple as Le Roy here makes out, for there are various other factors, such as the form of the spring's terminals, to be taken into account. His discovery is better stated in a less dogmatic manner, thus:

> *"A given balance spring will not necessarily produce isochronous motion in a balance, although particular lengths of it may be found which will do so."*

He had the courage of his convictions, for he refused to fit either a fusee or a remontoire to his machine, contenting himself with a going barrel, which allowed the torque at the escape wheel to vary directly as the tension of the mainspring.

He describes his method of adjusting the machine as follows:

> " . . . I set the marine watch (which, as we have seen, has no fusee) to go twelve hours in the long arcs and twelve hours in the short arcs; that is to say, twelve hours with the mainspring strongly wound, and twelve hours with it almost unwound. If, in the latter case, the watch goes faster than in the former, it proves that the balance springs are too long, and I shorten them. If, on the contrary, it goes slower, I lengthen them, and proceed in this manner until the watch goes equally with the mainspring up or with it down. I then diminish or increase the weight of the balance until the watch is brought to time . . ."

His escapement is shown in Fig. 22. It is a very simple detached one, with pivoted detent.

E is the escape wheel, having six long radial arms, each with a tooth at its extremity. These teeth, in turn, are normally locked upon one or other of the pallets *p*,*p'* mounted on the anchor A, pivoted at H, and having rigidly attached to it the two arms *c*,*c'*, which are situated one above and one below the rim B of the balance. The latter carries, on its nearer side, the vertical arc or partial rim *rrr*, and on its farther, the similar arc *ooo*, the latter being shown dotted. It also carries the impulse pallet I.

As drawn, the tooth 1 of the escape wheel is locked on the pallet *p*, and the balance is swinging in a clockwise direction. When the end of the arc *rrr* meets the arm *c'*, it brushes it aside, thus rotating the anchor A slightly around H, and unlocking tooth 1. Tooth 2 then falls on the impulse pallet (which is cut away so as to clear the arm *c*) and gives impulse to the balance. Tooth 1 then locks on the pallet *p'*, which is slightly undercut, so that it is drawn into deeper locking by the action of the tooth on it, and by so doing keeps the arm *c'* clear of the arc *rrr*. The balance swings to the full extent of its arc, some 100°*, and returns.

The end of the arc *ooo* now meets the arm *c*, and throws the anchor slightly over the other way, allowing the tooth 1 to clear the pallet *p'*. The escape wheel turns very slightly, and tooth 2 locks on the pallet *p*, which is undercut also, drawing it deeper into engagement and keeping the arm *c* clear of the arc *ooo*. On the return of the balance the cycle of operations starts again.

---

* The balance is banked to an arc of about 160° by means of a small flat spring, projecting into a cut-away portion of the balance staff just above the lower pivot. See fig. 21.

It will be seen that in this escapement the balance is almost completely detached, and that the unlocking and impulse occur very near the dead point, where they have least effect on the time of its vibrations. It is the pioneer chronometer escapement, and is remarkable for giving impulse at the balance rim instead of near its centre*—also for the fact that no springs are employed to control the detent, whose action is extraordinarily light and delicate, and yet perfectly safe. As will appear, almost every chronometer escapement produced since Le Roy's time has been less successful in this direction, requiring, generally, the employment of at least two springs.†

The remainder of the mechanism consists only of a very small and simple movement—a mainspring, going barrel, and four wheels and their pinions. By using a going barrel, Le Roy did away with both fusee and maintaining gear‡, while even the ordinary motion work for the hands is absent, the hour wheel being driven direct from a pinion on the centre wheel arbor, and consequently travelling backwards. The machine goes for 38 hours, and is wound from the face (which is the correct method, although the clumsy plan of winding from the back, which has not a single valid argument except cheapness in its favour, is in all but universal practice). The gimbals were damped by springs and restricted to an arc of about 20°. The inside of the box was padded, and a circular pad was also attached to the bottom of the balance casing.

If we contrast this marvellous machine with No. 4, which, in its own way, is equally wonderful, Le Roy's superiority as a horologist is evident. Harrison took the escapement, balance, and general arrangement of the ordinary watch of his day, and by fitting a remontoire and maintainer, an automatic regulator, and diamond pallets, aided by high-numbered wheels§ and pinions and lavish jewelling,¶ he compelled

---

* Le Roy's idea in arranging it thus was to give impulse at or near the radius of gyration of the rim. By so doing, he obtained a marked stabilising effect upon the extent of the arcs, since the blow given by the teeth of the escape wheel diminishes almost exactly as the arc of the balance increases, and *vice versa*.

† Chronometer escapements using only one spring have been devised by various makers, including Berthoud, Arnold, Earnshaw and Cole. Berthoud also invented a very simple and robust pattern without any springs, but did not make much use of it.

‡ A maintainer is not required with a going barrel, since the spring is wound by turning the fixed end forwards, not the free end backwards, and accordingly the act of winding increases the power exerted by the mainspring at the escape wheel, instead of reducing it to zero.

§ The higher the number of teeth in a wheel or pinion the greater, broadly speaking, is its mechanical efficiency. There is however, little actual benefit in using very high numbers, as the teeth are of necessity weaker, and also more expensive to cut. Harrison's third wheel had 140 teeth, and his centre pinion 21. Mudge, also, used a very high-numbered train. In Le Roy's machine, on the other hand, there is no wheel above 73, and no pinion above 12.

¶ There are no jewels whatever in Le Roy's timekeeper, the pivots revolving in plain brass holes. As explained in the footnote on p. 156 the process of jewelling was unknown, at the time, on the Continent.

PRECISION POCKET WATCH BY LES FRERÈS; GOYFFON OF PARIS.
Discovered since Commander Gould wrote this book.

PRECISION POCKET WATCH BY LES FRERES. GOYFFON, Paris.
Goysson, Paris. Discovered after this book was written. The photograph shows the bi-metallic compensation curb and rivets.

it to become an efficient timekeeper. Le Roy attacked the problem from an entirely different standpoint, and obtained his results not by nullifying defects, but by eliminating them. The difference in their machines is fundamental—Harrison built a wonderful house on the sand; but Le Roy dug down to the rock.

His entire originality cannot be too strongly emphasised. At the time when he completed his machine, he did not possess, and could not have possessed, any information as to the mechanism of No. 4.* Nor, if he had done so, would it have been of any assistance to him. To Sully, also, his work obviously owes nothing except the plan of using friction rollers at the balance staff,† and the only other Richmond in the field was Berthoud, who had published, in 1763, a description of his first timekeeper‡—a machine, however, designed on the lines of Harrison's early work, and quite as crude as the latter's No. 1, which Le Roy had seen in London in 1738. Le Roy's timekeeper was an entirely new departure, and the credit of having designed and constructed the first modern chronometer is entirely his, and his alone.

Le Roy entered his machine to compete for the prize offered by the Académie des Sciences in 1766§. The award of this was, however, postponed in the following year until a competitive trial of the machines should have been made at sea. This trial was carried out by the Marquis de Courtanveaux, who had a yacht, the "Aurore," specially built for the purpose. It proved, however, to be a walk-over, for although timekeepers had been entered by various other makers, such as Tavernier and Romilly,¶ none was produced for trial except this machine of Le Roy's and a duplicate by the same maker. Le Roy took these to Havre, where the "Aurore" was lying, in a post-chaise, and they received such violent shocks en route that the harpsichord wire supporting the balance of No. 1 was broken.‖ Nothing daunted,

---

* "The Principles of Mr. Harrison's Timekeeper" was not published until 1767, while Le Roy had presented his machine to King Louis XV. in the preceding year. However, the success of No. 4 in the trials of 1761 and 1764, of which several contemporary accounts had appeared in the press, undoubtedly stimulated the French makers. Berthoud, in a letter to Short, dated Paris, February 2nd, 1767, remarks:

> " . . . since the Knowledge of the Success of Mr. Harrison, and the Reward given him, every little Watch-maker is endeavouring to make Marine Watches, and we shall see what this Fermentation will produce."

† It is worth noting, however, that Julien Le Roy, Pierre's father, worked under Sully, and profited greatly by his instruction.

‡ In his "Essai sur l'Horlogerie."

§ Out of the endowment left them by De Meslay.

¶ Romilly's machine was accidently damaged by Prof. le Monnier, in whose hands the Académie had deposited it for a preliminary test on shore. Its aggrieved maker withdrew it, and Tavernier, another leading Paris clockmaker, followed suit in sympathy with him. Romilly once constructed a remarkable *tour de force*—a watch of ordinary size, *going a year for one winding*. As might be expected, it was not an accurate timekeeper.

‖ He subsequently took steps to prevent this from happening again by fixing the upper end of the suspensory wire to a weak spring, which would support little more than the weight of the balance, so that any shock caused the lower pivot to rest on an endstone, and relieved the wire from being tensioned further.

however, Le Roy fitted another (bought locally) at his inn that night and reached Havre with both his machines going. In the absence of other competitors, he was allowed to embark for the trial, a coastal cruise of three months duration, during which the ship frequently put into port in order to check the going of the watches by astronomical observations.

The following extract is translated from the report made by Courtanveaux to the Académie :—

> " . . . the rates determined at Amsterdam, by the observations made in that city, continued without any great alteration during our return, to such an extent that the error of the first watch, in 46 days, is but 38 seconds of time, which, even at the equator, would give an error of but 6½ miles . . ."
>
> " M. Le Roy's second watch* has kept its Amsterdam rate more exactly than his first watch : in 46 days it erred from it no more than 7¼ sec., which, even at the equator, would not produce an error in longitude of as much as 2 miles.
>
> " These errors must not be regarded as the sums of several errors which have, in great part, destroyed each other : the daily comparisons of the two watches, and the observations made during our time in harbour, testify the contrary.
>
> " There were, however, some inequalities in the going of the watches, but they appear far from considerable ; the greatest did not exceed the daily rate more than 1½ sec. : however, the 24 hours between noon on Aug. 29th and on Aug. 30th ought to be excepted, the error of the first watch amounting during that period to 5½ sec. . . ."

A second trial of these two machines was made in 1768,† in the frigate " L'Enjouée," comprising a voyage from Havre to Newfoundland, thence to Cadiz, and back to Brest—lasting, in all, some twenty-four weeks. The standard of the results obtained was much the same as that of the first trial—*i.e.*, an accuracy of the same order as that of No. 4—and Le Roy was awarded by the Académie a double prize for his timekeeper and his memoir describing it.

The Académie's report on the results of the trials, delivered on April 5th, 1769, concludes as follows :—

> " . . . the rate of M. Le Roy's watch, observed at sea in several voyages . . . has appeared in general sufficiently regular to merit the reward for the author : the principal intention of which is to encourage him to new researches ; for the Académie must not dissemble that in one of the trials which have been made of the watch, it appears to have accelerated, rather suddenly, 11 or 12 seconds per day, even while on land ; from this it appears that the desired degree of perfection has not yet been obtained."

In 1771 the Académie offered a second prize for marine timekeepers, to be awarded after a test at sea in the frigate " La Flore." For this Le Roy entered his two watches, and there were two other competitors, a weight-driven timekeeper made by Arsandeaux, and a pendulum

---

* During the first part of the voyage, Le Roy kept this machine in his own hands, for adjustment and experiment. Later, he formally delivered it to Courtanveaux, for trial under the same conditions as his first machine.

† Two of Berthoud's timekeepers, Nos. 6 and 8 (both weight-driven) were embarked also, but did not compete for the prize.

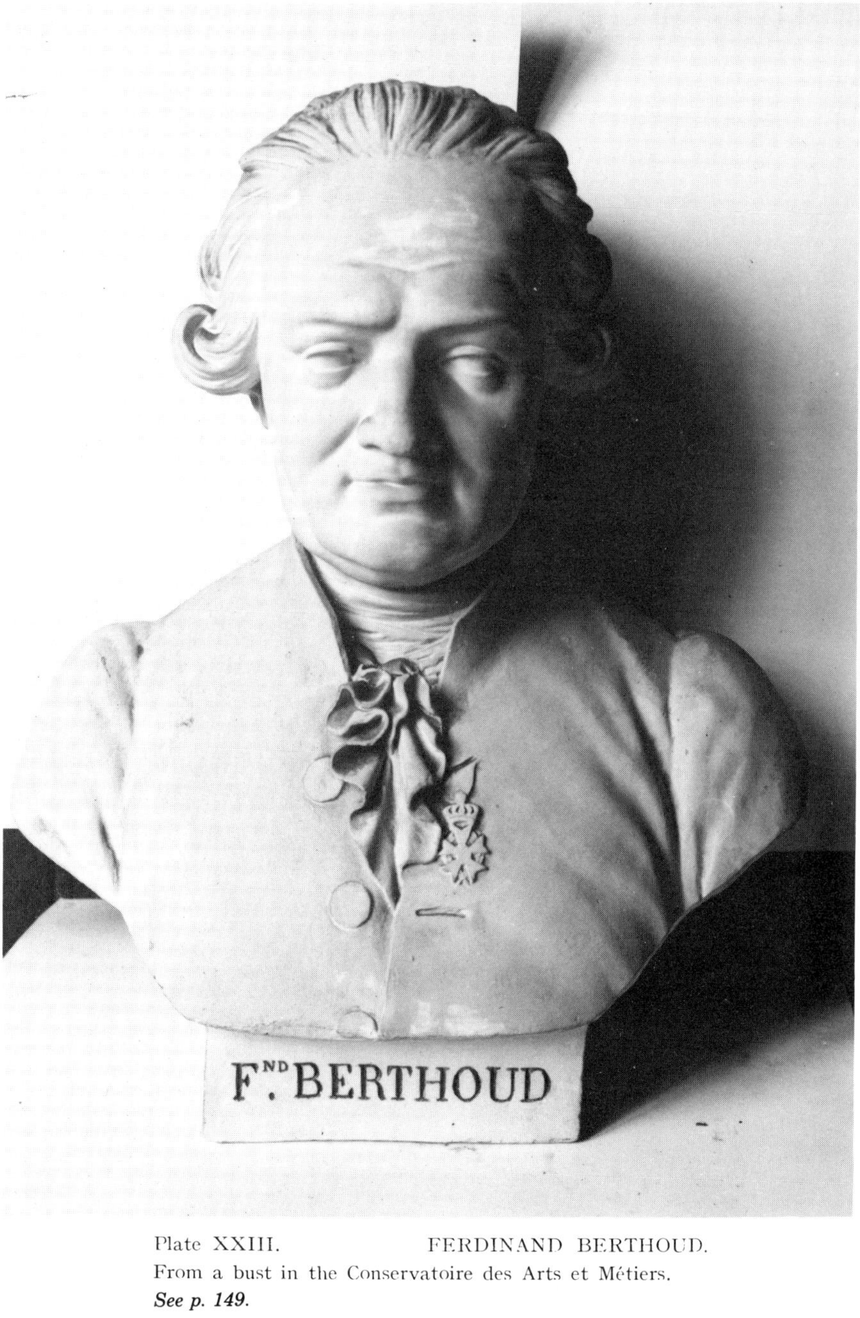

Plate XXIII. FERDINAND BERTHOUD.
From a bust in the Conservatoire des Arts et Métiers.
See p. 149.

FERDINAND BERTHOUD'S 'HORLOGE MARINE NO. 1'.
Completed in 1761, but not tried at sea.
(Conservatoire National des Arts et Metiers).

clock by Biesta, both of Paris.* Le Roy again carried off the prize, but the going of his machines was not quite so consistent as on former occasions. Biesta's machine proved a complete failure, and that of Arsandeaux went very irregularly. The latter was, however, commended for its very ingenious suspension.

During the voyage the ship touched on the Wilmington rock, off Antigua, and the resulting shock broke one of the thermometers of Le Roy's No. 1, which rendered it useless as a timekeeper.

After this trial, Le Roy seems to have rested content with the somewhat qualified praise expressed by the Académie in 1769, and to have abandoned, or at least suspended, further effort. He appears, indeed, to have persuaded himself that his machines were incapable of improvement, for he remarks :—

> " . . . All things have an end : since my last marine watch was finished, hardly a day has passed without my trying to find whether it was not susceptible of some advantageous alteration : useless attempt ! Theory and fact both persuade me that nothing remains to do except to devote myself to executing these machines well."†

However, he appears to have realised, later, that this was an overstatement, and to have begun the construction, during the last years of his life, of a new machine, of which no details, unfortunately, appear to have been preserved. He died on August 25th, 1785.

During his lifetime, his pen was by no means idle. He published several rejoinders to the attacks of his rival Berthoud,‡ a work entitled " Etrennes Chronometriques pour 1760," and a severe, but perfectly just comparison between the mechanism of No. 4 and of his own machines.§ He concludes this with a warm tribute of respect to " the toils of that venerable old man," and with a wistful hope that his work might meet with some similar recognition. But this, alas,

---

* Berthoud's No. 8 was also carried in this voyage, but did not compete, since its maker was in receipt of a salary as " Horloger de la Marine." Its going was better, in this trial, than that of Le Roy's machines. The latter also sent on board, but not for competition, a small marine watch called, from its shape, " la petite ronde," whose mechanism was much simpler than that of his larger machines, having a compensation curb like Harrison's, and a deadbeat escapement on the lines of that used by Sully. It did not perform well.

† He seems to have made several. In his " Memoir," after giving the dimensions of the rectangular box in which his first machine was contained, he adds : " I make them now circular, of the same diameter and height." Dr. Johnson, in the memoranda of his visit to Paris in 1775, notes that he visited " . . le Roy, the king's watchmaker, a man of character in his business, who showed a small clock made to find the longitude. A decent man."

A short-lived manufactory of marine timekeepers was founded, under Royal patronage, and with the co-operation of several members of Le Roy's family, in 1787.

‡ " Precis des Recherches faites en France pour la Determination des Longitudes en Mer, par la mesure artificielle du temps." Paris, 1773. 4to.
" Suite de precis sur les montres marines." 1774. 4to.

§ " Exposé succinct des travaux de MM. Harrison et Le Roy . . ." 1768.
Le Roy also wrote an anonymous critique of Rivaz' work. (Journal des Sçavans, 1751).

was denied him. As M. Gros has indignantly remarked* (I translate) " . . Harrison, for finding longitude by a mechanism which was abandoned almost immediately, received £20,000. The Frenchman of genius, who added one more to the glories of France, who sacrificed his fortune and twenty years of his life, received a medal !"

Le Roy might well have exclaimed, with Bacon, " . . For my name and memory, I leave it to men's charitable speeches, and to foreign nations, and to the next age." Although his labours, of which he made, as we have seen, no secret, provided an example and a basis which his rivals and successors were not slow to imitate and appropriate, they were never appreciated at their true value during his lifetime. He stands alone, the father of the chronometer as we know it.

NOTE.—I regret very much that I have not been fortunate enough to find any portrait of Le Roy for inclusion in this work, and I am inclined to suspect that none exists. But his memoir, and the wonderful machine preserved in the Conservatoire des Arts et Métiers, form his most worthy memorial—and he needs no other.

BERTHOUD.

Ferdinand Berthoud was born on March 19th, 1729, at Plancemont, in the canton of Neuchatel, Switzerland, a district which is now one of the largest centres of the Swiss watch and clock industry. Although practically the whole of his working life was passed in France, he is justly regarded in his native land as one of the greatest of all the Swiss horologists who have done so much to advance both the science of horology and the prosperity of their country.

He was originally destined for the church, but showed such outstanding mechanical ability that he was allowed to follow his own bent, and accordingly came to Paris in 1745 to perfect his knowledge of clock and watch making. He settled permanently there, and soon rose to eminence in his profession.

He is chiefly remarkable for his extraordinary industry, both as maker and author—he was the most voluminous writer on horology who ever lived—and for the marvellous variety of his conceptions. Some of his marine timekeepers were driven by weights, and some by springs : some were controlled by a balance, some by two balances geared together—one had a pendulum.† Some had compensation curbs, and others compensation balances—at least one had both. Some had their arbors pivoted vertically, and some horizontally. Some were fixed, and some slung in gimbals, while the diversity of their minor details is almost endless.

---

* " Echappements d'Horloges et de Montres." C. Gros. Paris, 1913 (p. 125).

† His No. 5. The machine, which was driven by a weight and beat three to the second, never got beyond the experimental stage. He proposed to make the pendulum describe a large arc, and to correct for circular error by suspending it rigidly from a pivoted arbor, carrying a balance spring left fast in the long arcs.

PLATE XXIV. BERTHOUD'S NO 2.
See p. 96.
Conservatoire des Arts et Metiers.

FERDINAND BERTHOUD.

MARINE WATCH NO. 3 of 1763.
His work shows the influence of John Harrison.

Berthoud began his work upon marine timekeepers in 1762, and was fortunate enough to obtain, soon afterwards, the appointment of "Horloger de la Marine," carrying with it a pension, which he enjoyed until the Revolution.*

He completed his first "Horloge Marine" in 1763.† This machine, which is preserved, among a representative collection of his timekeepers, in the Conservatoire des Arts et Métiers, is, like Harrison's No. 1, a comparatively clumsy affair. It has two very large horizontal balance wheels, suspended by short flat springs, and each controlled by a separate spiral balance spring. The balances are connected by toothed gearing—a method much inferior to Harrison's wires on account of the friction it involves. Their normal arc is small—some 20°. The escapement may be termed an undetached lever, the "fork" end of the lever carrying a roller moving in a slot cut in one of the gear wheels. (See Fig. 49.)

The compensation was effected by a large gridiron, which altered the position of two sets of curb pins. The train is of normal pattern, except that no maintaining gear is fitted, so that the machine is liable to stop while being wound.

The timekeeper had a wooden case, and was suspended by a pyramidal iron frame from a ball and socket joint.

It is impossible, within the limits of this chapter, to give more than a very brief outline of how Berthoud, by a process of gradual improvement and alteration, evolved his later timekeepers from this crude beginning.‡ His second machine§ follows very closely the lines of his

* Praslin, Minister of Marine, commissioned him to construct, for the King, his No. 6 and 8 machines, and promised a pension if they went well. After their trial in the "Isis," Berthoud was granted the appointment of "Horloger de la Marine," with a pension of 3,000 livres (with remainder of 1,000 to his wife) and other emoluments, totalling 7,500 livres per annum. Under a general law of the Republic, relating to such pensions, he was deprived of this income in 1793. Pomme, Deputy for Cayenne and French Guiana, made an eloquent speech in favour of restoring him to his appointment, with a salary of 6,000 livres, and proposed a decree in the Convention to this purpose. From the title page of Berthoud's "Supplement au Traité des Montres à Longitude," he appears to have held the office of "Mechanicien de la Marine," in 1807.

† An account of its mechanism appears in his "Essai sur l'Horlogerie," published in that year. It was tested off Brest in 1764, but the trial was a short one, as Berthoud unfortunately discovered that although he might be able to prevent the ship's motion from affecting his machine, he could not perform a similar office for himself.

‡ Berthoud himself always retained a very high opinion of this machine—but he must have been almost alone in doing so.

§ This machine bears a considerable resemblance, in its broad outline, to Harrison's No. 2. Berthoud was in London in 1766, as related in the previous chapter, and paid a visit to Harrison. The latter showed him Nos. 1, 2 and 3, but would not exhibit No. 4. The compensation of Berthoud's No. 3 (a large watch completed in 1764, but repeatedly altered later) is almost exactly on the lines of Harrison's curb, as fitted in that maker's third machine—a resemblance too great to be accidental. Berthoud also borrowed from No. 3 the idea of using an auxiliary "saddle piece," pressing upon a cam on the balance staff, to quicken the long arcs. His modification of this plan is illustrated in the "Supplement au Traité des Horloges Marines."

first, except that he fitted a remontoire, which proved unsatisfactory, and which he condemned, on principle, and never employed subsequently. This machine is shown in Plate XXIV.

He next evolved a weight-driven type of machine, fitted with a large balance beating seconds, a cylinder escapement with "pirouette," and a gridiron compensation. His No. 8, which he regarded as his chef d'œuvre of this kind, is shown in Plate XXV.

In view of the fact that this machine, in addition to being weight driven, had a compensation curb and a *cylinder escapement*, the closeness of its going at sea* is most remarkable. The following table† gives a selection of its rates during the 1771-2 trial:

Place.	Period.	Daily Rate.
Brest	Oct. 16-26, 1771 ...	1.19 sec. gaining
Cadiz	Nov. 22—Dec. 10 ...	0.05 ,, ,,
Teneriffe	Dec. 24—Jan. 4, 1772 ...	0.19 ,, ,,
Goree...	Jan. 16-25	1.46 ,, ,,
Fort Royal	Jan. 17—Feb. 26 ...	1.11 ,, ,,
Do.	Mar. 13—Apr. 7 ...	0.50 ,, ,,
Cape Francois ...	Apr. 18-30	0.63 ,, losing
St. Pierre	May 29—June 5 ...	3.60 ,, ,,
Copenhagen ...	Aug. 19—Sept. 4 ...	0.54 ,, gaining
Brest	Oct. 9-20...	0.04 ,, ,,

The extreme variation of daily rate in the course of the year was less than 6 seconds. MM. Verdun de la Crène, Borda, and Pingré, who took part in the voyage, and were commissioned by the Académie to report on the machine's going, computed that the errors in longitude which would have been committed in fixing that of various ports, on arrival, by means of the machine's going during the preceding six weeks‡ amounted to no more than the following:

Cadiz	1′
Teneriffe	1½′
Goree	¼′
Praya	—
Martinique	1¾′
,, again	½′
Cape Francois	¼′
Iceland	2′
Copenhagen	6′
Dunkirk	1¾′
Brest	1½′

* Together with No. 6, a machine of almost identical construction, it was tested in a twelve months' voyage in the frigate "l'Isis. An account of this voyage was afterwards published under the title of "Voyage fait par ordre du Roi, en 1768 et 1769, pour eprouver en mer les horloges marines inventees par M. Ferdinand Berthoud. Par M. d'Eveux de Fleurieu." Paris, 1773. At this period, it should be noted, Berthoud called his weight-driven machines "Horloges Marines," and his spring-driven ones "Montres de longitude." They were again tested, in the frigate "Flore," in 1771-2. An account of this voyage was published under the title of "Voyage fait par MM. Verdun, Borda et Pingré, . . ." Paris, 2 vols., 1778.

† Quoted from "Les Horloges Marines," by M. Henri Rosat.

‡ Presumably adopted to obtain a basis of comparison with Harrison's No. 4.

See p. 155.

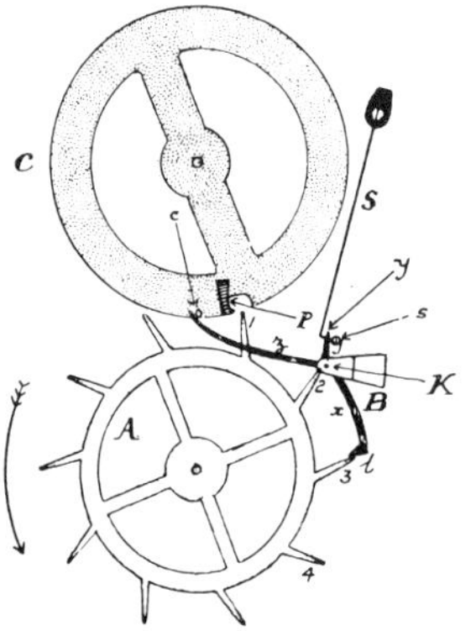

23

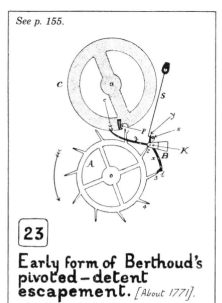

Early form of Berthoud's pivoted-detent escapement. [About 1771].

See p. 155.

24

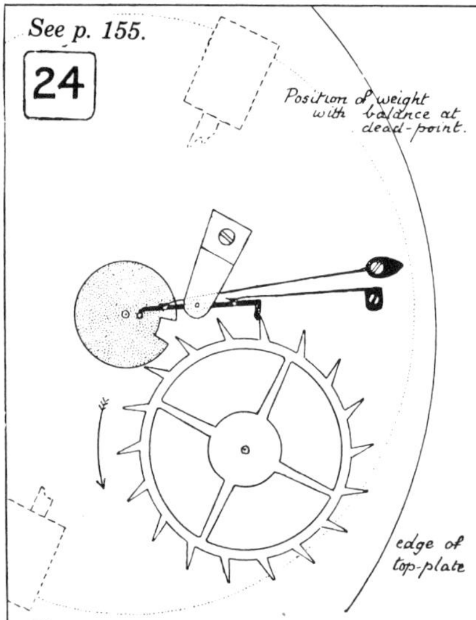

Pivoted-detent escape- -ment of Berthoud's no. 37.

[made about 1785]

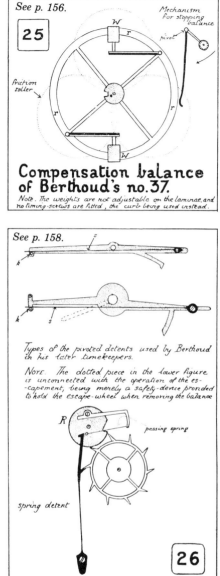

See p. 156.

25

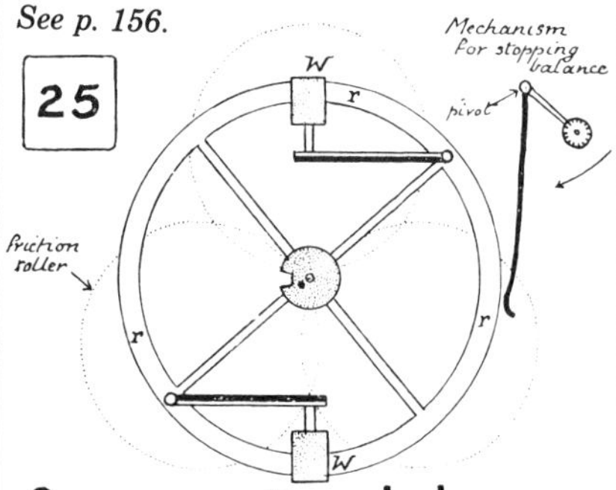

Compensation balance of Berthoud's no. 37.

Note. The weights are not adjustable on the laminae, and no timing-screws are fitted, the curb being used instead.

See p. 158.

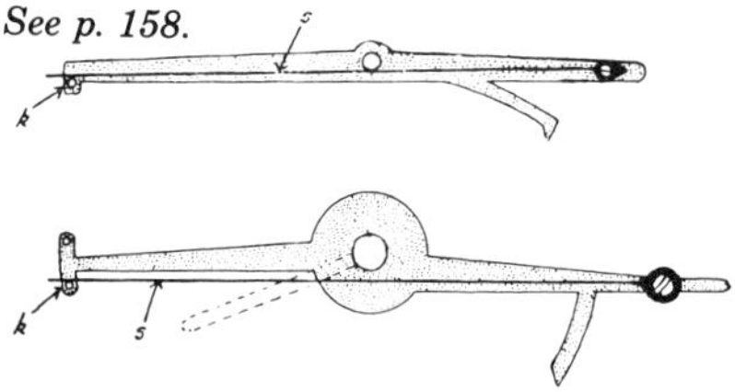

Types of the pivoted detents used by Berthoud in his later timekeepers.

NOTE. The dotted piece in the lower figure is unconnected with the operation of the es- -capement, being merely a safety-device provided to hold the escape-wheel when removing the balance

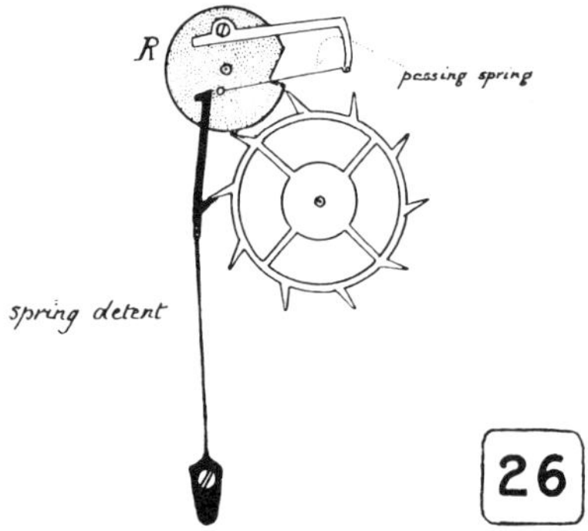

26

Berthoud's spring-detent escapement. [About 1782].

Gradually, however, Berthoud discarded all the features of this machine. The weight-driving was the first to go, and was followed by the cylinder escapement, for which Berthoud substituted a detached escapement of the form shown in Fig. 23. This is the simplest of several early forms devised by Berthoud, all of which show a steady progress towards the modern escapement.*

A is the escape wheel. B is the detent, pivoted at K, and having three projecting arms, *x*, carrying a pallet *l*, termed the "locking pallet"; *y*, engaging with the spring S, which keeps it normally pressed against the stop *s*; and *z*, which extends far enough for its extremity to intersect the path of a pin *c*, termed the "discharging pallet," mounted on the rim of the wheel C, mounted on the balance staff, which also carries the pallet P, termed the "impulse pallet."†

The action of the escapement is as follows. As drawn, tooth 3 of the escape wheel is locked on the locking pallet, and the balance swinging freely in the direction of the arrow. The discharging pallet meets the extremity of the arm *z*, rotates the detent slightly in an anti-clockwise direction, and unlocks tooth 3. Tooth 1 then falls on the impulse pallet, and impels the balance. In the meanwhile, the discharging pallet clears the end of *z*, and the spring S returns the detent to its normal, or "locking," position in time to meet tooth 4, and re-lock the escape wheel. The balance completes its swing, and on its return the discharging pallet again meets the extremity of *z*, but on the opposite side, which is bevelled. Accordingly, it bends it slightly upwards (*z* is made very thin and springy to allow of this), and passes by without disturbing the detent.

It will be seen that this escapement gives the same result as Le Roy's—an impulse in one direction at every complete vibration, the balance being entirely detached except at the moment of unlocking the detent and receiving impulse, the effect of the passing action being practically negligible.

While developing this escapement, also, Berthoud abandoned his gridirons, their place being taken by a compensation curb similar to Harrison's, and subsequently by a compensation balance with bi-metallic rims.

His No. 37 (1785), shown in Plate XXII., may be taken as a good example of his work at this period. It has the pivoted detent escapement and compensation balance shown in Figs. 24 and 25. The escapement is very similar to that described, except that the rather clumsy passing action is improved, the detent being controlled by two

* It would be impossible, within the limits of this chapter, to describe all Berthoud's numerous escapements, and I have accordingly confined myself to a selection of the most important. His earliest form (which Le Roy derided for its complication) was on the same lines as that shown in Fig. 23, but had two pallets, and the impulse was given by an intermediate fork. Berthoud claimed to have devised this as early as 1754. It was succeeded by a less complicated pattern, which dispensed with the fork and one of the pallets, and effected the passing action by means of a pivoted arm, controlled by a spring, mounted on the wheel C. The escapement now described is a simpler version of this second form.

† The terms enumerated in this paragraph are those which are given to the corresponding portions of a modern escapement.

springs instead of one, and the stop omitted, so that during the passing action the locking pallet is free to move slightly towards the centre of the escape wheel; its face being curved to the arc of a circle, the position of the escape wheel is unaltered while this occurs.

The balance has two bi-metallic rims * carrying the "balance weights" *WW*. The action of the rims (the brass being on the outside) causes the weights to approach the balance staff in heat, and to recede from it in cold, thus effecting part, but not all, of the compensation.

The movement, generally speaking, is on normal lines, except that it winds from the top, but it contains two curious and unnecessary devices which are survivals from Berthoud's earlier machines. In addition to the compensation balance, a compensation curb, on Harrison's plan, is fitted, which effects about one-third of the compensation, and the bottom pivot of the balance rests on a flat diamond endstone † and runs between friction wheels, although the upper one has an ordinary brass hole.

No. 37 also contains a very useful device which Berthoud fitted to nearly all of his machines—a means of locking the balance for transport. By moving a small stud on the dial, a thin brass spring is brought into contact with the circular portion *rrr* of the balance, and brings it to rest without the possibility of doing it any injury in the process.

In some of his later machines, Berthoud adopted the modified form of detent shown in Fig. 26,‡ in which the passing action is effected very simply and certainly by means of the small spring *s*, carried upon the detent. This "passing spring" is free to move away from the stop *k* to allow the discharging pallet to pass, but when pressed by it in the opposite direction it bears against the stop, and the detent unlocks.§

---

* Throughout this book, the laminated brass-and-steel strips on which the weights of a compensation balance are mounted are referred to as its "rims," and the member connecting them as the "cross-bar." Where the latter is replaced by several radial arms (as in some of Arnold's balances, and the non-compensated patterns used by the early makers) these are referred to as the "arms" of the balance.

† This is the only jewel in the movement, and even that is unpierced. It is an extraordinary fact, that, although jewelled pivot-holes for watches had been used in England ever since they were invented by Facio in 1703, the process of making them was, even so late as 1785, when this machine was made, practically unknown on the Continent. The first marine timekeeper (non-English) fitted with them appears to be one made by MM. Mole and Mangin, at Geneva, in 1798. Breguet was the first Paris maker to use jewels.

Berthoud affected to decry their usefulness, alleging that they tended to dry the oil and wear the pivots, but his nephew, Louis Berthoud, held sounder views. Some of his holes, which he made with his own hands, are beautiful pieces of work.

‡ See also the very similar patterns employed by Arnold (Fig. 30) and, later, by Louis Berthoud and Motel (Fig. 35).

§ As will be seen later, the passing spring is an integral feature of the modern escapement. I am inclined to ascribe its invention to Arnold, who used it in 1772 (see p. 107).

Berthoud's No. 8. The dial with bezel open.

He also devised the escapement shown in the same figure, which is practically a modern chronometer escapement, except that the passing spring is mounted on the roller R,* and not on the detent. Its action is similar to that of the previous patterns, but here the detent is no longer pivoted, but carried upon a thin spring, forming at the same time a frictionless pivot for the detent and a controller of its movements.

Probably no question in horology has been more hotly debated than the invention of this "spring-detent" escapement. It is, unfortunately, one on which no definite conclusion is possible. Berthoud, Arnold, and Earnshaw all have their warm supporters, but of actual evidence there is little beyond Arnold's patent of 1782, Earnshaw's (Wright's) of the following year and his *ex-parte* statements in his book "Longitude," the conflicting evidence taken by the Board of Longitude in 1804, and the fact that Berthoud published the description of his spring-detent escapement in 1787.† If we possessed as much information relating to the previous work of Arnold and Earnshaw as we have concerning Berthoud's, it would not be difficult to reach a definite conclusion—failing this, the verdict as to the claims of all three must, I think, be "not proven." It is not improbable that they all hit upon the same idea independently. It may at least be said that no one can show a *better* claim to the invention than Berthoud.

By this date he had finally abandoned his friction wheels and compensation curbs, and his machines presented, both in appearance and mechanism, a very close approximation to the chronometer of to-day. In all, he made upwards of seventy timekeepers, of which a considerable number have been preserved.‡

During his lifetime he received the distinctions of F.R.S. Membre de l'Institut, and Membre de la Legion d'Honneur. He died at his house at Groslay, Montmorency, on June 20th, 1807.

His deservedly great fame must rest at least as much upon his writings as upon his mechanisms. In the course of his life he produced three very important works: "Essai sur l'Horlogerie," 1763; "Traité des Horloges Marines," 1773; and "Histoire de la Mesure du Temps,"

---

* In the modern escapement two rollers are used, the "impulse" and "discharging" rollers, on which are respectively mounted the impulse and discharging pallets.

† In his "Supplément au Traité des Horloges Marines."

‡ There are thirteen of his "Horloges Marines" in the Conservatoire des Arts et Métiers: Nos. 1, 2, 3, (4), 6, 8, 9, (11), 20, XXIII., XXVI., XXVI., and XXXII; and six of his "Montres à Longitude": Nos. 1, 2, 3, 4, 7 and 52. "Horloges Marines" No. 16 and No. 65 are in the collection of M. Paul Ditisheim.
It may be noted that five of his timekeepers were lost with La Pérouse, including Nos. 18, 19 (which La Pérouse used as his standard), 25 and 29. La Pérouse also took with him an English pocket chronometer.

in two volumes, 1802.* These are not pamphlets, but bulky quartos, copiously illustrated. The first two, although containing a great deal of valuable information, are difficult reading, but the style and arrangement of the " Histoire " are easy and natural, and, being written towards the close of its author's life, when old animosities had subsided, it is not defaced by the carping criticism and charges of plagiarism, supported by misstatements, which in earlier years he had so liberally directed against his contemporaries, especially Le Roy.

No one can blame Berthoud for putting his own case in the most favourable light, but some of his statements will not stand examination. Thus, he claimed that he had ante-dated Le Roy both in the invention of the detached escapement and in enunciating the law governing the construction of an isochronous balance spring†, instancing in support of his claims an escapement made by him in 1754 and a passage from his " Essai " of 1763. Le Roy's first detached escapement was, as we have seen, presented to the Académie, and its description published in their transactions, in 1748, while the quotation from the " Essai " states only that Berthoud *intends to investigate* the relation between the long and short arcs. These points are typically of Berthoud's controversial methods, but the whole question of Le Roy's priority can, I think, be definitely settled by consideration of these facts—namely, that at the time when he constructed his marine timekeeper, fitted with detached escapement, isochronised balance spring, and compensation balance, and even when he published his account of it, four years later, Berthoud's faith was still firmly pinned to his weight-driven machines with cylinder escapement‡, and gridiron compensation—and that the latter soon afterwards abandoned this mechanism in favour of that used by his rival.

Still, one very valuable quality Berthoud undoubtedly possessed in far greater measure than Le Roy—that of dissatisfaction with his work and a keen desire to improve it as far as possible. In all his multitudinous timekeepers, a steady progress can be traced from start to finish, and while there is not one of them which can rival, as an original production, Le Roy's marine watch, they form collectively a series which, as the work of a single maker, is absolutely unique—ranging, as it does through several transition stages, from machines as crude as Harrison's earliest to a final development differing very little from the chronometer of to-day.

* Also several other works, including :—
" L'Art de conduire et de regler les pendules et les montres." Paris, 1760.
" Eclaircissements sur l'invention des nouvelles machines . . . pour la determination des longitudes . . ." Paris, 1773.
" De la mesure de Temps." (Supplement to the " Traité des Horloges Marines," 1773.
" La mesure de temps appliqué à la navigation." 1782.
" Les Longitudes par la mesure de temps." 1787.

† He attempted to obtain isochronism by tapering his balance springs.

‡ At p. 577 of his " Traité des Horloges Marines," published in 1773, Berthoud gives it as his considered opinion that he prefers his ruby cylinders to any form of detached escapement.

Plate XXVI. BERTHOUD'S No. 37.

The inscription on the dial runs: "horl. Marine N 37, PAR Ferdinand Berthoud." The dials are arranged thus: minutes / seconds hours. The small stud on the left of the minute dial is used for stopping the balance, and diametrically opposite to it is a sliding brass disc covering a keyhole in the glass.

The larger of the two keys is the original one, and is elaborately ornamented. The smaller is a recent addition, used to adjust the compensation curb.

See p. 155.

LOUIS BERTHOUD.

Berthoud's work is sometimes confused with that of his nephew, Louis Berthoud (1750-1813), who was also a celebrated chronometer maker. The latter adopted his uncle's final pattern, except that he adhered resolutely to the pivoted detent escapement. Occasionally, too, he reverted to the plan of mounting the lower end of the balance staff between friction rollers, and he also experimented with chronometers having very quick trains—amongst several specimens of his work which I recently examined was a box chronometer beating three to the second*. The finish of his work is very high, and his machines generally seem to have performed extremely accurately. Humboldt carried a chronometer of his make, No. 27, all through his great South American journey, and speaks very highly of it†.

In 1799 Louis Berthoud carried off a prize offered by the Institut for a chronometer showing decimal (or "Republican") time, and he was subsequently awarded an annual subvention of 10,000 frs. by Buonaparte, on condition that he instructed five pupils in the art of chronometer making. He died not long after his uncle, in 1813, leaving two sons whom he had brought up to follow his profession.

Postscript.

Intimately connected with the history of both the Berthouds is the prolonged and ill-fated attempt made by the Spanish government to establish a State manufactory of chronometers. Considerable encouragement was given by them both to John Arnold and Ferdinand Berthoud,‡ and as the result of representations made by the latter it was decided to select and send to Paris some young workman of proved ability, as apprentice to Berthoud, in order that he might acquire sufficient skill to enable him not only to repair the chronometers purchased for the Spanish Navy, but also to construct such as might be required in future, and to instruct a number of apprentices, thus rendering Spain entirely independent of foreign chronometer makers.

The choice of the Spanish government fell upon Cayetano Sanchez, a candidate strongly recommended by the Count of Florida Blanca,

---

* Until about the middle of last century, French box chronometers as a class were generally fitted with quicker trains than English ones, in which the 14,400 train (a train making 14,400 beats per hour, and therefore advancing every half-second) has been the standard ever since Arnold's time.

English chronometers with unusual trains are, however, occasionally met with. The Earnshaw shown in Plate XXXIII, beats 130 to the minute, and I have seen a letter from Capt. Wharton (afterwards Hydrographer) to the Admiralty, in which he complains strongly of the inconvenience caused him by a similar machine. One of the box chronometers used by Airy in the abortive Dolcoath experiments, for determining the earth's density, beat 160 to the minute—8 times in 3 seconds. It was made, I believe, by Frodsham.

† I am indebted to Mr. A. Hamilton Rice for calling my attention to this point in the course of an article published in the R.G.S. Journal for November, 1921.

‡ They purchased from Berthoud his chronometers Nos. 7-16 inclusive, and from Arnold his Nos. 3, 5, 6, 56, and 89.

who entered Berthoud's workshop in May, 1789. He appears to have made the most of his time, for in December of that year his master reported that he had made astonishing progress. A year later Berthoud informed the Spanish government that Sanchez was completely instructed, both in the actual making of chronometers and in the use of the instruments necessary for testing them, and that he had completed a pocket and a box chronometer.*

Sanchez was permitted by his government to remain for a further period at Paris in order to acquaint himself with the work of Louis Berthoud and other makers, and also to spend some time in London, where he took service under Emery† in order to study the work of the English chronometer makers.

Sanchez returned to Spain in March, 1793, and was directed to proceed to the Royal Observatory of San Fernando‡, in order to take over the superintendence of the government chronometers. He performed his duties with great ability, and was granted, in 1798, the dignity of honorary clockmaker to the King.

But in 1800 the plague attacked San Fernando, and amongst its victims were Sanchez, " chronometrista de la marina," and his assistant Eugenio Cruzado.

Meanwhile, another blow was dealt to the fortunes of the enterprise. Antonio Molina, a schoolmate of Sanchez, had been sent by the government to London in 1792, in order to learn the art of jewelling, which was then regarded in England as a valuable trade secret. However, an English maker was found (by Don Jose de Mendoza) willing, provided that his pupil did not establish himself in England, and for the further consideration of a hundred guineas, to betray his fellow workmen, and to impart the process which he had sworn never to divulge. Molina acquired in this manner the art of jewelling, and returned to Spain in 1795. While on a mission to Paris, however, in connection with the purchase of jewels on behalf of the Observatory, he died there in 1798.

Molina was succeeded by Carlos La Rue, but the ill luck of the enterprise still pursued him, and he died in 1800, a victim of the same epidemic which carried off Sanchez and Cruzado.

The moving spirit of the whole undertaking was Admiral Mazarredo, one of that small and select number of scientific and indefatigable seamen which counts in its ranks the names of Beaufort in England, Mouchez in France, and Maury in America. Equal to any of this band in courage and perseverance, Mazarredo refused to accept as final the several reverses which his project had suffered, and after engaging, and subsequently dismissing, Bernadino Coromina, " whose

* Berthoud was paid 20,000 frs. by the Spanish government in recognition of his services in instructing Sanchez.

† Emery received a bonus of £200 for instructing Sanchez, together with an undertaking that the latter would not set up a competitive manufactory in France.

‡ This observatory corresponds to that of Greenwich in this country.

LOUIS BERTHAUD. THE MOVEMENT OF NO.49
4¾in. square. circa 1805. 24 hour movement with pivoted detent. Conical balance spring, in silver engine-turned case in mahogany box.

LOUIS BARTHOUD.
The dial of No. 49. A Marine Chronometer now in the British Museum.

results did not correspond to the height of his pretensions," he procured the appointment of two apprentices, Agustin Albino and Blas Munoz, to study under Louis Berthoud. The proposal to train them came in the first instance from Berthoud himself*, and he offered to house and instruct them for four years for the sum of 20,000 francs.

His offer was accepted, and Munoz was sent to Paris (Albino was already studying clockmaking there when selected by the Spanish government) in 1801. They did not altogether hit it off with their master, who had several times to make official reports of Albino's idleness and dissipated habits, while his pupils in their turn complained to the Spanish ambassador that Berthoud neglected their instruction, and did not comply with the schedule laid down in his contract. At one time it appeared possible that the apprentices would be transferred from Berthoud to his rival Breguet. But the disputes were adjusted, and Berthoud was able to report in January, 1805, that Albino and Munoz had completed their training, while asking that they might be permitted to remain in Paris long enough to complete the chronometers on which they were engaged, and to construct two others and two astronomical clocks. During this later period Albino and Munoz also visited the workshops of Breguet and other leading makers.

In September, 1806, they returned to Spain, and were appointed to the Observatory of San Fernando, with the distinction of clockmakers to his Majesty, and a salary of 12,000 reales each.

But evil times were in store for the Spanish navy. The struggles of the Peninsula War left Spain with a depleted revenue, and the first point upon which, the economists of the period seized was, as ever, that least understood, and, as a consequence, least valued, by the Spanish public—the upkeep of that fleet which, since Trafalgar, had been allowed to rot behind the fortifications of Carthagena and Ferrol. Albino and Munoz found themselves not actually dismissed, but unable to obtain payment of their salaries, while, as if to add fuel to the fires of economy, they entered into an acrimonious dispute as to their respective merits. An enquiry was accordingly instituted as to their several pretensions†, but it led to no definite result, except that of still further delaying the payment of any sums due to them.

Albino died in 1813, as the result of a similar epidemic to that which had carried off Sanchez, and Munoz (who, greatly to his credit,

* In the course of a long memorial detailing his proposed scheme of instruction, dated November 17th, 1800.

† The results of the enquiry showed that Albino had constructed a regulator with Ellicott's compensation pendulum (in which a lever carrying the bob is actuated by the differential expansion of a brass and a steel rod—now abandoned on account of its jerky action), another after a design by Berthoud, and several chronometers, in addition to completely reconstructing F. Berthoud's No. 10, and training two apprentices: while Munoz had constructed a regulator and three chronometers, reconstructed L. Berthoud's No. 13, and instructed one apprentice. Albino actually trained four apprentices—Jose Maria Asino, Santiago Dufour, Benito de Lerua, and Jose Ocon, the last of whom continued his training under Munoz after Albino's death.

had refused a tempting offer from the Czar of Russia to transfer his activities to Petrograd), in 1823. He was succeeded by Antonio Bonfante, who had been apprenticed to him in 1808; but by this time the authorities of the Observatory had formed the conclusion that little good was to be expected from chronometer makers supported entirely by the State (and thus lacking the stimulus of commercial rivalry), and that it was in all respects preferable to obtain chronometers from English or French makers*, while retaining at the Observatory a workman capable of repairing them. As the result of a very adverse report made by Julian Canelas, Director of the Observatory in 1821, and acted upon, *more Hispanico,* by the government under the ægis of his successor, Jose Sanchez Cerquero, the manufacture of chronometers at the Observatory was discontinued as from February 20th, 1826, although Bonfante was retained as chronometer repairer, and was succeeded in turn by Jose Diaz Munio, Francisco de Paula Aguete, Jose Diaz Columbres, and, as the result of an arduous contest, by Joaquin Torres on August 4th, 1877†.

It should be added that in consequence of a Royal order dated May 17th, 1829, the obsolete chronometers then in the possession of the Spanish government, comprising examples of the work of Ferdinand and Louis Berthoud, John Arnold, Albino and Munoz, were disposed of as of no value. Fortunately, however, Berthoud (F.) No. 39 and Arnold's Nos. 5 and 89 were retained in the Naval Museum.

NOTE.—The foregoing account of the Spanish chronometer makers is chiefly based upon Capt. Duro's very interesting and valuable "Disquisiciones Nauticas," Vol. IV.

---

* In 1864, as the result of a competitive trial, there were purchased 38 chronometers made by J. E. de Losada (a Spanish maker resident in London, where he acquired a considerable reputation), 29 by Johannsen, and 13 by Dent.

† The terms of this contest are interesting. The competitors, who consisted, in addition to Torres, of Fritz Stebler, Carlos Sievert, and Ramon Antonio Iglesias, were required, in addition to giving descriptive drawings of their chronometers, and schemes for electrically synchronising a number of clocks from a central regulator, to deposit for trial a chronometer in good going order, and to replace in it, when called upon, the escapement, balance, maintaining gear and fusee by duplicate pieces, the machine's rates before and after this substitution being compared.

THE ESCAPEMENT ASSEMBLY OF A MARINE CHROMOMETER BY LEGO A L'ORIENT. Pivoted detent escapement with remontoire. Note the pierced escape wheel designed to retain oil. Courtesy British Museum.

Painted by R. Davy

MR. JOHN ARNOLD.

Engraved by S. E. Reid.

To the Society for the Encouragement of Arts, Manufactures and Commerce
this Plate is most respectfully inscribed by their most Obd.t humble Servant
Susan Esther Reid

Plate XXVII. JOHN ARNOLD.

From a mezzotint in the possession of Messrs. Charles Frodsham.

See p. 169.

CHAPTER VII.

JOHN ARNOLD.

We now come to the two men who developed the manufacture of the chronometer in England on a comparatively large scale, and brought it into widespread use. Their forerunners, as we have seen, did all, or nearly all, their work with their own hands, and were accordingly prevented from turning out more than a strictly limited number of machines. Harrison's later timekeepers—Nos. 4 and 5—took three years each to make: Kendal took the same time over his copy of No. 4, and two years apiece for K2 and K3. Mudge required three years for his first machine, and two years for the simultaneous construction of "Blue" and "Green": and although Berthoud made upwards of seventy machines in forty years, he was unable, even when he had developed a more or less standard model, to produce them at the rate of more than two or three per annum*.

On the other hand, both Arnold and Earnshaw were able to produce, in the same period, upwards of a thousand chronometers of satisfactory performance, and to sell them at prices far below those charged by any of the makers previously mentioned. The importance of the service thus rendered to navigation and commerce is difficult to over-estimate.

Such enormously increased production was, of course, only rendered possible by division of labour. Both Arnold and Earnshaw first developed, by their own efforts, a simple and commercially practicable design of timekeeper, and then employed other workmen to do such subsidiary work as the making of the plates, wheels, dial, etc., and also, after tuition, the more complicated portions such as the escapement and balance, while invariably reserving to themselves the final springing and adjusting (which were regarded as valuable trade secrets).

It should be added that they were no better friends than Le Roy and Berthoud, and that they jealously disputed the originality of each other's improvements in the escapement and balance.

John Arnold was born in 1736, at Bodmin, Cornwall. His father was a watchmaker of that town, and brought the boy up as his apprentice, but after a family quarrel the latter broke his indentures by the simple plan of running away from home. He made his way to Holland,

* Louis Berthoud worked somewhat faster. He produced about 150 machines in 27 years.

where he picked up a further knowledge of the watchmaking trade, and also learnt German.

He returned to England about 1755, and was for some time in very poor circumstances, working as a gunsmith and itinerant mechanic. Subsequently, however, he made the acquaintance of a Mr. McGuire, who lent him sufficient capital to start business as a watchmaker in London, at Devereux Court, Strand. There he prospered, and at once proved himself both a skilful and ingenious workman and a clever man of business. An audience of King George III., coupled with his knowledge of German, enabled him to push his fortunes by obtaining a considerable amount of court favour.

His ability as a mechanic was soon demonstrated in a very striking manner. In 1764, he requested His Majesty's leave to present to him a remarkable watch, no larger than a silver twopenny-piece, set in the bezel of a ring.* In spite of its absurdly small size, it was a half-quarter repeater,† and kept good time. Finger ring watches of ordinary pattern were not unknown in Arnold's day, and before it, while even smaller watches have been made since‡, but a *repeater* of such minute proportions was regarded, at the time, as a thing almost unheard-of.§ Even to-day it would not be easy to construct a duplicate.¶

Soon after completing this *tour de force*, Arnold began to experiment with a view to constructing a marine timekeeper. His first machine of this kind was completed in 1770, and in the Board of Longitude's minutes for May 26th of that year appears the following entry:—

> " . . . Mr. Arnold, a Watchmaker in Pall Mall, attended with a Timekeeper of a new construction, which he showed to the Board and strongly recommended.|| He was told that if he would construct one of the same kind** it should be tried."

---

* Its diameter was about half an inch, and its weight 5 dwt. 7¼ grs. It had a cylinder escapement, the cylinder, of ruby, being $\frac{1}{54}$ in. in diameter, and weighing $\frac{1}{200}$ of a grain.

† *i.e.*, it repeated the hour and quarter, followed by one blow if the succeeding quarter were more than half elapsed.

‡ A pocket chronometer the size of a shilling was exhibited by its maker, Mr. John McLennan, in the Exhibition of 1862. A watch constructed by M. Paul Ditisheim for the Paris Exhibition of 1900 is probably the smallest ever made. The diameter of the movement is .26 of an inch.

§ Guido Ubaldi della Rovere, Duke of Urbino, is credited with having possessed, in 1542, a repeating watch set in a finger-ring.

¶ Arnold declined an offer of 1,000 guineas, from the Czar, for a similar watch, stating that he wished King George's (for which he received half that sum) to remain unique. In view of this fact, it is curious that a very similar watch, made at about the same time, is preserved in the British Museum. King George's watch is now in the collection of the late Mr. James W. Usher, which was bequeathed by him, together with his other collections, to the Corporation of Lincoln.

|| This statement is highly characteristic of Arnold.

** The timekeeper made by Arnold in accordance with this decision was purchased by the Board and issued to Admiral Sir Robert Harland, who also bought the machine originally exhibited to the Board.

Plate XXVIII. ARNOLD'S No. 3.

As explained on p. **173** this is one of Arnold's earliest productions, and accompanied Captain Cook during his second voyage round the world.

Royal Society.

THE MOVEMENT OF JOHN ARNOLDS POCKET CHRONOMETER NO. 3.
The earliest serving pocket chronometer by Arnold with his pivoted detent escapement.
Modified by the addition of John Arnolds 'SS' balance probably before 1782.

Accordingly, Arnold constructed a second, which (after a satisfactory trial at Greenwich) he exhibited to the Board in November, 1771, stating at the same time that its cost was only about sixty guineas. The Board advanced him £200, and in the following March a further £100, these sums to be deducted from the cost of any timekeepers which they might subsequently purchase from him.*

Arnold was very anxious to have his new timekeepers tried against Kendall's K1 in the " Resolution " and " Adventure" which were then fitting out for their Antarctic voyage. Accordingly, he made two more, designated Nos. 2 and 3.† All were upon the same plan, differing only in minor details. Nos. 2 and 3 are now the property of the Royal Society, and through the courtesy of that body I am enabled to give some details of their mechanism, and also a photograph of No. 3 (Plate XXIV.).

The arrangements for compensation are strongly reminiscent of Harrison's work. A plain steel balance is employed, and a spiral steel balance-spring, whose effective length is controlled by a compensation curb composed of two strips of brass and steel soldered together. The curb pins are mounted at one end of a pivoted lever, whose opposite end engages with the free end of the curb. A projection on this lever also carries a cycloid pin, but this is arranged in a different manner from Harrison's, since it is further from the stud than the curb pins are, and touches the outside of the outermost coil of the balance spring when the latter is uncoiling. From this it may be inferred that the balance spring was slow in the long arcs.

The escapement, which is shown in Fig. 27, is a detached one, of peculiar design. The escape wheel has two sets of teeth, those for giving impulse being flat, while those for locking were a series of short steel pins standing up at right-angles to the rim of the wheel. These locked in turn upon a pallet of black flint carried at one end of a pivoted detent, mounted diametrically across the wheel. At the opposite end of the detent was mounted a small passing-spring, extending into the path of a small steel inclined plane set obliquely on the balance staff.

The action of this escapement is as follows:—Prior to impulse being given, the inclined plane, being carried round with the balance, bears down on the passing-spring and raises the locking pallet clear of one of the pins on the escape wheel. The latter turns, and one of the impulse teeth falls on the impulse pallet, and impels the balance. The plane then clears the passing-spring, and the detent returns to its place in time to meet and arrest the next locking tooth.

On the return swing, the opposite side of the inclined plane meets and raises the passing-spring (without disturbing the detent).

* Up to 19th July, 1783, the Board's accounts show that Arnold had supplied them with chronometers valued at £378.

† Arnold's numbering of his machines is somewhat chaotic. There is a " No. 1 " of obviously much later date in the Guildhall, while a No. 3, which cannot have been that now in the possession of the Royal Society, was purchased from him by the Spanish government. He stated to the Committee on Mudge's petition (1793) that he had twenty No. 1's, which may imply that he used several series of numbers.

In No. 2, whose escapement is shown in the figure, the escape wheel has 10 locking teeth and a corresponding number for giving impulse, the latter having cycloidal faces. The detent is returned to its place by a small straight spring. In No. 3, which may be regarded as an improved pattern, there are twelve teeth of each kind, and those giving impulse are of the ordinary pointed type. No spring is used for the detent, which is returned to the locking position by a second (inclined) pallet acted upon by the tooth diametrically opposite to the released one. In both patterns, the detent is prevented from unlocking accidently by means of a small roller mounted on it underneath the passing-spring, and normally kept just clear of the surface of a disc carried by the balance staff. This disc is cut away at one point to allow of the unlocking.*

This escapement, although a great advance on those used by Harrison or Kendal, is open to the objection that the surfaces of the inclined plane, which have an oblique wedging action upon the passing-spring, require to be oiled, and that any thickening either of this oil or of that at the pivots of the detent may cause sufficient friction to impede the motion of the balance seriously. Arnold abandoned it soon afterwards in favour of that shown in Fig. 30.

The remainder of the mechanism needs little description. The mainspring, fusee, train, etc., were of ordinary pattern. The maintaining gear, however, was an adaption of the epicyclic pattern often found in turret clocks.† Both machines go for about thirty hours, No. 2 beating 94 to the minute and No. 3 112.

A remarkable feature of the machines is that they have no inner cases, the naked movement being simply dropped into a recess in the box and kept down by the lid. To allow of winding, a hole, normally covered by a sliding shutter, is cut in the bottom of the box. Arnold continued to adhere to this clumsy plan until about 1795, when he adopted the ordinary brass case suspended in gimbals.‡ Prior to his doing so, at least two instances had been brought to his notice of timekeepers of his make having been deranged through *spiders* making their way into the movement via the winding hole.

No. 3 was sent aboard Cook's ship, the "Resolution," which also carried Kendall's K1, while Nos. 1 and 2 were entrusted to Furneaux,

* This safety gear misled the late Mr. J. U. Poole, who cleaned these chronometers in 1890, into stating that the escapements were a compound of the lever and the spring detent.

† The fusee rides loose on its arbor, which carries a fixed pinion engaging with an intermediate epicyclic wheel (provided with a ratchet and click) mounted on a stud set in the end of the fusee. This intermediate wheel also engages with a ring of internal teeth on the great wheel. Except when winding, the click on the intermediate wheel is engaged, and the whole arrangement revolves as one piece. When winding, the great wheel becomes a fulcrum, and sufficient power is thus transmitted to it to keep the train in motion. This arrangement is much simpler than Harrison's maintaining power, but it is liable to jam, and the winding takes longer.

‡ Gimbals were used in one of his earliest box chronometers—that carried by Phipps in his North Polar Expedition of 1773. Its performance was not good, and this may have prejudiced Arnold against the use of gimbals.

See p. 173

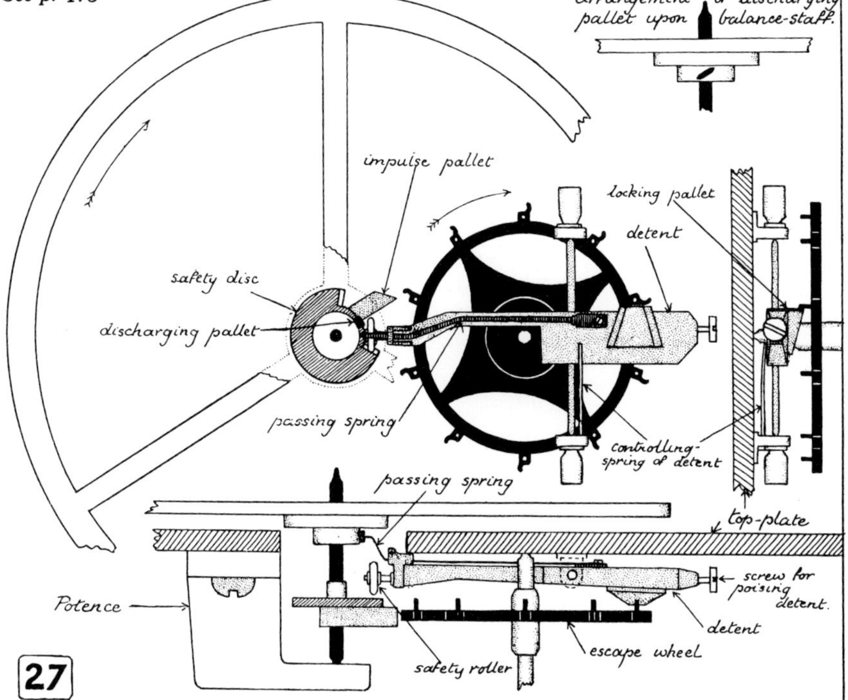

27

Arnold's first pivoted-detent escapement.

Drawn from his no. 2 [1772], in the possession of the Royal Society.

See p. 177

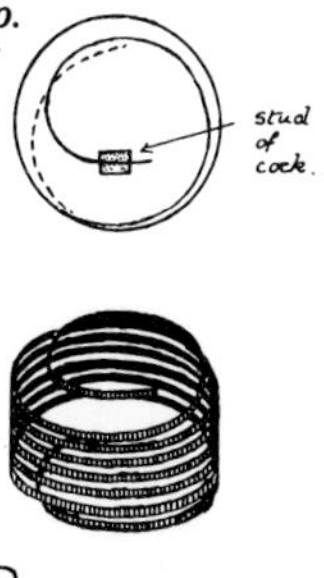

28

Arnold's helical balance-spring. [Drawn from that of his no. 24.]

See p. 177

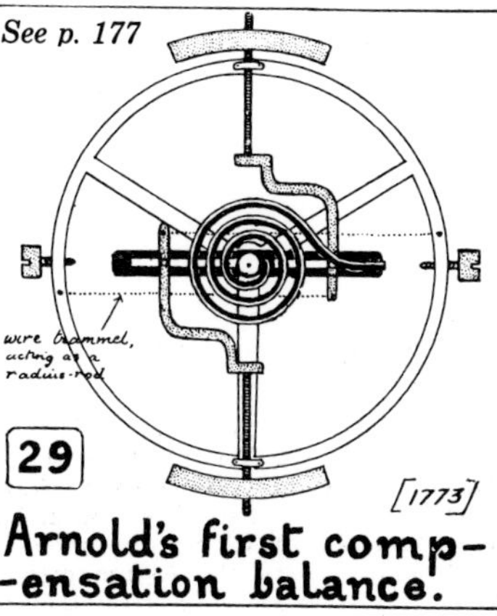

29

Arnold's first compensation balance.

See p. 177

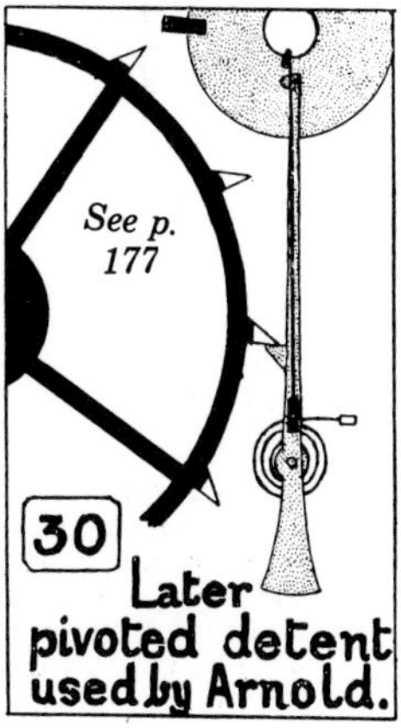

30

Later pivoted detent used by Arnold.

Cook's consort, in the "Adventure." All four machines were kept in locked boxes, which could only be opened with three conjoint keys, entrusted to the vessel's captain, first lieutenant, and astronomer respectively.

While K1, as we have seen, went magnificently, the performance of the Arnold chronometers was extremely bad. No. 2 began to go very wildly soon after leaving Plymouth, and stopped altogether before the "Adventure" reached the Cape of Good Hope. Its companion, No. 1, also stopped at the Cape owing to rough handling while being taken ashore. After being restarted, it continued to go throughout the voyage, but its fluctuations of rate were enormous. As for No. 3, Cook dryly remarks, in a passage omitted from the published version of his journal—

> " . . . little can be said in favour of the one of Mr. Arnold's on board of us, . . ."

Later, he says, on June 8th, 1773 (page 131, Vol. I.),

> "To-day, when we came to wind up the watches, the fusee of Mr. Arnold's would not turn round, so that, after several trials, we were obliged to let it go down."

after which comes another suppressed passage,

> " . . . this is the second of this gentleman's watches that have failed: one of those on board of the 'Adventure' stopped at the Cape of Good Hope, and has not gone since, but the other bids fair to answer well."

By an unfortunate coincidence, the box of No. 3 had to be forced open about a fortnight before it stopped, owing to a wrong key having been used to lock it the previous day. This was not, however, the cause of the stoppage,* which was obviously due to the maintaining gear having jammed.

The erratic going of all three machines was apparently due to defective compensation. Thus, in three periods about three months apart, the extreme rates of No. 3 were as follows:—

Average temperature.	Daily rate.
73° Fahr.	57 sec. losing
63° ,,	14½ ,, ,,
56° ,,	101 ,, gaining

Since the mean values of its rate at various temperatures approximate to those of an uncompensated watch, it is probable that the

* George Forster, a German, who, with his father, accompanied Cook as naturalist, and subsequently, after the manner of his kind, forestalled the latter by publishing (in violation of his father's pledge to the Admiralty) an account of the voyage, mentioned this stoppage in his book, and, having quarrelled with Cook (and, indeed, with practically all of his shipmates) naturally represented it as due to ill-usage. William Wales, the Astronomer of the "Resolution," who was responsible for forcing the lock, took up the cudgels for Cook, who was then (1777) absent on his last voyage, and replied to Forster's malicious inuendoes in an indignant pamphlet. When dealing with this particular incident, he pointed out the true facts of the case, and mentioned that he had met Arnold since Forster's book was published, and that Arnold had accepted his explanation, but stated that he would complain of Cook to the Board. This, however, he did not do.

lever carrying the curb pins had jammed in some manner. It may be noted that Arnold used a balance spring, balance, and compensation curb of much the same size as Harrison's.

In view of the failure of these machines, the Board refused to give him any further assistance "until they have better proof of the merits of the watches they have had of him, or are satisfied that he has made some very considerable improvement." Being thus put on his mettle, Arnold set to work to better his timekeepers, and soon evolved several noticeable improvements, which he patented.*

In 1776 he protected in this manner the helical (or cylindrical) spring† and compensation balance shown in Figs. 28 and 29. The balance, in which two weights are shifted towards or from the centre by the action of a spiral brass-and-steel curb at its centre, is the first attempt to follow up Le Roy's suggestion, published in 1770. At the same time Arnold discarded his original escapement, and adopted the form of pivoted detent with passing spring shown in Fig. 30.

Before long, the efficacy of these improvements was clearly demonstrated. As if conscious of his powers, and seeking for fresh difficulties to conquer, Arnold proceeded to make a number of *pocket* chronometers‡ fitted with his new spring, balance, and pivoted-detent escapement. It may not be superfluous to explain that any pocket chronometer labours under a number of disadvantages from which a box chronometer is free. The latter is kept always horizontal and comparatively free from shocks or rapid twisting, while the pocket chronometer is sometimes horizontal, sometimes inclined, sometimes vertical, and exposed to more violent changes of temperature and much rougher handling. Accordingly the going of a watch, No. 36, which Arnold sent to Greenwich for trial in March, 1779, produced, when published the following year §, a great and well-merited sensation.

It was officially¶ tried for a period of thirteen months, being constantly worn in the pocket, and during that time its total error, after

---

* Nos. 1113 of 1776, and 1328 of 1782. As was the custom of the time, the terms of the specifications were very vague (those of the 1782 patent especially so) and if contested they would probably have afforded Arnold little protection. On the other hand, they undoubtedly operated to his detriment with the Board. By 1792 the latter had laid down the invariable rule that they would give no assistance to any inventor who secured his inventions by a patent.

† The helical spring was not really patentable. It had previously been used by Hook in 1664, and (in tension) by Hautefeuille and Harrison. Emery, also, stated in his evidence to the Committee on Mudge's petition that he had read of a watch fitted with a helical balance spring a year or two before Arnold took out his patent for it.

‡ One of the first of these was that carried by Phipps in his polar expedition (1773). It proved a better timekeeper than either of the box chronometers (one by Kendall and the other by Arnold) which he carried with him. In fairness to Arnold, however, it should be pointed out that the box chronometer of his make was returned from the voyage in a very rusty condition.

§ "An Account kept during Thirteen Months in the Royal Observatory at Greenwich, of the Going of a Pocket Chronometer made on a New Construction by John Arnold, having his new-invented Ballance Spring and a Compensation for the *Effects* of Heat and Cold in the Ballance." London, 1780.

¶ An unofficial continuation of the trial for a further five months was added by Arnold when the register of No. 36's going was reprinted in his "Certificates and Circumstances."

John Arnold & Son No. 26
CAE / 1952

JOHN ARNOLD AND SON MARINE CHRONOMETER NO. 26.
Similar in appearance and construction to No. 32/122. See Plate XXIX — Gould.

A CHIMING CLOCK MOVEMENT BY SMITH CLOCKS LTD. OF CRICKLEWOOD. 'Floating balance'. Arnolds patent for a helical balance string was granted in 1775. The idea was that the helical spring would partially support the weight of the balance thus reducing friction on its pivots. Here the idea is taken to its ultimate development in a mass produced clock of the 1950s.

applying a mean rate taken from its going in the first month of the trial, was only 2 m. 33.2 sec., while its daily rate never varied more than 3 sec. on two consecutive days. Its going in positions was as follows :—

Position.	Daily Rate.
Vertical, XII up	0.35 sec. gaining
,, III up	0.35 ,, losing
,, VI up	3.85 ,, ,,
,, IX up	0.29 ,, ,,
Horizontal, dial up	1.72 ,, ,,
,, ,, down	2.83 ,, ,,

Arnold's account of this watch's going was attacked by an anonymous writer,* who seems to have been a disciple of Hutchinson. His chief criticism is directed against an account, written by Mayer, of the going of an astronomical clock by Arnold (which certainly is somewhat high-flown and bombastic, as were Arnold's own writings), but he also decries the latter's education, ability, and mechanical improvements, of which last he claims to have had considerable practical experience. He falls particularly foul of the method of employing a mean rate as a criterion of No. 36's going, alleging that such a plan begs the whole question, and is much too favourable to the machine. Arnold replied unsparingly in the following year, and, after demolishing his opponent's arguments, concluded with a tag from Pope—" I wage no war with Bedlam."

In the same year, he obtained a second patent, comprising, though not at all definitely, the escapement shown in Fig. 31, and, more explicitly, three new forms of compensation balance, and the application of incurved ends to a cylindrical balance spring. Of the latter improvement, which is discussed in Chapter 10, it is sufficient to note here that such ends have a very great influence on the isochronism of the balance. Arnold appears to have abandoned the use of the spiral balance spring about 1773, giving as his opinion of it, that " it is never a spiral, but when it is at rest."

The escapement is very similar in its action to those of Berthoud, and that introduced at about the same time by Earnshaw, which is universally employed to-day. It is a simplified form of Arnold's original escapement, as fitted to the chronometers used by Cook and Furneaux. The teeth of the escape wheel stand up above the plane of the escape wheel, and are locked in turn upon a ruby pallet on the detent, which is not pivoted, but attached to the top plate by a thin spring. This spring acts both as a pivot and as a controlling spring, returning the detent to the locking position after displacement.

* " On the Longitude : in a letter to the Commissioners of that Board . . ." London, 1781.

This pamphlet is extremely rare. There is no copy in the British Museum or the Bodleian. The only example I have ever seen is in the Vulliamy collection. It contains a clue to the anonymous author, who appears, from a pencil note upon the title page, to have been " The Rev. — Smith." He was therefore, in all probability, the Rev. William Smith, who, while in Jamaica, had originally bespoken No. 36. Arnold refused to deliver it on completion, as Smith's mother, acting for her son, proposed that the watch, before payment, should be tested by a local *wheelwright.* It was eventually purchased by Governor Johnstone, of Jamaica, for 120 guineas.

A small passing spring, similar in its action to that previously described, is mounted at the free end of the detent.

On the balance staff are mounted the impulse and discharging rollers and their pallets, both of which, in the original patterns, were of ruby.

The action of this escapement is similar to that of the earlier form. The escape wheel is unlocked by the discharging pallet pressing inwards on the passing spring, and impulse is immediately given by the tooth of the released wheel upon the impulse pallet. The detent then returns under the influence of its spring in time to lock the next tooth.

The teeth of the escape wheel are of epicycloidal* shape—not, apparently, in any attempt to diminish friction between the tooth and the pallet, but to ensure that during the whole period of impulse the effective radius of the escape wheel should be exactly the same. This escapement was used by Arnold in all his subsequent chronometers, and by his son for many years after his father's death. But, although a perfectly workable arrangement†, it proved inferior to the escapement introduced at about the same time by Earnshaw, which is now in general use.

Arnold's last balance is shown in Fig. 32. It is much simpler than his earlier ones, consisting of a steel cross-bar carrying two rims formed of brass and steel strips soldered together. Its action is similar to that of Berthoud's balance described on p. 98. The weights can be screwed towards or away from the roots of the arms to alter the amount of the compensation, all but a few threads at the centre of the weight being turned off to allow of using a curved bolt, instead of a straight one. The latter would cause the moment of inertia of the balance to alter on any movement of the weights. The circle carrying three small weights was a later addition used by the younger Arnold in pocket chronometers, to allow of adjustment for position. The screws S,S are the "timing screws," which are screwed in or out to regulate the going of the chronometer by altering the moment of inertia of the balance.

While bringing his design to this point, Arnold had been producing chronometers in considerable numbers. He established a manufactory of them at Chigwell, in Essex‡, and in 1785 quitted Devereux Court for 112, Cornhill.

---

* An epicycloid is the curve described by a point on the circumference of a circle rolling upon that of another circle. The great majority of the wheels used in clocks and watches—and, indeed, in all wheel gearing—have teeth of epicycloidal section.

† It is curious to note that there is at least one watch known to have been made by Earnshaw with Arnold's escapement, and with the hall-mark of 1798 (*i.e.*, a year before Arnold's death). See the "Horological Journal" of January, 1898.

I have a pocket chronometer by J. R. Arnold, with the hall-mark of 1810, fitted with this escapement. It is still an excellent timekeeper.

‡ This factory is not now in existence. It seems to have been discontinued shortly after J. R. Arnold's death in 1843. Two of his workmen, John and Roger Glover, were still living in 1885, and a chronometer by John Glover took the seventh place in the Greenwich trial of that year.

See p.180.

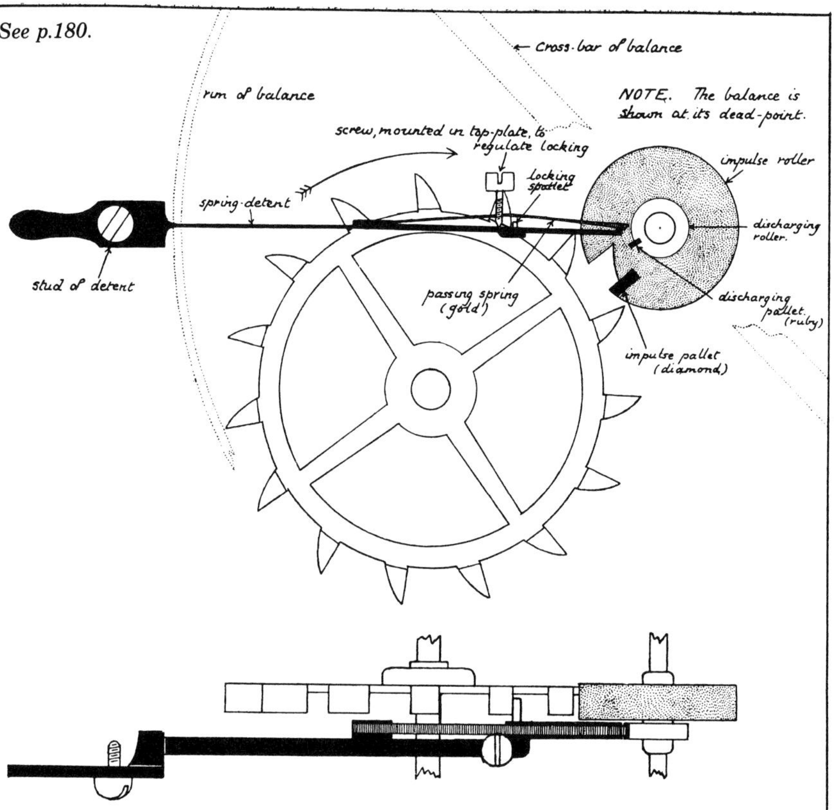

31 **Arnold's spring-detent escapement.**

Drawn from that of a box-chronometer, marked "John Arnold, London, no 26" (about 1790,) in the possession of Messrs. Ch. Frodsham & Co.

See p.181.

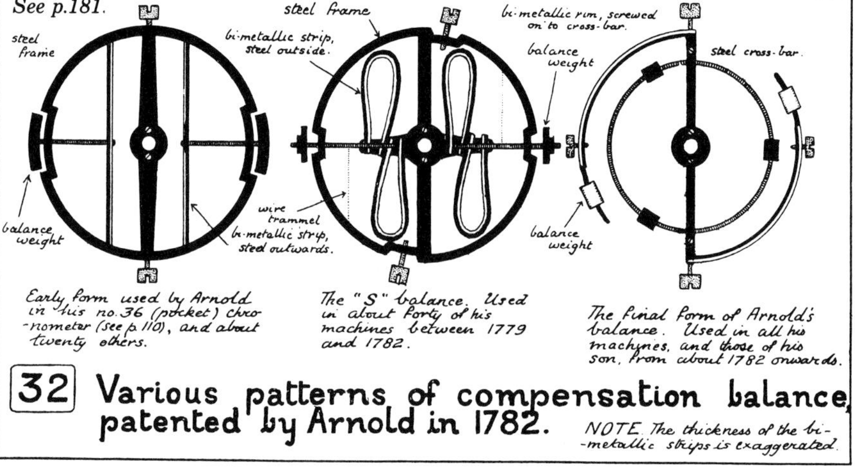

Early form used by Arnold in his no.36 (pocket) chronometer (see p.110), and about twenty others.

The "S" balance. Used in about forty of his machines between 1779 and 1782.

The final form of Arnold's balance. Used in all his machines, and those of his son, from about 1782 onwards.

32 **Various patterns of compensation balance, patented by Arnold in 1782.**

NOTE. The thickness of the bi-metallic strips is exaggerated.

MOVEMENT OF A ONE DAY MARINE CHRONOMETER BY JOHN ARNOLD NO. 12.
With Arnolds double T balance with trammels.

On the occasion of Mudge petitioning the House of Commons in 1791, Arnold issued a pamphlet* in which he put forward his own claims—quite justly, in the main, but with a certain amount of clap-trap. Thus, he remarks:—

> " . . . That I have been of infinitely more service to my country than any other man, the great number of my Chronometers which have now been, for many years, in constant use at sea, will irrefragably evince. . . ."

and again

> " . . . Let me add, that I have lately invented a new mode of *escapement*, of such a nature, that friction is utterly excluded from it; and, in consequence, the use of oil, that bane to equality of motion, is rendered wholly unnecessary: and, whether the material be a diamond, steel, brass, or piece of wood, is perfectly indifferent, as they are all equally proper for the purpose."†

He also gave some very interesting evidence before the Committee which examined Mudge's‡ petition, stating in the course of it that up to that time (1793) he had made upwards of nine hundred chronometers, " but never made Two alike, while I was able to improve the Principles."

In spite of the pressing cares of a large and growing business, and the routine work of springing and adjusting, Arnold continued his experimental work, chiefly in connection with the balance and balance-spring. He also devised an escapement which, like Mudge's, gave impulse concentrically with the balance.

He took his son, John Roger Arnold, into partnership about 1790, having previously sent him to Paris to study watchmaking under Breguet§.

Arnold received from the Board, at various dates between 1771 and 1784, a total of £1,322 to assist him in his experiments, on the understanding that he should compete for the reward, and that this sum should be deducted from it if won. He offered, in 1782, to surrender his patents and make public the construction and adjustment

---

* " Certificates and Circumstances relative to the going of Mr. Arnold's Chronometers." London, 1791. It contains six pages of statement and a number of certificates, including the register of No. 36's performance at Greenwich, and one, claimed to surpass it, of No. 68's performance in the hands of its owner, Mr. Everard, a wine-merchant of Lynn.

† Earnshaw comments upon this: " Hear it, ye watch-makers! Friction is utterly excluded from scape and balance pivots; and whether the material be a diamond, steel, brass, or a piece of wood, they are all equally fit for the purpose. Joyful news indeed for the watchmakers, as now they may all make wooden timekeepers." (" *Longitude*," p. 144).

‡ The Committee's report was published in full as a Parliamentary paper (1793). Very valuable evidence was given by Maskelyne, the younger Mudge, Emery, Banks, Gilpin (Secretary to the Board of Longitude) and others.

§ The elder Arnold once told Urban Jurgensen, the celebrated Danish chronometer maker, that he considered Breguet to be the finest horologist in Europe.

of his chronometers, if the Board would grant him a suitable reward, but this proposal was declined, and from then onwards his dealings with them appear to have diminished to the mere cleaning and repair of such machines as they had purchased from him.

Although he had more than once expressed to the Board his intention of competing for the £10,000 reward, and had had several of his chronometers tried at Greenwich, he never formally entered the two demanded by the terms of the Act. In view of the fine performance of No. 36 this seems curious, but it is probable that, as a business man, he considered that his time would be more profitably spent in attending strictly to the commercial side of chronometer-making, and declined to engage in a speculation which, while uncertain in its result, would most undoubtedly absorb a good deal of his time and energy for several years.

The elder Arnold died in 1799 at the comparatively early age of 63.*

An obituary notice † states :—

> " On Sunday morning last died, Mr. John Arnold, of Well Hall, near Eltham, in Kent. As a mechanic his *abilities* and industry will be ever remembered by his *country*. He *was* the Inventor of the *Expansion Balance*, of the *present Detached Escapement*, and the first artist who ever applied the Gold Cylindrical Spring to the balance of a Timepiece. He retired from business about three years since, but his active mind still labouring for the completion of his favourite object, and for what he called the ultimatum of timepiece making, has produced a *Chronometer*, far different and infinitely superior to any thing yet made public. *His Son* who succeeded him, we understand is in possession of *all* his father's drawings and models, and from *him* we may now hope for the completion of that grand object—the discovery of the Longitude by Timekeepers." ‡

This remarkable combination of filial piety with advertisement contains, of course, a number of over-statements. Arnold was undoubtedly not the original inventor of the " Expansion balance "—that honour belongs to Le Roy—and his claim to the " Present form of detached escapement " is very disputable, since both Berthoud and Earnshaw have one at least as good. Moreover, from a remark in Dalrymple's pamphlet against Earnshaw (see p. 207), it appears that

* All the other " old masters," except Sully (46) and Le Roy (68), considerably exceeded threescore and ten. Thus, Graham lived to be 78, Harrison 83, Mudge 79, Kendall 74, Berthoud 80, Breguet 76 and Earnshaw 80. This goes far to disprove the assertion of Rousseau (himself the son of a watchmaker), that the very nature of the employment tries the temper.

† " The Times," August 17th, 1799.

‡ Earnshaw's remarks upon this advertisement are not complimentary: " There is no truth in this publication, except that of his father living at Well Hall, dying on Sunday morning, his having retired from business about three years, and his son succeeding him. If he was the first who applied gold springs to watches, it was because the corrosive matter which (unfortunately for him) always ouzed from his hands, rusted all the steel ones. The truth of this all his workmen knew . . . The public are likewise told, that the present Mr. Arnold is in possession of all his father's drawings, and . . . were led to expect something very wonderful indeed . . . ; but, the devil take it, eight years has passed away, and the son seems to have forgot his promise . . . Oh Mr. John Roper (*sic*) Arnold, young man, it was too soon for you to begin puffing, you should have known a little more of your business . . . ." " *Longitude*," pp. 142, 143.

Courtesy of the Worshipful Company of Clockmakers.

The movement of No. 28 fitted with the '02' balance in Gould figure 32 opposite page 181. It appears as the right hand drawing.

a dentist named Vanbutchell had had a watch fitted with a spiral gold spring before Arnold's time. On the other hand, the notice does less than justice to his many good qualities—his determination, business ability*, fine craftsmanship, love of experiment, and, above all, his reduction of the chronometer to a simple and efficient machine of moderate price, suitable for production in quantity.

JOHN ROGER ARNOLD.

The younger member of the firm of " Arnold and Son " deserves little more than passing notice. He appears to have been a poor workman, and a poorer man of business. He received a windfall from the Board of Longitude in 1806, when he was awarded £1,678 in final recognition of his father's efforts to develop the chronometer. He became master of the Clockmakers' Company in 1817, and migrated in 1820 from Cornhill to 27, Cecil Street, and afterwards, in 1830, to 84, Strand. His business had declined very considerably, but in the same year he took a very able and energetic partner, E. J. Dent, on a ten year's agreement†. Dent speedily restored the reputation of the firm, but as soon as the agreement had expired he set up for himself next door, at 82, Strand, subsequently migrating to 61.

J. R. Arnold continued at 84, Strand until his death in 1843, when his business was taken over by Charles Frodsham.

---

* It should not be forgotten that he was greatly assisted in his business by his wife, who acted as his " first lieutenant," and during his severe illness in 1791 took charge of his business.

It may be noted as a curious fact that prior to the introduction of the factory system into watchmaking, in which a considerable quantity of female labour is now employed, there are very few recorded instances of women watchmakers. A watch in the Pierpont Morgan collection, made about 1660 and signed " J. Lalement, Autun," is believed to be the work of Judith Lalement, who died in 1670, while in more modern times (and, indeed, at the present day) women have occasionally pursued the springing and balance-making branches of the trade. But, in general, it is none the less true that neither in watch-making nor in the game of billiards have women made their mark in a province where, it might be thought, their deftness and delicacy of touch would enable them to compete, on something more than equal terms, with the majority of the opposite sex.

† A clause in the agreement runs " One object of the said Copartnership being, to relieve the said John Roger Arnold from the fatigues of business." During Dent's consulate, or rather dictatorship, the younger Arnold was little more than a sleeping partner.

CHAPTER VIII.

THOMAS EARNSHAW.

Last in point of time among the little band who made the chronometer a reality, but not inferior to any of them in skill and invention, is Thomas Earnshaw, to whom, as Britten remarks, " must be ascribed the merit of having devised the chronometer escapement and compensation balance precisely as they are now used."

This perfectly correct statement derives its force from the fact that these two devices are the most essential features of a chronometer, and practically the only ones which differentiate it from a common watch. It is, therefore, all the more remarkable, in view of the enormous advances which mechanism in general has made in the last century, that in spite of all the attempts made by hundreds of highly skilled horologists to devise a better escapement and balance, examples practically identical with the form of the present day can be found in chronometers constructed by Earnshaw as long ago as 1783.

As regards the first fifty years of his life, we know more about Earnshaw than any other of the early chronometer makers, since he is the only one of them who has left what may be regarded as an autobiography. This is a work entitled " Longitude—an Appeal to the Public," which he published in 1806, and in which he has, quite unconsciously, revealed his personality as well as any realistic novelist could have done it.

It was an outstanding personality—of that there can be no doubt. There is a striking similarity of character between Earnshaw and Harrison—of whom, by the way, he spoke and wrote with something less than reverence.* Both had the same power of dominance and leadership, and the north-country shrewdness and dogged grit (also, it must be admitted, its vanity and lack of self-criticism). The book is full of unconscious humour (there are also one or two examples of the other kind), but it is honest and straightforward, and although its style may be rugged its matter, as far as can be tested by outside evidence, is neither overdrawn nor distorted.

According to his own account, Earnshaw was born at Ashton-under-Lyne, on February 4th, 1749, and was apprenticed to a watchmaker.† When out of his time, he worked independently for several

* " . . . a reward has been given more than 6 times the amount of that which I ask, and that to a person whose productions were an hundred times inferior to mine." (" *Longitude* " p. 188).

† Probably in London, but he does not say so.

Plate XXXI. THOMAS EARNSHAW.

From an engraving after a portrait by Sir Martin Shee. A copy of the portrait is in the Science Museum, South Kensington.

See p. 11[illegible]

POCKET CHRONOMETER BY JOHN ANTES, LONDON, 1787.
Clockmakers Co. (C.C. Cat. 423).

makers, including John Brockbank, of Cornhill, and Thomas Wright, of the Poultry, and soon became well known, first as a watch-finisher, and subsequently as a watch-jeweller and ruby-cylinder maker. He married early in life, and had a numerous family.

While working for Brockbank, in 1780, he conceived the idea of his new escapement. After making for his employer two detached escapements with pivoted detents, as used by Berthoud and Arnold at that time, it struck him that if the detent, instead of turning on pivots, were mounted upon a spring, the irregularities caused by the thickening of the oil in the pivots would be abolished, and the spring itself would serve both as a pivot and a means of returning the detent, when displaced, to its normal position. The escapement then assumed the form shown in Fig. 33. The escape wheel is normally locked by a tooth (No. 3 in the figure) taking against the "locking stone" *l*, on the detent D, which is mounted on the thin spring S, whose end is fixed to the top-plate. On the tip of the detent is a small gold passing spring, as in Arnold's escapement. The balance staff carries the impulse and discharging rollers and their pallets (*i* and *p*).

The action of this arrangement is similar to that of the Berthoud and Arnold escapements. As the balance swings in the direction of the arrow, the discharging pallet presses on the passing spring, bends the spring S, and unlocks the escape wheel. The tooth 3 then falls on the impulse pallet, gives impulse, and disengages as the pallet swings clear. Tooth 2 then locks on the locking stone, the detent having been brought back by S to its position. On the return swing, the unlocking pallet passes the passing spring, deflecting it slightly in doing so, but without moving the detent.*

This plan is preferable to Berthoud's system (see Fig. 26) of placing the passing spring on the discharging roller, as it is less liable to derangement.

As compared with Arnold's, in which the escape wheel, turning the other way, is unlocked by moving the detent inwards, this escapement has the advantage of easier unlocking (the escape wheel being locked on the point of the tooth instead of its root), and of giving impulse with less friction. The impulse being given by a direct blow from the point of the tooth, no oil was required on the pallets, while it was needed on the epicycloidal faces of Arnold's teeth. This, however, could have been avoided by altering the shape of the teeth and there is really little to choose between the two escapements,† although Earnshaw's was easier to manufacture. Arnold's possesses one advantage, in that the spring of the detent, which must of necessity be very weak, is in tension instead of compression.

* As originally patented (Wright's Patent No. 1354 of 1783), there was no passing spring, the spring of the detent banking against a pin on the return swing and bending slightly to allow the impulse pallet to pass. This construction of the detent was frequently used by J. F. Cole (1799-1880). It is also possible to use one piece of spring both for the detent spring and the passing spring.

† Earnshaw claimed that Arnold's method of unlocking involved a recoil of the escape wheel, but this is incorrect. Actually, as explained on p. 218, there is a slight recoil in his own escapement.

The question of priority in the invention of the spring detent was hotly disputed between Arnold and Earnshaw. Earnshaw's account is, that having planned his new escapement he fitted it to a watch and showed it to John Brockbank under a pledge of secrecy, which, however, did not prevent the latter from immediately divulging it to Arnold, who patented his own arrangement eight days later.* Meanwhile Earnshaw, being unable to afford a patent, took the watch to Wright, who kept it for some twelve months, and then patented the escapement in his own name,† bargaining with Earnshaw that the latter should work off the cost of the patent (100 guineas) by making them for the trade at his own price, and charging on each watch a royalty of a guinea, payable to Wright. Watches made under these conditions were stamped [Wright's Patent.].

Earnshaw studied the properties of his escapement (which remains to this day the best of all for balance timekeepers) very carefully. The proportions of the original model were found to be faulty, since the impulse roller was only about one-quarter the diameter of the escape-wheel, while about 120° of its circumference intersected the path of the escape wheel teeth. If the vibrations of the balance were reduced below this amount by external motion, the watch would stop. Accordingly Earnshaw, after bitter experience of this fault‡, made the impulse roller half the diameter of the escape wheel (reducing the intersection, and the consequent minimum arc of the balance, to about 60°). The proportions which he finally adopted may be seen in Plate XXXII., which shows a large model of his escapement which he made for the Board of Longitude in 1804.§

Earnshaw also introduced the method now universally employed for making compensation balances.¶

Unlike Arnold, who made the arms separately (soldering the brass and steel together)‖, bent them to correct shape with special pliers, and screwed them on to the cross-bar, Earnshaw cut both arms and

---

* Earnshaw, in the course of a trade wrangle, once taxed Arnold openly, before the Lord Mayor, with stealing his invention.

† Patent No. 1354 of 1783. The description and figure of the escapement are much less obscure than Arnold's, but still not entirely satisfactory.

‡ The first dozen watches, made on the original design, were always stopping, and Earnshaw altered them at his own expense. "I endeavoured to persuade Mr. Wright to bear half the expense, but he refused, nor could I ever get one shilling from him on that account. I then had a wife and four young children, and not a guinea before-hand."

§ On 23rd March 1804 the Board, who were then investigating the rival claims of Arnold and Earnshaw, asked the latter and J. R. Arnold to make, at the Board's expense, models of their respective escapements, five times the natural size. Descriptions of these were published with the Specifications. Earnshaw charged the Board £52 10s. for his model, much to their dismay. J. R. Arnold asked only £10 10s. Earnshaw's model (see Plate XXXII.) is still preserved at Greenwich, but Arnold's has disappeared.

¶ Dr. Pearson, in his article "Chronometer" in Rees' "Cyclopædia," stated that this plan was introduced by Brockbank. His bias is pretty apparent throughout (the whole article, although containing valuable information, is a piece of pro-Brockbank propaganda), and little importance need be attached to the statement, which is entirely unsupported.

‖ In his later machines, the brass and steel of the rims were united by fusion, but these were still screwed on to the cross-bar.

See p. 217.

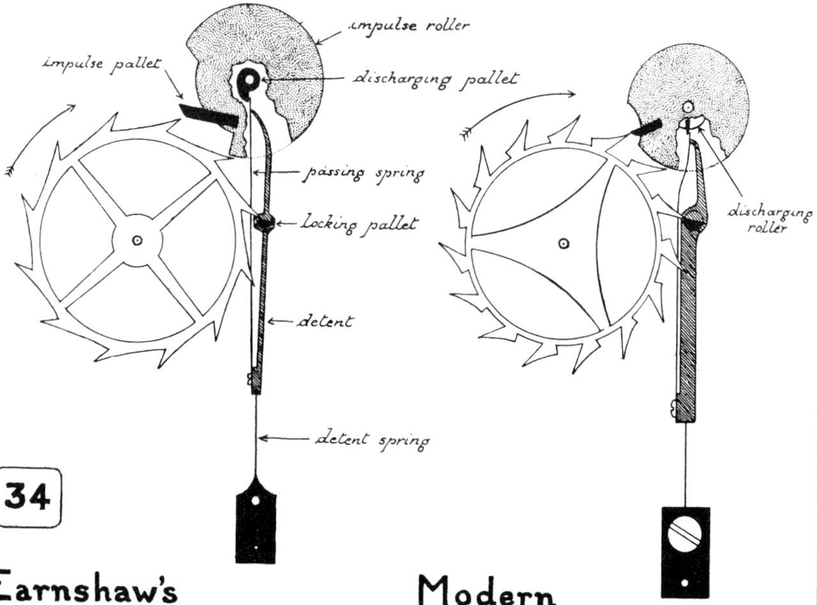

34

Earnshaw's spring-detent escapement. [1784]

Modern chronometer escapement.

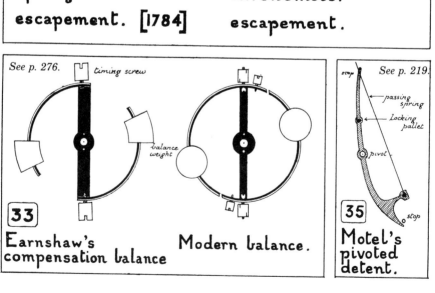

See p. 276.

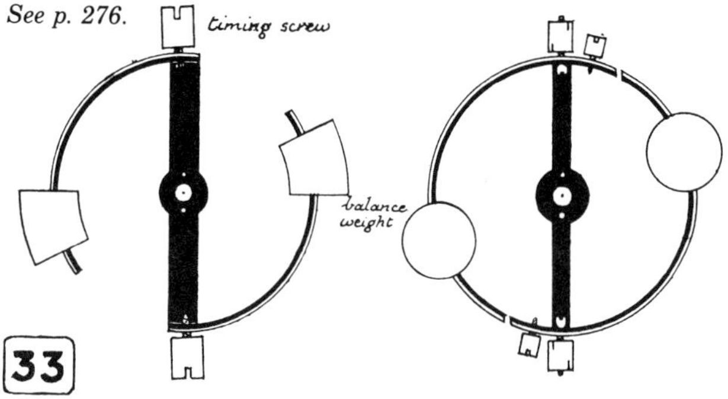

33

Earnshaw's compensation balance

Modern balance.

See p. 219.

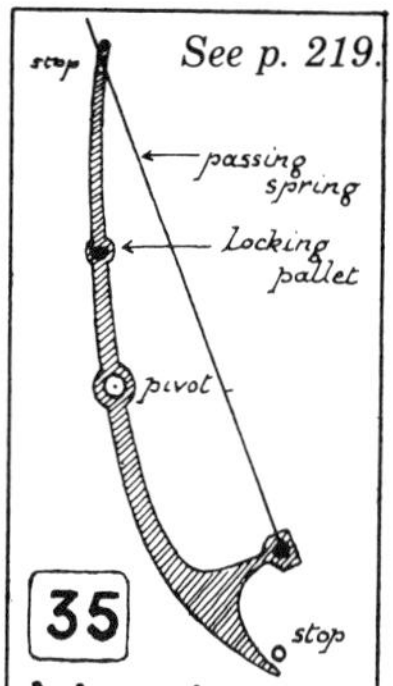

35

Motel's pivoted detent.

cross-bar out of the solid. A disc of steel of the thickness required for the breadth of the rims had molten brass run on to its edge, this making a perfect connection between the two metals. It was then hollowed and turned to the correct thickness inside and out, thus becoming the shape of a flat dish, and two segments of the bottom of the dish were cut away, leaving the cross bar and bimetallic rim, which was cut into a pair of arms of the required length. The weights of the balance were cut from a turned brass ring with the help of a dividing engine, and the whole (shown in Fig. 34) constituted, as Earnshaw justly remarks, " a Ballance in the full sense of the word, equal in all its parts."

In his escapement and balance, Earnshaw undoubtedly surpassed Arnold or any one else, but in his method of spring-making he was not equally sound. He made his balance springs from soft-drawn wire hardened by rolling, and did not temper them,* so that as time went on they were liable to lose on their rates. To get over this he left them fast in the short arcs, in order that as the arc diminished by thickening of the oil in the balance pivots the vibrations might be quickened by this cause about as much as they were slowed by the weakening of the spring. He also claimed to be able to obtain a perfectly isochronous spring (although, as stated, he did not use one) by tapering the spring from the outer end to the inner.† He used spiral and cylindrical springs indifferently in both chronometers and pocket chronometers.‡

It took Earnshaw a long time to obtain enough profit and reputation from his improvements to let him emancipate himself from his employers and set up on his own account. Thus when Maskelyne was induced to make a private test of one of Earnshaw's chronometers in 1789, he observed that the maker's name on it was " Wm. Hughes," and asked Earnshaw for an explanation.

> " I informed him that as I had invented things which my connections did not understand, and could not purchase, I was under the necessity of making them for the watch-makers, who had customers for them, and the watch-makers, for whom I made them, in course (*sic*) had their own names put on them ; although they had no more to do with the making of the timekeeper than the person who bought it of them."

Maskelyne was very pleased with the going of this timekeeper,§ and, according to Earnshaw (but the statement seems improbable),

* His No. 549 (made about 1795) which I recently examined, still has the original spring. It is a very short helical steel spring, of four turns only. Arnold generally used tempered springs, but sometimes one of rolled steel, not tempered, or of gold.

† This was the direct opposite of Berthoud's method.

‡ He remarks (" *Longitude*," p. 15) : " . . . It is of no consequence what shape the spring is, whether spiral or cylindrical, so it be tapered accordingly." Although he produced a large number of pocket chronometers, he made no secret of his opinion that such machines were, of necessity, inferior to those of the box pattern.

§ He reported its performance to the Board (15th August, 1789), its maker's name being entered in the minutes as " Hemshaw." The uniformity with which the names of the pioneer chronometer makers were mis-spelt is surprising. Harrison, abroad, was generally " Harisson," or sometimes " Harrisson," and other variants such as " Kindil," " Earnschaw," " Emeril " and " Mugde," are to be found in numerous Continental authorities.

commissioned him to put in hand two others for the purpose of competing for the £10,000 reward. This commission, however, if given, was never executed. Maskelyne seems to have formed a very high opinion of Earnshaw's ability and honesty of character, and the minutes of the Board of Longitude, together with Earnshaw's own statements, leave no doubt that Maskelyne repeatedly went out of his way, in the face of very powerful opposition, to serve Earnshaw's interests, behaviour which the latter did not always appreciate at quite its full value.

In 1791 Earnshaw's reputation was enhanced by a semi-official trial at Greenwich in competition with several other makers.

The ill-fated " Bounty " had been sent out with the intention of transplanting bread-fruit trees from Tahiti to the West Indies. Bligh was now ordered on a second expedition designed to effect the same purpose, and, being instructed by the Admiralty to purchase a timekeeper, he invited various makers to send samples to Greenwich for a comparative trial. Earnshaw entered five pocket chronometers, while Arnold sent four box chronometers, and Brockbank one. The result of the trial appears from the following certificate:—

> " This is to certify the principal Officers and Commissioners of His Majesty's Navy, That Mr. Tho. Earnshaw has delivered into my possession a Metal Case Chronometer, No. 1503, at the price of forty guineas. And I do further certify that this Chronometer was compared at Flamstead House*, with watches of much higher prices, and that its rate was preferable, and on that reason taken by me on Government Account.
> July 1791. (Signed) WM. BLIGH."

By this time Earnshaw was in a good way of business, employing several workmen to make chronometers under his direction.

Soon after this trial he petitioned the Board for some assistance in his work on the improvement of timekeepers, but unsuccessfully. At about the same time, Maskelyne requested him to make an astronomical regulator for the Archbishop of Armagh. Earnshaw accepted the order with diffidence, remarking that he had never made a clock, and did not even know how many wheels were in one. However, he produced a very fine regulator, which was tried at Greenwich, to Maskelyne's entire satisfaction, before delivery. He also pointed out and remedied several defects in the Greenwich standard clock.†

In 1792 he again petitioned the Board for assistance and, this being declined, gave up for the time, any thought of competing for the reward. His application, however, led to the question being raised, at the Board, of whether he was entitled to the credit of inventing the improvements in chronometers claimed by him. Maskelyne spoke strongly in his favour, and the Board appeared satisfied, although, as will appear, the question was raised again twelve years later.

* Flamsteed House (after John Flamsteed, 1646-1719, the first Astronomer Royal) was the old name for the Royal Observatory, and it is still retained for the original portion of the building.

† He simplified the motion work, setting the hour hand to turn backwards, and strengthened the gridiron pendulum by cross-bracing the various pairs of rods, thus preventing them from moving by jerks if one rod expanded or contracted a little faster than the other.

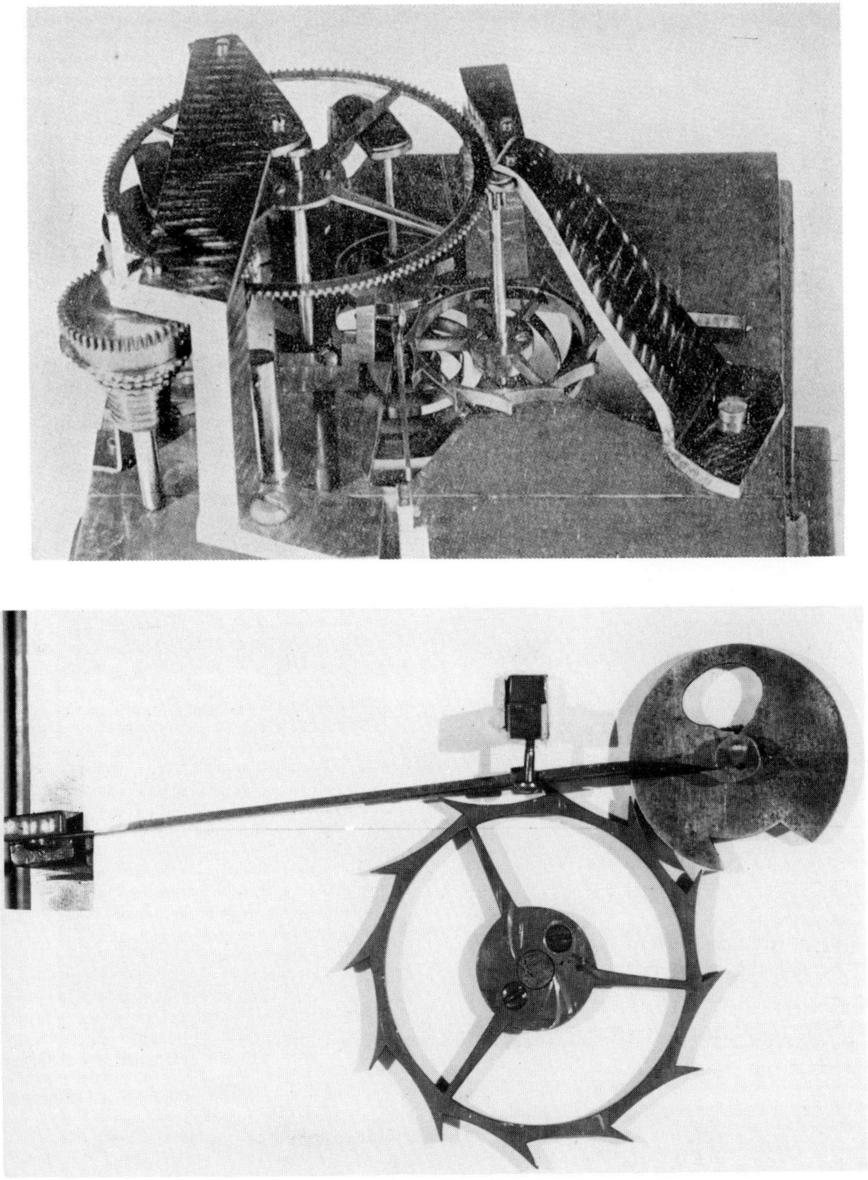

Plate XXXII. EARNSHAW'S MODEL OF HIS ESCAPEMENT.

The lower photograph shows the essential portions of the model in their correct relative positions.

Earnshaw used 13 or 15-toothed escape wheels in his chronometers, although that of the model has 12 teeth only. The Board of Longitude published an illustrated description of the model as an appendix to Earnshaw's specification.

See p. 194. Royal Observatory, Greenwich.

EMERY NO. 1.
Clockmakers' Company (C.C. Cat. 602).

CHRONOMETER NO. 1 BY JOSIAH EMERY, CHARING CROSS, LONDON 1792.
One of four submitted to Royal Observatory.
Clockmakers' Company (C.C. Cat. 602).

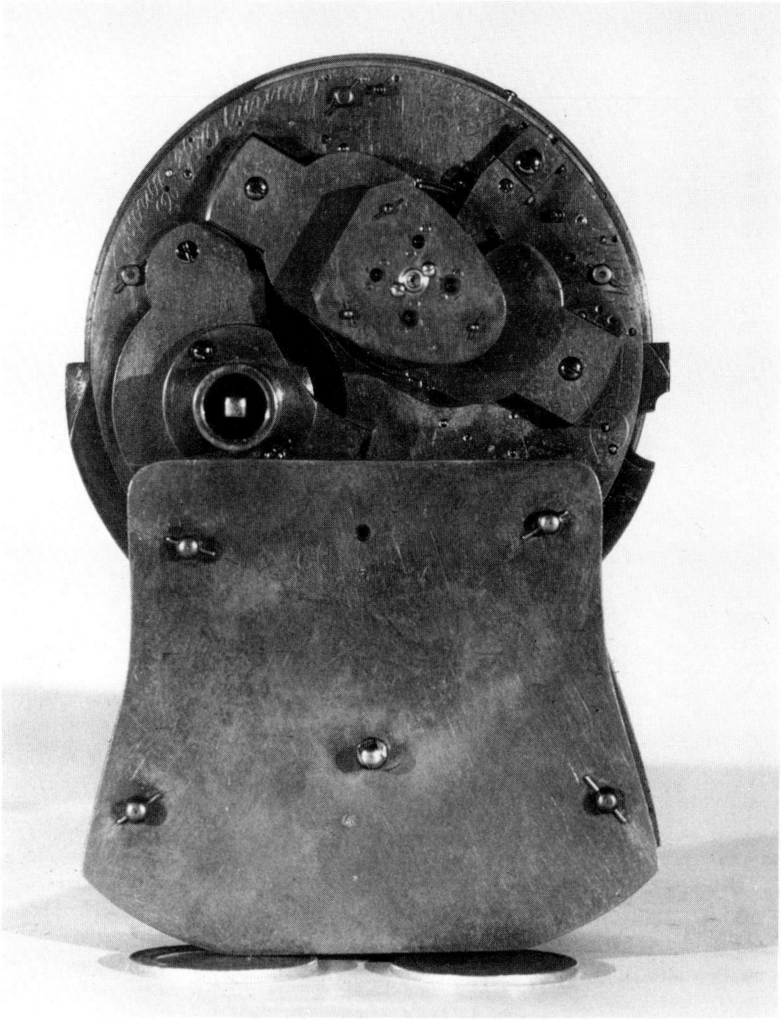

EMERY NO. 1.
Clockmakers' Company (C.C. Cat. 602).

Earnshaw's attention was recalled to the reward by the unsuccessful efforts of Josiah Emery* to win it by means of two chronometers of his construction. Earnshaw spoke scornfully of these machines to Maskelyne, and offered to excel their performance with an old timekeeper of his make, No. 265, just back from an East India voyage, and very dirty.† This being reported by Maskelyne to the Board, the trial was allowed, and the machine tested for a year. It quite justified its maker's confidence, its total error on mean time, in twelve months, being only 1 m. 56.46 sec. By Maskelyne's method of rating‡, however, which adopted the rate of going of the first month as the standard for the remainder, its errors were outside the limits allowed by the Act.

The Board then offered Earnshaw £200 if he would send two chronometers for trial, such machines to become, in any event, their property ; but this offer he declined, thinking the sum insufficient, and the condition degrading.

The Board, however, helped him indirectly by bringing him to the notice of the Admiralty, who instituted three comparative trials at sea§ between his chronometers and those of Mudge, Arnold, and other makers. The results of the trials were decidedly in his favour, and no doubt helped to increase his business considerably.

In 1798, and succeeding years, Earnshaw made three attempts to win the £10,000 reward, and although he failed, yet the circumstances of his failure, and the very narrow margin which finally divided him from complete success, showed that in his day he had no equal as a chronometer maker. Not only did he completely distance the efforts of the only two¶ who, like himself, had endeavoured to comply with the very rigorous conditions of the Act, and submitted two machines for simultaneous trial, but he even beat the very remarkable performances of Arnold's two celebrated watches, Nos. 36 and 68, made in non-competitive trials (and, in the case of No. 68, under the supervision

* Emery was a Swiss, but had long been settled in London. He was a fine workman, and employed several able assistants. He made a number of splendid lever watches on Mudge's plan for wealthy patrons. The register of one made for Count Bruhl was adduced by Banks in his protest against Earnshaw's reward. The machines tried at Greenwich had compensation balances, and most peculiar escapements, a combination of the lever with two remontoires. The pivots of the balance ran between two sets of friction-rollers (with jewelled pivots), all the arbors being horizontal. The design was evidently based upon that of Mudge's machines. Two (Nos. 1|| and 2) were tried at Greenwich in April—November, 1792, July, 1793—February, 1794, and two others (Nos. 3 and 4) in July, 1795—February, 1796. None of them kept time within the limits of the Act, although No. 4 went for five months with a total error of not quite a minute. Emery died early in 1796, before the last trial was concluded, and his wife petitioned the Board unsuccessfully for assistance, stating that her husband had spent over 25 years in the improvement of timekeepers, to the detriment of his other business.

† *i.e.*, with thickened oil in its pivot-holes. ‡ See Appendix I.

§ In H.M.S. "Sans Pareil," during 1796, 1797 and 1798, in competition with Mudge's "Blue" and "Green," one on Mudge's plan by Howells, Barraud and Jamison, and one by Brockbank.

¶ Mudge and Emery. || Now in the possession of Mr. Percy Webster.

of a private owner, who was believed, in some quarters, to have exaggerated its performance). He showed that the reward was not, as had previously been stated on very respectable authority, impossible to win*, and, indeed, had it depended upon the going of one chronometer only, instead of two, he would have secured it at his first attempt.

Earnshaw's attempts were made with two new machines, which took only two months each to make. The movements, of his normal pattern, were securely locked into their cases, so that no details of the mechanism could be seen. The trials lasted from January to December 1798, October 1799 to June 1800, and July 1801 to September 1802.

In the first trial, in which Maskelyne's method of applying the mean rate of the first month to successive periods of six months was employed, both machines were outside the limit of error (4m. 0s. in 6 months) imposed by the Act, No. 1's errors being successively 2m. 15s., 3m. 6s., 3m. 59s., 4m. 46s. and 5m. 17s., while those of No. 2 were 2m. 40s., 3m. 20s., 4m. 53s., 7m. 10s. and 10m. 19s.† If, however, the method which Earnshaw advocated (that of applying to each period of six months the mean rate of the previous month) had been used, No. 1 would have been completely within the Act for all periods, and No. 2 for all but one. He withdrew both machines for further adjustment.

In the second trial, the performance of the machines was not quite so good. By Maskelyne's method, in seven overlapping periods of six months each, No. 1 was outside the limits of the Act for four, and No. 2 for two. By Earnshaw's method, on the other hand, No. 1 was inside the Act for six periods, and No. 2 for all of them. This notable difference emphasised the importance of selecting the fairest possible method of obtaining the mean rate, and as the Board were unable to dispute Earnshaw's contention that Maskelyne's method held the timekeepers to their rates for twelve months, while the Act only prescribed six, they adopted his proposal, although with characteristic reserve and ineptitude they intimated that they would use their own discretion, *after the trial*, as to which method should be adopted. In the meanwhile, they voted him £500, to be subsequently deducted from the reward, if won.

In the third trial, Earnshaw had the mortification of finding that he had been his own worst enemy. Confident that the Board could no longer refuse to adopt his method of rating, he had altered his compensation accordingly, and that of No. 1 a little too much. In this trial, by his method, No. 1 was inside the limits of the Act in five periods out of ten, and No. 2 in all of them, but by Maskelyne's method

* The Parliamentary Committee on Mudge's petition stated, in the course of their report, that " . . . The present Act does indeed impose conditions so difficult, and so impossible to be surmounted, if enforced to the full extent of which they are capable, that it is to be feared few artists will quit the certain gains of their profession, to enter into things so discouraging and precarious."

† The remarkable acceleration of No. 2 was caused by dirt getting into the lower pivot-hole of the balance. The vibrations were reduced to about half a turn, and, as the balance spring was intentionally left fast in the short arcs, the machine accelerated considerably in consequence.

Plate XXXIII. CHRONOMETER No 549, BY EARNSHAW.

The movement is held in the case by two small screws at XII and VI which were not in place when the photograph was taken,

See p. 195,f.

ONE DAY MARINE CHRONOMETER BY THOMAS EARNSHAW.

their performance was even better, as appears from the following letter to Earnshaw :—

" Sir,

The errors of your timekeepers, after correcting them for the mean daily rate of the first month, applied equally throughout the year, were at the end of the year as follows : No. 1, 3′ 44″ 72 : No. 2. 3′ 7″ 93.

I am, Sir,

your humble servant,

N. MASKELYNE."

Still, this letter only referred to twelve months going (No. 2 ran out of the limits of the Act in the final four subsequent months of the trial)* and it only gave the average errors, while in one period during the year No. 1 had gone a few seconds outside the Act. It was in vain that Earnshaw protested that the Act required a method that was " generally practicable and useful," and that therefore the average going of the machines, and not the exceptions, should be the criterion of their performance. The Board resolved, on December 2nd, 1802, that the trials of the chronometers should be discontinued.

Earnshaw then gave up all thoughts of further attempts to win the £10,000, but petitioned the Board for such reward as they might think fit, in view of his having come so near to complying with the requirements of the Act. They replied by communicating to him the following resolution :—

" Resolved—

That the Board are convinced that Mr. Earnshaw's watches have gone better than any others that have been submitted to trial at the Royal Observatory, and therefore are of opinion that he deserves a reward equal, at least, to that given by Parliament to Mr. Mudge, provided he will disclose the construction of his timekeepers in such a manner as shall satisfy the Board that other watch-makers will be able to construct them with equal accuracy."

But Earnshaw was destined, before receiving this reward, to meet with formidable opposition from more than one quarter. Sir Joseph Banks, at that time President of the Royal Society and (politicians apart) one of the most influential men of the day, was, *ex officio*, a member of the Board, and, being an enthusiastic patron of the Arnolds, both father and son, set himself, seconded by Alexander Dalrymple, Hydrographer of the Navy, to oppose, tooth and nail, anything tending to exalt or reward another chronometer maker to the detriment of their reputation. He at once drew up and printed, for private circulation, a protest against the Board's resolution, advancing the going of No. 36 and other watches of Arnold's make against those of Earnshaw. This was answered in the same manner by Maskelyne, and after full discussion at an extraordinary meeting of the Board, held on March 17th, 1803, the previous minute was confirmed.

* However the Board may have chosen to construe the letter of the Act, there can be no question of its spirit, which intended that the timekeepers competing for the reward should undergo a *six months'* trial. There was absolutely no warrant for extending this to a year, or, as in the present instance, to sixteen months. Its duration appears to have been left entirely to Maskelyne's discretion, and it might with equal justice, or want of it, have been prolonged until the machines stopped for want of cleaning.

A more serious attack was made on Earnshaw from another quarter. Not unnaturally, it came from his brother makers. Reports reached the Board's ears that the improvements for which they were about to reward Earnshaw were, in reality, due to John Arnold.

They accordingly investigated the matter with characteristic thoroughness and deliberation, and examined a number of watch and chronometer makers*, who indulged in a good deal of hard swearing, and obscured the issue with all manner of envy, hatred, malice and other Christian vices. When the air had cleared a little, it was apparent that the issue was narrowed down to "Banks contra mundum." All the remainder of the Board were of opinion that Earnshaw had shown, if not his absolute priority of invention over Arnold, at least his entire originality, while the balance of evidence was in favour of the truth of his statement that Arnold had learnt of the Earnshaw escapement before patenting his own. Also, it could not be gainsaid that Earnshaw had repeatedly asserted this, and that Arnold had never exerted himself to deny it. But Banks refused to admit the force of these arguments, and as a final compromise it was agreed to give both Earnshaw and J. R. Arnold £3,000 each, less such sums as the former and John Arnold had previously received for encouragement. In return, they were to give the Board, as Harrison had done, a full description with drawings) of their respective chronometers.

This compromise was satisfactory to all parties concerned, except Earnshaw. He wanted the money, it is true, but, far more than that he wanted to show his superiority to Arnold—and here they were officially bracketed equal for all time! He resolved to comply with the Board's requirements, take his reward, and then appeal to Parliament. Accordingly he delivered, on March 7th, 1805, his drawings and specification to the Board, at the same time as Arnold.

These were immediately circulated by the Board to about a dozen of the trade, who remarked on them, chiefly to Earnshaw's disparagement. From their remarks the Board framed a number of supplementary questions, designed to clear up doubtful points. Answers to these having been received, the specifications were next published, for the benefit of the public.†

---

* Amongst those who gave evidence in Earnshaw's favour were Robert Best, who returned very opportunely from Constantinople in time for the enquiry, and William Frodsham. On the other side were John and Miles Brockbank, Peto, Barraud and others. As illustrating the unscrupulous methods of Earnshaw's rivals, the following fact may be instanced. His early chronometers were very highly finished (as was natural to expect from one who had formerly earned his living as a watch finisher), and his opponents promptly said that his mechanism required, to work at all, the utmost accuracy of execution. (A similar complaint was made about Maxim's first gun.) To disprove this, Earnshaw, in his later machines, left the parts "in the grey" (*i.e.*, he did not polish them), with the natural result that his rivals spread it about that the workmanship in his chronometers was inferior to that which they were in the habit of putting in a £5 watch.

† "Explanations of Timekeepers, constructed by Mr. Thomas Earnshaw and the late Mr. John Arnold. Published by order of the Commissioners of Longitude." London, 1806. Price 5s.

The two specifications are curiously contrasted. Arnold's is by far the clearer and better written. I do not imagine that he had much to do with it himself; but it is not improbable that Banks or Dalrymple had. Earnshaw's, on the other hand, is as full of his personality as "Longitude" is, and appears crude by comparison with that of his rival*. One seems to be the work of a scientist writing about chronometers: the other, that of a chronometer maker trying to write about science.

On December 12th, 1805, Earnshaw received his £2,500 (Arnold at the same time being paid £1,672), and he at once inserted a long advertisement in the press, recounting his struggles and triumph, and pouring abuse upon Banks and Gilpin (Secretary to the Board). Banks endeavoured to persuade the Board to prosecute Earnshaw for libel, and, on their excusing themselves, obtained copies of their minutes in order to do so on his own account—but thought better of it. From his own point of view, this was probably wise, but he deprived posterity of a great deal of amusement. Banks in the witness box against Earnshaw would have been a sight for the gods.

However, Dalrymple took up the cudgels for his patron, and wrote a pamphlet†, which vigorously contested the assertions of Earnshaw's advertisement. Although ably written, it suffers from a superfluity of italics and rhetoric, and a lack of any knowledge of horology. It reads unpleasantly, and there can be little doubt that it was written merely to oblige Banks, and hence strengthen Dalrymple's position as Hydrographer. If so it was, in itself, a judicious move, since its author was then beginning to feel the first breath of the official displeasure which caused his dismissal two years later.‡

Earnshaw countered, almost immediately, by publishing "Longitude." Although actually a book (it runs to some 300 8vo. pages), it is technically a pamphlet, filled with invective directed, primarily, against Dalrymple. The following passage will serve as a specimen:—

> "In your late puffing publication, you appear to have had two motives, one to puff off your darling boy, the present Mr. Arnold, son of your old tutor and friend: and another to please Sir Joseph. The first was, to be sure, an act of friendly generosity, the other a tolerably good step to please a great man, who keeps a great and a good table; and every one knows how necessary it is to have a good table at every quarter of the town. It is so convenient when you take your departure

* There is some reason to believe that it was not all Earnshaw's work, but partly compiled by Firminger, Maskelyne's assistant at Greenwich. Earnshaw is probably responsible for the vituperation, which is very marked in the MS., but was discreetly omitted from the version published by the Board.

† "Longitude—a full answer to the Advertisement, concerning Mr. Earnshaw's Timekeeper, in the 'Morning Chronicle,' 4th Feb., and 'Times,' 13th Feb." London, 1806.

‡ He had been Hydrographer for eleven years, and had produced a number of excellent charts, but would not issue them to the fleet, intending to wait until a set could be produced which would enable a ship to navigate the world. It must be remembered that we were then at war, and that the charts which were badly needed afloat were, thanks to Dalrymple's obstinacy, lying in hundreds on the shelves of the Hydrographic Department.

from Arnold's in the east, and sail west, to know the exact longitude of a good table, in order to step in and take a plate. In fact, such conveniences as these are not only irresistible, but very comfortable indeed, and not by any means the worst port a man can make. What a pity it is that the dirtiest means so generally obtain such comforts ; and that these were your reasons for writing against me I really believe. My readers will in course take the same liberty of forming their own opinions, and if after reading this book through (with that attention you ought to do, in justice to a man whom you have so unjustly attacked, and that too without the least provocation on his part) you cannot eat your dinner with the comfort you intended, it will at least be an honour to you, and some atonement and great satisfaction to me, to know that you have yet a blush."

Earnshaw, after offering his two prize chronometers to the Board for 400 guineas, and refusing to take 300 for them, proceeded with his plan of petitioning Parliament, and, after some demur, prevailed on the Board to grant him copies of all papers and minutes relating to them. He also complained to them, at the same time, of a mysterious allegation that he "had forfeited his life to the laws of his country," of which they disavowed any knowledge.*

He presented his petition to Parliament in 1808, recounting his struggles to improve timekeepers and the results of the various trials, and praying for some further reward. The Board promptly circulated a minute to the First Lord, Chancellor of the Exchequer, and the Speaker, disclaiming any intention of supporting him by granting copies of their minutes, and stating that they had only done so to avoid any suspicion of their wishing to decline investigation. On account of the lateness of the session, no action was taken by the House, but the indefatigable Earnshaw renewed his petition the following year, and procured the appointment of a committee to investigate it.

The Committee made a thorough investigation, and obtained evidence from Earnshaw himself, various members of the Board, several other makers of chronometers, and a large number of officers who had had practical experience of chronometers at sea. They presented an adverse report on May 31st, 1809, from which the following passage is extracted.:—

" . . . they cannot take upon themselves to decide as to the priority of Inventions claimed by different persons, which seem in part to have been borrowed from foreign artists, and rather to have proceeded gradually from one contrivance or suggestion to another, than to have started into excellence by the discovery of any one individual. . . . timekeepers of great merit have been constructed by Mr. Arnold, and by different watchmakers, but they are led . . . to believe that *a larger number, as well absolutely as relatively, of excellent Timekeepers have been made by Mr. Earnshaw, than any other Artist;* but, . . . observing that the Board of Longitude, . . . have awarded to Mr. Earnshaw the sum of three thousand pounds, as an adequate public reward, according to the scale of Rewards established . . . by the Act of Parliament : the Committee are of opinion, that no sufficient ground has been laid for calling on the House to interfere with the determination of that Board."

There is no doubt that Earnshaw honestly considered himself very hardly used; but, like Mudge before him, he allowed his judgment to

* This emanated, I believe, from P. P. Barraud.

be prejudiced by the fact that Harrison had been granted a far larger reward for what was, relatively, an inferior timekeeper, and he did not reflect sufficiently upon the difference between the horology of 1725 and of 1785, nor upon the legal peculiarities which made the winning of the first reward contingent solely upon complying with certain simple and arbitrary conditions.

He continued in business as a chronometer maker, but appears to have retired shortly before his death*. One catches a glimpse of him as the innocent victim of a typical piece of Theodore Hook's effrontery. Hook and a friend, when out driving near Uxbridge, found themselves dinnerless, and with their money exhausted by paying the last turnpike, close to Earnshaw's villa. Hook, who had never met him, but knew of his history, promptly introduced himself and his friend as two devotees of science who could not deny themselves the pleasure of paying their respects to "an individual famous throughout the civilised world." The good-natured old man, much flattered, insisted upon their staying to dinner. Still, he had by no means the worst of the bargain. A dinner with a wit like Hook was well worth the saddle of mutton and half-dozen of Madeira with which he regaled the two jokers.

Earnshaw died at Chenies Street, Bedford Square, in 1829. His son succeeded him, and carried on business until about 1850, removing to Fenchurch Street. Earnshaw's shop, 119, High Holborn, was pulled down when that thoroughfare was widened in 1901.

His grandson, Thomas Earnshaw, was also brought up to the trade, but devoted his attention principally to the manufacture of compensation balances, in which he obtained considerable reputation.

POSTSCRIPT.

In Earnshaw there passed away the last of the great pioneers of chronometer making. By 1829, and indeed much earlier, it had become an important and systematised branch of the watch trade, conducted on lines which are well described in the article "Chronometer," in Rees' "Cyclopædia":—

> "At present the *movement*, that is, the frame containing the barrel, fusee, wheels and pinions, all but the escapement-wheel, is made, like the movement of a watch, by the different workmen employed for this purpose in Lancashire; the motion or dial-work is next added by a workman in London, who has the mainspring, chain, face, and hands, from the respective makers in town; then the escapement-maker and the jeweller are employed to finish their departments; and, lastly, the *maker*, as he is called, finishes the adjustments, and puts the works into the box, or case, or both, as may be required.

It is curious, as illustrating the conservatism with which the English chronometer trade has been conducted ever since, that the foregoing description of the process of manufacture, although written in 1819, is almost equally applicable, with the exception of one particular firm, to the makers of the present day.

* It may be noted that the "Astronomiche Nachrichten" for 1823 contains a letter from him in which he strongly opposes Urban Jurgensen's plan (see p. 135) of improving his escapement by the use of a duplex escape wheel.

And, this being the case, and the chronometer having, in Earnshaw's hands been transformed, not only in its broad outlines but in its details, into what is, substantially, the machine of to-day, the *personality* of its makers becomes relatively less important from that time onwards. The lives and work of the early makers are interwoven, and it would be impossible to give a clear notion of one without the other. But the chronometers of the nineteenth century are the work of many men's hands, and their development is best traced through their mechanism alone. Accordingly, no attempt will be made in the latter part of this book to give such connected biographies as hitherto.

Some slight reference must, however, be here made to one maker who forms, like Earnshaw, a connecting link between the pioneers and the later makers, and who is world famous. I refer to Abraham Louis Breguet. For sheer mechanical skill and ingenuity it is doubtful whether any one ever surpassed him, and the beautiful workmanship and finish of his productions make them an abiding joy to the connoisseur. Some of his inventions, too, such as the Breguet spring and the "tourbillon," presently to be described, are not (like his watches repeating hour, minute and *date*, and his clock which will *wind, set* and *regulate* your watch for you) merely diabolically clever, but also of great scientific value. Unfortunately, although the Stradivarius of watchmaking, he spent much of his time in satisfying the whims of wealthy clients, and while he held the appointment of "Horloger de la Marine," and made a number of chronometers, his chief fame was reaped in other fields, and does not come within the scope of this book.*

Nor is it necessary to refer in detail to the other makers of Earnshaw's time, such as Brockbank, Pennington, Haley, Grimaldi, Hardy, Motel, and others. Points in which their work excels, or differs from, the standard are enumerated later, and in comparison with the little band of pioneers they are of relatively little account.

"The iniquity of oblivion blindly scattereth her poppy," but it is to be hoped that even when Macaulay's New Zealander, in years to come, visits the ruins of Greenwich Observatory, and finds the chronometer room long deserted and forgotten, there may yet be some living who still remember the little band of men who bequeathed us the chronometer of to-day: Le Roy, Mudge, Berthoud, Arnold, Earnshaw, and, above all, John Harrison.

* Those wishing to learn more about one of the greatest horological artists who ever lived should consult Sir David Salomons' beautiful monograph "Breguet" (London, J. & H. Bumpus, 1921).

PART II.

THE LATER DEVELOPMENT OF THE CHRONOMETER.

As was stated in the postscript to the last chapter, the making of chronometers had come, by the beginning of the nineteenth century, to be a considerable branch of the watch and clockmaking trade—indeed from about 1800 to 1840 the demand for them far exceeded the supply. Like many other new inventions, of course, they had to establish their value in the eyes of the public by means of a tedious process of demonstration extending over many years. At first, the chronometer makers found customers chiefly in those Governments which required chronometers for exploring expeditions and for other scientific purposes, in such corporations as the East India Company, and amongst those naval officers whose means allowed of their purchasing a chronometer for their private use. The general issue of chronometers to H.M. Ships only came into force about the year 1825, and for many years later it was restricted to *one* chronometer per ship, with the proviso, however, that a second might be supplied, if available, in cases where the captain or master of the ship possessed a chronometer of his own.* British merchant seamen appear to have taken more readily to chronometers than to "lunars," and amongst the sealers and whalers, whose work took them into high latitudes and uncharted regions where navigation was difficult, they soon became comparatively common. Thus when William Smith, in 1819, discovered the South Shetland Islands and so brought about that stampede of sealers to the new rookeries which, in four short seasons, practically exterminated the Southern fur seal, he carried a chronometer in his little brig, the "Williams" of 450 tons,† and Weddell, who with two tiny ships, the "Jane" of 160 tons, and the "Beaufoy" of only 65, made his way through the pack and reached the extraordinarily high latitude of 74° 15′ S. in the Weddell Sea, beating Cook's furthest by over three degrees, writes thus of his preparations :‡

> "Of chronometers, I had one of eight days (No. 820) made by James Murry; of which I shall speak in another place. One of two days, by Murry and Strachan (No. 403). One of 24 hours, also made by Murry, and they all performed sufficiently well to recommend the makers for their very improved mechanism in this useful art."

On the other hand there were many seamen who, either from extreme conservatism or recklessness, declined to interest themselves at all in chronometers. Of the first class may be instanced the admiral

---

* The reason for this was, of course, that a second chronometer, except as a stand-by, was of little use to the navigator. If he carried *three*, he could be reasonably certain that two of them would not suddenly change their rates by the same amount (although coincidences of this kind have sometimes occurred), and, accordingly, if the daily comparisons showed that one had started to disagree with the other two, it was a fair assumption that it was in error, and should be disregarded. But with only *two* chronometers, he had no means, except by lunar observations (if he could trust them), of determining which was in error and which was keeping its rate.

† It is noteworthy that when in 1819 Capt. W. H. Shirreff, R.N., the Senior Naval Officer on the South American station, chartered the "Williams" for a survey of the South Shetlands, his flagship, the "Andromache," was only provided with one chronometer, and had it not been for Smith's, Bransfield, the master of the "Andromache," who was in charge of the survey, would probably have had to do without one.

‡ "A Voyage towards the South Pole," London, 1825, p. 4.

who, perceiving one of his officers bringing on board a mysterious box, demanded with some heat what it might be, and on receiving the reply "a chronometer, Sir," ordered the picturesquely-described instrument to be discharged to shore immediately, adding that he would have no *necromancy* on board his flagship. On the other hand, during the Napoleonic wars an American vessel, having crossed the Atlantic, was seized and condemned at Christiania, the authorities of the port holding that, *as she had no chart or sextant on board*, she must have come from the British Isles. The other American ship-masters at Christiania made an indignant protest, stating that "we have frequently made voyages from America without the above articles, and we are fully persuaded that every seaman with common nautical knowledge can do the same." It was their dependence upon navigation of this kind that led Messrs. Bryant and Sturgis, of Boston, when informed in 1823 by the captain of one of their ships that he had thought it expedient to purchase a chronometer for $250, to reply that he must foot the bill himself, adding:

> "Could we have anticipated that our instructions respecting economy would have been so totally disregarded, we would have sett fire to the Ship rather than have sent her to sea."*

Nor is this spirit extinct to-day, as witness Capt. Joshua Slocum, of U.S.A.:†

> ". . . The want of a chronometer for the voyage was all that now worried me. In our new-fangled notions of navigation it is supposed that a mariner cannot find his way without one; and I had myself drifted into this way of thinking. My old chronometer, a good one, had been long in disuse. It would cost fifteen dollars to clean and rate it. Fifteen dollars! For sufficient reasons I left that timepiece at home, where the Dutchman left his anchor.
>
> ". . . At Yarmouth, too, I got my famous tin clock, the only timepiece I carried on the whole voyage. The price of it was a dollar and a half, but on account of the face being smashed the merchant let me have it for a dollar.
>
> ". . . My tin clock and only timepiece had by this time lost its minute hand, but after I boiled her‡ she told the hours, and that was near enough on a long stretch. . . ."

But as early as 1800 or so seamen in general, not gifted with that fine old Viking spirit, that splendid contempt of ordinary seaman-like precaution which sometimes sends vessels speeding through ice or fog at full speed, but, perhaps, more commendable in their modest way as

---

* Quoted from "The Maritime History of Massachusetts," by S. E. Morison, Boston, 1921.

† "Sailing Alone around the World," London, no date (*circa* 1895). As a feat of single-handed sailing, Capt. Slocum's circumnavigation in the "Spray," a sloop (altered to yawl-rig during the voyage) of 36½ ft. in length and 12.7 tons net register, has never been equalled. She is believed to have foundered, with her brave master, in the course of a subsequent voyage.

‡ This drastic treatment is not to be recommended for any timepiece costing more than a dollar and a half, although it is somewhat reminiscent of the methods once used at Greenwich. In the record of K1's trial at the Royal Observatory a note on January 16th, 1772, relates that it was found stopped, and continues: ". . . I could not make it go again, tho' I warmed it by the fire and gave motion to the ballance."

careful navigators, attaching a reasonable value to the lives of their crews and passengers, and the safety of their cargoes, had discovered that, as a means of finding longitude, a chronometer was a long way ahead of the method of lunar distances, and that the purchase of one was a sounder investment than a multiplicity of insurance premiums. And, accordingly, a widespread demand for them gradually arose, which quickly caused, on all hands, a general agreement as to the lines of their construction and the essential portions of their mechanism. This accepted specification, which included a mainspring, a maintaining spring, a fusee, a train of five wheels, a detached escapement, a helical balance spring, and a compensation balance, was followed both in the chronometers produced in England, which very soon took the lead in the new manufacture, and in those of France, Denmark, Spain and other countries.

But although a satisfactory form of the chronometer had been evolved, it had not yet been proved, or, indeed, suspected, that it was the best form, and it was not until after an immense amount of ingenuity had been expended upon other designs that it came to be generally recognised that the strong and simple construction embodied in Earnshaw's chronometers was better fitted to do the work required of it than any other, and that except in minor details its mechanism could not be materially altered with advantage. As often happens, practice had far outstripped theory, but had kept to the right road. It remained for theory and experiment to fill up the gaps in the technical knowledge of chronometer makers, and to supply reasons for the results which they obtained in the course of their work.

To the ordinary observer there may not appear much difference between the chronometer of 1800 shown in Plate XXXIII., and that of 1920 appearing in Plate XXXVIII.—certainly nothing would lead him to suspect that one was over a century older than the other. And even if the two movements were taken out of their cases for the purpose of comparison he would still be unable to detect much difference in their mechanism. The lovely finish of the Kullberg would probably contrast rather painfully with the comparative roughness of the Earnshaw, intentionally left " in the grey " and not polished, but this is a difference which is more apparent than real, and when apprised of the respective dates of the two machines he could hardly be blamed for coming to the conclusion that chronometer makers, as a class, were extremely conservative and unprogressive.

But this conclusion would be most unjust, as could easily be proved to him by a simple comparison of the recorded rates of the two machines. The Earnshaw was doubtless found quite adequate to the needs of the navigator of his day, but, as appears from Appendix I., it could not hold a candle to the modern machine for close and consistent timekeeping under severe conditions of test. And since the sole function of a chronometer is to measure time accurately, it must be admitted that there is just as much real difference between a modern machine and an Earnshaw as there is between the Earnshaw and Harrison's

No. 4. That the difference is not more apparent at first sight is due to the fact that it resides chiefly in small and apparently not very important details.

The century and a quarter which separates the two machines was filled with research and experiment conducted by hundreds of clever men, some working on right lines, and some otherwise, but all playing their part in producing the chronometer of to-day. Some of their work is dross, some alloy, and some pure gold. And even the dross is interesting and deserving of record—if the only result be to prevent wasted effort in days to come. Accordingly, it is proposed, in the following chapters, to give some account of the various improvements, real or imaginary, practical or otherwise, which have been applied, or proposed to be applied, to the chronometer as left by Earnshaw and his contemporaries. The principal points of improvement and alteration were, as might be expected, found to be the escapement, the balance spring, and the balance, while one chapter contains an account of such miscellaneous work as does not come under any of these specific heads.

CHAPTER IX.

THE ESCAPEMENT.

Figure 34 shows, side by side, the chronometer escapement devised by Earnshaw, and that in use at the present day—the Alpha and Omega, in fact, of the period (1782-1922) which we are now discussing. It will be noted that the differences between the two do not appear to be very great, while the essential parts—escape wheel, impulse roller, discharging roller, and detent—are almost alike. Between the initial and final forms, however, there has taken place a considerable amount of research and experiment, which will be briefly described.

ESCAPE WHEEL.

As originally made by Earnshaw, this was flat, the teeth being in the same plane as the rim. In the modern form the teeth are raised above the rim as in the old Arnold pattern of escapement. They are thus enabled to be much broader, giving an increased acting surface and reducing the wear on them without materially increasing the moment of inertia of the wheel.

In order to decrease the work of unlocking the detent, it has several times been proposed to use a duplex escape wheel, with two sets of teeth, one for giving impulse, and the other, at a larger radius, for locking. This was tried by Owen Robinson (one of J. R. Arnold's workmen) and Urban Jurgensen, amongst others. It was found better to have two separate wheels of different radii, rather than to form both sets of teeth on a single wheel; but, although this construction proved extremely easy to adjust, the practical benefit gained from the duplex wheel was extremely slight, and by no means made up for the extra labour involved.

A reversal of this plan was tried by Charles Frodsham at Airy's suggestion—an impulse roller considerably larger than the escape wheel, instead of being, as now, about half its diameter. Airy's idea was to diminish the side friction of the balance pivots due to the blow of the escape wheel falling near to the axis of the balance staff. The plan necessitated, however, an entire reconstruction of the movement, including an extra wheel in the train, while the increased angular velocity of the impulse pallet rendered it extremely difficult to get the escape wheel, after unlocking, under way in time to give the former any impulse at all.† It must be remembered that in the chronometer escapement the escape wheel, starting from rest, has to overtake, and give impulse upon, the rapidly swinging impulse pallet, and in consequence its moment of inertia must be very considerably less than

* An escapement on the lines of the old Arnold pattern, with an escape wheel and impulse pallet very like those of the duplex escapement, was proposed by H. Ganney in 1903. In an escapement designed to effect the same end—easier unlocking—patented by Massey in 1838 (Patent No. 7678 of that year) two separate detents were employed.

† It will be remembered that the escapement of Le Roy's timekeeper was of this type. Frodsham died while the new design was under trial, and the experiments with it were not continued.

that of the balance. In fact, a perfectly proportioned escapement, set correctly in beat, might be rendered absolutely useless by the fitting of too heavy an escape wheel.

IMPULSE AND DISCHARGING PALLETS.

Little change has been made in these since Earnshaw's time. The acting surfaces of the pallets are faced with ruby or sapphire.* It will be noted, however, that while Earnshaw undercut the face of his impulse pallet considerably, that of the modern escapement is set radially.

R. Webster proposed, in 1849, to use epicycloidal curves for both impulse pallet and escape wheel teeth, and thus obtain a rolling impulse without any sliding friction.† This construction, however, is open to the objection that unless the impulse be given absolutely instantaneously (which is a practical impossibility) the radius at which it is applied will vary very considerably, and that the point of contact must always be before the line of centres‡. It may be noted that in several of his chronometers Ferdinand Berthoud employed a small pivoted roller for the impulse pallet.

THE DETENT.

Here, again, there is little difference from Earnshaw's construction. The face of the locking stone (generally a ruby) does not point exactly to the centre of the escape wheel, but slightly to one side of it, so that the pressure of the escape wheel tooth tends to draw the detent slightly further into engagement. This makes the locking safer, while involving a barely perceptible recoil of the wheel at the instant of unlocking.

For many years it remained a moot point whether the spring detent was preferable or otherwise to the pivoted form used by Berthouds,

* The impulse and discharging rollers are of steel. It may be noted that the edge of the impulse roller forms a safety device in the event of the detent being accidentally unlocked by some sudden shock. In such a case, a tooth of the escape wheel would fall on the rim of the roller, and rest on it until the impulse pallet came round. The friction so caused would not be enough to stop the balance, although, of course, it would lengthen its time of vibration. I once came across an old chronometer, made by Margetts and Hatton, about 1810, going in a very extraordinary manner. It sounded badly out of beat, and at every beat there was a very perceptible recoil of the second hand. Believing K3, made some forty years earlier, to have been the last chronometer to have a recoil escapement, I opened up the movement and found that the spring detent had broken at the root of the spring and dropped clear, leaving the machine going as if with a modified form of duplex escapement, the teeth of the escape wheel resting on the edge of the impulse roller for the greater portion of the balance's swing, and escaping one by one through the notch cut away in front of the impulse pallet, giving impulse on the latter as they did so. The recoil was caused by the pallet meeting the teeth on the return swing, and pushing them backwards.

† His idea in so doing was to reduce the sliding friction of the tooth on the pallet, but in the modern escapement this end is best obtained with the radial pallet.

‡ The line joining the centres of two geared wheels—in this case the escape wheel and impulse roller. In all questions of gearing this line serves as a standard of reference by which the suitability or otherwise of the design can be judged. The position at which the teeth engage is determined by the number on the smaller wheel, and if too far before the line of centres there is danger of the engaging friction of the teeth preventing any rotation. The nearer to the line of centres the engagement takes place, the less power is wasted in friction; similarly, in an escapement, the nearer to the line of centres the impulse is given, the better.

by Arnold in his early models, and by several later French makers. Fig. 35 shows the form of pivoted detent used by Motel, a pupil of Louis Berthoud, who brought it to very great perfection, and was renowned for the beauty and exactitude of his work. Its merits, as compared with the spring detent, were hotly debated, but the question, as far as it relates to box chronometers, has for many years been definitely settled in favour of the latter, while for pocket chronometers it has merely an academical interest, since both have been beaten out of the field by the lever escapement.

On the score of expense and difficulty of manufacture there is little to choose between the two forms. The pivoted detent has the advantage that it can be exactly poised, so that its action is the same in all positions, while that of the spring detent is slightly affected by its position, *e.g.*, it offers less resistance to unlocking when assisted by gravity, and *vice versa*. On the other hand, the pivots of the former need oil, and its action is liable to be impeded by the thickening of this oil with age—a fault from which the spring detent is entirely free. *A priori*, then, it might be concluded that the spring detent is preferable for box chronometers, and the pivoted form for pocket ones.

Several pivoted detent escapements have been designed, having as their principal aim the securing of unlocking with a less motion of the balance than is required with the spring detent. An escapement of this pattern, called the "American Chronometer" for pocket watches, was patented in 1864 by J. Karr, of Washington, and the idea was revived in 1882 by E. Storer.

It should be added that it is possible to counterbalance a spring detent so as to be unaffected by position, but it then becomes practically a pivoted detent controlled by a straight spring instead of a spiral.

A modification of Earnshaw's escapement, termed the "cross-detent" and shown in Fig. 36, was devised by Peto, a pupil of his who subsequently left him and worked for Brockbank. The latter used it in a number of chronometers.* It is an attempt to retain the principal

* Earnshaw's account of the genesis of this escapement is amusing:—"Mr. Peto enquired of me concerning the difference and superiority of my Escapement over Arnold's; I . . . proved to him the great disadvantage of Arnold's scape unlocking *towards* the centre, and how much better it would be if it were to unlock *from* the centre, but that could not be done with Arnold's wheel, on account of the shape of the teeth, and the side on which Arnold had placed his spring, unless the end of the detent spring was carried round to the back of the verge,† which would likewise be another great inconvenience. Mr. Peto set to work, and made one in that way which I had then described, and took it to Brockbank . . . Although this was a spring detent without pivots, yet it was so inconsistent, and inferior to the manner in which I made them, that it was like a person going round a house to get in at the back door, when the front door stood fairly open to him. But when I mentioned this absurdity to Mr. Peto, he said it was different from mine, and evaded the Patent, and that I could not prosecute him for it." When opposing the £3,000 reward granted to Earnshaw, Brockbank claimed this escapement as his own, but subsequently admitted that it was not entirely so. He described it, of course, as superior to all others. A chronometer by Brockbank, No. 70 (made about 1785), fitted with this escapement, is preserved in the Museum of the Clockmakers Company.

† Formerly, the balance-staff was sometimes called the "verge," and the word is so used in this instance.

advantage of Arnold's escapement—that of keeping the detent spring in tension instead of compression. But the arrangement is clumsy, and takes up a lot of room.

REMARKS ON THE CHRONOMETER ESCAPEMENT.

This escapement still holds pride of place as the most perfect form of escapement for balance timekeepers of high precision. It owes this pre-eminence to two features—the balance is more detached than in any other escapement, and since the impulse is given very rapidly by a direct blow on the impulse pallet close to the line of centres, the isochronism of the balance is interfered with as little as possible, while no oil is required on the pallet. All these conditions combine to render it capable of performing its function of unlocking and giving impulse in a manner which approximates very closely to the theoretical ideal, and exhibits no perceptible change over a very long period.

The one unavoidable defect of this escapement is its liability to stop, or "set," as it is generally termed. If any external motion, such as a sudden twist, should bring the balance to rest, or nearly so, close to its dead point, the chronometer will probably stop.

The reason of this is that the design of the chronometer escapement demands that the balance should turn through a considerable arc while effecting the unlocking—an arc which, in box chronometers, amounts to about 35°. In order to reduce this arc, it would be necessary to increase the radius at which the discharging pallet acts, which would have the disadvantage of inflicting a much greater check upon the motions of the balance at the instant when the pallet met the passing spring. Actually, in pocket chronometers, the size of this unlocking angle (and, with it, that of its complementary arc on the other side of the dead point*) is slightly reduced, in order to render it more difficult for the watch to be stopped accidentally. In either case, however, should the relative motion of the balance and the detent be accidentally reduced, by a twisting being given to the chronometer, below twice the unlocking angle, the escape wheel will not be unlocked, no impulse will be given to the balance, and the machine will stop, the balance gradually coming to rest at the dead point.

If once stopped, the chronometer will remain so until it is again set going by giving the balance sufficient motion. No plan has yet been suggested to overcome this defect, but in practice it is not so formidable as it may at first sight appear. The normal arc described by the balance is in the nature of 270° on either side of the dead point, and the twist required to reduce it below the amount necessary to maintain its motion is therefore upwards of half a turn in $\frac{1}{4}$ sec. A box chronometer is never likely, except when carelessly

* If the escapement is correctly in beat, the arc described by the balance between the moment when the discharging pallet meets the passing spring and that when the escape-wheel tooth falls on the impulse pallet should be exactly equal to that which it describes between the latter point and that at which the escape-wheel tooth drops off the impulse pallet. When so adjusted, the balance must be turned through the same minimum angle in either direction before the chronometer will go.

MARINE CHRONOMETER BY J.F. COLE INSCRIBED 'DOUBLE ROTARY DETACHED ESCAPEMENT' JAMES F. COLE LONDON AD 1840

Courtesy Worshipful Co. of Clockmakers. C.C. Cat. 621.

See p. 219.

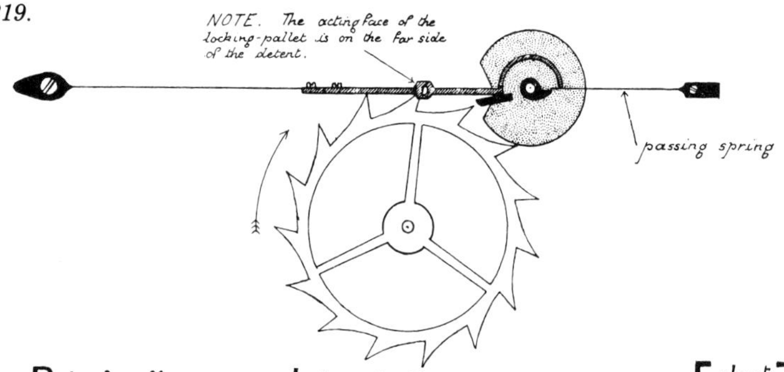
NOTE. The acting face of the locking-pallet is on the far side of the detent.
passing spring

36 Peto's "cross detent" escapement [about 1785]

See p. 223.

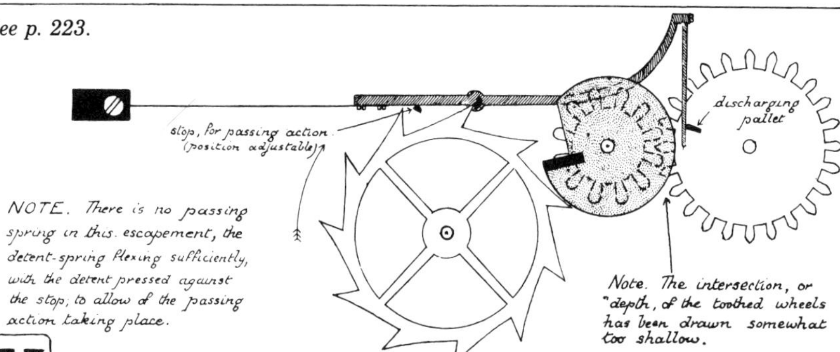
stop, for passing action (position adjustable)
discharging pallet
NOTE. There is no passing spring in this escapement, the detent-spring flexing sufficiently, with the detent pressed against the stop, to allow of the passing action taking place.
Note. The intersection, or "depth, of the toothed wheels has been drawn somewhat too shallow.

37 Cole's "double rotary" escapement [1840]

See p. 223.

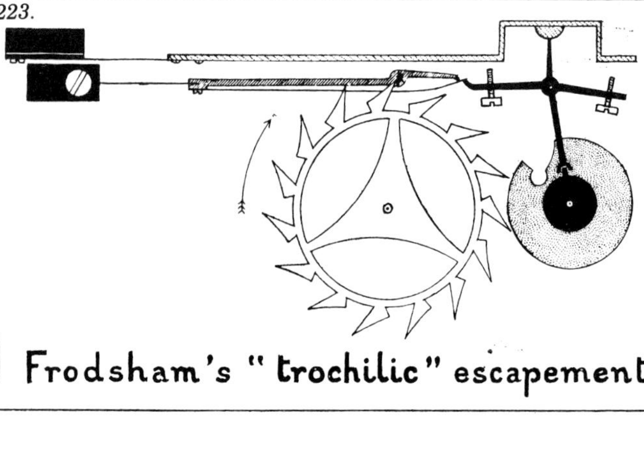

38 Frodsham's "trochilic" escapement.

transported, to experience such a rapid angular motion, and even in a pocket chronometer such treatment would argue great carelessness on the part of the wearer.

TRIPPING.

A twisting motion given to a chronometer may, however, operate in the contrary way, and, instead of bringing the discharging pallet to rest, or nearly so, relatively to the detent, cause the extent of this relative motion to be considerably above the normal. It is obvious that if, after the unlocking has been effected, the balance make a complete turn, it will again unlock the escape wheel, and receive a second impulse, which will send it still further, while the seconds hand, being in connection with the escape wheel, will jump forward half a second. If the twist occur on the opposite swing, the discharging pallet will "pass" twice, and this "tripping" will occur on the return swing. In addition, tripping may occur at any time, without a double unlocking, if the detent spring be too weak, or if the detent be jarred out of the locking position by a blow on the chronometer case.

To cure this defect, several plans have been put forward. The balances of some chronometers have been banked to prevent them from describing a complete turn, but this is only a palliative, since the shock of touching the banking affects the time of vibration. Attempts were also made by Arnold, Ulrich, Dent, and others, to add some form of safety gear, as used in the lever escapement, which should prevent the detent from unlocking except at the right moment; but these were found to involve too much complication. In addition, at least two* forms of escapement have been devised—Cole's double rotary escapement, and Frodsham's "Trochilic," which permit the balance to describe more than a complete turn without ill effect.

Cole's double rotary escapement is shown in fig. 37. The discharging pallet is carried on a separate arbor, and geared to the balance staff (which carries the impulse pallet in the usual manner) in the ratio of 2 to 1. Hence it follows that the balance can make almost two revolutions (or, by varying the gearing, even a higher number) without causing tripping. The friction of the gearing, however, involves a constant impediment to the free vibration of the balance.†

The "Trochilic" escapement‡, shown in fig. 38, is still more ingenious, since it involves no additional friction, and permits of the

* A third form, of rather fantastic appearance, is described by M. Gros, p. 177.

† I recently examined a chronometer by Cole, with this escapement, fitted up as a table clock. It is preserved in the Nelthropp Collection, which forms part of the Museum of the Clockmakers' Company. The balance describes about a turn and three-quarters, and the operation of the escapement is attended with an audible buzz from the gearing. The workmanship is very fine. A diagram of a very similar escapement is given in M. Gros' work, but there is nothing to indicate its authorship. It is there stated that, with the object of diminishing wear, the tooth of the discharging pallet wheel which was in gear at the moment of giving impulse was formed of ruby.

‡ This name, which is not remarkable for its aptness, is formed from the Greek τροχος "a wheel."

balance making any number of revolutions without any possibility of tripping taking place. The discharging pallet does not actuate the detent directly, but through the medium of a fork and T piece, which is driven to one side or the other by the pallet and retained there by a separate spring detent until its position is reversed by the balance on its return journey. Should the latter perform more than a complete turn, the discharging pallet merely presses on the outside of the fork, and passes it, without moving the detent.

The foregoing remarks give an outline of the principal modifications attempted in the standard escapement, but many attempts have also been made to produce chronometer escapements of entirely different pattern, generally with the idea of giving a constant impulse to the balance, notwithstanding such fluctuations of force as must, in spite of the fusee, occur in even the most accurately cut train. These attempts have, however, long been discontinued, for it is now generally recognised that isochronism must be sought, not in the maintenance of a constant arc of vibration (which is impossible in practice) but in the proportion and adjustment of the balance spring.

CONSTANT-FORCE ESCAPEMENTS.

These escapements are best described by the above title. They are frequently termed "remontoire escapements," but the expression is a misleading one. The remontoire, *per se*, is not an escapement, but a mechanism interposed at some point between the mainspring and the balance, and designed to render that portion of the force of the former which reaches the latter constant, or nearly so, by transmitting part of it in the form of a series of small and equal increments, and discarding the remainder. The power of the mainspring must be sufficient to ensure that the minimum amount which, in the course of the fluctuations inseparable from its transmission, reaches the remontoire is sufficient for its purposes, and it follows that constant-force escapements, from their construction, require a stronger mainspring for a given size of balance than a chronometer escapement of the ordinary pattern does, and that a certain proportion of the latter's force is unavoidably wasted.*

The remontoire may be, and has been, installed at any point in the train. It will be recalled that Huyghens fitted his in the crown wheel, Sully in the centre wheel, Harrison in the fourth wheel (in Nos. 2, 4, and 5), or the escape wheel (in No. 3), and Mudge on the balance staff itself. In later times, chronometers were constructed

---

* W. G. Schoof once remarked of Grimthorpe's double three-legged gravity escapement, in which a fly is fitted to absorb the excess force of the train, that it reminded him of a captain taking thirty tons of coal on board for a trip that only required one ton, and then hiring a stoker named Fly to throw the other twenty-nine tons overboard.

The locking pallet of a standard chronometer escapement plays, in a sense, the part of a remontoire-fly in absorbing the surplus power transmitted through the train, which is converted into heat. In a *frictionless* chronometer, the angular speed of the balance would increase until the teeth of the escape wheel no longer fell on the impulse pallet. The force stored in the mainspring would then be expended in gradually raising the temperature of the locking stone.

Plate XXXIV. CHRONOMETER BY J. G. ULRICH.

The size of the machine may be gathered from the chronometer (a Dent, of normal size) on top of it.

In the centre of the upper dial, but barely discernible, are the Royal Arms, and below them the up-and-down indicator.

by Scrymgeour (1828)* and Dent (1842) with remontoires in the escape and third wheels respectively, while a patent taken out by Weber in 1854† covers the use of a remontoire in the great wheel itself (in lieu of a fusee).‡

Since the fluctuations of driving force which the remontoire is intended to correct are largely due to the varying friction of the toothed wheels composing the train, it follows that its efficacy will be greatly diminished if placed near the mainspring, and that if situated farther back than the fourth wheel it can be of no practical value. The best position for it is obviously either at the balance staff itself, or immediately next to it.

This last position is that generally adopted by those inventors who have proposed constant-force escapements. In general, all their plans are a modification of the Earnshaw escapement upon the following lines.

The escape wheel, instead of being allowed to impel the balance direct, does so indirectly through the medium of a small auxiliary spring, which is wound by it and then locked upon a detent until released by the discharging pallet on the balance staff. The auxiliary spring then gives impulse to the balance, and, having disengaged itself from the latter, unlocks the escape wheel, and so causes itself to be re-wound and re-locked ready to give the next impulse. Some form of passing spring is fitted, as in the ordinary chronometer escapement, to prevent the auxiliary from being unlocked on the return swing of the balance. In theory, there is nothing to be said against escapements of this pattern, which ought to give the balance a practically constant impulse (and, therefore, cause it to describe a practically constant arc), but in practice their complication, and the alterations in their action caused by the ageing of the oil in their pivots and on their pallets, nullify most of their theoretical advantages, while they have the further defect of being considerably more expensive, both in construction and adjustment, than the ordinary pattern. In addition, it has never been demonstrated that they actually give any better results from the point of view of timekeeping.

The first escapement of this pattern appears to be that patented by Haley, a London maker, in 1796§. It was complicated and easily deranged, and its inventor never succeeded in rendering its action even reasonably safe. His invention was the forerunner of a number of others on the same lines, amongst which may be instanced those of Breguet (*circa* 1800), Hardy (*circa* 1810), Ulrich (1825 and 1828), Hedgethorne (1899), Pettavel (1900), and Cox (1912).

* This machine competed in the Greenwich trial of 1850, but with the remontoire thrown out of action as unreliable.

† No. 1335 of 1854.

‡ A remontoire patented by Poncy in 1840 (No. 8062) is remarkable as being, in all essentials, a reversion to the type employed by Harrison. The following points are common to both: a remontoire in the fourth wheel, a circle of eight pins in the latter to effect the unlocking, and the use of a fifth wheel and fly.

§ Patent No. 2132 of 1796.

All these differ only in their detail arrangements. Figs. 39—42 show four of them—Hardy's, Breguet's, Ulrich's of 1828, and Pettavel's. In all four figures the following lettering has been adopted, viz., B the balance, E the escape wheel, S the auxiliary spring, I the arm conveying the force of that spring to the impulse pallet, D, the detent which locks the escape wheel, and *d* that which locks the auxiliary spring.

HARDY'S (Fig. 39).

The relatively enormous size of the escape wheel will be noticed. The piece P, which is pivoted, serves to communicate the impulse of the remontoire spring by means of the arm I, and a second arm J unlocks the detent *e* after I has disengaged from the impulse pallet, thus causing the piece P to be returned to its initial position (locked by the detent *d* with the spring S wound).

No other maker appears to have made use of this escapement (or, indeed, of any of the forms described, with the exception of Pettavel's).

BREGUET'S (Fig. 40).

In this design the auxiliary spring is a straight one. The escape wheel is duplex, one set of teeth being employed for locking, and a second for re-winding the auxiliary spring. A fly, F, driven from the escape wheel, is provided to ensure that the re-winding does not take place too quickly, and so cause damage. It may be noted that although it might be thought that the use of a remontoire would enable the fusee to be eliminated from the movement, this has not often been found to be the case in practice. The remontoire is necessarily a delicate piece of mechanism, and if exposed to considerable variations of force its action and adjustments are liable to be impaired.

Saunier, in his classic work*, says of this escapement of Breguet's that it gave no better results than one of ordinary pattern, and did not even maintain these, although it was executed with all Breguet's inimitable skill.

ULRICH'S (Fig 41).

This is perhaps the most complicated escapement which has ever been devised for a marine timekeeper. In essentials, its operation is exactly the same as that of Hardy's and Breguet's: *i.e.*, the train winds the auxiliary spring and then locks. The auxiliary spring is unlocked by the balance, gives the latter impulse, disengages, and then unlocks the train, which re-winds the auxiliary—and so on. Ulrich, however, added a number of auxiliary devices designed to render the unlocking both of the auxiliary and the train easier and safer†. As

---

* "Traité d'Horlogerie Moderne," Paris, 1861. English translation by Tripplin and Rigg, London, 1871.

† I examined the escapement of the machine shown in Plate XXXIV. recently. There is a quality of suspended animation about it suggestive of catalepsy. The slightest touch to it when at rest starts a whole cycle of complicated reactions, one following closely on the heels of another.

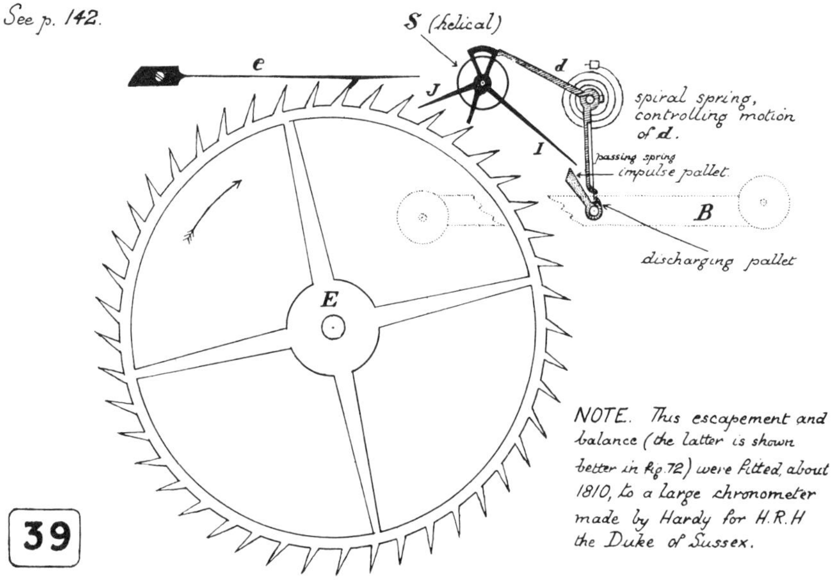

39

Hardy's constant-force escapement [about 1810].

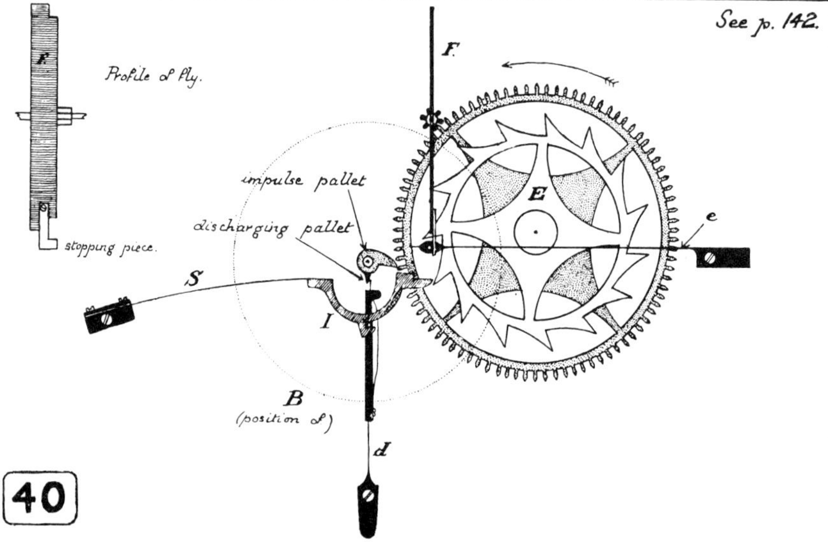

40

Breguet's constant-force escapement [1795].

MARINE CHRONOMETER BY JOSEPH CROUCHER.
c.1830, made on J.G. Ulrich's patent.
Clockmakers Company. (C.C. Cat. 619).

may be gathered from the figure, this escapement was very expensive to make and very difficult to adjust. Of necessity, its size was considerable. It was fitted to a number of very large chronometers made by Ulrich in 1828-1832 in collaboration with Joseph Croucher*, of Cornhill, who found the capital for the enterprise, and became a heavy loser by it. The general appearance and movement of these gigantic machines are shown in Plates XXXIV. and XXXV., which are photographs of an example preserved in the museum of the Clockmakers' Company. They present several features of interest, as in addition to having this escapement they are fitted with non-magnetic balances of brass and platinum, the (non-laminated) arms of the balance being moved by means of a central tubular gridiron, while the escapement and balance are mounted on a detachable plate, and can be removed without affecting the remainder of the mechanism.

None of these machines was ever entered for an official trial, although one was tried privately at Greenwich for some time by one of the assistants, with poor results. Airy, in the course of an official report upon Ulrich's claim for a reward for his work, remarks scathingly upon a similar escapement designed by Ulrich.

> "The escapement submitted to the Board of Longitude in 1824 is the most complicated piece of mechanism that I ever saw: for instance, seven springs are in it employed to do the same work which is done by one in the ordinary escapement. It is perhaps the most remarkable instance of misapplied ingenuity that ever was seen. It is utterly useless."†

This is an extreme opinion, but it is incontestable that any slight advantages which such constructions may theoretically possess over the ordinary pattern are far more than counterbalanced by their cost, delicacy, and complication.

PETTAVEL'S (Fig. 42).

This has, I believe, the distinction of being the only constant-force escapement at present in use for balance timekeepers. It is fitted in some of the high-class watches produced by the firm of Paul Ditisheim. Its action is similar to that of those previously described, but it is simpler and more robust than any of them, and has been found, in practice, to give excellent results.

Before leaving the subject of constant-force escapements, it may be noted that after having been formerly tried unsuccessfully in various classes of clocks they have, in recent years, come into widespread use for that purpose. For example, the Grimthorpe double-three-legged gravity escapement (which, after its amazingly successful debut in the Westminster clock, has become the standard escapement

* Croucher issued a description of the machine, in pamphlet form, entitled "Analytical Hints on the Patent Marine Timekeeper made by Joseph Croucher, No. 27, Cornhill, London" (no date). It is a pure advertisement, of no scientific value as a correct description.

† Quoted from an official report by Airy to the Admiralty. This paper, reprinted in Parliamentary Paper, No. 142, of 1859, is valuable as containing a full statement of matters relating to J. G. Ulrich's claims to reward for his improvements in chronometers.

for large turret-clocks*), that used in the "Synchronome" and other similar types of electric clocks, and the Riefler escapement used in the high-class astronomical clocks made by the firm of that name, are all constant-force escapements. And it might be thought that the undoubted advantage derivable from the use of such escapements in clocks ought to be equally marked in chronometers and watches. But the two cases are by no means analogous. In a clock the variations of train and pallet friction generally exceed those of the pivot friction, and accordingly a constant-force escapement is of decided advantage; but in chronometers and watches the pivot friction varies considerably more than that of the train and pallets, and accordingly the advantage obtainable from a constant-force escapement is not so great. It is possible that some escapement of the kind, as simple, relatively speaking, as Grimthorpe's (which, it must be remembered, is by far the youngest of all the escapements now in common use, and appeared at a time when *all* constant-force gravity escapements were regarded as being demonstrably inferior to the dead-beat)† may yet be produced, and provided that it eliminates the fusee and gives a constant impulse with a minimum of moving parts, it will no doubt have a future. At present, all that can be said of the many constant-force escapements which have been proposed for chronometers is that hardly any one of them has ever proved to be worth the trouble and expense of its manufacture.

"Free Balance" Escapements.

The above term seems the best suited to describe that small and seductive class of escapements in which the balance has no connection with the movement other than the balance spring itself, the impulse being transmitted through this spring and the unlocking of the escapement being effected in the same manner. To all appearance, such an escapement gives a *perfectly* detached balance, and it might accordingly be thought that if it were mechanically feasible it would constitute the best of all escapements. But in practice this is not so. There is no great difficulty in merely maintaining the motion of a balance by this means, but it is extremely hard to ensure that the isochronism of its vibrations is unaffected by such a method of impelling it.

The force exerted by the balance spring upon a swinging balance takes effect at two points—the stud at which the fixed end of the spring is attached to the top-plate, and the collet‡ by which the other and of the spring is affixed to the balance staff. These forces are

* It should be noted that this escapement differs only slightly (principally in the provision of a fly) from that previously invented by Mr. J. M. Bloxam, a barrister. His original clock is now going in the Science Museum, South Kensington.

† This opinion was due to a paper by Airy in the Cambridge Philosophical Transactions for 1826, in which it was generally thought that he had conclusively proved this point: but it was subsequently shown by Denison (afterwards Lord Grimthorpe) that his argument involved a fallacy.

‡ A small metal collar fitted friction-tight to the balance-staff.

See p. 227.

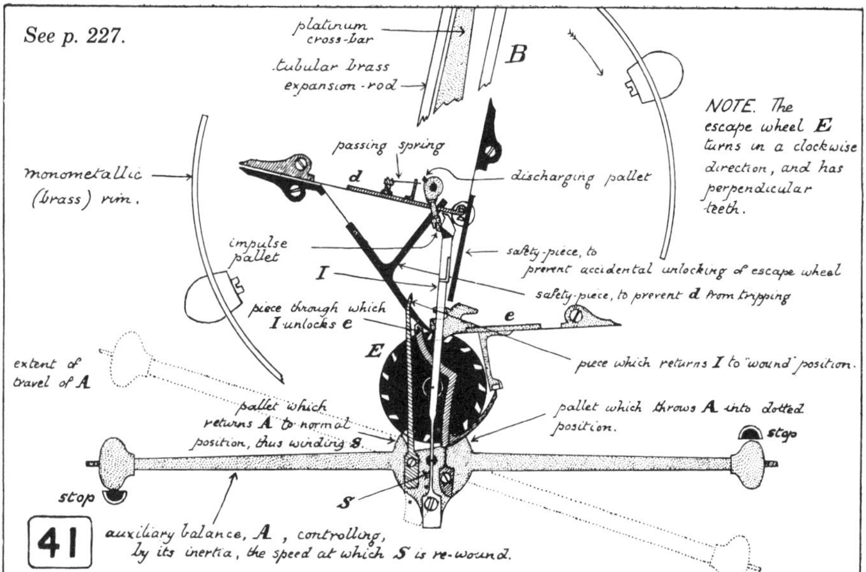

41

Ulrich's constant-force escapement [1828]

See p. 230.

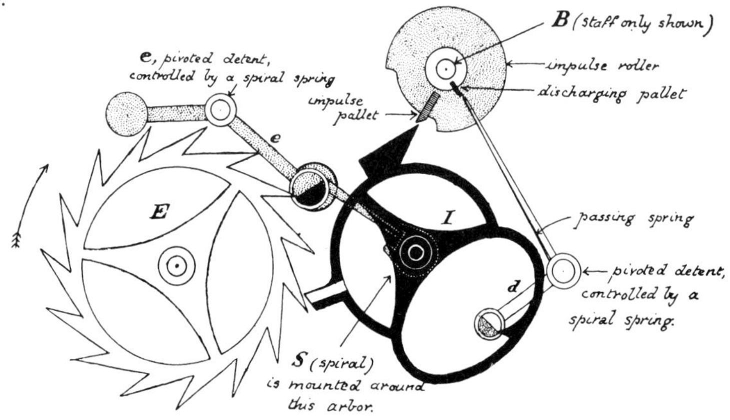

42

Pettavel's constant-force escapement.

equal and opposite, *i.e.*, there is as much force tending to make the stud move towards the balance as there is tending to make the balance return to the dead-point.

Now if the stud, instead of being fixed, be mounted on a movable arm pivoted concentrically with the balance, and this arm be moved through a small arc in the opposite direction to the force exerted by the balance spring on the stud, and then held, the tension or compression of the spring (and, accordingly, the force acting upon the balance) will be augmented—or, in other words, impulse will be given to the balance. Since the amount of impulse needed to maintain its vibrations is slight, it is obvious that the motion required to be given to the stud is not great, and that since the spring, so long as the balance is in motion, will continue to exert alternating forces upon the stud, these forces can be utilised to effect the unlocking of the escapement controlling the movements of the arm.

So long as the movement of the fixed end of the spring takes place in the correct direction, impulse will be given, and it is immaterial, strictly speaking, whether this be done at every complete vibration, or at a shorter or longer interval. All such arrangements as have so far been proposed, however, give impulse either at every half vibration (as in the lever escapement) or at every whole one (as in the chronometer escapement). In the first case, the fixed end of the spring oscillates through a small arc, and its mean position is constant: in the second, it gradually describes a circle around the axis of the balance, and the latter's motion may be regarded as compounded of two—a rapid periodical vibration, and a slow rotation around its own axis. It follows that in this case the arc which it describes on one side of the dead-point (which moves round with the stud) is always slightly greater than that described on the other.

The objection to such escapements is that unless the movement of the stud can be arranged to be absolutely constant, not only in amount, but in *speed*, the time of vibration of the balance will vary: and this necessitates the employment of either a remontoire or a fly to obviate what would otherwise be a source of considerable error.

Very few escapements have been made on this principle. The earliest, I believe, is that patented by Robert Leslie in 1793, while since his time various other plans have been proposed by Gowland (1849), Benoit (1853), Hillgren (1882), and Riefler (1889). These, with the exception of Hillgren's, are illustrated in figs. 43—46.

LESLIE'S (Fig. 43).

In this escapement the outer end of the balance spring is attached to a fixed stud planted in the top-plate, but the spring is gripped about one turn from this stud by two pins mounted on a moveable arm projecting through a hole in the plate and moved by means of an escapement planted so that the pivot of the arm is concentric, or nearly so, with the balance-axis. The action of the escapement (which, as illustrated in the specification, is a cylinder) is normal, its only difference from the ordinary pattern being that instead of the balance being rigidly mounted with the cylinder it is connected with it by the balance spring, and is thus enabled to describe a much larger arc. From the point of view of accurate timekeeping, this construction presents no advantage over the ordinary cylinder escapement.

Leslie stated that his invention was equally applicable to any escapement, but this could not be effected in the case either of the chronometer or lever escapements without very considerable modification. Its chief defect is that as the unlocking can only be accomplished by the action of the spring after the balance has swung considerably past the dead-point, the impulse is given more or less at the extremity of the arc of vibration, instead of at its centre.

GOWLAND'S (Fig. 44).

This escapement is much more complicated than the foregoing, and while the impulse is transmitted through the balance-spring, the unlocking is effected by a discharging pallet mounted on the balance staff.

The outer end of the balance spring is attached to a stud carried on a cross-bar which is revolved slowly around the balance by the action of the train, the amount of its advance at every beat being limited by a circle of step-cut projections on the top-plate, against which a locking pallet carried at the end of the bar engages, until unlocked by the discharging pallet on the next swing.

There is little merit in this escapement, and it never came into practical use. The use of a discharging pallet to effect the unlocking allows of the impulse being given at or near the dead-point, but involves an abandonment of the principal feature of this class of escapements—that of suppressing all obstacles to the unrestricted motion of the balance.

BENOIT'S (Fig. 45).

A much simpler and better arrangement than the foregoing is that devised in 1853 by C. Benoit, a well-known French maker. In this escapement the stud of the balance spring is mounted on the escape wheel, which is controlled by the lever L, carrying the pallets *p*,*p'*. The action is as follows. If it be imagined that the escape-wheel has just given impulse by turning in the direction of the arrow, and is now locked on *p*, the balance will be free to swing to the full extent of its arc, and will then return. On the return swing, the escape wheel will be set back a little by the compression of the balance spring and the back of tooth will press against the pallet *p'*, thus rocking the lever slightly and lifting *p* clear of the path of the teeth. The escape wheel will therefore be left free to give impulse as soon as the stress in the balance spring diminishes, and in doing so the tooth will meet the pallet *p'* and rock the lever back to its former position in time to lock the tooth.

See p. 233.

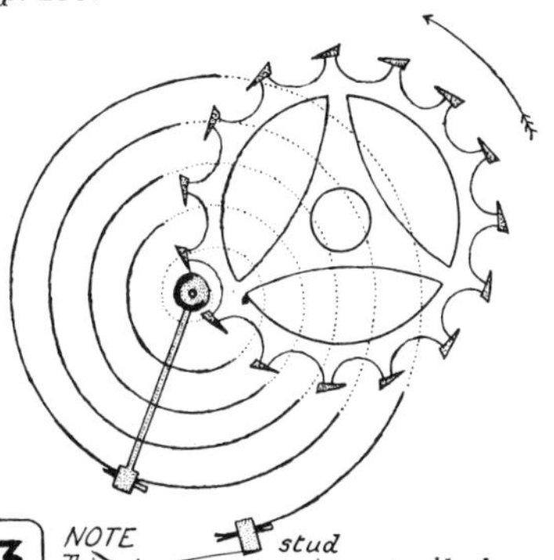

43

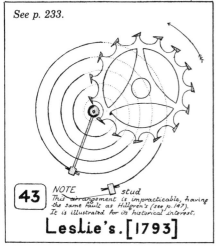

NOTE stud
This arrangement is impracticable, having the same fault as Hillgren's (see p. 147).
It is illustrated for its historical interest.

Leslie's. [1793]

See p. 234.

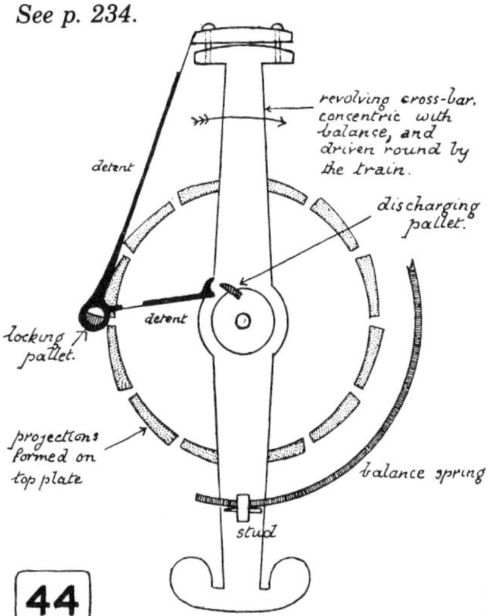

44

Gowland's. [1849]

"Free balance" escapements.

See p. 234.

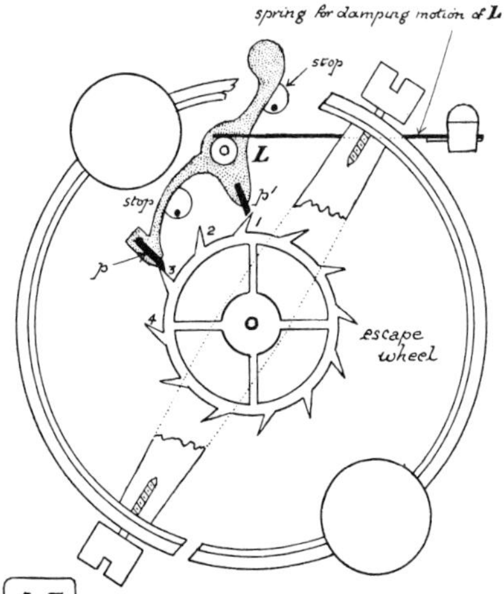

45

Benoit's. [1853]

See p. 236.

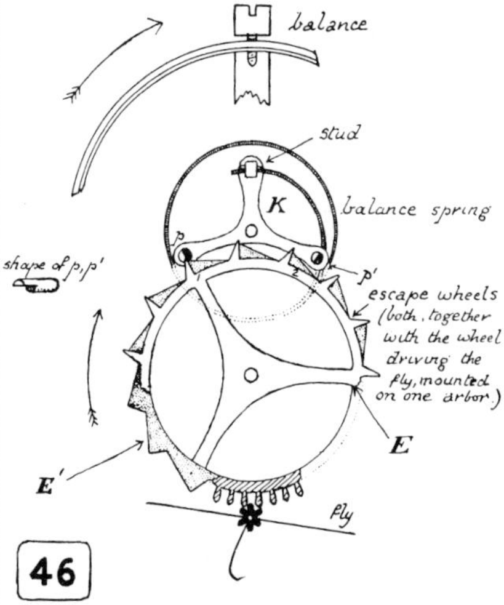

46

Riefler's. [1889]

The method of balancing the force of the train against that of the balance spring allows of the impulse being given not far from the dead-point, and the gradual rotation of the escape wheel (and, accordingly, of the balance itself) produces a "tourbillon" effect which eliminates practically all position errors.

HILLGREN'S.

In 1882 A. Hillgren, of Geneva, proposed an escapement in which the stud was carried on a movable frame attached to a form of lever escapement. As drawn by him, the arrangement could never have worked, since the motion of the stud took place in such a manner as to diminish, instead of increase, the tension of the balance spring at every half vibration*. This curious oversight suggests that Hillgren had never experimented with his device, and indeed it was at once asserted by A. H. Potter, an English watchmaker resident at Geneva, that Hillgren's escapement was a garbled version of one of many forms of the same plan with which he had been experimenting for some time past, and which he had shown to Hillgren when the latter was working under him. He omitted, however, which is somewhat strange, to remark the fact of Hillgren's plan being unworkable; but a similar oversight was also committed by so sound a horologist as Lord Grimthorpe, who, in the sixth edition of his "Rudimentary Treatise on Clocks and Watches," praised it highly†.

RIEFLER'S (Fig 46).

Last amongst this class of escapements comes that patented by Dr. Sigismund Riefler in 1889, which is an application to chronometers of the escapement used in his celebrated astronomical clocks‡. Like Hillgren's, the escapement proper is a form of the lever, but here the pallet-and-tooth action is correctly planned, *i.e.*, it impels the lever in the opposite direction to that in which it has moved to unlock. There are two escape wheels, E, E, mounted co-axially, with their teeth cut in opposite directions. The T-shaped piece K is pivoted concentrically with the balance, and carries the two pallets p,p' and the stud S.

---

* A similar mistake appears in a pamphlet entitled "Chronometers, Watches, and Clocks," published by E. J. Dent, in 1841, in which there is a wood-cut of the chronometer escapement, with the escape wheel teeth cut the wrong way round.

† Hillgren also proposed a second arrangement somewhat like Leslie's, in which the movable frame was eliminated. A similar plan is illustrated in M. Gros' work, but no indication of its inventor is given. On account of the fundamental error in Hillgren's first design, I have not illustrated it. His drawing is given in the "Horological Journal" for April, 1882. Potter's counterclaim appeared in the May issue, and Hillgren replied, singularly ineffectively, in the following number.

‡ The Riefler clock escapement is of practically identical design, except that the rocking T-piece carries the suspension spring of the pendulum, through which the impulse is communicated and the unlocking effected.

Riefler devised the original form of his escapement in 1869, while a student at the Gymnasium, Leipzig.

As drawn, the pallet p is locked on the tooth 1 of the wheel E, while the balance is swinging in the direction shown by the arrow. When the stressing of the balance spring has reached a certain point, it will rock K slightly, and tooth 1 will be unlocked. Both wheels will then turn in the direction shown, and the surface of tooth 2 on the wheel E′ will come into contact with the pallet p', throwing K over into the position shown by the dotted lines, and giving impulse to the balance. On the return swing, a similar cycle of operations will occur in the reverse direction.

A fly, geared to the escape wheel arbor, is fitted to regulate the speed at which K is moved, and this feature, combined with the simplicity and robustness of the design, makes it probably the best " free balance " escapement which has yet appeared, although it sacrifices the " tourbillon " effect obtainable in Benoit's. But although it performed well in an experimental chronometer, it has never been marketed.

All the foregoing escapements, except Gowland's (which was far too complicated) and Benoit's suffer from the additional defect that the time at which the unlocking is effected by the tension of the balance spring (and, accordingly, the time at which impulse is given), will vary considerably if the friction of unlocking should alter with use, as it inevitably must do. In general, it may be said that the advantages which, even in theory, can be obtained from such escapements are slight, while their practical disadvantages are numerous and difficult to eradicate.

The Lever Escapement.

To deal adequately with the lever escapement would need the whole of a book considerably larger than this one. It is used in 99 per cent. of the millions of pocket watches which are made to-day, or which have been made in the past twenty years, and has shown itself to be, for such timekeepers, by far the best escapement yet invented. Here, however, I am only concerned with the attempts which have been made to apply it to marine chronometers, in which its particular advantages have not, up to the present, been found sufficient to compensate for its one defect as compared with the chronometer escapement—that of requiring oil on its pallets, and of accordingly suffering an alteration of its rate (due to the thickening of this oil) when kept going for a long period without being cleaned.

The lever escapement really takes its origin from the " dead-beat " escapement for clocks invented by George Graham about 1715, which, in its turn, was a modification of the " recoil " escapement formerly used in them. Both these escapements are shown in fig. 47, and it will be noticed that while in the recoil escapement the teeth of the escape wheel fall upon the inclined surfaces of the pallets themselves, and, as in the verge escapement, are first driven backwards and then run down the pallet to escape, giving impulse as they do so, in the dead-beat they drop upon a surface concentric with the arm carrying the pallets, and there is accordingly no recoil. Being intended for use

Plate XXXV. MOVEMENT OF ULRICH CHRONOMETER.

The piece like a bar-balance to the right of the balance spring is really a shock-absorber connected with the escapement. The fusee chain is almost big enough to fit the sprockets of a bicycle.

The top-plate is double, and the upper portion, carrying the escapement and balance, can be detached without disturbing the rest of the movement.

See p. 230.

Clockmakers' Company Museum.

with a pendulum, however, the arc described by the pallets was not designed to be more than a few degrees, and accordingly it was obviously impossible, without some modification, to apply this plan to a balance swinging even so little as a quarter of a turn.

Graham himself modified this escapement into the well known cylinder, or "horizontal," escapement (once much in favour for watches), which, in its way, is a good escapement, although undetached, but it was left for later inventors to find a better plan, in which the balance is detached during the greater portion of its swing, and, consequently, unaffected by the friction of the teeth on the dead faces of the pallets.

The first attempt at what we should now regard as a lever escapement was made by the Abbé Hautefeuille, in 1722. His plan is shown in fig. 48. Here the "anchor" of Graham's escapement carries an arm, or lever, whose end is formed into a curved rack, which engages with a pinion on the balance staff. It will be seen that a small motion of the lever produces a large one in the balance, and allows the escapement to act as though it were driving a pendulum. But the balance is never detached, and the friction of the rack is fatal to accurate timekeeping of the order required in chronometers or high-class watches. The escapement has, however, one good feature—the impulse and unlocking take place exactly on the line of centres.

Fig. 49 shows an even simpler plan used by Berthoud in his first timekeeper (1764). It is simply a dead-beat escapement, arranged as if for a pendulum swinging an arc of some 20°, and connected with the balance by a roller at the end of the lever engaging in a hole cut in a roller mounted on the balance staff. It will be remembered that in Berthoud's first machine the arcs of the twin-geared balances were designedly left very small—indeed, they could not well have been otherwise, since the staff of each balance was embraced by the rim and two of the arms of the other. The friction in this escapement and in the gearing connecting the balances must have been considerable.

But shortly before Berthoud produced his machine, the first true lever escapement had been invented and constructed by Mudge. This is shown in fig. 50*.

* This escapement of Mudge's, although quite clearly described and figured in his son's work, was completely transfigured, and rendered unworkable, by Berthoud in his "Histoire de la Mesure du Temps," and this action on the part of so eminent an authority has greatly misled subsequent writers as to the actual operation and arrangement of Mudge's escapement. M. Gros, in attempting to correct Berthoud's error, has evolved an arrangement which, unlike Berthoud's, is perfectly practicable, but departs somewhat from the original (which is correctly depicted in Fig. 50).

Mr. A. Mallock, the owner of Mudge's original timekeeper, also possesses a small bracket clock of uncertain date made by him (at present lent to the Science Museum, South Kensington), which is fitted with a lever escapement in which the two sectors on the balance staff are replaced by a single pallet. The clock has a circular brass balance, about six inches in diameter, and the compensation is effected by two laminated curbs in the same manner as in Mudge's marine timekeepers.

The arrangement of the anchor and pallets is much the same as that used by Hautefeuille, but instead of a rack the lever carries the fork *f*, which engages with the two quadrantal pieces *q*,*q*′. The two prongs of the fork are set at different levels so that each engages with one sector and clears the other.

In the position shown, the tooth 1 of the escape wheel is locked upon the "dead" face of the pallet *p* and the balance is swinging in the direction shown by the arrow. As it nears the dead-point, the sector *q* meets the upper arm of the fork and rotates the anchor slightly. This allows the tooth 1 to pass from the dead face of the pallet *p* to its acting face, down which it immediately runs, throwing the anchor further over, and causing the lower arm of the fork to strike the sector *q*′, and so give impulse to the balance. This then swings clear of the fork, while the motion of the escape wheel is stopped by tooth 6 coming in contact with the dead face of the pallet *p*′. On the return swing the cycle of operations is repeated in the reverse direction.

Thus it will be seen that the balance unlocks the escapement by impinging on one arm of the fork, and immediately afterwards receives impulse from the other arm, while except for the moment during which this occurs its motion is entirely detached.

To prevent the lever from being thrown over too far, its motion was restricted by the two banking pins *d*,*d*′, while to ensure that it was not accidentally displaced during the detached arc of the balance (in which case the sectors would not be able to engage correctly with the fork on the next swing), a safety device was added, consisting of a roller carried on the balance staff, having a notch cut in it, allowing a projection carried on the end of the lever to pass the notch at the correct moment, while at other times any motion of the lever was prevented by this projection coming into contact with the rim of the roller.

As related on p. 108 Mudge did not make much use of this escapement, and displayed no anxiety to bring it into notice. However, he made a large model of it for his patron, Count Bruhl, who, with Mudge's consent, showed it to several London makers, two of whom, Emery and Margetts, fitted it to a number of their high-class watches, and also in some marine timekeepers. Both men introduced modifications of Mudge's plan at the fork end of the lever, Margetts evolving the form known as the "crank roller," in which the unlocking and impulse are effected by a single pin carried on a short arm projecting from the balance, while Emery, in some of his watches, went a step further, and mounted this pin in jewelled pivots, so that it rolled into and out of the fork. He also used adjustable banking pins.

But the principal improvement introduced by Emery was one of far greater importance. In Mudge's original escapement, nothing but the friction of the escape wheel teeth on the dead faces of the pallets prevented the lever, after having been moved over until it met the banking, from starting, under the influence of its own weight (or, if

See p. 237.

47

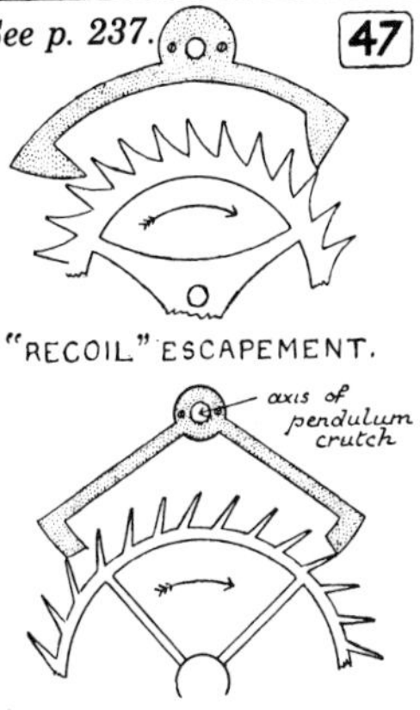

"RECOIL" ESCAPEMENT.

"DEAD-BEAT" ESCAPEMENT.

See p. 239.

48

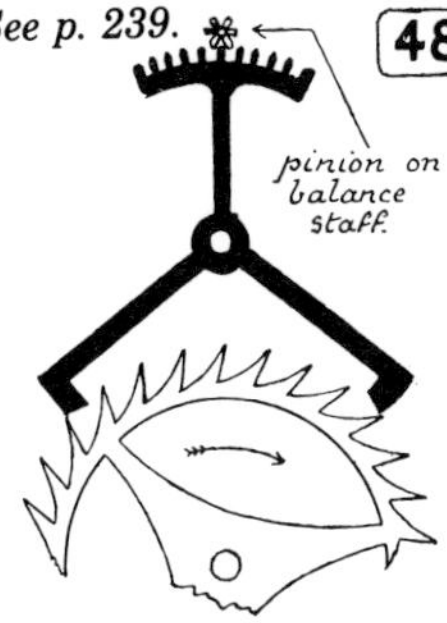

Hautefeuille's "rack-lever" escapement. [1722]

See p. 239.

49

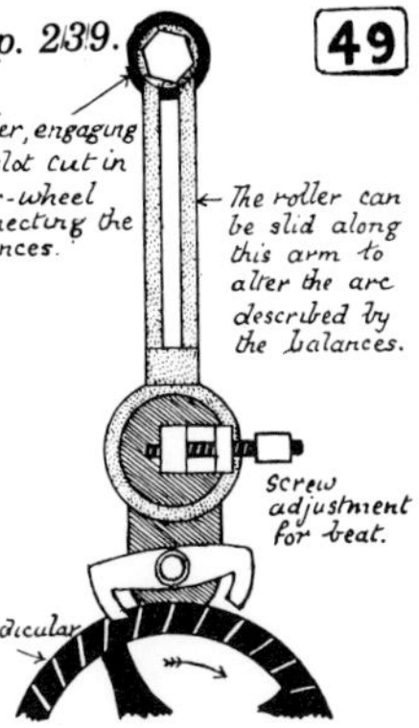

ESCAPEMENT OF BERTHOUD'S 'HORLOGE MARINE NO. 1'.

See p. 240.

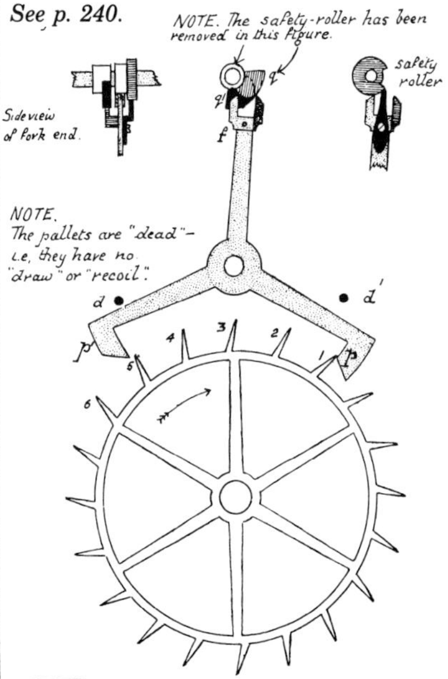

50

Mudge's lever escapement. [1757]

The first true detached-lever escapement ever made

Notes on the figures.

47. These two escapements are, of course, only used in pendulum clocks.
48. Diagrammatic only. I have failed to find a contemporary drawing of this escapement.
49. From the "Traité des Horloges Marines"
50. From a drawing by Pennington in "A Description .... of the Time-keeper invented by the late Mr. Thomas Mudge".
51. From a drawing in Schoof's pamphlet (see p. 152 f.)

See p. 246.

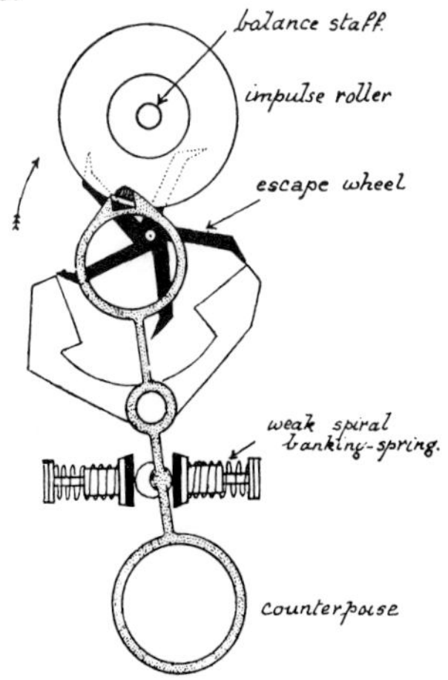

51

Schoof's "five-toothed" Lever escapement.

laid flat, of any slight shake), to unlock the wheel again. True, it could not do this, for the projection on the end of the lever would first come into contact with the safety roller: but the extra friction of this contact would seriously affect the time of vibration of the balance.

Emery cured this fault by making the locking faces of his pallets not quite dead (*i.e.*, not absolutely concentric with the axis of the lever), but slightly inclined, in such a manner that the pressure of the teeth upon them tended to draw them further into engagement, thus keeping the lever pressed against the banking pins, and the projection safely clear of the roller. The slight inclination given to the locking faces of the pallets is termed "draw,"* and with this addition Mudge's escapement, as developed by Emery, became, except for the additional and superfluous refinement of the pivoted impulse-pin, substantially the "double-roller" lever escapement of to-day,† in which the unlocking and impulse are effected by a jewel mounted in a roller set on the balance staff, and engaging in a fork on the end of the lever; the safety action being provided by a second smaller roller with a notch cut in it, and a small gold finger screwed to the end of the fork.

At the time of the inquiry into Mudge's petition (1793), Emery stated that he had made some 32 or 33 watches on the former's plan, at 150 guineas each, and that he had sent two timekeepers for trial at Greenwich with this escapement, but he added that he was then at work on a new escapement with only one pallet. This was probably the pattern described on p. 201*f*.

---

* It will be remembered that Le Roy, in 1705, employed "draw" in an analogous manner in the escapement of his marine timekeeper. (See p. 140)

Pearson, in his article "Escapement," in Rees' Cyclopœdia, stated that Mudge, in his first lever watch (Queen Charlotte's) used a slight recoil on the locking-faces, keeping the lever in contact with the safety roller: but Mr. H. Otto, who has examined this watch, assures me that the locking-faces are "dead," having neither draw nor recoil.

† Several other patterns of the lever escapement have been made, and some are still in use, such as the "table roller" (the commonest form) in which the impulse roller and safety roller are combined; the "two-pin," designed by George Savage to effect the unlocking nearer to the line of centres than can be accomplished in the ordinary pattern (this is now almost obsolete); the "club-tooth," in which the impulse faces are half on the pallet and half on the teeth; and the "pin-lever," in which they are wholly upon the teeth (fitted in the Roskopf and other cheap forms). In addition, the lever can either be of the "anchor" or "straight line" pattern, *i.e.*, directed towards the centre of the escape wheel, as in Mudge's original design, and in the majority of present day lever escapements, or tangentially to the wheel, as in the "right angle" pattern used in the majority of high-class English lever watches. Mention should also be made of Cole's "resilient" lever escapement, described in a later portion of this chapter, and of his "repellent" escapement, in which the draw on the pallets is reversed and the extremity of the lever bears continuously upon a small notched roller on the balance staff, as in the duplex escapement.

The wonderful successes achieved in the Kew trials, and elsewhere, by M. Paul Ditisheim, have been accomplished with watches having double-roller club-toothed lever escapements of the "anchor" pattern. One of his watches of this type, with a Guillaume balance (see p. 308), holds the record at Kew (or, rather, Teddington) with 96.9 marks out of a possible 100.

After Emery's death, the lever escapement lay dormant (or nearly so) for many years,* although Hautefeuille's much inferior "rack-lever" was re-invented and patented by Peter Litherland in 1791. This was made in large quantities by Litherland, Whiteside & Co. early in the last century. The lever itself, often called, in its early days, the *detached* lever, to distinguish it from the other, gradually made its way into favour from about 1820 onwards, and its obvious advantages have, for many years past, established it as the best, and practically the only, escapement for pocket timekeepers.

The pre-eminent feature of the lever escapement which makes it so suitable for this purpose, is that it combines in a high degree the qualities of detachment (which, of course, is an essential requirement of accurate timekeeping) and certainty. Giving an impulse at every half vibration, and commencing this slightly before either side of the dead-point, it is practically impossible, with fair usage, for it to stop in the pocket.

Here, however, we are only concerned with the attempts made to substitute it for the chronometer escapement in box chronometers, and these, up to the present, have been neither numerous nor successful. Breguet fitted, in some of his marine chronometers, a peculiar variant which he termed "échappement naturel," in which two escape wheels, geared together, give impulse alternately to a lever placed between them.† Some chronometers of the kind were made by Messrs. Roskell about 1850, but served only to demonstrate that when safeguarded from rough treatment, the chronometer is a better escapement than the lever, and can preserve a steadier rate over a longer period, without requiring to be cleaned. And the same fate befel the prolonged attempt which was made, in quite recent times, by W. G. Schoof to introduce box chronometers fitted with a lever escapement of most original design.

Schoof (1830-1901) was a man of the Harrison type,‡ a trained watchmaker and a clever man of business, but a rule-of-thumb mechanic. His escapement, which is shown in fig. 51, was extremely

* It was, however, used to a limited extent during this period by various makers, particularly Breguet, for high-class watches. I recently examined a very fine "right-angle" lever watch by Earnshaw, in the possession of Mr. A. F. G. Leveson-Gower.

† The Breguet chronometer illustrated in Plate XXXVI. has this form of escapement. It possesses the great advantage of requiring no oil on the pallets, as the escape wheels impel them by a direct blow at right angles, and not, as in other forms of the lever escapement, by a sliding diagonal action. The objections to it are the friction of the gearing between the two wheels, and their increased inertia as compared with a single escape wheel.

‡ He published a pamphlet, entitled "Improvements in Clocks and Marine Chronometers," in which he put forward a plan for what he termed a "Giant Clock," which was to have a semi-gravity escapement of his design, and a pendulum some 120 feet in length having a period of *six seconds*. This would have been a "World-beater" if it had ever been made, for the longest pendulums with which I am acquainted are one of 54 ft. 3 in., beating 4 seconds, fitted long ago by Hindley in a Yorkshire turret clock, and one of 67 ft. said to exist in a clock at Avignon.

Schoof's original clock with his "gravity" escapement is now in the Science Museum, South Kensington, bequeathed by the inventor, and is remarkable for the smallness of the arc (about ½°) described by the pendulum. Even when standing close to it it is difficult at first to determine whether it is going or not.

W.G. SCHOOF 1830-1901

DETAIL OF SCHOOF'S 5-TOOTH LEVER ESCAPEMENT.

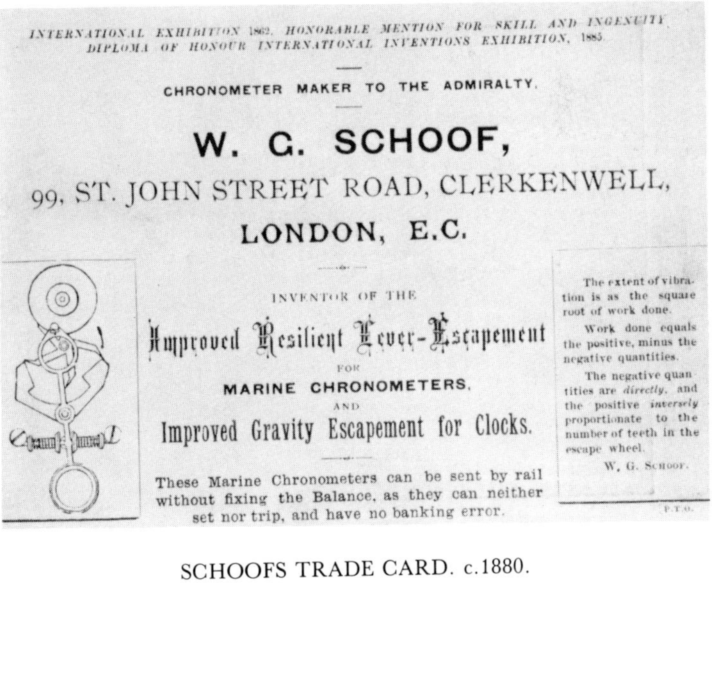

INTERNATIONAL EXHIBITION 1862. HONORABLE MENTION FOR SKILL AND INGENUITY. DIPLOMA OF HONOUR INTERNATIONAL INVENTIONS EXHIBITION, 1885.

CHRONOMETER MAKER TO THE ADMIRALTY.

W. G. SCHOOF,

99, ST. JOHN STREET ROAD, CLERKENWELL,

LONDON, E.C.

INVENTOR OF THE

Improved Resilient Lever-Escapement

FOR

MARINE CHRONOMETERS,

AND

Improved Gravity Escapement for Clocks.

These Marine Chronometers can be sent by rail without fixing the Balance, as they can neither set nor trip, and have no banking error.

The extent of vibration is as the square root of work done.

Work done equals the positive, minus the negative quantities.

The negative quantities are *directly*, and the positive *inversely* proportionate to the number of teeth in the escape wheel.

W. G. SCHOOF.

P.T.O.

SCHOOFS TRADE CARD. c.1880.

ingenious and suggestive, but his inadequate knowledge of mechanics and mathematics led him to make various claims for it which were obviously absurd*, and his attempts to bolster them up by some second-hand and rather agricultural mathematics and by copious and wonderful arguments are positively painful reading. This, however, cannot be allowed to detract from the great mechanical ingenuity shown in the design of the escapement itself.

The escape wheel has *five* teeth only,† Schoof considering that the power lost in "drop"‡ was thereby lessened, and a steadier impulse secured. The teeth are of the "resilient" pattern introduced by J. F. Cole. If, in the ordinary lever escapement, the balance be made by a sudden shake or twist, to describe more than a complete turn, the impulse pin will come into contact with the *outside* of the fork, which is resting against the bankings, and the result may, in extreme cases, be a broken balance pivot, while in any case the timekeeping of the watch will be affected. To prevent this, Cole devised the resilient form of tooth shown in the figure, and did away with the banking pins. Should the balance overturn, the impact of the pin on the outside of the fork forces the locked pallet further into the wheel until it meets the lower part of the tooth, below the angle, and backs the escape wheel slightly, thus using the mainspring as a banking.

The objection to this, and to most other forms of resilient arrangements,§ is that for a pronounced overturn they are admirable, but that if the amount be only just sufficient to bring them into play there is a risk of the impulse pin jamming against the fork and stopping the balance. Schoof claimed to have overcome this by using, in addition to Cole's resilient teeth, very weak spiral spring bankings, acting on the tail of the lever. He stated that with these the escapement could not be set—but this was not strictly correct.¶

* He originally claimed that his design, as compared with the ordinary 15-toothed lever escapement, gave an increased efficiency of no less than 66¾ *per cent.* It was, however, clearly shown by Mr. T. D. Wright that the utmost possible amount that could be claimed for it was 8½ per cent., and that in all probability the actual increase, if any, was far less than this.

† This, however, is not a record (or, as "The Times" would print it, a "record") for fewness of teeth. An escapement invented by Deshays in 1827, and patented, probably in ignorance, by MacDowall in 1851, has an escape wheel with one tooth or pin only. This necessitated, of course, an extra wheel in the train. MacDowall sold his patent to Messrs. Dent, who had a number of watches on this plan made in Switzerland. These performed well, but did not succeed in establishing themselves permanently in public favour.

‡ The space through which the escape wheel moves without communicating impulse to the balance.

§ The form devised by R. Whittaker is practically free from this objection.

¶ The Schoof chronometer in the possession of the Admiralty (No. 6059) can be set without much difficulty. Still, this is hardly a fair test, since it is not kept going, and is, indeed, only preserved at Greenwich on account of its historical interest. It is, however, possible (although not so easy) to set the one at South Kensington, which is wound daily.

The balance made 7,200 vibrations per hour, instead of the usual 14,400, a heavy balance and weak balance spring being employed. Due to the lower number of vibrations, a weaker mainspring could also be used, and Schoof wrongly interpreted this as a proof of the superior mechanical efficiency of his escapement.

He made several of these machines, and repeatedly entered them in the Greenwich trials, but the results were far from satisfactory. Their performances may be thus tabulated :—

Date of trial.	No. tried.	Place.	Number competing.
1883	1	36	38
1884	2	28 & 31	32
1885	2	38 & 40	40
1886	—	—	—
1887	1	28	28
1888	—	—	—
1889	—	—	—
1890	2	41 & 45	45
1891	—	—	—
1892	2	41 & 49	51
1893	1	46	48
1894	2	34 & 41	42
1895	—	—	—
1896	1	54	83

As luck would have it, the Admiralty, after the 1896 trial, purchased no less than 55 chronometers, instead of the usual twenty or so, and thus, by the narrowest of margins, Schoof's No. 6059 became their property, and its gratified maker was enabled to style himself "Chronometer maker to the Admiralty,"* whatever that may have been worth. It is only fair to state, however, that although the performances of this machine at Greenwich had been far from first-rate (its trial number was 18.3s. + 18.4s. as against 5.6s. + 7.2s. for Kullberg 5512, the first machine)†, it gave good service at sea for a number of years. But in spite of this *opéra comique* finale, the net result of Schoof's prolonged experiment was to demonstrate afresh that for box chronometers, in long trials, the lever escapement is inferior to the spring detent. It cannot be gainsaid, in view of the magnificent performances of the lever watches made by M. Ditisheim and others, that the modern high-class lever watch is capable, when clean, of satisfying every requirement of the most exacting navigator. But for extended use over a long period, it is probable that the chronometer would have the best of it.

On its own ground, for use in pocket timekeepers and machines exposed, as in destroyers and light craft, to rough usage, the lever escapement is unsurpassed and at present unsurpassable.

* See the remarks on "John Forrest, maker to the Admiralty" on p. 372.

† An explanation of the method of calculating "trial numbers" used at Greenwich is given on p. 371.

THE BACK PLATE OF MARINE 2 DAY CHRONOMETER
by W.G. Shoof. No. 6059 with Shoof's 5-tooth lever escapement.

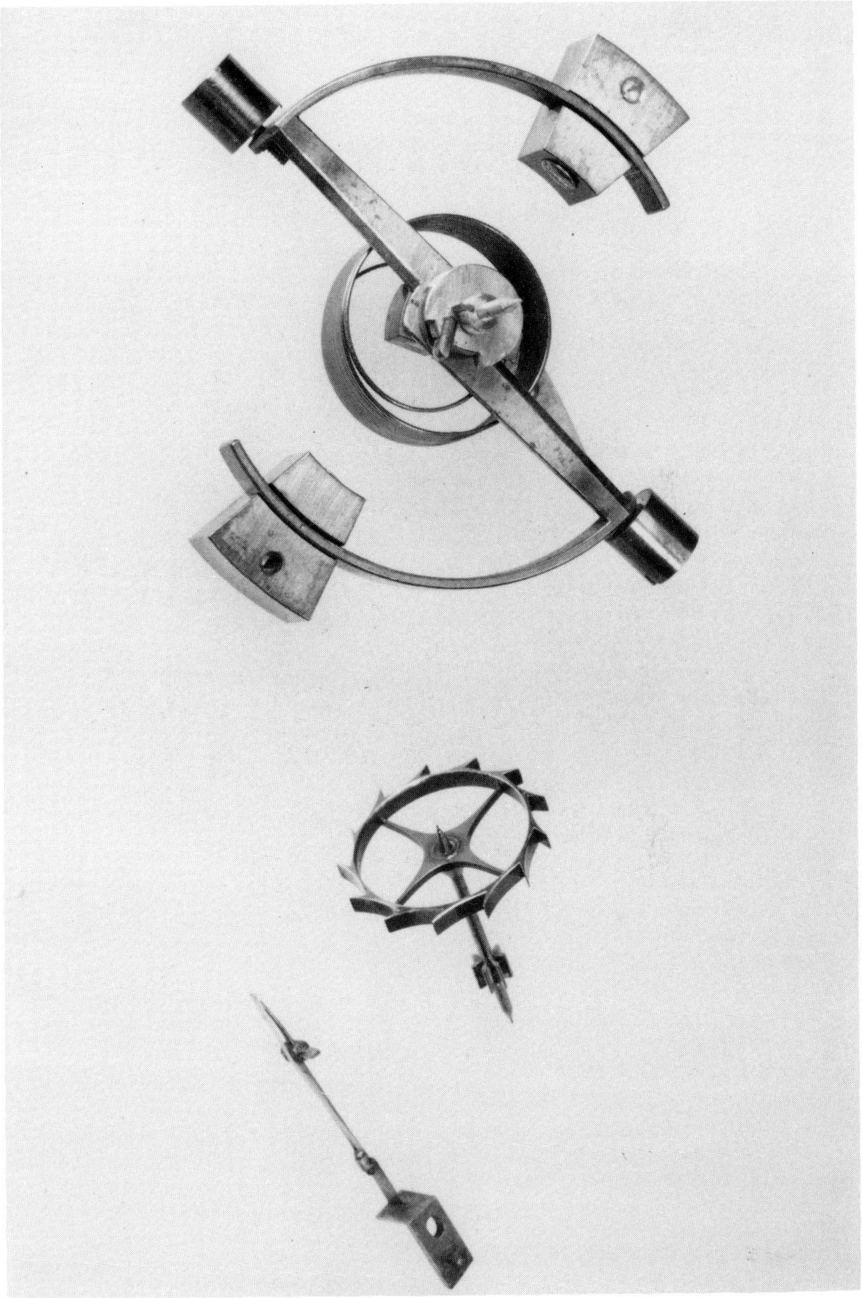

THE BALANCE & ESCAPEMENT FROM THO. EARNSHAW CHRONOMETER NO. 509.

Half-Chronometer Escapement.

The term "half-chronometer" was often used in former times to denote a watch with lever escapement, helical spring, and chronometer balance, and it is now sometimes given, in order to attract purchasers, to any finely adjusted lever watch of ordinary pattern. But there have been several attempts made to combine the lever and chronometer escapements, and to such the name "half-chronometer" can be quite correctly applied.

The various schemes which have been proposed differ very little in detail. The end proposed is always the same—to effect the locking as in the lever escapement, by means of a pair of pallets having locking faces only, to effect the unlocking by means of a fork, and to give impulse, as in the chronometer escapement, by means of the impact of a tooth of the escape wheel upon an impulse pallet on the balance staff. During the return swing, the locking is merely transferred from one pallet to the other, the escape wheel advancing a very minute amount.

The first escapement of this pattern was constructed by Robin, a French maker, in 1791. The plan has been several times re-invented and re-patented. The pallets need oil, and the unlocking friction is liable to variation. On the other hand the unlocking is more certain, and less affected by the position of the escapement.

Breguet, in some of his pocket chronometers, employed a most singular escapement somewhat on these lines, in which the balance receives impulses alternately from the teeth of the escape wheel and from the fork of the lever.*

Half-chronometer escapements have also been made on a slightly different plan, in which only one pallet is used for locking, the other engaging the escape wheel during the impulse and returning the lever to the locking position.

The Tourbillon.

Like the remontoire, the "tourbillon" is often spoken of as if it were some particular form of escapement. Actually, the term is used to denote a mechanism in which the balance and certain other portions of the movement revolve around a fixed centre in some short period of time, thus causing it to run through all its position errors at short and constantly recurring intervals, producing, for all practical purposes, no more effect upon the machine's timekeeping than if they were non-existent.

Although tourbillons have occasionally been fitted in box chronometers†, possibly with the idea of eliminating the effects of the ship's magnetism, it is obvious that their valuable property of nullifying all, or nearly all, position errors renders them chiefly useful for pocket chronometers.

---

* A description of this escapement, with drawing, is given by M. Gros in his work, but he has omitted to remark the impulse given via the lever.

† A box chronometer constructed by Frédéric Houriet, and presented to the Société des Amis des Arts, Geneva, in 1828, was fitted with a tourbillon.

They have been made on several plans, all embodying the same principle—that of causing the balance and escapement to revolve gradually in a circle. The genesis of the invention is due to Breguet, who devised it in 1795, and took out a "brevet d'invention" in 1801. In his arrangement, the balance and escapement are carried upon a platform driven by the third wheel, and revolving concentrically with the fourth, which is a fixture, screwed to the top plate. The escape wheel pinion engages with the teeth of the fourth wheel, and power is thus transmitted from the third wheel to the balance. The period of rotation of the "tourbillon," as the revolving platform is named, is one minute. This is considerably quicker than is really necessary for the purpose of balancing the position errors, and it necessitates the revolving portions being kept very light, in order to diminish their inertia as much as possible. A very high standard of workmanship is also required, and while this, of course, presented no obstacle to Breguet and his workmen, it prevented the invention from coming into the extended use which its ingenuity and performance warranted, and restricted it to an occasional appearance in high-class watches.

As if in a spirit of sarcastic comment upon this restriction, a form of tourbillon made its appearance many years later (1881) in what was, at the time, the world's cheapest watch—the famous, or rather notorious, original Waterbury. At the time, the watch-making world in general was not disposed to admit that this watch, which retailed at $2.43 cents,* was anything more than a toy, but the ingenuity displayed in its design was extreme. Its keynote was simplicity and the reduction to a minimum of the moving parts.† The centre wheel was fixed to the dial-plate, and the whole movement rotated round it, under the influence of a huge mainspring *eight feet* in length, once an hour. The design had many other points of interest, including a duplex escapement consisting of only two pieces, and an extremely simple motion-work based on the principle of "Ferguson's Paradox."‡

In 1894, B. Bonniksen, of Coventry, patented a very ingenious modification of Breguet's tourbillon which he termed a "Karrusel,"§ and which removed such objections as could be raised against the original pattern. There were no fixed wheels in the train, and the revolving platform, instead of turning once in a minute, geared with

* The explanation of this remarkably precise sum generally offered, not entirely seriously, by the Waterbury Watch Company, was that the 3 cents represented the actual cost of the watch, and the $2.40 cents the net profit. The adverse impression created by the low price was enhanced by the methods employed to distribute the watches: for example, various enterprising tailors advertised that every 30s. suit of reach-me-downs would be delivered with a Waterbury ticking in the waistcoat pocket.

† Its inventor, Mr. D. A. A. Buck, succeeded, after two unsuccessful attempts, in reducing the number of separate parts in his watch to 57 all told. The suppression of the great wheel, and the consequent necessity of using a mainspring having upwards of 30 turns, rendered the winding of the watch so prolonged and laborious as to become a bye-word.

‡ A method of gearing in which two or more wheels having slightly different numbers of teeth engage with a common pinion, so that the wheels have a relative motion in opposite directions.

§ This word is the Swedish equivalent of "a roundabout."

POCKET CHRONOMETER BY HUNT & ROSKEL, LONDON
with Tourbillon & spring detent escapement.
Courtesy of the British Museum.

SULLY MARINE TIMEKEEPER.
Courtesy of the Worshipful Co. of Clockmakers.

the third wheel and was driven round at a comparatively slow speed—one turn in $52\frac{1}{2}$ minutes which, however, was found to be amply fast enough for all practical purposes. This device at once became popular. In 1903 its inventor produced a modification of the original design, termed the "Bonniksen tourbillon," in which the karrusel was pivoted top and bottom (thus removing an objection raised against the former pattern, which had only one large flat pivot) and driven by a separate train from the centre wheel at the rate of one turn in 39 minutes. This design embodied a centre seconds hand, showing fifths of a second.* At almost the same time Messrs. W. and E. A. Holland patented two arrangements which, to the ordinary mind unversed in the intricacies of patent law, appear to be almost identical with Bonniksen's, except that an upper pivot is provided for the direct-driven form of karrusel.

Mention should finally be made of the "annular tourbillon," patented in 1903 by A. Taylor, of Brixton. This is more on the lines of Breguet's design—*i.e.*, the power required to keep the balance in motion is derived entirely from the rotation of the tourbillon.

The revolving platform's rotation-period is reduced by making it carry not only the balance and escape wheels, but also the fourth wheel. The third wheel is of annular form, with internal teeth, and is a fixture, the fourth wheel pinion engaging in it, and the platform being driven round by an intermediate wheel gearing with the centre wheel. The time of rotation (one hour in the original design) can be varied as desired by changing the proportions of the gearing.

Both Bonniksen's karrusel and Taylor's tourbillon have been frequently employed in pocket chronometers and lever watches, while the original pattern invented by Breguet is still often fitted, especially abroad.

---

* The original pattern of karrusel watch made 17,657.1 beats per hour, instead of 18,000 (the usual number for a watch beating five to the second), the remainder being absorbed in consequence of the rotation of the platform. Accordingly, it did not indicate exact fifths of a second. In the later (centre-seconds) pattern, however, this was rectified by means of a slight modification of the train.

CHAPTER X.

THE BALANCE SPRING.

The balance spring is the most vitally important portion of any chronometer. The escapement merely maintains the vibrations of the balance, and this latter in turn serves only as a *point d'appui* for the balance spring, and as a means of correcting the alterations produced in the action of the latter by the effects of heat and cold. The timekeeping of the instrument depends principally on the free and consistent action of the balance spring.

As related on p. 30, the balance spring was first introduced about 1660, having been invented by Robert Hooke (followed, a little later, by Hautefeuille and Huyghens). Prior to this time it is possible that one or two attempts may have been made to provide some similar form of controlling agency for the balance, but it is indisputable that they were stillborn, and attracted no general attention.

Hooke's enunciation—*ut tensio sic vis*—of the uniform manner in which the force of a balance spring varies directly as the extent to which it is tensioned (or, in effect, as the angular rotation of the balance from its dead-point), and other passages in his writings, show him to have been acquainted with the fact that the motion of a balance swinging freely under the influence of its balance spring ought, theoretically, like that of a pendulum whose bob moved in a cycloidal path, to be isochronous: *i.e.*, it should describe its arcs, whether of large or small extent, in some constant unit of time. The importance of this property cannot be overestimated, and its enunciation first demonstrated the possibility of obtaining really accurate timekeeping—accurate enough for the finding of longitude—from balance timekeepers, and so made the chronometer possible, but its revolutionary character was not fully appreciated at the time, for two reasons. In the first place, it was not until a century later that a detached escapement was produced, and until this was accomplished the balance was never free from the influence of the escapement, so that although the balance spring might exert a stabilising effect on the time of its vibrations, it could not be expected to render them isochronous, or anything like it. And, in the second place, even if a detached escapement had been available, experimenters would have found that although Hooke's law rightly postulated the isochronous motion of a balance swinging without friction (and hence requiring no external impulse) under the impulse of a perfect spring, yet that in practice the disturbing effects of friction and air resistance (with their necessary corollary, the imparting of regular impulses to the balance), the imperfection of the spring, and the necessity of using a certain percentage of the kinetic energy of the balance to unlock the escapement, considerably modified the degree of isochronism which the addition of a balance spring should theoretically have imparted to the motions of the balance. Even Harrison, as we have seen, although he gave a satisfactory solution of the problem of keeping the spring unaffected by changes of temperature, found himself unable (principally for lack of a detached form of escapement) to equalise the times of the long and short arcs, except by such shifts as his "cycloid-pin" (which was tantamount to using two balance springs of different lengths) and the devices which he fitted to vary the force exerted by the escape wheel on the balance at different portions of the latter's vibrations.

But after the various forms of detached escapement invented by Le Roy, and subsequently by Mudge, Berthoud, Arnold, and Earnshaw, had liberated the balance, almost entirely, from the influence of the escapement, and thus removed a most formidable obstacle which had blocked any real progress towards the attainment of isochronous motion by means of the balance spring, the true conditions of the problem and the true direction in which to seek for a solution soon became apparent. Although, as related in the last chapter, there remained many makers of the utmost ingenuity who were led astray by the glamour of the remontoire, and endeavoured, by the use of a constant force escapement, to keep their balances vibrating in an invariable arc (in which case the equality or otherwise of the long and short arcs became a matter of little importance), yet, side-by-side with these efforts of misdirected ingenuity, there went on a painstaking investigation of the best material and form of the balance spring, of the molecular changes which take place in it, and of the conditions governing the isochronous motion of the balance to which it is applied. Within the limits of this chapter it is not possible to give more than a brief outline of the progress of this investigation and of the results which have been obtained. Started by the laborious experiments of practical chronometer makers, it has also attracted the attention of mathematicians, and the balance spring of to-day forms an outstanding example of the benefits arising from a sagacious union of theory and practice.

Materials used in Balance Springs.

The balance springs of Hooke's time were made of soft steel wire, hardened to a certain extent by rolling, and springs made in this way held the field for a very long period, and were employed in a number of the early chronometers. Earnshaw, in particular, always used them. It was found, however, that the chronometers in which they were fitted gradually lost on their rate.*

To obviate this defect, recourse was had to the process of hardening and tempering, by which the spring's tendency to lose strength is, in

* As noted on p. 195, Earnshaw, whose chief objection to the tempered spring appears to have been that Arnold used it, regarded this gradual losing as a necessary evil, and compensated it by leaving his springs fast in the short arcs.

great measure, removed. This was employed by Harrison, who tempered his spring by immersing it in a molten mixture of lead and pewter, and after the correct temper, indicated by the changing colours of the spring, was obtained, transferred it to an oil bath. This method, with various modifications, was adopted by Le Roy, Berthoud and Arnold, and soon drove the untempered spring out of the field for chronometers. At the present time it is universally employed for all classes of balance springs. The spring is also "blued" after tempering, which renders it less liable to rust.*

Rust and magnetism are the two chief enemies of steel balance springs. The latter defect, which is relatively of less importance, is ineradicable, but various plans have been tried to prevent them from rusting. E. J. Dent had some springs electro-gilt after tempering, but it was found that the gilding was liable, after a time, to crack and to flake off the steel of the spring, affecting the strength of the latter (and, accordingly, the rate of the chronometer) considerably. Experiments were made in 1861 with some Admiralty chronometers fitted with balance springs left white after tempering, and not blued, but the results were not very conclusive. In the course of a correspondence on the subject between the Astronomer Royal and various chronometer makers, Messrs. Litherland & Davis stated that in their experience chronometers fitted with permanently attached keys, and having, accordingly, no winding aperture in their cases, were more liable to rust through moisture forming on the inside of the case than chronometers not so fitted. Various lacquers and varnishes have been used by different makers for coating their springs.

GOLD SPRINGS.

Springs of this material have been used to a limited extent in former times, but are now obsolete. The Arnolds, both father and son, fitted them occasionally, and they were strongly advocated by Urban Jurgensen. As compared with a steel spring, it is, of course, impossible for them either to rust or to become magnetised, but against these two great advantages must be set the defects that gold is much heavier than steel, and consequently has a much greater inertia; that it is not so elastic, and that therefore a considerably longer spring is required; that it cannot be tempered, and is accordingly liable to lose its strength, and that the amount of its progressive loss of elasticity in heat is considerably greater than that of a steel spring, so that more compensation is required. These considerations have been generally held to outweigh its advantages of freedom from rust and magnetism. The extra cost of the gold spring is a negligible factor.

---

* The slightest spot of rust upon a balance spring is sufficient to impair its action so much as to destroy entirely the accuracy of the chronometer in which it is fitted.

The process of "bluing" steel, by heating it to a lower temperature than that of tempering, and allowing it to cool slowly, produces an initial film of hard xide on the surface of the steel, and so affords less scope for the formation of rust.

PALLADIUM SPRINGS.

These were introduced by Paillard about 1880, and have gradually come into general use for high class chronometers. As compared with the steel spring, they have the advantage of being rustless and non-magnetic, and of reducing the "acceleration" presently described. On the other hand, like the gold spring, they are heavier and softer than a steel spring, and hence more liable to be distorted—nor can they be tempered.

GLASS SPRINGS.

At first sight, it might appear that glass was one of the most unsuitable materials for a balance spring that could well be found, but as a matter of fact the construction of a glass spring is perfectly feasible, and such a spring possesses one important advantage over any of the foregoing, namely, that it is much less affected by heat and cold. In fact, the change in elasticity produced in a glass spring by a given alteration in temperature is only about one-tenth of the corresponding change produced in a steel spring.

As the result of experiments conducted by E. J. Dent in 1833, it was determined that a chronometer with an uncompensated (glass) balance, and keeping correct time at 32° Fahr., lost, at 100° Fahr., the following daily amounts :—

With a gold balance-spring	...	8	min.	04	secs.
,, steel ,,	...	6	,,	25	,,
,, palladium* ,,	...	2	,,	31	,,
,, glass ,,	...	0	,,	40	,,

Glass springs, however, are difficult and expensive to make, the few experiments which have been made with them appear to show that they cause much greater and more persistent acceleration than a steel spring—and, last but not least, there is a widespread impression that such springs must necessarily be fragile, although that is by no means the case.

In addition, glass has a tendency to de-vitrify, *i.e.*, to lose its original homogeneity, and become an agglomeration of small crystals. This effect, some times called "vegetation," is noticeable in photographic and other lenses.

From all these causes, glass springs have received, in the past, very little attention from chronometer makers, and they are never likely to now, since "elinvar" possesses their characteristic advantage—insensibility to temperature—in a much greater degree, and is, moreover, much more suitable in other respects.

Glass springs appear to have been proposed by Berthoud, but not actually tried by him*. Experiments in this direction were, however,

* The "palladium" springs used in modern chronometers require slightly more compensation than a steel spring. These, however, are by no means of pure palladium, but composed of an alloy of several metals.

† I make this statement on the authority of Lord Grimthorpe and others, but I must confess that I have not succeeded in tracing the assertion in any of Berthoud's voluminous works.

made by his younger contemporary, Breguet. A chronometer by the latter, with a glass balance and balance spring, is preserved in the Conservatoire des Arts et Métiers*.

In 1828 experiments with glass springs were also made by James Scrymgeour, a Glasgow maker†, and about the same time Frederick Rippon (afterwards Dent) also constructed some glass balance springs and fitted them in chronometers. He was a stepson of E. J. Dent, and some of the results of his work were published by the firm of Arnold and Dent in 1833. There is little doubt that the springs made by him were superior to those of Breguet and Scrymgeour, and he completely disproved the idea that a glass spring must of necessity be fragile—on one occasion a chronometer so fitted was accidentally knocked off a table on to the ground without breaking the spring, although both of the balance pivots were fractured—while the rate of a chronometer of this pattern sent to Greenwich was exceedingly good; but his tests revealed a previously unsuspected fault of the glass spring—its tendency to accelerate the motions of the balance to which it was fitted was found to be much more pronounced and continued than that of a steel spring‡.

In 1853 a very interesting paper on the manufacture of glass springs was read before a meeting of the Society of Arts§ by Mr. F. H. Wenham, and a discussion followed, in which E. B. Denison and a number of leading chronometer makers took part. It is to be regretted, however, that their comments evinced much more trade jealousy than knowledge of the subject¶.

---

* It is a small machine with going barrel, and has a helical glass spring (diameter about .45 inches) with 15 turns. The balance was a glass cylinder, fitting over the spring, but it has been broken, and only its glass cross-bar remains.

† He appears to have been a very keen experimenter. His remontoire is referred to in the preceding chapter, and his mercurial balances in the following one. He made his glass springs from window glass, as being stronger than flint glass, but from the account of his experiments I suspect that the quality of the glass which he used was not very high. His principal trials were made with a chronometer fitted with two glass springs, but he complains that it was extremely sluggish in following changes of temperature.

‡ His springs, which were about two feet long, were found to be unaffected by gunfire, and did not deteriorate when used at sea. The balance used was a glass disc, fixed on the balance staff with shellac (often used for the same purpose by John Arnold), and the compensation required was extremely slight: in fact, as Lord Grimthorpe once expressed it, the machine had no secondary, and hardly any primary compensation. The ordinary pattern of laminæ were found, *even without any weights on them,* to give too much compensation, and the form finally adopted was a pair of very short vertical laminæ, composed of platinum and silver, and devoid of weights.

§ Published in the Society's Journal, Vol. I. (1852-3), p. 325.

¶ It seems to have been assumed that Wenham's paper was a trade puff inspired by Dent, instead of being, as it was, a *bona fide* attempt to "broadcast" the results of independent experimental work. The parties to the discussion included Charles and George Frodsham, John Poole, and E. T. Loseby, who found themselves (possibly on this occasion only) in complete agreement—as regards the worthlessness of the paper—although they contradicted each other's statements as to the bad qualities of the glass spring in a manner irresistibly recalling the famous triple defence offered in the case of the borrowed vase: "In the first place, it was cracked when borrowed; secondly, it was flawless when returned; and, in addition, my client denies that he ever borrowed it."

Denison, who had called attention to the subject in the Jury Report of the 1851 Exhibition, and whose connection with the firm of Dent was well understood, also came in for a certain amount of the adverse criticism.

GLASS BALANCE & BALANCE SPRING
By Frederick Dent (formerly Frederick Rippon)

Bi-Metallic Springs.

It has several times been suggested to use a bi-metallic laminated spring, composed of brass and steel, on the assumption that by this means the spring could be made to increase its strength in heat. It is to be presumed that the proposers were not aware of the metallic thermometers made on this plan by Breguet*, Urban Jurgensen, and others, in which similar springs are used to move a pointer and so indicate the temperature. The principal effect noticeable when using a bi-metallic spring would be that any considerable alteration of temperature would throw the escapement out of beat, and stop the chronometer.

Elinvar.

It is probable that the balance spring of the future will be formed of this alloy or a similar one. It is a nickel steel alloy, the invention, like "invar," of Dr. C. E. Guillaume, head of the International Bureau of Weights and Measures, at Sèvres. Its elasticity is practically unaffected by changes of temperature.

Form of the Balance Spring.

The balance springs used in the earliest chronometers—*e.g.*, those of Harrison, Le Roy, Kendall, and Mudge—were flat spirals (see fig. 4), such as had been employed in watches ever since the invention of the balance spring. As related in Chapter VII., the first maker to employ the helical spring was Arnold, who set his face against the spiral spring, and used the helical in both box and pocket chronometers. In the former case, his example was soon afterwards followed by the great majority of makers, but for pocket chronometers the spiral spring continued to hold its ground, and has, indeed, beaten its rival out of the field. The helical spring, in fact, is not well suited to pocket timekeepers, since, unless the watch be made very thick, it is difficult to find room for a sufficiently long spring†.

Terminal Curves.

A very important feature of the helical spring was discovered empirically by Arnold. He made his springs with their ends incurved, as shown in fig. 28, and soon found that the form of these curves, and the use of a length of spring sufficient to make slightly under or over a complete number of turns, had a very important bearing upon the isochronous qualities of the spring.

It is a curious coincidence, but nothing more, that the helical balance-springs used in Harrison's No. 1 (1735) and No. 2 (1739) exactly resemble, in the arrangement of their coils and terminal curves, the helical spring subsequently patented by Arnold. Harrison's

---

* Breguet, in his metallic thermometers, and also in his compensation balances, used a thin film of gold between the brass and steel of the laminæ.

† I possess what was originally a very fine pocket chronometer movement by Earnshaw, subsequently converted by some botcher into an inferior lever watch. The original helical balance spring and balance were, however, retained, and although there is room for no more than five turns of the spring, the thickness of the watch makes it very clumsy for wear in the pocket.

springs, however, were used in *tension*, not in *torsion*, and the terminal curves were employed merely to centralise the pull at each end of the spring.

The method of utilising the terminal curves as an aid to improved good timekeeping was discovered by experiment, and it is probable that neither Arnold nor the rival makers who subsequently evolved and employed similar methods—which were kept strictly secret*—could have given any explanation of the causes which produced the results.

An analogous discovery was made by Breguet, who found that if the outer coil of a spiral spring, instead of being simply pinned at its maximum distance from the centre of the balance staff, were brought inwards in a sweeping curve, as shown in fig. 52, the isochronism of the spring was much improved. But, like Arnold, he was content to put this discovery into practice without investigating its theory†.

During the lifetime of Arnold and Breguet, the laws governing the operation of balances and balance springs had been made the subject of a mathematical investigation‡ by George Atwood, F.R.S. (1746-1807), but his work, although correct and laborious, was vitiated by lack of data, and it was not until 1861 M. Phillips, a well-known French mathematician, published the results of his investigations, and placed the theory of the balance spring upon a sound mathematical basis, that any explanation was given of the action of the terminal curves invented by Arnold and Breguet.

Phillips' memoir§, though of the first importance as a mathematical investigation, was written by a scientific man for scientific men, as were his subsequent publications on the subject, but his work was reshaped into a more practical form by M. Jules Grossman¶, and still further simplified by M. Lossier||, who produced a most excellent and comprehensive manual of the theory of timing**.

Here it is only possible to give a brief synopsis of the principal result obtained by Phillips, and discussed by his successors. It is that, for any spring to be isochronous, it is necessary that the centre of gravity of the spring shall coincide with the axis of the balance. Phillips demonstrated that if a spring comply with this condition when at rest it will also do so when deformed as a result of the vibration of the balance. Furthermore, that there will be no side pressure on the pivots of the balance.

---

* Arnold's specification, delivered to the Board of Longitude in return for his reward of £3,000, mentions the fact that the spring is formed with incurved ends, but gives no hint of their importance in the adjustment of the chronometer.

† Such springs are in almost universal use to-day for high-class pocket watches, and are correctly termed "Breguet" springs, after their inventor. Unfortunately, however, his name is, more often than not, mis-printed "Brequet."

‡ "Investigations for Determining the Times of Vibration of Watch Balances." In the "Philosophical Transactions" for 1794.

§ "Sur le spiral reglant." Paris. 1861.

¶ Director of the School of Horology, Locle.

|| Director of the School of Horology, Besançon.

** This work was translated into English by Messrs. Walker and Barber, and appeared in the "Horological Journal" for 1895 and 1896.

See p. 262

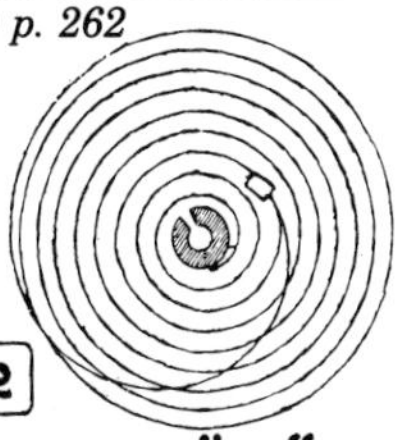

52

"Breguet", or "over-coil" spring.

See p. 264.

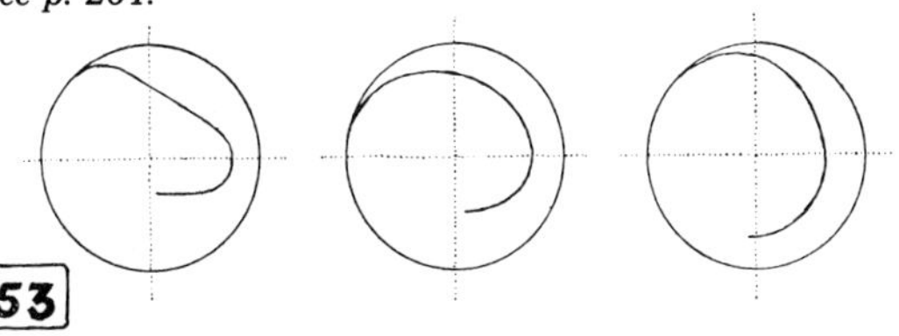

53

Various theoretically-correct terminal curves. [From Phillips' treatise.]

See p. 264.

54

Conical spring [Used by L. Berthoud.]

See p. 264.

55

Spherical, invented by Frédéric Houriet.

See p. 264.

56

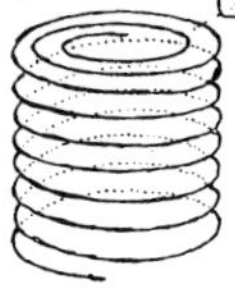

"Duo in uno" [outline only]

See p. 264.

57

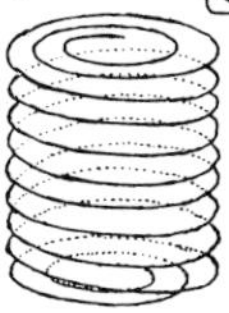

"Tria in uno" [outline only]

See p. 269.

58

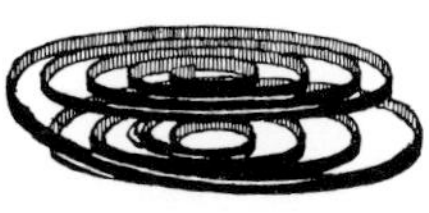

Cole's "double overcoil" spring.

See p. 269.

59

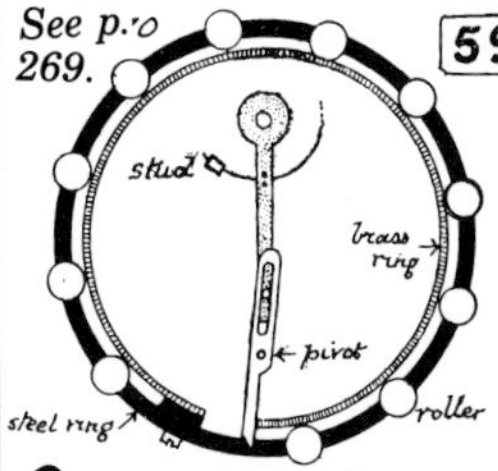

Cummings' compensation curb.

See p. 273.

60

Breguet's compensation curb.

See p. 274. NOTE. The thickness of the compound strips is slightly exaggerated.

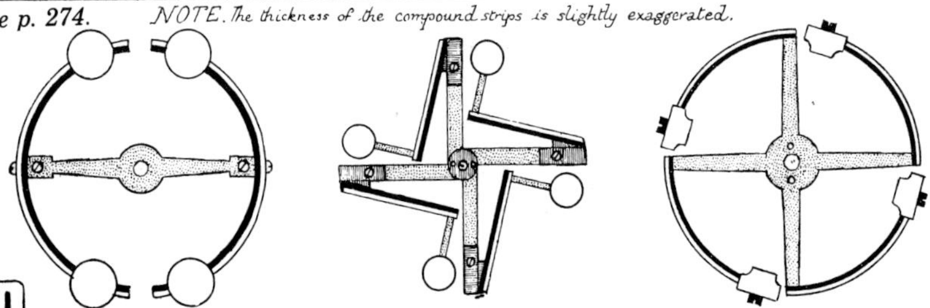

61

Le Roy, about 1769. F. Berthoud, about 1773. L. Berthoud, about 1800.

Various early forms of compensation balance.

He gave a number of examples of theoretically correct terminal curves, three of which appear in fig. 53. It will be noted that they differ very little from the forms of terminal used by Arnold and Breguet. In the helical spring, there is little difficulty in complying with the requirements of theory, since in calculating the position of the centre of gravity the *complete* turns can obviously be neglected, and all that is necessary is to ensure that the two terminal curves, and the portion of a complete turn intercepted between perpendiculars through the two points where they commence their incurvature, have a common centre of gravity at the centre of the balance staff. Phillips gave a graphical method of shaping the curves. It may be noted that they need not necessarily be identical.

With a spiral spring it is not possible for the inner terminal curve to comply absolutely with the requirements of theory, but the difference need only be slight, and the errors, if any, caused by this difference can be corrected by subsequent adjustment. In any case, so long as the escapement remains, experiment must have the last word in the adjustment of the final shape of the terminal curves, and an account of the method of doing this will be found in the works cited, and in Britten's " Watch Springing and Adjusting." It is too big a subject to be treated within the limits of this book.

OTHER FORMS OF SPRING.

Various other forms of balance spring have been tried, but are no longer used. Louis Berthoud thought highly of the conical spring, shown in fig. 54, and considered it preferable to the helical spring. Springs of a less exaggerated conical form were sometimes used by Motel, and Breguet occasionally employed a helical spring with the middle turns much thinner than the end ones, so that during the vibrations of the balance the spring alternately assumed the shape of an hour-glass and of a barrel*.

Spherical springs (see fig. 55) were strongly advocated by Frédéric Houriet, of Locle (1743-1830) but they have no real advantage, and are very difficult to make†. Amongst other fancy shapes are the " duo in uno " and " tria in uno " shown in figs. 56 and 57.

A peculiar form of spring, termed the " double overcoil," was devised and used by J. F. Cole, and is shown in fig. 58. It was practically two spiral springs, of opposite curvature, formed from a single length of wire, and having the stud at the same radius from the balance staff as the point of attachment of the free end of the spring at the collet. Hammersley subsequently produced a very similar form of spring.

In connection with the escapement shown in fig. 37, in which the balance vibrates nearly two turns in each direction, Cole used another form, like a Breguet spring with several turns of overcoil instead of one.

---

* He used this form of spring in some of his four-barrelled chronometers, such as the one shown in Plate XXXIII.

† A chronometer by " Barthet, Marseilles," in the museum of the Clockmakers Company, is fitted with one of these springs.

DOUBLE SPRINGS.

The use of more than one balance spring has often been suggested*. As related on p. 116, Mudge employed two spiral springs in his time-keepers, one acted upon by the compensation curbs, and the other by the regulator. Le Roy also used two springs, but avoided the errors introduced by Mudge's method of regulation.

The idea was revived in a patent taken out by J. G. Ulrich in 1836, in which there are two helical springs, one above and the other below the balance, the object being to reduce the side friction at the pivots, and make the end friction constant. It must be remembered that with a helical spring there is always a longitudinal pull or push on the balance staff while the balance is in motion, and this causes the friction at the endstones to vary. Incidentally, in the early Arnold chronometers, the balance was practically suspended by the spring, very little of its weight being taken by the end stone. This plan was, however, found to weaken the spring.

A patent taken out by G. Philcox, a chronometer maker, in 1846, covered the application of two helical springs in practically the same manner as that of Ulrich, whose patent was still in force†. The underlying idea, however, was simply absurd. Philcox seems to have considered, quite correctly, that the lengthening of the balance spring in heat makes the dead-point alter its position slightly with regard to the escape wheel, and so throws the escapement slightly out of beat. So it does—but the amount is negligible. Philcox, however, succeeded in convincing himself (it is hard to conceive how—it cannot have been by experiment) that it would amount to 1° of arc for every 1° Fahr. rise of temperature. Accordingly he proposed to obviate this supposed defect by using two opposed springs. It does not seem to have occurred to him that, if his springs lengthened by anything approaching this fantastic amount, the balance would, on any rise of temperature, pass into a state of constrained equilibrium‡ and have its motion much accelerated, so that by adjusting the length of the springs a point could easily be found at which no compensation would be required. Ulrich, with sounder views, had proposed to effect the same end by mounting the studs on moveable collets controlled by a compensation curb, which would, in theory, be quite a feasible plan, affording a complete compensation without either using a compensation balance or altering the length of the balance spring.

---

* The mathematical conditions governing the application of several balance springs have recently been investigated by M. Jules Andrade. See his "Les organes réglants des chronometres," Bésançon, 1922.

† It should be noted that in this country the grant of Letters Patent implies no official guarantee that the invention is novel, or that it does not infringe some existing patent. The onus of ascertaining this rests upon the patentee.

‡ This term is due to Daniel Bernoulli (see p. 267), who discussed the application to a marine timekeeper of a balance controlled by two opposed springs, of equal initial tension. Some experiments with this device were made by Romilly, of Paris, who stated that the motion of a balance so fitted was found to be so rapid and free that he had some little difficulty in stopping it.

ACCELERATION.

Intimately connected with the material of the balance spring, and possibly with its form also, is the phenomenon of "acceleration." It has been known for over a century that chronometers fitted with hardened and tempered steel springs tend, when first set going, to accelerate their rates. Some outline has been given, in the chapters relating to Kendall, Mudge, and Earnshaw, of their experiences of this phenomenon, but, strictly speaking, only Kendall's was a normal case, since the action of Mudge's two balance springs was affected by that of his remontoire springs, while Earnshaw's springs were not tempered. The later makers, however, who followed Arnold in using hardened and tempered steel springs, found that chronometers so fitted had a uniform tendency to accelerate. The amount of this acceleration varies, but a change in the daily rate amounting to a second in a month and continuing for a year or more is quite common.

It is now fairly certain that this acceleration is due to two causes—the molecular change which the outer surface of the spring undergoes during the process of hardening, and the stresses set up in the ends of the spring when forming the terminal curves. A spring formed by rolling from soft steel wire, and not subsequently hardened—such as was used by Earnshaw—does not produce acceleration, but on the other hand a chronometer so fitted will have a constant tendency to lose on its rate. Generally, too, although not invariably, the amount of acceleration is found to vary in accordance with the degree to which the hardening process has been carried. Palladium springs, which are made by a process of annealing, and not hardened, do not accelerate so much as steel springs.

The effect of forming the terminal curves in assisting to produce acceleration is shown by the fact that if such curves have been much altered from their original shape during the process of isochronising the spring, the amount of the acceleration is generally found to increase considerably. It was asserted by Hammersley, an English maker, that an old spring which has run through its period of acceleration, and settled down, can be made to re-accelerate by distorting the terminal curves, and then restoring them to their original shape*, but this is denied by others. In any case, it is certain that the less the terminal curves are manipulated the better and steadier will be the performance of the spring. A spring without any terminal curves —*e.g.*, an ordinary flat spiral spring—accelerates less than one with an overcoil.

Many other theories have been advanced to account for the phenomenon of acceleration, such as wear taking place in the escapement, distortion of the rims through centrifugal force, and a gradual alteration in the amount of their action. But such theories cannot be made to square with the results of experimental investigation, and the balance of proof is strongly in favour of the conclusion that

* It was for this reason that he devised the "tria in uno" spring, in which sharp curvature of the terminals is avoided.

acceleration is produced, almost entirely, by the two causes already mentioned—the hardening of the spring and the formation of the terminal curves.

In practice, of course, acceleration is no longer the bugbear that it was to the early makers. It is evident that a steel spring must be hardened to obtain a permanent rate, and that, accordingly, some acceleration is unavoidable, as is also the case, though in a less pronounced form, with the palladium spring. But once the spring has settled down, the acceleration disappears. To hasten this end, the plan is sometimes adopted of "running in" a new spring by fitting it to a chronometer with a lightened balance, going, say, twelve months in six.

EFFECT OF HEAT AND COLD ON THE BALANCE SPRING.

This is, of course, the most important point connected with the employment of a balance spring in any machine designed for the accurate measurement of time. Ever since the introduction of the balance spring, it has been known that unless some form of compensation be fitted such a machine will go slower for an increase of temperature, and faster for a decrease. This is due to an actual change in the modulus of elasticity of the spring, and not to a mere increase or decrease in its length*, which would, in any case, be quite insufficient to produce an effect of the magnitude observed.

For a long time after the introduction of the balance spring—and, indeed, for many years after a practical solution of the difficulty had been found in the compensation balance—the action of heat and cold upon such springs remained obscure. Daniel Bernouilli (a mathematician of much note in his day), writing in 1747, went so far as to remark that if springs were found to vary their force in different temperatures (as, of course, they do) this property would always preclude them from being successfully employed in timekeepers†. Again, Arnold, in adopting the helical spring, contended, at first, that it possessed the property of being unaffected by temperature. But even after both of these random assertions had been effectually disproved, it remained quite uncertain whether the rate of increase or decrease of the spring's elasticity was constant or otherwise, and what law, if any, it followed.

To determine this point, a series of experiments was made in 1840 by E. J. Dent, who employed for the purpose a chronometer having a glass balance (uncompensated) and a hardened and tempered

* Berthoud, in his "Traité des Horloges Marines," tabulated the effects of a change of temperature of 60¾° Fahr. on his No. 8 timekeeper as

Expansion of balance	62.4 sec.
Decrease of spring's elasticity	309.9 „
Lengthening of spring	20.2 „

This was accepted for many years, but in 1882 it was pointed out by Mr. T. D. Wright that the effect ascribed to the lengthening of the spring was non-existent. The strength of a given spring varies directly as the breadth of the spring and the cube of its thickness, and inversely as its length, and, as all its dimensions are increased in the same ratio, it would actually be slightly stronger for a rise of temperature.

† "Recherches Mechaniques et Astronomiques sur la meilleure maniere de trouver l'heure en mer, etc." Paris, 1747.

steel spring. He obtained its rate at various temperatures, ranging betwen 32° Fahr. and 100° Fahr., and deduced from his results that the elastic moment of the balance spring per unit angle of displacement of the balance (or, in other words, the strength of the balance spring to resist torsion) varied directly as the temperature.

Similar experiments were made at Greenwich by Sir George Airy in 1859, using two chronometers, one by Molyneux (No. 5174) and one by Frodsham (No. 3148) with steel helical springs (hardened and tempered) and plain (uncompensated) circular brass balances. Analogous experiments were made at the same time in France by MM. Delamarche and Ploix, who employed a chronometer by Breguet, similarly fitted*.

The results of both sets of experiments were practically the same. Airy deduced from an analysis of the rates that the change of daily rate produced by varying temperatures ranging over 60° Fahr. was, in all cases, directly proportional to the temperature, and amounted to 6.11 secs. for 1° Fahrenheit. Or, in other words, that an uncompensated chronometer, in going from a temperature of 30° to 90°, would change its daily rate by *over six minutes*. From this may be gauged the magnitude of the problem which confronted the early constructors of marine timekeepers, and which was first solved by Harrison.

The results obtained by MM. Delamarche and Ploix similarly pointed to an exact correspondence between the changes of rate and of temperature. The constant obtained by them was a change of daily rate of 11.01 sec. per day for 1° Centigrade, or 6.12 sec. for 1° Fahrenheit.

The importance of the facts thus established by the concurrence of three independent sets of experiments will become apparent in the following chapter.

THE COMPENSATION CURB.

Before going on to discuss the method universally employed to obviate the effect of heat and cold on the balance spring—namely, the compensation balance—it may be as well to give some account of the compensation curbs previously used to effect the same purpose. At first sight the compensation curb appears to have the preference, since it is an attempt to correct the errors of the spring *in the spring*, and not by a roundabout method. And it is incontestable that the old masters who employed it obtained, for a time, and by a process of patient and laborious experiment and adjustment, excellent results†. It has, however, the fatal defect of interfering with the isochronism of the

* "Note sur les marches d'un chronomètre à balancier non compensé." "Comptes Rendus de l'Académie des Sciences." Vol. 48, 1859.

† Earnshaw was stated, by his grandson, to have got as good results with a compensation curb as with a compensation balance.

balance spring, and this has caused its abandonment as a primary compensation*, although it has once or twice been suggested in more recent times for use as an auxiliary.

The compensation curbs used by Harrison, Kendall, Mudge, and Berthoud have already been described. It is worthy of note that Harrison's claim to be the first man to compensate a balance spring has been contested in favour of Tompion (1638-1713), "the father of English watchmaking," who is stated† to have experimented with a compensation curb consisting of a simple brass split ring, one end of which carried the curb pins, and to have abandoned it through his inability to get sufficient travel of the pins. In the absence of corroboration, however, and of more mechanical details, this claim must be taken *cum grano*. I have not been able to find any contemporary account of the experiment, and unless the curb were secured to a steel plate it is difficult to see how any motion of the curb pins could have been obtained at all.

The first pocket watch to have a compensation curb is generally stated to have been that sold by Berthoud to George III. in 1763, but as a matter of fact Ellicott exhibited a watch so fitted at a Council meeting of the Royal Society on Feb. 15th, 1752. In the absence of a detached escapement, however, such devices could have had but little effect upon the timekeeping of a watch of ordinary pattern‡.

After the publication of "The Principles of Mr. Harrison's Timekeeper" in 1767, considerable attention was devoted to the compensation curb, but not always intelligently. Hatton, writing in 1773§, remarks :—

> "Since Mr. Harrison's method to correct the expansion of metals came out, we have had many and strange fancies of expansion slides; but most unfortunately for most of the constructors, their famous inventions have been found of no use; nay, some of disuse, as some of their performances have had a contrary effect."

A compensation curb which did not employ a bi-metallic strip was proposed by Alexander Cumming (1732-1814) in a work published in 1766¶, and is shown in fig. 59. He used a brass ring, encircled by a number of rollers pivoted into a steel frame, the travel of the free end of the ring being multiplied by a lever carrying the curb pins.

* The idea died hard, however. A compensation curb was patented by Massey, an English maker of experience, in 1842, and proposals of a similar kind have been put forward occasionally since his time—but chiefly by persons having only a rudimentary knowledge of the subject.

† This statement is due to J. G. Ulrich, who made it in several articles and pamphlets. I have not been able to trace his authority for it.

‡ The watch made by Berthoud was fitted with a cylinder escapement, as was a similar watch subsequently made by Mudge, who repaired Berthoud's. The escapement selected for both was about the worst possible choice that could have been made. The cylinder escapement possesses a rough form of inherent compensation, due to the oil on its resting faces thinning in heat and thickening in cold, and accordingly the addition of a compensation curb to a watch with this escapement would probably overcompensate it considerably, while in any case its effect would be quite masked by that of the oil.

§ "An Introduction to the Mechanical Part of Clock and Watch Work." London. 1773.

¶ "The Elements of Clock and Watchwork adapted to Practice, in two Essays." London. 1766.

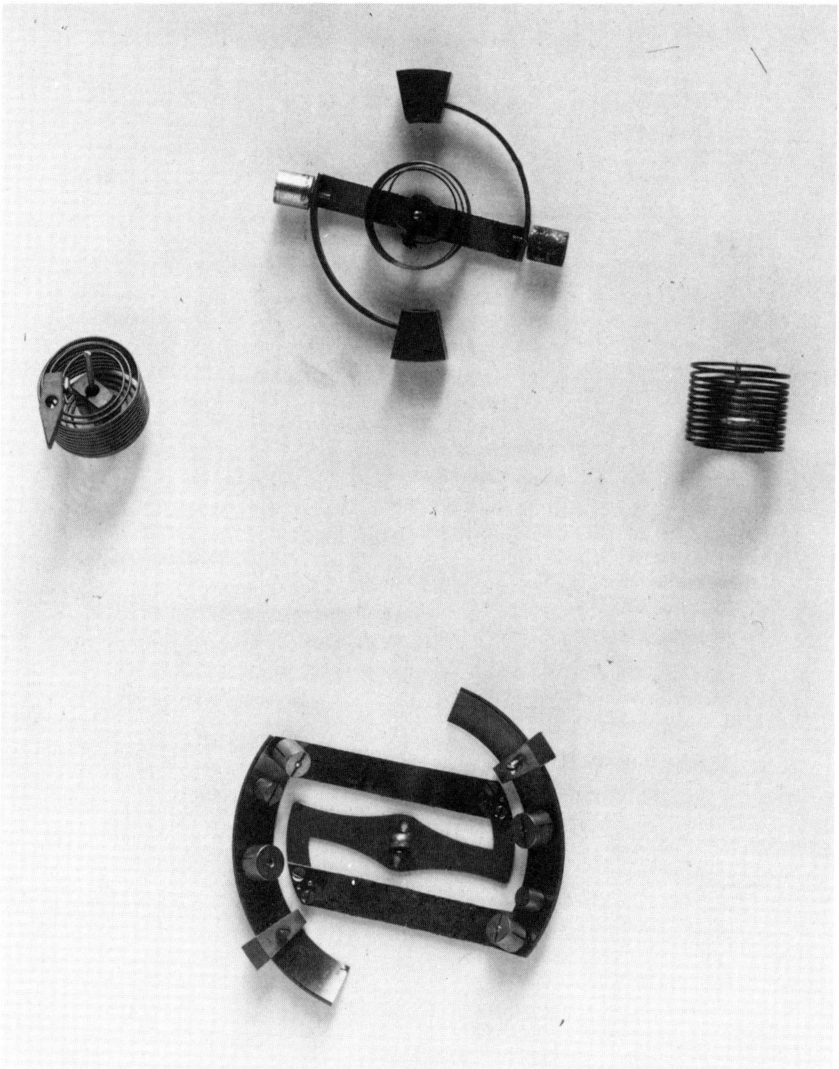

EARNSHAW BALANCE (TOP)
'TRIO IN UNO' BALANCE SPRING (LEFT)
CONVENTIONAL HELICAL BALANCE SPRING (RIGHT)
JOHN HARTNUP'S BALANCE (BOTTOM)

MOVEMENT OF POCKET CHRONOMETER BY THOMAS EARNSHAW.
No. 504/3163. Showing the 'Sugar Tongs' compensation.
Courtesy B.M.

Compensation curbs of a different character were employed by Breguet in a number of his watches, and similar examples made by Berthoud* and Earnshaw are also to be found. In these, the length of the spring is unaltered, but compensation is obtained by a still more objectionable method—that of varying the amount of play which the spring has between the curb pins.

In Breguet's, shown in fig. 60, the laminated curb is bent into the form of a U, whose extremities carry the curb pins, and cause them to approach in heat and recede in cold. The effect produced was analogous to that of Harrison's "cycloid pin," in that it practically involved the use of two balance springs of different lengths, the shorter spring being used for a longer period in heat, and a shorter in cold. The method affects the isochronism of the spring considerably, and also introduces large position errors. Breguet, of course, was fully aware of these defects, and in his high-class timekeepers he used the compensation balance†.

The forms used by Berthoud and Earnshaw employed two separate curbs, but the principle involved is the same, and they present the same defects.

Attempts have also been made, by many inventors from Berthoud onwards, to use the compensation curb as an auxiliary compensation. This was proposed, for example, by Hardy (*circa* 1810), who mounted the stud of a helical spring on a short bi-metallic strip, and by Eiffe (*circa* 1840), who moved in the same manner a cycloid pin similar to Arnold's, acting on the outer coil of the spring. A similar plan to Eiffe's was patented in Switzerland by Paul Nardin in 1893, but in this case the cycloid pin, which was adjusted by hand, was carried on a small spring, and employed to obtain isochronism.

For ordinary watches, the problem of compensating the balance spring has now been solved by the employment of a nickel-steel spring and an uncompensated balance. The errors introduced by this construction are only about a twelfth to a fifteenth of those involved by the use of a steel spring. As described on p. 309, it is quite possible that in the future the employment of an "elinvar" spring may similarly obviate the necessity of using a compensation balance: but the difficulty which stands in the way is that although *almost* all the errors of the balance spring can be removed in this manner, the problem of eliminating or cancelling the very small residual errors is an exceedingly complicated one.

---

* Berthoud's is illustrated in his "Histoire de la mesure de Temps," and there is a large unsigned silver watch fitted with it in the museum of the Clockmakers Company (Nelthropp collection). This watch also has a very peculiar escapement, a compound of the lever and the cylinder. Earnshaw's may be seen in a watch of his make in the Science Museum, South Kensington (Evan Roberts' collection).

† In some of his very small watches, where economy of space was an object, he employed plain balances made of platinum, whose expansion is very small compared with that of steel.

CHAPTER XI.

THE COMPENSATION BALANCE.

PART I.

The principal facts in connection with the early history of the compensation balance—its invention by Le Roy in or about 1765, its adoption by Arnold and Berthoud, and the improvements in its manufacture introduced by Earnshaw—have already been related. By 1785 it had definitely ranged itself alongside the chronometer escapement as an essential requirement of any marine timekeeper.

As related in the preceding chapter, the errors produced by changes of temperature in the going of any balance timekeeper arise chiefly from two causes—an alteration in the elasticity of the spring, and a change in the dimensions (and, therefore, in the moment of inertia) of the balance. The effect of the latter, however, is much less than that of the former, and it is almost entirely counterbalanced by the corresponding increase in the radius of the coils of the spring.

To counteract these changes, two methods have been devised—the compensation curb, which corrects the errors of both balance spring and balance by means of the *spring*, and the compensation balance, which corrects them by the agency of the *balance*. Efforts have also been made, chiefly by Berthoud, to combine the two—a compromise which, like many others, succeeded in combining the defects of both in far greater measure than their advantages.

From about 1765 to 1780, or thereabouts, the compensation curb may be regarded as holding the field, but after that time the superiority of the compensation balance became manifest, and ensured its universal adoption. The principal defect of the curb is, of course, the alteration it produces in the isochronism of the spring, whether it acts by altering the length of the spring, or by varying the distance between the curb pins. If it were not for this crucial defect, the principle of the curb—especially if fitted on the lines adopted by Berthoud, who used a massive and solidly constructed "gridiron" of brass and steel rods—might be thought to promise more permanent and more easily controlled results than could be obtained from a rapidly vibrating balance, in which the rims, which must of necessity be comparatively weak,* have to carry a pair of heavy weights, and are exposed to considerable centrifugal forces. But in practice the compensation balance has proved itself to be so decidedly superior to the curb that the latter has been, for over a century, a mere obsolete curiosity.

* The curvature produced in a bi-metallic strip by a change of temperature is directly proportional to the difference of the co-efficients of expansion of the two metals, and inversely proportional to their relative thickness. It follows that if the rims are made too thick in proportion to their length, their action in heat and cold is diminished, or, in extreme cases, totally impeded.

For the purposes of the present chapter, it will be convenient to take as a starting point the simple form of compensation balance evolved by Earnshaw, and already described on page 195. He was not, and did not claim to be, its inventor, but he simplified it as far as possible, and his plan of fusing the brass and steel together and turning the rims on a lathe—a plan in sharp contrast to the rule-of-thumb methods employed by Arnold and others*—is followed, in all essentials, at the present time.

The simplicity of Earnshaw's balance will become apparent by comparing fig. 33 with fig. 61, which shows several forms used by the early chronometer makers. All are based on the same principle—that of using compound rims of brass and steel to carry the balance weights and to alter the distance of the latter from the axis of the balance, in varying temperatures, thus increasing or decreasing the moment of inertia of the balance sufficiently to compensate for the effects of heat and cold upon the balance spring and the balance itself. The actual number and shape of the rims has no bearing upon the operation of the balance, but any increase beyond the minimum number—two—involves a correspondingly increased difficulty in poising the balance, i.e., in ensuring that its centre of gravity coincides exactly with its axis. Furthermore, when using a number of rims it is difficult to ensure that the action of each is precisely the same: such a balance, if correctly poised in any particular temperature, may easily be found to be out of poise in a different temperature. In addition, it is more costly to make and to adjust, and there is no corresponding advantage to be gained from using it. Accordingly, the standard balance of ordinary pattern—that is to say, one not provided with any of the forms of auxiliary compensation described later—has come to be that shown in fig. 33, which exhibits very little difference from Earnshaw's, either in appearance or construction.

The actual shape of the weights is of little importance, so long as they are exactly alike. Earnshaw cut his weights out of a turned ring, which explains their somewhat peculiar form. In the modern balance they are made cylindrical, which simplifies their manufacture considerably, and have their axes parallel with the balance staff. In the early Arnold balances (see fig. 32) they were also cylindrical, but placed tangentially, while Brockbank and Jurgensen (see fig. 62) sometimes used weights of a "streamlined" shape, with the object of diminishing air resistance. The practical advantage of such weights is, however, negligible, and they are difficult to make and to poise.

The rims of the modern balance are considerably longer than those used by Earnshaw, and slightly thicker. The proportionate

* Pearson, in his very able article "Chronometer," in Rees' "Cyclopædia," defends Arnold's method of forming the rims separately with pliers, but his arguments are not convincing. The objection made at the time to Earnshaw's plan of turning them out of the solid, was that they did not retain the circular form thus imparted after they were cut open, but sprang outwards a little. This, however, is unimportant in comparison with the much greater facility this plan affords of making both rims alike in all respects, to say nothing of the great advantage of having them in one with the cross-bar.

thickness of the brass and steel is also slightly different. Earnshaw made his with the brass twice or three times as thick as the steel, but the modern practice is to have the proportion of brass to steel approximately as 3 to 2, although this is not an invariable rule. On theoretical grounds, Yvon Villarceau has suggested that the correct thicknesses should be in the inverse proportion of the square roots of the moduli of elasticity of brass and steel, which gives roughly 17 of brass to 12 of steel.

The central bar of the standard balance is formed, as described on p. 189, in one piece with the rims, and carries two small bolts with heavy nuts, which are termed the "timing screws." These can be screwed in or out to bring the chronometer to time without affecting the action of the compensation.* As related on p. 138 this plan is due to Le Roy, and it was employed by him in the first compensation balance ever made.

COMPENSATION BALANCES FOR POCKET TIMEKEEPERS.

Fig. 63 shows a modified form of the Earnshaw balance, which only differs from the former in having the mass of the balance weights distributed amongst a number of pairs of heavy-headed screws instead of being concentrated in two larger weights. Balances of this type were found to be better adapted for use in pocket chronometers,† where the obtaining of a perfectly poised balance is of far greater importance than in a box chronometer, whose balance is always horizontal; and, although the pocket chronometer is now practically obsolete, the same type of balance is used in the high class lever watch which has taken its place.

Balances of this kind, which are not, as a general rule, fitted with any of the forms of auxiliary compensation‡ described in the following pages, present very little difference in design, and while the method of their adjustment is one of great technical interest, it must, I am afraid, be regarded as outside the scope of this book.

The balances evolved by Earnshaw and his contemporaries represent, of course, a very considerable amount of experimental research in a virgin field. Thus we find Arnold, in 1781, reporting to the Board of Longitude that in the past three years he had expended £300 in experiments "on the single article of compensation balance," and doubtless similar claims might have been put forward by Earnshaw,

* Actually, any change in the position of the timing screws causes a minute alteration in the effect produced by the motion of the weights for a given alteration of temperature, since this depends upon the ratio of the moment of inertia of the weights to that of the remainder of the balance, which latter is slightly changed by an alteration in the position of the timing screws.

† Some of the older pocket chronometers are fitted with balance weights similar to those of a box chronometer, but these take up a lot of room, and it is by no means easy to adjust such a machine in positions.

‡ The pocket chronometer by Earnshaw, alluded to in the footnote on p. 261, has a modification of Uhrig's plan—two wire trammels which restrict the outward movement of the laminæ. I imagine that this was added after Earnshaw's time.

Berthoud, and the rest. But it is a curious fact that none of them appears to have discovered or suspected a perceptible defect in the action of such balances.

Their method of applying this form of compensation was as follows: The balance having been made and poised, the weights (whose size and approximate position had been previously determined, for a given size of balance, as the result of experience) were set roughly in position, and the going of the chronometer observed in various temperatures. If it lost in heat, the compensation was obviously insufficient, and the weights were accordingly moved towards the free ends of the rims, causing them to move further for the same change of temperature. If the chronometer gained in heat after this change, they were moved the other way, and so on until the correct position was found, the balance being re-poised after each alteration. This was necessitated by the fact that if the weights were placed somewhere near the correct position to begin with, the subsequent displacement required was slight, and it was practically impossible to ensure that each weight was moved exactly the same distance*. A position having been found for the weights in which a considerable rise or fall of temperature, say 20° Fahr., did not affect the timekeeping of the machine, the adjustment of the balance was regarded as completed, and the machine was brought to correct time by means of the timing screws, these being, of course, screwed in (equally) to make it go faster, and *vice versa*.

Middle Temperature Error.

Although the standard type of balance used in the ordinary chronometer of to-day is still, in all essentials, that of Earnshaw, its limitations are now clearly understood, and it has been recognised for a long time that it has an inherent defect, and that although it compensates in a general sense for the effects of temperature changes, yet a chronometer in which such a balance is fitted, no matter how carefully it may be made and adjusted, will only keep absolutely correct time at *two particular temperatures*, some distance apart. Between those two temperatures the machine will gain slightly on its rate, while at higher or lower temperatures it will lose. The amount of the change of rate in a chronometer keeping, say, correct time at 50° and 80°, may be as much as 2½ seconds per day at 65°, midway between the two. The name "middle temperature error" is given to this peculiarity of the standard balance, although it is rather a misnomer, since in the above case the amount of the error at 35° and 95° would be considerably greater than that at the middle temperature, and would increase rapidly as the extreme temperatures diverged further from it.

It is uncertain who was the first discoverer of this defect. It has been claimed, by such authorities as M. Paul Ditisheim and Dr. Ch. Ed. Guillaume, that the honour should be given to Ferdinand Berthoud, who undoubtedly published, in 1773, a table of corrections to be

* In this connection, see the account of the genesis of "Airy's Bar," on p. 309.

applied to his No. 8 timekeeper, exhibiting what is apparently a well-marked middle temperature error. This table is as follows :—

Table of corrections which must be applied to the time shown by the marine clock No. 8, to judge of its going in different temperatures.

898. The clock No. 8 is assumed to keep correct time at a temperature of 15 degrees above freezing point; it goes more slowly in cold and also in high temperatures.

Degrees above freezing point.	Loses.	Seconds.
At 5°	In 24 hours	$1\frac{5}{7}$
10°		$0\frac{5}{7}$
15°	Assumed correct	0
20°	Loses	$1\frac{1}{4}$
25°	Loses	$2\frac{1}{2}$
32°	Loses	$6\frac{1}{4}$

Had Berthoud's machine been fitted with a compensation balance, there could but be one opinion as to his discovery of the middle temperature, or " M.T.," error.

But, actually, No. 8 had a plain circular brass balance, and its compensation, as noted on p. 153 was effected by means of a " gridiron " compensation curb of brass and steel rods, which altered the position of the curb pins. The error noticed by Berthoud in the going of the machine was probably due to the curb, whose action was slightly greater, for a given range of temperature, at middle temperatures.* Accordingly, it may be said that although he detected an analogous error in the going of this early machine, this was not the M.T. error which is inherent in the ordinary pattern of compensation balance.

In the early part of the last century the discovery was claimed by several makers. Lord Grimthorpe, *more suo*, went so far as to assert that . . . " I believe it has never been disputed that Mr. Dent (E. J. Dent) was the first person to explain the cause of this error, in the 'Nautical Magazine,' in 1833; and he gave the following explanation of it :— . . ."† but since Dent's alleged explanation, as quoted by Grimthorpe, was rather vague, and it was not claimed for him by his very able advocate (and executor) that he was the discoverer‡ of the fact in question, the way is clear for the assertion that, as far as I know, the first recorded investigations relating to middle temperature error were made by J. G. Ulrich, a London maker (already noticed in the previous chapter as the inventor of a

* The gridiron was employed to rotate an arm, carrying the curb pins, by a direct push upon its shorter end, which was kept in contact with it by a spring. The motion of the arm was therefore quickest when at right angles to the axis of the gridiron.

† I am inclined to consider that this statement (which was also made by Dent himself in a pamphlet entitled " On the Errors of Chronometers," 1842), is untrue. I have been unable to trace any such statement in the " Nautical Magazine " for that year, or in any of the articles on the chronometer contributed by the firm of Arnold and Dent during the period 1833-1840. Moreover, in the course of an article in the volume for 1833, entitled " Glass Balance Springs," and signed " Arnold and Dent," a statement appears which evinces complete ignorance of the existence of M.T. error.

‡ Dr. Guillaume ascribes to Dent the re-discovery of the M.T. error, but, I think, incorrectly. See previous footnote.

remontoire, in 1814. It has also been ascribed to William Hardy, another London maker, but I have not been able to substantiate this.*

It may be as well here to point out the essential requirements of a *perfect* compensation balance.

The compensation balance aims at removing, by the movement of the weights which it carries, and consequently by an alteration of its moment of inertia, the errors produced by the alteration of the elasticity of the balance spring, and of its own dimensions, in changes of temperature.

The time of oscillation of a given balance is given by the following formula :—

$$T = 2\ \pi \sqrt{\frac{IL}{Ei}}$$

where I is the balance's moment of inertia, L the length of the balance spring, E its modulus of elasticity, and i the moment of inertia of the balance spring about its neutral axis.

This formula, although it provides a complete statement of the facts, is not of much practical value, since in order to apply it to find the time of vibration it would first be necessary to obtain some of the data, such as I, by experiment†, in which case the result would be no more accurate than if the time of vibration were found directly by experiment. It leads the way, however, to a modification which is of interest.

The elastic moment of the spring per unit angle of displacement of the balance in the foregoing formula is $\frac{Ei}{L}$, and calling this S, and substituting it, we have—

$$T = 2\ \pi \sqrt{\frac{I}{S}}$$

from which it is apparent that for the compensation afforded by the balance to be perfect, the ratio of I to S must remain the same for all changes of temperature to which the machine is exposed. Consequently, if we know how these two quantities actually vary in alterations of temperature, it can at once be seen whether this condition is likely to be fulfilled or not.

* Glasgow, in his "Watch and Clock Making," p. 242, says of Hardy's balance (see p. 292) " . . . . He called it a permanent compensation balance," and in his description of it he says: "It will carry the weights to the centre quicker in heat than they are made to recede in cold." This would go a long way to show that Hardy had discovered the M.T. error in 1804, but after a careful search in all likely quarters I have failed to find the statement which Glasgow attributes to him.

† It is impossible to compute the moment of inertia of a given balance from such data as its dimensions, specific gravity, etc., as accurately as it can be found by experiment. Moreover, the formula assumes that the construction of the balance is theoretically perfect, which is, *a priori*, impossible.

Although the exact path taken by the weights of a standard compensation balance is not exactly known, it may be taken as roughly accurate that the weights move inward in heat, for a given rise of temperature, as much as they move outwards for a similar fall*. It remains to be investigated what effect, in either case, is produced upon the timekeeping of a chronometer fitted with such a balance.

If r be the distance of the weights from the axis of the balance, and M their combined mass, then if dr be the movement of the weights for some given decrease of temperature, the moment of inertia of the balance, which before was Mr^2 will now be $M(r^2 + 2r\,dr + dr^2)$, and the ratio of the new moment of inertia to the old will be $1 + \frac{2dr}{r} + \left(\frac{dr}{r}\right)^2$.

Again, for a similar increase of heat, the motion of the weights may again be taken, as previously stated, to be dr, and the new moment of inertia will be $M(r^2 - 2dr + dr^2)$, and *its* ratio to the original moment of inertia will be $1 - \frac{2dr}{r} + \left(\frac{dr}{r}\right)^2$. Consequently, the *change* of moment of inertia is greater for a fall of temperature than for an equivalent rise by the amount $2\left(\frac{dr}{r}\right)^2$. In other words, in the standard balance, the weights move slightly faster from the centre than they should for a fall of temperature, and slightly slower towards the centre than they should for a rise.

It has thus been shown that I varies for a change of temperature t by an amount depending upon the square of the alteration in the radius of gyration of the weights, and since this alteration may be expressed as the product of a constant multiplied by t, it follows that I varies as t^2, and that its representation by means of a graph will be a curve, as shown in fig. 64, the inclination of the curve depending upon the extent of the compensation, and hence upon the position of the weights along the rims. Such curves, for six positions (at 0°, 30°, 60°, 90°, 120°, and 150° from the roots of the laminæ), are shown in the figure.

From the experiments of Dent, Airy, and of Delamarche and Ploix, on the other hand, it appears that S is a function of t, not of t^2, and that, if plotted to a temperature base, its graph is a straight line, as shown in the same figure.

From this, it follows that although, by adjusting the mass and position of the compensation weights, an I curve can be obtained which will intersect the S line in two points, *it can never coincide with it except at those points*, and that in consequence a machine fitted with the standard type of balance can only be compensated with *absolute* correctness at two temperatures, corresponding with the points of intersection of the two graphs. Between them, it will gain, since the I curve is below the S line, which shows that the moment of inertia

* This was first established, experimentally, by Le Roy, *circa* 1764. See his "Mémoire sur la meilleur maniere de mesurer le tems en Mer," 1770.

See p. 274

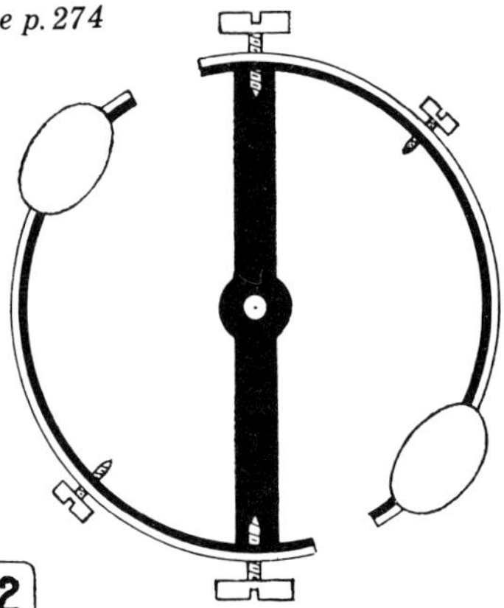

62

Jurgensen's balance.

See p. 275.

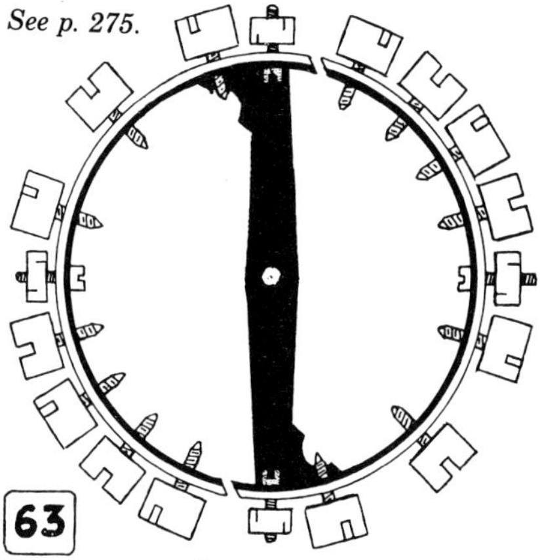

63

Pocket-chronometer balance.

See p. 279.

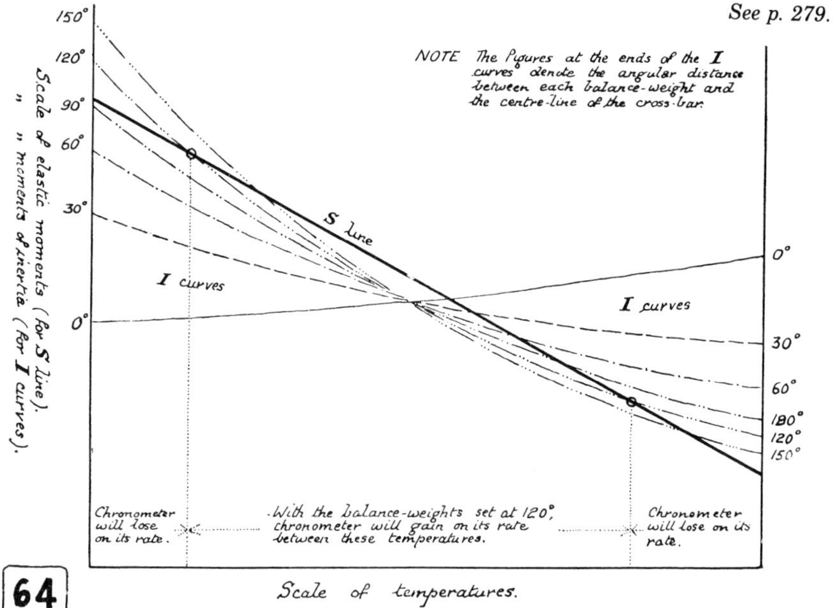

64

Diagram showing effect of compensation, and cause of "middle temperature error."

MINIATURE CHRONOMETER BY CHARLES YOUNG.
London. No. 503. 3⅞ in. square. A one day movement, with three arm balance.
Courtesy B.M.

of the balance is slightly too small: while, conversely, at temperatures outside the two points of intersection, the machine will lose, since the I curve is then above the S line, and the moment of inertia is accordingly shown to be slightly too great.

As previously pointed out, the inclination of the I curve to the S line can be altered by shifting the weights along the rims, and in a similar manner the distance between the points of their intersection can be varied by altering the mass of the weights themselves, which has the effect of raising or lowering the I curve bodily. This does not in the least affect the *total* amount of the machine's error for a given range of temperature, since a reduction in the amount of the error between the points of intersection produces a corresponding increase of the error in the extremes, and *vice versa*.

AUXILIARY COMPENSATIONS.

The existence of the M.T. error having once been established, and the means of correcting it—the acceleration of the motion of the weights in heat as compared with that in cold—having been pointed out (as was done by Ulrich), it is natural that the attention of those chronometer makers who were desirous of exhibiting their ability by obtaining a high place in competitions (such as the Greenwich trials), should have been directed towards some means of removing it. The standard form of balance, however, had been in use for a long period, and had given convincing proof of its power to nullify all but a very small portion of the total error caused by changes of temperature. It is natural, therefore, that there were but few makers who considered the possibility of abandoning it *in toto*. The general attention was, rather, directed to the provision of some auxiliary compensation which should remove the middle temperature error while leaving the rims to do their work of nullifying the far greater errors which would otherwise be caused by changes of temperature.

The auxiliaries which have from time to time been suggested and, in many cases, brought into practical use, may be divided into two classes. The former, which are only intended to come into action at some predetermined temperature, and are inactive above (or below) it, may be termed " discontinuous " auxiliaries. The second class, which are always in action, may be termed " continuous " auxiliaries. The latter involve a re-arrangement, or, in extreme cases, a reconstruction, of the standard form of balance. It will be convenient to give some examples of both classes.

DISCONTINUOUS AUXILIARY COMPENSATIONS.

POOLE'S AUXILIARY COMPENSATION.

This is the first form of auxiliary compensation known to have been applied to a compensation balance. The name by which it is generally called is that of the maker (John Poole, 1818-1867) who brought it into prominence, but although there appears no reason to doubt that he re-invented it independently about 1845, it had previously been employed by John Pennington. Even Pennington, moreover, was not the original inventor, since there is a watch in the museum of the Clockmakers' Company, by John Leroux, hall-marked 1785, fitted with what is undoubtedly an early form of "Poole's auxiliary."

In its simplest form,* which has been used in a large number of chronometers, this auxiliary is shown in fig. 65. It consists simply of two small screws carried upon rigid arms united to the cross-bar of the balance, and so adjusted as to meet the rims, near their roots, as they move outwards in low temperatures. The effective length of the latter (and, accordingly, the motion of the weights which they carry) is thus reduced slightly below its normal amount. This action is made use of by adjusting the chronometer fitted with such a balance to keep correct time, say, at 90° and 60°, which would normally cause it to have a considerably increased error at 30°. The action of the check screw, however, counteracts this.

The effect of this, as of the other auxiliaries of the same kind shortly to be described, is to reduce the *total effect* of the middle temperature error very considerably, but it does not remove it altogether, nor does it distribute the remaining error uniformly. A chronometer fitted with it would still have a slight (gaining) error between 90° and 60°, and a slight but increasing losing error between 60° and the temperature at which the rims met the check screws. For a further reduction of temperature, the error would either remain constant or gradually diminish, this depending upon the distance of the check screws from the roots of the rims. In the latter case, a third temperature might be reached at which the machine would keep correct time, beyond which it would have a slight gaining error. (Long before this, however, the oil would probably have frozen in the pivot holes.)

The practical effect of the device is, then, to halve the M.T. error between the two standard temperatures, and greatly to reduce the error which would normally be produced in low temperature by this adjustment. Balances of this pattern are simple to make, and their popularity may be ascribed to this reason.

Apart from the main objection that its action is discontinuous, the principal fault that can be found with Poole's auxiliary is that as its correct operation depends upon the extremely slight motion of the rims close to their roots, its adjustment is of necessity very delicate†, and liable to be upset by any foreign matter which may find its way between the point of the screw and the rim. Still, it has been found to work very well in practice, although it is not employed so much now as formerly.

* It should be added that Poole also experimented with a number of other forms of auxiliaries, including one on Molyneux' plan. He did not patent his auxiliary, and it was largely responsible for the success of several other competitors in the Greenwich trials. A request from Airy for a description of it was met by a polite, but very decided, refusal. It is amusing to note that soon after its first introduction descriptions of it were sent to Greenwich by two other makers, each of whom stated that it was his own invention.

† This is increased by the fact that, in contrast to most other forms of auxiliary, it acts upon the main weights, and not upon separate and smaller auxiliary ones.

Auxiliary compensations, mostly discontinuous.

See p. 283

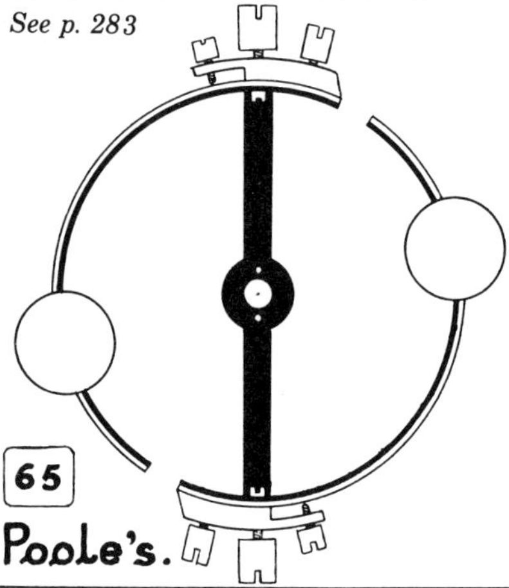

65

Poole's.

See p. 287.

66

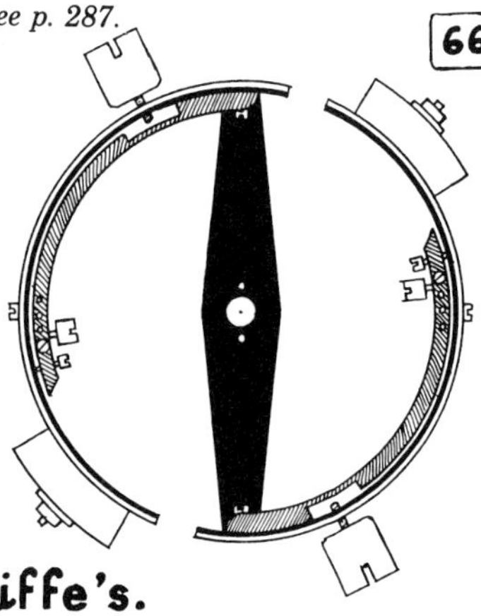

Eiffe's.

See p. 288

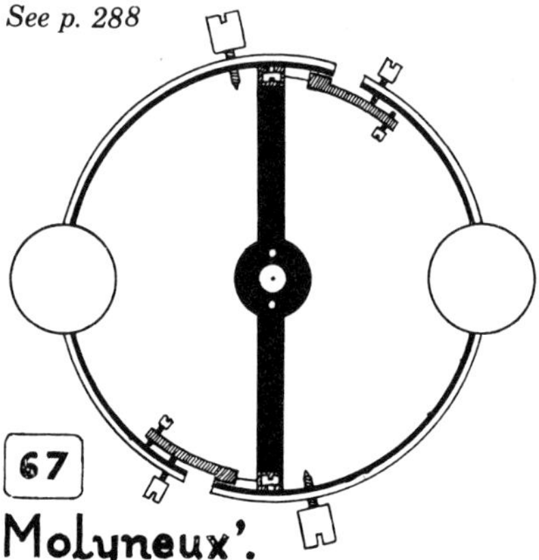

67

Molyneux'.

See p. 289.

68

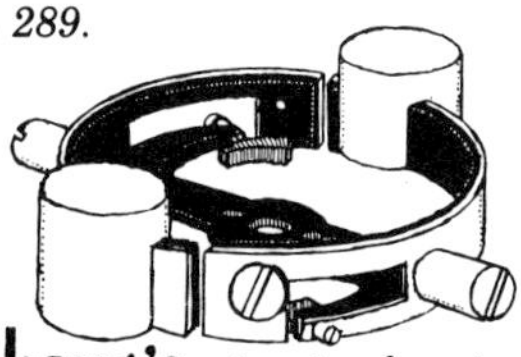

Kullberg's, (early form).

See p. 289.

69

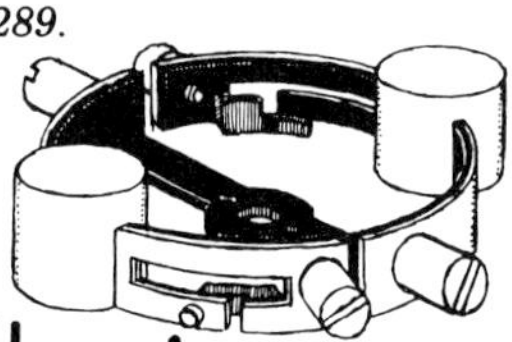

Kullberg's, (later form).

See p. 290.

71

Dent's "prismatic" rim (sections of)

See p. 289.

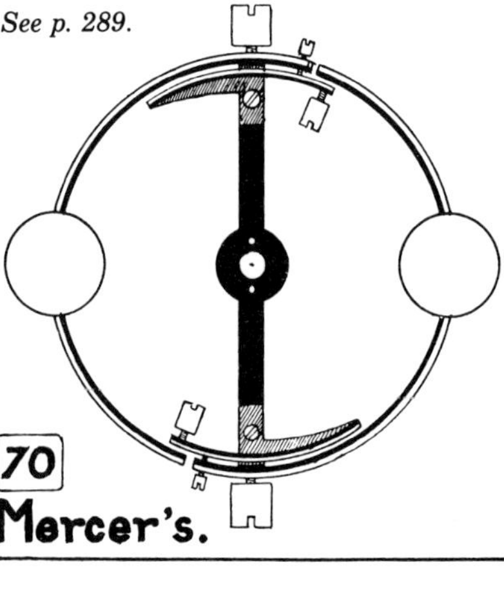

70

Mercer's.

See p. 292.

72

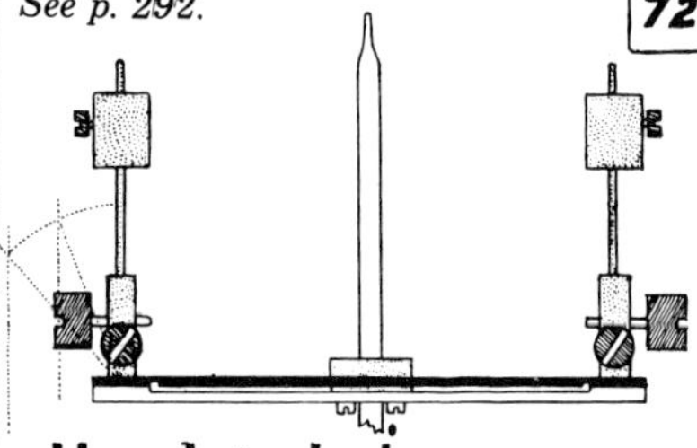

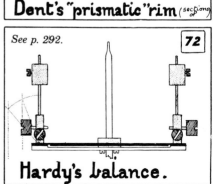

Hardy's balance.

ONE DAY MARINE CHRONOMETER BY WILLIAM HARDY No. 53.
With Hardy's patent bar balance. (Circa 1805).
Lot 12 in the Ilbert Sale Catalogue.

EIFFE'S (MOLYNEUX') AUXILIARY.

This invention provides one more example, if any were needed, of the fact that the same idea often occurs to more than one inventor at the same time.

In the winter of 1835 John Sweetman Eiffe, a London maker, communicated to Sir George Airy, Astronomer Royal, particulars of an auxiliary compensation which he had invented. Two chronometers fitted with this invention were tried at Greenwich, and Airy made, in June of the following year, a very favourable report upon their performance. In January 1840 Eiffe addressed a memorial to the Admiralty asking for a reward for this invention.

But in the meanwhile Airy had been informed by Robert Molyneux, another London maker, that he, also, had brought out an auxiliary, and was about to patent it: and although Airy recognised that it was, in essentials, identical with Eiffe's, he was unable, Eiffe having communicated his plans in confidence, either to warn Molyneux that the invention was not original, or to dissuade him from taking out a patent. Meanwhile, Molyneux fitted his auxiliary to two chronometers which he deposited at Greenwich for the annual trial (Jan.-June, 1840), and requested that, in addition to undergoing the ordinary tests, they should also be subjected to extreme natural temperatures, both of heat and cold*. Both performed very well: in fact, considerably better than Eiffe's had done.

Molyneux obtained his patent in September, 1840, and at the end of that year both he and Eiffe addressed memorials to the Admiralty, claiming rewards for their improvements. They relied on the precedent afforded by the rewards previously granted to Arnold and Earnshaw, and also upon an official announcement issued by the Admiralty when discontinuing the abortive "premium" trials of 1822-1836.

> "Their Lordships being, however, still very desirous of advancing, to the utmost perfection, a machine of such value to navigation as the chronometer, they will occasionally reward any important improvement, either in its principle or construction, by which it may either be so simplified as to be materially reduced in cost, without being deteriorated in excellence, or by which a greater uniformity of rate can be insured with more certainty under all varieties of position, motion, and climate."

These memorials, together with one from Parkinson & Frodsham, were transmitted by the Admiralty to the Royal Society for their opinion as to the novelty and value of the invention, and the allotment of the award to be granted, if any.

The Royal Society appointed a committee† to examine the matter, and upon their report the sum of £300 was awarded to Eiffe on condition that he made a complete disclosure of his invention. It must be confessed that this reward does not appear to err on the side of over-generosity, but it must be remembered that the error removed by

---

* Until 1849, in which year it was made compulsory, this was only done at the maker's request.

† Airy was a member of this committee.

Eiffe's device was diminutive in comparison with the improvements in timekeeping effected by Arnold and Earnshaw, and that, furthermore, the method employed by him to remove it was far from a perfect solution of the problem of M.T. error.

Justly or otherwise, Eiffe (in common, it is to be feared, with many another chronometer maker) regarded himself, to the end of his life, as a deeply-wronged man. In a letter* to Airy, written shortly before his death in 1880, he gives full vent to his feelings :—

> " . . . As for myself, . . . I must feel as a feeble old dog, who has been working for a very requiring harsh master for very many years ; unmindful, for that harsh master's sake, of his simple food and shelter (for is it not a simile proper) I must feel, I say, like such poor animal *begging for* a few crumbs. . . .
>
> " What signifies, by comparison, that which was done by Arnold or Earnshaw : and for the *little*, the one received £4500 the other £3000—but for me, how serious the remembrance ! Yet of all things for the said comparison, or for a parallel, how ridiculous the trifle which Harrison brought to Science, yet for which (by his heir) he received 20000 £. Harrison's was but a feeble attempting—while in comparison, I repeat, to my inventions, the product was as a mole to a mountain.
>
> " What ? Shall it be said that Eiffe who Domed the Building, which had been for so long time without roof, therefore unfinished, must be deemed rightly remunerated for having achieved the most difficult of all the requirements by £300. Which for the incomparable advantage brought to Science itself must be valued as a *few halfpence* compared with £20000 or rather £27500 Harrison, Arnold, and Earnshaw included. Truly it cries out that those who did not even raise the Building to which Eiffe added the roof or Crown, were greatly rewarded.
>
> " Arnold and Earnshaw left the chronometer as they found it—Still the Common Chronometer—while Eiffe shall have left it, *Never to be Surpassed*. Eiffe's'is as the racehorse unapproachable by the inferior animal contending however well amanaged (honestly) always vainly.
>
> " . . . To be silent, hereupon, should be named the abjectness of the basest considerations, or the unperceiving nature of the most pitiable imbecile. . . ."

And now for the not very marvellous invention which was the cause of this " old abusing of God's patience and the King's English."

Eiffe devised several forms of auxiliary, some of which were designed as additions to existing balances, and others as integral portions of balances of his improved pattern. A typical example of the latter kind is shown in fig. 66.

The object of Eiffe's auxiliary compensation is to cause a small additional weight to be picked up by the rims, when moving inwards in heat, at a certain temperature and carried onwards with them, producing, roughly, the same effect as if their motion had been accelerated, and thus reducing the moment of inertia of the balance more rapidly. To effect this there are carried, inside the circle of the rims, two additional steel arms, carrying screws at their free ends, and thinned near their roots like a chronometer detent, so that they can pivot about these thin portions with practically no friction. The roots of the arms are secured to those of the rims, into which are tapped, at about 90° from their roots, two small screws. When the rims have moved inwards in heat to

* The arrangement and punctuation are those of the original.

a certain extent, which can be adjusted by these screws, the latter bear against the steel arms and carry those inwards also. On the rims moving outwards for a fall of temperature, the steel arms move with them, owing to the slight tension previously set up at the thinned portions, until the temperature is reached at which the screws originally met them. If the temperature falls further, the arms are left behind, and the balance functions as one of ordinary pattern.

It will be seen that the principle on which this auxiliary acts is the reverse of Poole's. The action of the rims is unchanged at low temperatures, but in heat the mass of the balance weights is slightly increased, and the rate of the chronometer slightly accelerated. Accordingly, the method of adjustment is to correct the timekeeping of the chronometer for say, temperatures of 30° and 60°, and then to adjust the action of the auxiliary so as to compensate, or nearly so, for the increased error which would, in a normal balance, be caused at higher temperatures.

Following the plan adopted in the cases of Harrison, Arnold, and Earnshaw, in which a reward was given from public funds for an improvement in chronometers, a full description of Eiffe's auxiliaries was given in a pamphlet published by the Admiralty under Airy's superintendence. It embodied the substance of a paper drawn up by Eiffe for presentation to the Royal Society, containing an account of the M.T. error, and of his various auxiliaries, illustrated by a number of drawings. To this was added a preface by Airy and a copy of Molyneux' specification, with its accompanying engravings. The whole was in 1842 issued under the title of "Account of improvements in chronometers, made by Mr. John Sweetman Eiffe, for which a reward was granted to him by the Lords Commissioners of the Admiralty."

Eiffe, in this pamphlet, describes several other ways of effecting the same end, but they present little or no difference in principle. One of them, however, in which the cross-bar of the balance is also laminated, foreshadows the continuous compensation balances of Hartnup and Kullberg, described further on. Eiffe's account of it is in the Harrison manner:

> " . . . Here we have the bar itself, made to do double duty; it is to be regarded no longer as the diameter line; it will be deprived of a great part of its polarity. It presents to the eye a spherical action, and forms one grand universal compensating power, in connexion with the arcs of the circle. It scarcely requires any definition. . . ."

It should be added, however, that his pamphlet is not entirely written in this style, and that it contains the results of considerable experience and acute observation.

Molyneux' Auxiliary.

The principle of this auxiliary is identical with Eiffe's, but it differs considerably in details. Instead of the auxiliary arm and the rim which moves it having a common root, the former, which is much shorter than Eiffe's, points in the opposite direction, as shown in fig. 67. Molyneux also described and illustrated a second arrangement in which the auxiliary arm is reversed and carried upon the free end of the rim. In this arrangement it can move freely towards the centre, but is checked from moving outwards more than a certain amount by a check screw in the short portion of the opposite rim.

In a third arrangement, also described and illustrated by Molyneux, the motion of the auxiliary weights is independent of that of the rims. They are carried upon small secondary rims of their own, mounted upon the cross-bar inside the main ones, and provided with check pieces which restrict the extent of their motion outwards, although they are free to move inwards to any extent in heat.

It has been mentioned that Molyneux obtained some very remarkable results with this auxiliary. This was, however, due in some measure to his very fine and painstaking workmanship. Glasgow mentions* having seen some of his balances in which the auxiliary pieces were jewelled with rubies at the points where they met the check screws.

The plans of Eiffe and Molyneux were adopted for some time by the trade, but it was found that they called for very careful manufacture and laborious adjustment. They formed, however, the groundwork for the improvements of other makers, notably Kullberg and Mercer.

KULLBERG'S IMPROVED AUXILIARY.

The balance shown in fig. 68 is one of many forms used by Victor Kullberg (1824-1890), one of the most brilliant and successful chronometer makers of the last century. It is, in principle, a modification of Molyneux's third form, but it possesses one important advantage. The secondary rims, instead of being separately made and subsequently attached, are cut out of the tail ends of the main rims themselves, the resulting form being both stronger and easier to make.

Another form of auxiliary used by Kullberg is shown in fig. 69. Here the action and construction of the auxiliaries is the same, but they are placed at the free ends of the main rims, in front of the weights, instead of being formed from the non-acting portions.

MERCER'S BALANCE.

Fig. 70 shows a form of balance devised and used by Thomas Mercer (1822-1900), another well-known English maker. It is, in essentials, the same as Molyneux's third form, but is of more robust construction.

Many other forms of discontinuous auxiliary compensation have been put forward from time to time, but those which have had any measure of success will generally be found to have followed, more or less closely, the arrangements of Molyneux or Poole. It may be pointed out that the operation of these two plans is, to a certain extent, convertible. Thus, by arranging the rims of the Molyneux auxiliary

* In his "Watch and Clock Making."

weights so that the brass is on the inside, they can be made to move inwards in cold, and so produce the effect of Poole's auxiliary. This has been practised by Cole, Dent, and others.

A modification of Poole's plan which has sometimes been proposed, and which was used with great success by Uhrig, is to connect the rims by a wire, so as to restrict their outward motion.

Before leaving the subject of discontinuous auxiliary compensations, it may be well to summarise their advantages and disadvantages. All of the forms described have shown themselves capable, if well made and adjusted, of removing very nearly all the M.T. error. On the other hand, they add considerably to the cost of manufacture, and the majority of them, except Poole's, are deficient in the robustness which is, comparatively, so marked a feature of the Earnshaw balance. In consequence, they are less adapted to bear rough usage on board ship. The theoretical objection to them—that their action is discontinuous—has not, in practice, proved objectionable. True, it is impossible, theoretically, to make a chronometer fitted with them keep time at more than three particular temperatures, but the errors at intervening temperatures, and their rates of change, are much less than those of the ordinary balance. It was, indeed, asserted by Kullberg that the action of such auxiliaries was, in reality, continuous, since, by reason of the effects of centrifugal force, such devices were *always* in action in the middle of a vibration, when the balance was moving fastest, and that the effect of temperature was only to bring them into action for a greater or less period. This is, however, a rather extreme view.

Continuously Acting Auxiliaries.

As has been stated, the attempt to produce a balance whose moment of inertia at any given temperature should bear the correct relation to the elasticity of the balance spring has generally necessitated a complete departure from the standard type. One or two attempts to produce this result by slight modifications of the rims of the ordinary balance have, however, been made.

Dent's Prismatic Balance.

This plan was based upon the fact that a loaded beam of triangular section, if supported at its ends and weighted at its centre, bends more readily with the apex of the triangle downwards than with it upwards. Accordingly, E. J. Dent, in 1851, invented a balance whose rims were of the section shown in fig. 71. This was subsequently modified by his successor, Frederick Dent, into a second form, also shown, in which the steel is of the usual section, while that of the brass is a thin obtuse-angled prism. This was, no doubt, a better and stronger balance than the ordinary pattern, but the amount of secondary compensation which it afforded was not sufficient to bring it into general use, although good places were obtained in the Greenwich trials by several chronometers in which it was fitted.

KULLBERG'S HOLLOW RIM BALANCE.

In this arrangement the brass portions of the rims, instead of being, as usual, flat, are formed into a hollow groove, like that of a pulley. The rims are somewhat broader than usual, and the effect of the lateral expansion of the brass in heat tends to flatten the groove and diminish the resistance which the rim offers to bending. Conversely, in cold the groove deepens, and the rim becomes stiffer and less easily bent. The effect, thus, is the same as that of the prismatic balance—the weights are more easily brought inwards for a given degree of heat than taken outwards for the same degree of cold. Still, the results which this plan gives in practice have not been sufficiently in accordance with theory to render it generally acceptable.

Kullberg also suggested that, to diminish as far as possible the effects of centrifugal force, the rims of balances should be made considerably wider than the usual, which would strengthen them without affecting their action in heat and cold, and he published in 1887* the results of some very remarkable experiments which demonstrated, beyond all doubt, that the effect of centrifugal force upon the action of the ordinary balance was far greater than had hitherto been suspected. The experiments were made with a chronometer with an isochronous spring, and kept in a practically uniform temperature. Balances of the ordinary pattern, but with rims of different thicknesses, were fitted in turn, and with the thinnest rims the mean daily rates in the long and in the short arcs differed by no less than 30 seconds.

* In the "Horological Journal" for September of that year.

CHAPTER XII.

THE COMPENSATION BALANCE.

PART II.

Hardy's Balance.

As stated on p. 278*f*, it has been claimed that the first recorded enunciation of the M.T. error was made by William Hardy, when introducing, in 1804, a compensation balance of an entirely different pattern to that of Earnshaw. This balance is shown in Fig. 72*.

It consists of a cross-bar carrying two vertical pillars, one at each end, the balance weights being slid on to the pillars, and secured by set screws.† The cross-bar is composed of two portions, one of brass and the other of steel, the latter being uppermost. These strips, however, are not fused or soldered together, but left unconnected except at the centre (where they are both screwed to a collet on the balance staff) and at the extremities (where they are pinned together by the feet of the pillars). Just outside these feet the steel strip is filed very thin, so that it is free to bend at these points.

The action of the balance is as follows: The pillars may be regarded as levers having their fulcra at the thinned portions of the steel strips, the short arm of each lever being the portion of the pillar between the fulcrum and the centre of the thickness of the brass strip, and the long arm the portion between the fulcrum and the centre of the weight. As the brass and steel strips are not pinned or fused together, there is no tendency for the cross-bar to bend as a whole, but the greater expansion and contraction of the brass causes a push or pull to be exerted at the short arms of the levers, and the balance weights, carried on the long arms, accordingly are brought nearer the balance staff in heat and further from it in cold.

This balance has, I think, been rather under-estimated by writers on the subject, nor has it generally been described correctly. Thus the usually accurate Britten, both in his "Watch Springing and Adjusting," and his "Watch and Clockmakers' Handbook," states that the cross-bar is laminated, and does not notice that the laminæ are unconnected. Again, Glasgow, in his admirable handbook "Watch and Clockmaking," published in 1885, remarks: ". . . his balance never could have answered the description he gave of its action." This opinion is probably based on the supposition that if the pillars were parallel with the balance staff *at the middle temperature*, the weights, as in the ordinary balance, would move inwards for a rise of temperature approximately the same amount as they moved outwards for a corresponding fall.

* Hardy received a gratuity of thirty guineas from the Society of Arts for this invention, and accordingly did not patent it.

† In an earlier form of this balance, the pillars were threaded, so that the weights could be screwed upwards or downwards.

But, if it be assumed that the pillars are parallel to the balance staff at the extreme upper temperature, the case is altered, and the weights will be found to move outwards at the lower temperatures with diminishing speed. This is due to the fact that, as shown by the dotted perpendiculars in the figure, the amount by which the radial distance of the balance weights from the balance staff increases for a given increment of temperature is greatest when the pillars are perpendicular, and decreases as they diverge from that position. In addition, owing to the sliding action of the brass past the steel the angular rotation of the pillars for a given change of temperature is not strictly constant, although the manner in which it varies and the point at which it becomes a maximum is difficult to determine except by experiment. From the latter cause it may easily have arisen that Hardy found, even with the pillars parallel to the balance staff at the middle temperature, that his balance was capable, in practice, of doing, what subsequent writers have alleged, *a priori*, on insufficient grounds, it could not do—namely, bring the weights to the centre in heat more rapidly than they receded in cold.

But it should be noted that this property does not necessarily imply the removal of the M.T. error. To do this, *the weights must move in one definite manner, and in that manner only*. For any given temperature there is one corresponding radius of gyration of the balance which will give accurate timekeeping, and, unless the operation of the compensation can obtain that corresponding radius for every temperature, errors will appear.

It used to be thought that the great point to aim at was to make the weights move radially—direct towards and from the centre—but, in fact, the problem does not depend solely upon either the *path* described by the weights, or upon the *amount* which they move along that path for unit change of temperature—*but upon both combined.* We know that the standard balance makes a chronometer gain at middle temperatures, and lose in extremes, and that this arises from the weights not approaching the centre sufficiently fast in heat, and receding too fast in cold—but although some of the continuous compensation balances now to be described can be made to reverse this error, and cause a gain in the extremes and a loss at middle temperatures, it does not necessarily follow that, even then, they can be made correct at all temperatures. Moreover, some of the attempts which have been made to achieve this end by piling rim upon rim, and weight upon weight, are reminiscent of the manner in which the astronomers of the Middle Ages, wedded to Ptolemy's theory of circular orbital motion, sought to explain the paths of the planets by adding epicycle to epicycle, until they drew from King Alphonso of Castile the celebrated remark that, had he been consulted at the creation, he could have given the Almighty some useful hints in the way of arranging matters more simply.

To return to Hardy's balance. It is quite possible that he found that it removed a considerable portion of the M.T. error. But it was liable to the objection that it was very much weaker than the ordinary pattern. This weakness was due to the fact that in order to get sufficient compensation, the pillars had of necessity to be so long that the torque set up when their motion was reversed imposed a very severe strain upon themselves and upon the cross-bar, this strain being augmented by that produced by centrifugal force. It was, therefore, very difficult to ensure that the balance, if once correctly adjusted, remained so, and it may be said that in its original form it was far too delicate for use at sea, however well it might perform under easy conditions on shore. This objection applies also to a number of the other balances described in this chapter.

Later Balances on the Lines of Hardy's.

Massey's Balance.

In 1814 Edward Massey, a well-known chronometer and clock-maker, and patentee of many inventions (including various forms of keyless mechanism, and a sounding machine, on the principle of a patent log, which was for some time supplied to H.M. ships*), patented† a balance resembling Hardy's in appearance, except that the cross-bar was solid and the pillars laminated, and also slotted, with the idea of making them approximate to the balance spring in sensitiveness to changes of temperature.

Arnold's Auxiliary Bar.

This was patented by J. R. Arnold in 1821.‡ Although like Hardy's in appearance, it is of simpler construction, the cross-bar being a bi-metallic strip, with the brass and steel fused together. The outward motion of the weights is accordingly not retarded so quickly as in Hardy's balance, but a slight effect of the kind is produced. Originally designed as a complete balance, this device was latterly used by Arnold as an auxiliary, acting in heat only. The cross-bar was fitted on top of that of the main balance, and was prevented by stops from curving so as to take the auxiliary weights outwards, although it was left free to bring them towards the centre.

Dent's Balance.

In this balance, shown in Fig. 72A, the effect of the Arnold cross-bar is enhanced by mounting the weights upon bi-metallic strips of U or S shape, so that the radius of the arc through which the weights are carried by the action of the laminated cross-bar is increased in heat and decreased in cold. On this account the motion of the weights is slightly greater for a rise of temperature than for a corresponding fall. Dent experimented with many forms of this balance, the one shown being that which he considered the best. It is certain that a very near approximation to a correct compensation at all temperatures could be obtained by its use, but the fragility of its construction is obvious, and would always prove a bar to its general adoption. Later forms of this balance used the U-shaped pillars, and kept the weights as low as possible in order to avoid the effects of torque and centrifugal force.

---

* It was superseded after a few years by the much simpler "Burt's Bag and Nipper."

† No. 3854 of 1814.

‡ No. 4531 of 1821.

HARTNUP'S BALANCE.

This balance was designed about 1845 by John Hartnup, Superintendent of the Liverpool Observatory.* Being able to scrutinise the going of a large number of chronometers at first hand, he was favourably placed for investigating the amount of the M.T. error in the standard form of balance, and for drawing conclusions as to the best method of removing it.

An early result of his researches was the balance shown in Fig. 73, whose design was governed by the two following conditions, which his experience led him to consider essential.

1. The balance should be so constructed that the weights moved towards the centre with an accelerating velocity in an increasing temperature, and receded from it with a decreasing velocity in a decreasing temperature.

2. That the rims should be of circular form, so as to admit of their being easily brought to correct form and thickness in the lathe.

After a number of experiments, made in conjunction with William Shepherd, a Liverpool chronometer maker, Hartnup evolved, in 1849, a balance complying with these conditions. Instead of the single steel cross-bar of the Earnshaw balance, there are three, all laminated, and connected together in the form of a Z, the brass side of the laminæ being uppermost in the central bar, and undermost in the other two, which are attached to the central one by means of screws. The two outer bars carry a pair of laminated rims, having, as in the ordinary balance, the brass outside and the steel inside, but these, instead of being placed vertically, are bevelled so that at the middle temperature they are inclined at an angle of 45° to the vertical. These rims carry the balance weights and the timing screws.

The action of this balance, which from its appearance was sometimes known as the "gridiron" balance, is roughly as follows.

Neglecting, for the moment, the action of the cross-bars, that of the rims is substantially the same as that of the corresponding portions of the ordinary balance: i.e., the weights are brought towards the centre in heat, and away from it in cold. The inclination of the rims reduces the actual amount of this effect, but this could, of course, be allowed for by making their acting length greater than that which would be

* This Observatory, founded in 1844 as the result of private subscription, was intended primarily for the rapid and accurate rating of ship's chronometers, a service to commerce which it continues to render at the present day. The selection of Hartnup as its first Superintendent was a most fortunate one, and the success of the Observatory must be attributed in very great measure to the thorough and scientific methods which he immediately introduced into its work. In many points (including the provision of an oven, for testing chronometers in heat, whose temperature could be accurately controlled and altered at will), the Observatory was, for a long time, considerably in advance of Greenwich in matters relating to chronometer-testing. It has also, apart from its main duties, accomplished a considerable amount of astronomical investigation and research.

needed if they were placed vertically. Were the cross-bars not laminated, therefore, the balance would exhibit much the same M.T. error as the standard pattern.*

Owing, however, to the action of the laminated cross-bars, the inclination of the rims varies in different temperatures. At a temperature above the middle one, they become more vertical, and accordingly bring the weights further towards the centre than if they remained at their former inclination. Conversely, at temperatures below the normal their inclination from the vertical is increased, and in consequence they do not carry the weights outward quite so far as they otherwise would.

Actually, the action of the balance is not quite so simple as this, since the bevelled rims have also a slight tendency to twist, as well as to move horizontally, and in consequence the actual motion of the balance weights is not entirely in the plane of the rim. Still, the action of the laminated cross-bars in producing a modification of their motion is indisputable, and hence this construction certainly offers a means of eliminating, to a great extent, the M.T. error. On the other hand it is much more difficult to make than the ordinary pattern of balance, and has to be slightly larger.

Comparative tests, made at the Liverpool Observatory with one of Shepherd's chronometers fitted alternately with the new balance and one of standard pattern, showed that the new balance practically abolished the M.T. error. A repetition of the trials at Greenwich with three chronometers by the same maker was not quite so successful. One performed well enough to be purchased by the Admiralty, but the others exhibited discordances in their rates, of which no satisfactory explanation could be found. Hartnup suggested that this was due to the chronometers having been taken out of their gimbals, but Airy took pains to demonstrate that no ill effect could have been caused to the machines' going by this practice, which, in order to save space, was often adopted at the Observatory when a large number of chronometers were under trial.†

Hartnup refused to patent his balance, and made no secret of its construction, but gave it freely to the chronometer trade, and published its description widely. However, it must be confessed that in the hands of other makers it was not so successful as it had been originally with Shepherd, and in consequence it never came into very general use. In later years Hartnup devoted himself chiefly to studying the operation of the standard pattern of balance, and (as the result of trials with over 1500 chronometers) deduced the following empirical formula, from which, if the rate of a chronometer fitted with the standard form of balance be accurately known at three particular temperatures, its

* The original pattern of Hartnup's balance had the bevelled rims but a single solid cross-bar. The results which it gave were promising, but inadequate, and it was in order to increase the action of the rims that the triple and laminated cross-bar was added.

† The practice has, however, been discontinued in later years.

rate at any other temperature can be approximately predicted by obtaining the values of R^1, x^1 and K in the following formula :—

$$R = R^1 + K (x - x^1)^2$$

where R is the known daily rate for a known mean temperature x, R^1 the unknown daily rate for an unknown mean temperature x^1, and K is an unknown constant.*

It should be borne in mind that this formula is strictly empirical : that is, it makes no claim to being based upon mathematical demonstration, but merely embodies, in convenient form, the average amount of the results of M.T. error, change in consistency of oil, and other effects of temperature, as exhibited in a large number of chronometers of very similar construction. Its application presents little difficulty—a matter of a few minutes' work per day—and there can be no question that its use increases very greatly the dependence which can be placed upon a chronometer of the ordinary pattern (*i.e.*, one not provided with auxiliary compensation).

KULLBERG'S "FLAT-RIM" BALANCE.

This balance, shown in Fig. 74, is a modification of Hartnup's, but is of simpler and stronger construction, the arms of the balance and the single cross-bar being made in one piece. The foundation of the balance is a disc of steel, on to which brass is fused, and the whole cut to form the two arms and cross-bar, the brass being on top of the cross-bar and underneath the arms. In spite of their circular form, the arms do not move outwards and inwards, but mainly up and down—in fact, their action is similar to that of the two straight outer cross-bars of the Hartnup balance. The weights are mounted on short pillars, and this, as in the case of the Hardy and Arnold balances previously described, causes their motion inwards to be more rapid than outwards for an equal change of temperature. The approximate path of the weights (exaggerated) is shown in the figure.

The "flat-rim" balance, like Hartnup's, affords a continuous compensation approximating very closely to the theoretical ideal, but it presents considerable constructional difficulties. It was once very popular, but is not often used nowadays. Kullberg subsequently devised a modification of it, which he called the "low-rim" balance. In this, the laminated cross-bar is retained, but the rims are of the ordinary laminated pattern, except that they are somewhat thicker and narrower, while the dividing line between the brass and steel, instead of being vertical, runs diagonally from the top of the outer edge of the rim to the bottom of the inside edge. It did not come into general use.

---

* As the result of an investigation similar to Hartnup's, an analogous, but somewhat more complicated formula was evolved by a French contemporary, Aristide Lieussou. Like Hartnup's, it is empirical, but it has the additional merit of taking into account the ageing of the oil in the pivot-holes. See Lieussou's "Recherches sur les Variations de la marche des Pendules et des Chronomètres. . . ." Paris, 1854 (reprinted from the "Annales Hydrographiques" for 1853).

Balances with continuous auxiliary action.

See p. 294.

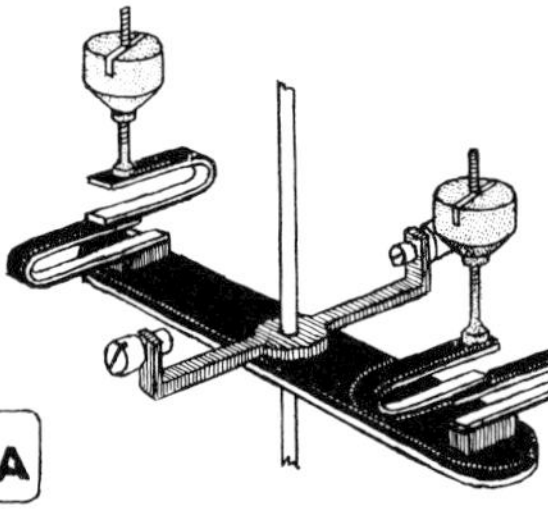

72A

Dent's.

See p. 295.

73

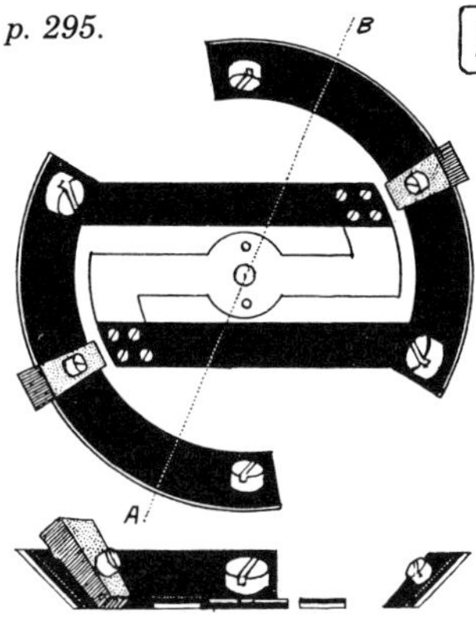

Section along the line AB.

Hartnup's.

See p. 299.

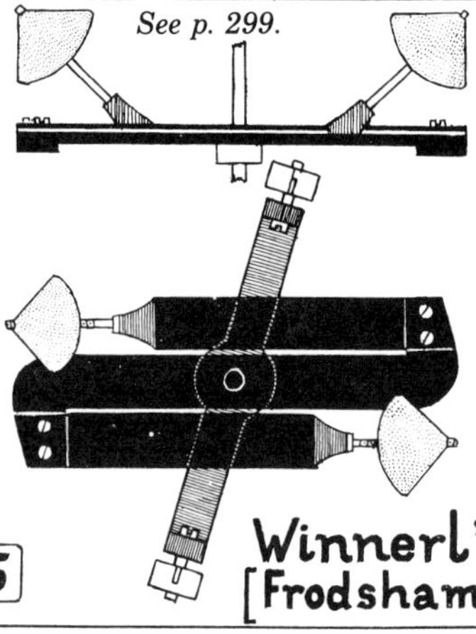

75

Winnerl's [Frodsham's]

See p. 297.

74

Kullberg's "Flat-rim."

See p. 302.

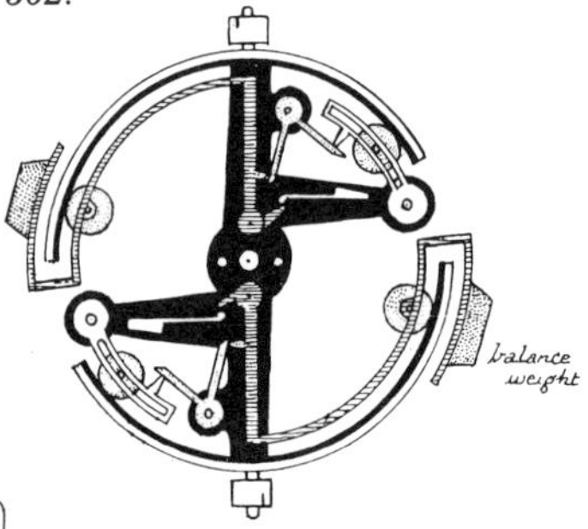

76

Ulrich's. [early form].

See p. 302.

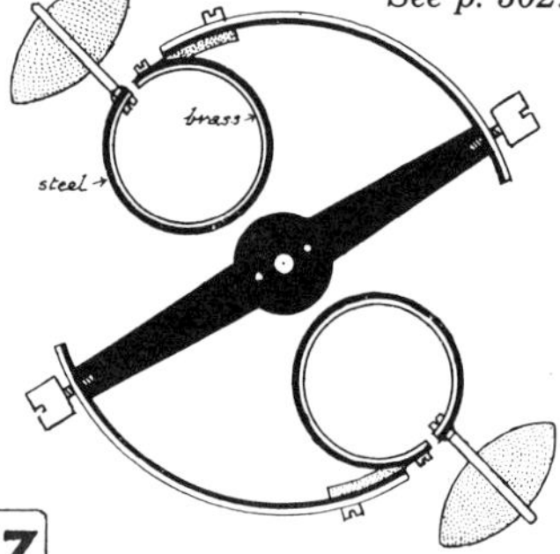

77

Ulrich's. [final form].

FRODSHAM'S (WINNERL'S) BALANCE.

Fig. 75 shows a balance devised in 1876 by H. Winnerl,*—a well-known Parisian maker. It was pointed out at the time, however,† that a balance of very similar character had been devised by Chas. Frodsham at some date anterior to 1871, and that a chronometer fitted with it competed in the Greenwich trial of 1874. There is, however, no reason to doubt that Winnerl hit upon the idea independently. In any case, it possesses no great originality, being a combination of Arnold's auxiliary with Hartnup's cross-bars. Theoretically, there is no reason why it should not be perfectly satisfactory, but presumably the difficulty of getting a sufficiently rigid construction was found in practice to outweigh its theoretical advantages. In all built-up balances of this kind, it is difficult to get an absolutely rigid connection of the laminated rims to the cross-bars carrying them. In this respect, Hartnup's arrangement was superior to those of Frodsham and Winnerl, since the former employed four, or sometimes six, screws for this purpose, while the latter provided two only.

OTHER CONTINUOUSLY-OPERATING BALANCES.

Amongst the continuous-acting balances previously described, from Hardy's to Frodsham's, there is a family resemblance, which can be traced to the employment of a laminated cross-bar or bars. This, however, although the commonest method upon which balances of this character have been constructed, is not the only one. Several other plans have been put forward from time to time, of which a brief account will be given.

ULRICH'S BALANCES.

Many efforts, extending over more than fifty years, were made by John Gottlieb Ulrich (1795-1875), a London maker (whose ingenious but over-complicated remontoire is described on p. 227), to perfect the compensation of the chronometer. His personal skill, perseverance, and ingenuity, were of a high order, but he suffered from a persistent tendency to prefer a complicated mechanism to a simple one, and from an entire lack of business adroitness and prudence.

It is regrettable that the only tangible reward of a tremendous amount of experimental work directed towards the production of a perfect compensation balance, a non-magnetic balance, a perfect remontoire escapement, and other ideals, was his admission as an inmate of the Clock and Watchmakers Asylum, Colney Hatch,‡ where he died in 1875. Even there he continued his experiments, and in

* He was also the inventor of many other ingenious devices, including a form of gravity escapement for clocks possessing a very high degree of detachment, which created a great sensation on its first appearance. In the Conservatoire des Arts et Métiers is a most ingenious (but too delicate) calculating machine of his construction. It is remarkable for the quickness of its operation.

† "Horological Journal," Nov., 1877.

‡ The conjunction of title and locality is unfortunate and misleading. The Asylum was, and is, an almshouse, not a *maison des aliénés*. Its name has now been changed to the Watch and Clockmakers' Home, and, as an institution, it reflects great credit upon its organisers and supporters.

an article contributed to the "Horological Journal" shortly before his death he confidently states:*

> ". . . there is more going forward that I think will supersede anything of the kind that has yet been done, and I verily believe that in a few months I shall succeed in producing a Compensation to act upon the spring (whether at the collet or the stud, or at both, I am not yet certain). If so, a simple plain balance with two small mean-time screws (or nuts) will suffice."

No particulars of this invention appear to have been preserved, but it was probably a form of compensation curb. Ulrich, however, was well aware of the defects of the ordinary pattern of curb, and it seems likely that he intended to use the arrangement described on p. 265, in which the length of the balance spring remains unaltered although its strength is artificially diminished or increased.

Ulrich began his experiments with the compensation balance in 1813, and soon discovered the existence of the M.T. error. He next devoted himself to the production of a form of balance which should eliminate it by moving the weights slightly along the rims, away from the roots in heat and towards them in cold. This requirement he postulated as a *sine qua non*, and it is undoubtedly true that it is *one* way, although, of course, not the only way, or the best, of removing the M.T. error. The effect of lengthening the rims slightly in heat, and shortening them in cold (for that is what the proposal amounts to) is to cause them, for an equal change of temperature, to move the weights slightly farther in the former case than in the latter. If the lengthening or shortening can be made to be exactly the right amount at all temperatures, a perfect compensation balance is secured. The difficulty is to obtain sufficient control of the (almost microscopic) motion of the weights along the rims.

Ulrich regarded the principle enunciated above as the only method by which the M.T. error could be removed, and his enthusiasm for it not only blinded him to the mechanical difficulties which stood in the way, but also induced him to regard *any* other contrivance, such as Molyneux's or Dent's† balances, as deliberate infringements of his work.‡ It was on this account that he petitioned for a reward at the same time as Eiffe and Molyneux, and subsequently bombarded the Hydrographer, the Board of Admiralty, the Astronomer-Royal (Airy), and the House of Commons for many years with petitions, memorials, claims, imprecations, patent specifications, &c., &c. Airy, whose position peculiarly fitted him to make an independent investigation of the matter, made a most thorough inquiry into Ulrich's claims in 1845, and satisfied himself that there was no ground for supposing that Eiffe and Molyneux plagiarised Ulrich's ideas, or for believing that the performance of Ulrich's double-acting balance was any better than that of one fitted

---

* "Horological Journal," Jan., 1875.

† Vulliamy, of course, supported and made capital of this allegation against Dent.

‡ There is, however, this much to be said for his contention—that he seems to have "talked shop" in season and out of it, with all and sundry, and that it is not unlikely that his peculiar combination of ingenuity and garrulity was found, as Fuseli said of Blake, "damned good to steal from."

A BARRAUD'S COMPENSATING WEIGHT.

with the Eiffe-Molyneux auxiliaries, On the point of whether Ulrich discovered the existence of M.T. error in 1814, as he claimed, thus ante-dating both Eiffe and Molyneux very considerably, he offered no opinion.* He reported that in his opinion a claim for reward was inadmissible, and, armed with this report, the Admiralty turned a consistently deaf ear to Ulrich, although the latter, with unabated persistency, and a pathetic inability to recognise a *res adjudicata*, went on hammering away at them until within a few years of his death.

Figs. 76 and 77 give two examples of Ulrich's double-acting balances, in which the balance weights are shifted, along the rims, slightly further from the cross-bar in heat and nearer to it in cold. Fig. 76 shows the first pattern he designed, in which his bent towards complication can be appreciated. In this device, the motion of the weights along the rims is caused by the action of the short ends of the latter, the power thus obtained being transmitted through a system of bell-crank levers. The amount of travel obtained can be varied by altering the position of the rollers upon which the short ends of the rims bear.

Fig. 77 shows a much simpler and more practical modification of the same plan. Here the weights, instead of being directly mounted upon the rims, are carried on short pillars attached to the free ends of small laminated circles, with the *steel* outside, whose fixed ends are attached to the rims. The action of these secondary rims moves the weights slightly forward in heat and back in cold, the amount of action being regulated by sliding the latter up or down the pillars.†

Theoretically, there is little objection to be raised against this plan, but in practice a balance of this type is found to be difficult to construct, and lacking in strength, while it takes up considerably more room than the ordinary pattern.

BARRAUD'S COMPENSATING WEIGHTS.

This device, illustrated in Fig. 78, is a very ingenious attempt to remove the M.T. error by means of an auxiliary mechanism fitted within the balance weights themselves, so that a balance of the ordinary pattern could be improved, without any structural alteration, by simply substituting a pair of such weights for the original ones.

---

* In a letter to the Admiralty, dated July 30, 1868, seven years before Ulrich's death, Airy states that he is quite ready to believe that the latter discovered the existence of M.T. error as early as 1817, although his plans for dealing with it were then impracticable.

It may not be out of place to mention here that Airy, while rigidly performing his duty of scientific adviser to the Admiralty upon chronometers (and many other subjects), showed himself, invariably, a considerate and painstaking critic of any plans submitted to him by chronometer makers. His correspondence (he generally declined an interview) contains a large number of instances in which he took enormous pains to encourage a well-grounded improvement or to point out a fallacy.

† This plan has been re-invented several times. See, for example, the balance described by F. J. Garrard in a letter to the "Horological Journal" for April, 1900.

The "Patent Correcting Weights" consisted of a brass plate carrying two pivoted levers, one of which carried a brass weight, while the other was attached to one end of a brass-and-steel curb encircling the whole mechanism and having its other end secured to the plate. The levers were inter-connected by means of screws operating upon two jewelled inclined planes, in such a manner that any motion of the curb, in either direction, would move the weight slightly inwards, towards the balance staff, against the resistance of a weak spring, provided to keep the inclined planes always in contact with the adjustable screws which bore on them. The point of contact between the curb and the similar screws in the other lever was also jewelled.

Although the mechanism and its description may appear complicated, its action was simple. At the middle temperature, the weight is at its farthest from the balance staff, and both screws bear equally upon the inclined planes. As the temperature rises, the ends of the curb tend to separate, the lever K rotates slightly clockwise, and the screw *s*, bearing on the plane *p*, overcomes the resistance of the spring S, and moves the weight slightly towards the centre. Similarly, for a fall of temperature, the weight is moved towards the centre, in a similar manner, by a reverse motion of the curb.

At first sight it may not appear quite obvious why the weight should need to go inwards both for a rise and for a fall of temperature, but a little reflection will soon make this clear. The whole mechanism forms the balance weight proper, and is moved inwards and outwards by the main rim as if it were one solid mass. The small weight within the mechanism is the auxiliary, and the effect of its motion relative to the remainder of the mechanism makes it approach the centre of the balance in heat slightly faster than the remainder of the mechanism: *i.e.*, slightly faster than the balance weight proper. The effect of the compensation, therefore, is slightly greater than it would be if the weight were a solid mass, and the difference increases with the temperature.

Conversely, the effect of the mechanism in cold is that the auxiliary weight recedes from the centre at a slightly slower rate than the weight proper, and accordingly the effect of the rims is slightly less than it would be if they carried weights of the normal pattern. Here, again, the difference increases in proportion to the change of temperature.

The objection to this most ingenious plan is the necessarily small size of these elaborate weights, and the very high standard of skill required to make and adjust them. Moreover, it is hardly to be expected that the results produced by so minute and complicated a mechanism should be permanent and unvarying in their amount. Messrs. Barraud subsequently brought out a modification of this plan, in which the operation of a single large laminated rim was employed to move two bell-crank levers, carrying the main balance weights, by means of a similar system of jewelled inclined planes.

HUTTON'S AUXILIARY COMPENSATION.

An auxiliary compensation of unique character, based upon a principle which has not, I think, yet received the attention which it deserves, was invented by John Hutton, a London maker, in 1845. He employed a cap of boxwood, fitting closely around and over the balance, and found that by increasing or decreasing the clearance between the cap and the balance he could effect a considerable alteration in the rate, the chronometer going faster for a larger clearance, and slower for a smaller.* Having ascertained that his balance spring was isochronous, and that accordingly the effect produced was not to be attributed to the chronometer being slow in the short arcs, he mounted the cap upon a system of levers controlled by a compensation curb, which reduced the clearance at middle temperatures and increased it at the extremes.

I have not been able to obtain any information as to the performance of chronometers fitted with this auxiliary, but, from the fact that when one of Hutton's make fitted with this device was cleaned by Messrs. Frodsham† in 1876 Airy asked for the cap to be removed, it is to be inferred that it was not very successful. The idea, however, as affording a means of effecting very slight and delicate corrections to the motions of a balance—and of doing this by mechanism which does not vibrate with the balance, so that it can be of far more solid construction—is a valuable one. A modification of this device is, I understand, now being adopted by M. Paul Ditisheim in his chronometers, but with a different object—namely, to correct the barometric error referred to in a later portion of this chapter. This adaptation, indeed, points out the defect of Hutton's original plan, which is that a chronometer to which it was fitted would be found far more sensitive to barometric changes than an ordinary one, and that for its successful operation there would have to be used, in conjunction with it, some form of hermetically-sealed or vacuum case (see next chapter).

MERCURIAL BALANCES.

Balances employing mercury as a compensating agent have often been proposed. As related on p. 138 Le Roy's compensation balance, the first ever made, embodied two thermometers, whose tubes were filled partly with mercury (used chiefly as a balance weight) and partly with alcohol (used chiefly as a source of power for displacing the mercury, its expansibility being much greater than that of the heavier fluid). Theoretically, such a balance can be made perfect, since by altering the curvature of the tubes the radius of gyration can be brought to coincide exactly, at all temperatures, with the theoretical amount requisite for perfect time-keeping. But in practice, this result has proved very difficult of attainment.

* A controlling device of this nature has been employed in various patterns of chronographs, and Grimthorpe, in his "Clock and Watch-making," fourth edition, gives an illustration (p. 221) of a similar plan applied to regulate the remontoire of a turret clock.

† Hutton was then no longer in business, and his successor, to whom the chronometer would in the ordinary course have been sent, had brought himself within the grasp of the law by pawning a number of chronometers entrusted to him, for repair, by the Admiralty and other customers.

After Le Roy, the first maker who appears to have experimented with mercurial balances was J. G. Ulrich, already mentioned. In 1824 Ulrich produced several forms of balance weights formed of iron, steel, or glass tubes containing mercury. These were all adversely criticised by Dr. W. H. Wollaston,* of the Board of Longitude, on the ground that the glass tubes might be accidentally fractured through a shock (as happened, it will be remembered, in one of Le Roy's time-keepers), while those of metal prevented the adjuster from knowing whether the thread of mercury in the tube was continuous or disconnected at any particular moment. Thus, the balance might be poised with the thread continuous, and this might become disconnected (thus throwing the balance out of poise) later. Or, conversely, the thread might be disconnected during the poising and unite subsequently. Ulrich did not proceed further with his plans for such balances.

A number of experiments with mercurial balances were also made, during the period 1824-1830, by James Scrymgeour, a Glasgow maker, already referred to on pp. 226, 259, as the inventor of a remontoire escapement and of a glass balance spring. Scrymgeour made his first experiments with a balance embodying two mercurial thermometers, whose action was found to be insufficient, and subsequently tried another form in which three were used. He found, however, that the continuity of the mercury in the tubes was easily upset by a jolt or a blow on the chronometer's box. Some experiments with very similar forms of balances were also made by R. Webster about 1849.†

Loseby's Mercurial Auxiliary.

But the most successful—indeed, the *only* successful—attempt to use mercury in the balance of a modern chronometer, was that made by E. T. Loseby, of Islington, who, in 1843, submitted to the Admiralty a chronometer fitted with the balance shown in Fig. 79.‡ In this construction the thermometers are no longer used as the primary compensation—that is provided by rims and weights of the normal pattern.

* William Hyde Wollaston, celebrated in his day as the inventor of a secret method for working platinum, by which he gained a large fortune.

† It should be noted that, in contradistinction to the thermometers used by Le Roy and Loseby, those of Scrymgeour and Webster were of the ordinary straight form, and that the balances to which they were fitted would accordingly possess a M.T. error. The amount of the compensation, in Webster's balance, could be varied by rotating the thermometers, with their bulbs as centres, so that their tubes were more or less inclined to the cross-bar.

‡ Loseby published, about 1855, a small pamphlet entitled "Loseby's Improvements in Chronometers," in which he gave an account of his balance, and also of some improvements in the ordinary type of mercurial pendulum. The information this contained, together with a short biography of the inventor, and an account of a very remarkable turret-clock made by him for the Market Hall, Coventry (it was really two clocks, the mechanism of the turret-clock being controlled by an astronomical clock), was re-published in 1914 under the title of "An Account of Mr. E. T. Loseby's Improvements in Chronometers, Watches and Clocks," edited by Mr. J. J. Farmer, of Coventry. I am indebted to Mr. Harold Gimson, of Leicester, for drawing my attention to this pamphlet. The account of Loseby's dealings with the Admiralty, however, is not from this source, but condensed from the original papers at Greenwich.

Mounted on the rims, however, in front of the weights, are two glass thermometers, containing mercury, and having their extremities brought inwards in a cycloidal curve towards the centre of the balance. The tubes of the thermometers are sealed with a little air in them, to prevent such discontinuity of the mercury as was noted by Ulrich and Scrymgeour, and it is obvious that for a rise of temperature a small quantity of mercury will be driven towards the centre of the balance, and that for a fall of temperature it will recede from it. It is also obvious that by varying the curvature of the tubes, and their original position, the amount of the change in the radius of gyration at any temperature can be made to coincide exactly with that theoretically requisite, and that accordingly complete power can be obtained over the M.T. error. Indeed, one of the chronometers sent for trial by Loseby had a reversed error, losing in the middle temperatures, and gaining at the extremes.

To make a balance of this kind, however, was, and is, a difficult problem. It is extremely hard to form two thermometers alike in all respects, and, this once done, their mounting in the balance presents considerable difficulty. Loseby blew and mounted his own tubes, but he was possessed of much more manipulative skill than the common, and he had the further advantage of having designed the balance, and therefore knowing exactly what was required. As a commercial proposition, in competition with other types, balances of this character can only be produced at a considerably enhanced price, and they are further handicapped by the quite unfounded suspicion that they are fragile, and liable to break with a slight shock—or even without it. As far as I am aware, the only maker who has used them since Loseby's time is Mr. Robert Gardner, who has effected various improvements in the manufacture and mounting of the tubes.

Chronometers with Loseby's balance were specially tried at Greenwich in 1844 and 1845, and Airy reported very favourably on them, as witness the following :—

> " . . . Remarking that the error of the ordinary chronometers is in the direction of losing at the extreme temperature of heat or cold, I deduce :
>
> " 1. That Mr. Loseby's construction has reversed the nature of the error, and therefore that he has complete power over it ; so that, by arrangements somewhat more delicate, it might be sensibly annihilated."

Loseby, accordingly, applied to the Admiralty for a reward, on the grounds of the announcement, previously quoted*, which had been made by them when discontinuing the premium series of Greenwich trials. He received a reply which undoubtedly contained an implied promise of reward, although, after reading through the papers in connection with the case, there can be no doubt that this was done inadvertently, and was at variance with the settled policy both of the Admiralty and of the Royal Observatory. This implied promise was contained in the following passage—

> " . . . Before they can venture to bestow a reward for the same by any grant of public money, my Lords require further proof of its practical utility by subsequent trials at the Royal Observatory."

Actually, Airy, who had been consulted by the Admiralty prior to the drafting of this reply, had expressed himself as strongly averse to granting a money reward to Loseby, on the ground that his claim was based merely upon the invention of an improved construction for removing M.T. error, while Eiffe had already pointed out the same error, and had been rewarded chiefly for that discovery, and not for the actual construction of balance proposed by him. "For very obvious reasons," however, as Admiral Beaufort, then Hydrographer, pointed out, referring to the decision that no reward should be given for further improvements designed to remove M.T. error, "Their Lordships did not think it prudent to establish that as an inflexible rule, and much less to publish it."

Accordingly, Jacob-like, Loseby proceeded to serve seven years for his reward, deferring, meanwhile, any attempt to patent his invention.

He concentrated his energies upon proving the merits of his balance by obtaining a high place in the annual trials at Greenwich, with the following results :—

Year.	No. of chronometers entered by Loseby.	Place.
1845	1	First.
1846	3	First, second and third.
1847	1	Sixth.
*1848	none entered.	
1849	1	Third.
1850	1	First.
1851	1	First.
1852	1	First.

In spite of these performances—and it must be admitted Loseby had fairly provided the "proof of . . . . . practical utility by subsequent trials" stipulated by the Admiralty—a memorial from him in 1852, praying that a reward might now be granted to him, was met by a polite, but firm, refusal. In justice to the Admiralty, however, it must be pointed out that, as suggested by Airy, they had given a certain amount of encouragement to Loseby in another manner. In addition to purchasing his trial chronometers for the use of the Navy, they also ordered supplementary ones year by year, which had not competed in the trials, and paid a higher price than usual for them.† It might be said that this roundabout method of reward was in itself an acknowledgment of the justice of Loseby's claim, and that they should have done more, but, in view of the very decided attitude adopted by Airy, their scientific adviser, it is difficult to see what more they could have been expected to do.

Disheartened by his experience, Loseby retired from the Greenwich trials altogether, and soon afterwards moved to Leicester, where he continued as a high-class clock and watch maker until his death in 1890.

* Prior to 1849, in which year it was made compulsory, chronometers sent to Greenwich for trial were not tested in extreme temperatures except at the specific request of their makers. All of Loseby's entries underwent this ordeal.

† Altogether they purchased 13, for which they paid a total of £630.

The Integral (Nickel-Steel) Balance.

Finally, we come to the latest and best solution of the problem of M.T. error, the " integral," or nickel-steel, balance. It is a remarkable fact that the foundation of this solution is not a piece of mechanism, but a discovery in metallurgy. The credit for having rendered possible the construction of a balance which, although no more complicated than that of Earnshaw, has *practically no middle temperature error,* is entirely due to the well-known metallurgist and metrologist, Dr. Ch. Edouard Guillaume, head of the Bureau international des Poids et Mesures, at Sèvres. In view of the remarkable strides which the horological industry—and, side by side with it, the higher horological art—has made in Switzerland of recent years, it is peculiarly fitting that the greatest improvement which has been introduced in horology since the invention of the compensation balance should have its genesis in the mind of a Swiss savant who is the son of a horologist.

A long and elaborate investigation as to the varying properties of the nickel-steel alloys, conducted by Dr. Guillaume, has resulted in the discovery of various alloys exhibiting an abnormal development or lack of some characteristic property, such as expansibility or elasticity. The alloy named " invar," for instance, has a negligible coefficient of expansion, so that its length is practically the same in all temperatures. That known as " elinvar " has practically a constant modulus of elasticity in all temperatures. For use in the compensation balance, however, Dr. Guillaume has developed an alloy whose *quadratic* coefficient of expansion is negative.

To explain. In the majority of metals or alloys, the amount of expansion for an increase of temperature t is given by the formula $l_1 = l_0 (1 + \alpha\theta + \beta\,\theta^2)$, in which α and β are known as the *linear* and *quadratic* coefficients of expansion.

Now, for brass and steel, the metals employed in the standard balance, all these coefficients are positive, and the quadratic ones do not differ much. Hence, although the actual expansions of brass and steel are, of course, dissimilar, the *rate* at which the expansion per unit change of temperature varies in different temperatures is practically the same for both. And, consequently, it is correct to assume, for the range of temperature to which the balance of a chronometer is likely to be exposed, that the weights move inwards in heat as much as they do outwards in cold—and, as we have seen, it is this fact which is the cause of the M.T. error.

But suppose that for steel we substitute in the rims an alloy whose quadratic coefficient of expansion is negative. Its rate of expansion per unit change of temperature will be less at a high temperature than at a low one, and, that of the brass remaining as before, the *weights will move further for a rise of temperature than for an equivalent fall.* Here, then, is a way of constructing a balance in which the middle temperature error is eliminated by the simple substitution, in the rims, of a nickel-steel alloy, possessing the correct negative quadratic coefficient of expansion, in place of the ordinary steel. The requisite proportions of this alloy have been determined by Dr. Guillaume, and it is now on the market. A balance, termed the "integral" balance, using this new alloy, is shown in Fig. 80, and is used by several leading chronometer makers. It will be noticed that there are no auxiliaries of any kind, and that its construction is identical with that of the Earnshaw type, except that there are four rims and four weights instead of two. Owing to the diminished expansibility of this particular alloy as compared with steel, the requisite amount of compensation can be obtained with a much shorter rim, and in consequence it is possible to adopt the construction shown, in which, by lessening the weight carried by each rim, the effect of centrifugal force is greatly reduced. Balances of the type shown are capable of giving an I-curve practically indistinguishable from a straight line. It seems probable, however, that even this wonderful achievement is not the last word in connection with the application of the nickel-steel alloys in horology, and that the chronometer of the future will be furnished, not with a balance of this type, but with a plain circular balance of "invar" in conjunction with an "elinvar" spring, the very small residual errors of the pair being designed to oppose each other, and any final compensation that may be required being effected by a pair of very small secondary rims, devoid of M.T. error*.

And so we find the trend of modern horological development returning to old Harrison's plan, which he left half executed, of a balance whose expansion shall be negligible.†

AIRY'S BAR.

Before leaving the older forms of compensation balance, mention should be made of a device invented by Sir George Airy in 1871 to facilitate the final adjustment of the compensation. Airy had noticed that if a chronometer happened to be slightly under or over-compensated, it was difficult to shift the weights the extremely small amount necessary to correct this, without overdoing it. Accordingly, he cast about for some method of effecting the same end without moving the weights, and evolved the device shown in Fig. 81. It became generally known in the chronometer trade as "Airy's bar," or, from an entirely mistaken notion of

---

* A balance of this kind has been designed and constructed by M. Paul Ditisheim, who informs me that he is also experimenting with another form in which the (continuous) rim and cross-bar are of dissimilar metals, so that the rim is only circular at one temperature, its moment of inertia altering as it becomes more or less oval. This construction is reminiscent of the "rhomboidal" pendulum designed long ago by Hooke, and subsequently modified by Troughton.

† A chronometer with a balance on Harrison's plan—namely, with its arms formed of wood, baked and varnished, in conjunction with several other features of singular inanity—was proposed by Muller in 1880. It is a typically Teutonic combination of obtuseness in plan and ingenuity in detail.

its functions, as "Airy's Supplementary Compensation."* It consists simply of a cross-bar, fitting friction-tight on the balance staff, and carrying at either end a small weight, about a tenth of the main weights, or less, mounted on a slender steel spring, of just sufficient strength to keep the weight pressed against the rim. Accordingly, it moved inwards and outwards with the latter, and practically became part of the main weight as far as its effect upon the timekeeping of the chronometer was concerned. Slight alterations in the amount of the compensation could now be effected by rotating the bar slightly, and thus altering the amount of travel of the auxiliary weights, producing the same effect as if the main weights had been moved a much smaller distance.

This device was ingenious, but it is liable to the objection that the pressure of the auxiliary weights against the rims is bound to affect their action slightly, and that the amount of this interference varies with different positions of the bar. It is inferior to the plan practised, long before, by Brockbank, and subsequently by R. F. Bond (an American maker) in which the adjustment is effected by altering the position of screws tapped tangentially through the balance weights.

If the chronometer trade had been left free to adopt this device, or otherwise, as they saw fit, it is improbable that it would have obtained much consideration. Airy, however, obtained Admiralty approval for the issue of an order, dated October, 1876, directing that all chronometers competing in the 1877 trial were to be fitted with the new device.

This order produced a good deal of very reasonable dissatisfaction. The "bar" was a new device, whose properties and merits had not been fully investigated: moreover, there were several balances, such as Hartnup's, and Kullberg's flat-rim, to which it could not possibly be fitted, while the effect of its action upon any balance other than the standard pattern (which stood very little chance of obtaining a high position in the trial, owing to its M.T. error) was problematical, although that it would in some degree interfere with its action was obvious.

Representations to this effect were made by the Council of the Horological Institute, and their force, it is pleasant to say, was admitted by the Astronomer-Royal, who obtained a second order rescinding, temporarily, the compulsory fitting of the bar, although he nevertheless intimated explicitly that purchases of chronometers for the Admiralty would, in future, be restricted to those which possessed it. Actually, its adoption was never made compulsory, and, the fact soon being

* In looking through Airy's correspondence with various makers relating to this invention, it is amusing to note with what unanimity they at once decided that it was some form of auxiliary compensation, a conviction which remained unaffected by the laborious explanations of its true function given by its inventor.

An account of "Airy's Bar," from the pen of W. Ellis, for many years head of the Time Department at Greenwich, appears in the "Horological Journal" for July, 1875.

generally recognised that it was, at best, a *succes d'estime*, the condition requiring it to be fitted in chronometers purchased for the Navy was quietly dropped.*

NON-MAGNETIC BALANCES.

The extent to which the going of chronometers is affected by a magnetic field, causing induced magnetism in the balance-spring and balance (the only parts whose magnetisation is liable to affect the going of the chronometer), has been the subject of much discussion and experiment.† The three kinds of fields in which a chronometer may be placed are—

1. The earth's magnetism.
2. The field due to the magnetism (permanent or induced) in the ship's hull.
3. Local fields, such as may be produced by permanent magnets (*e.g.*, compass needles) or by electrical circuits, near the chronometer.

1. The earth's field is incapable, under ordinary conditions, of causing any perceptible difference in the rate of a chronometer. Airy, in the whole course of his experience, only came across one case of a chronometer whose going was (as evidenced by its varying rate when placed with the XII. pointing successively to the four cardinal points) sensibly affected by the earth's magnetism. And in this instance it was found that, through some unexplained cause, practically every steel portion of the chronometer had become strongly magnetised.‡ In such a case, of course, the cross-bar of the balance, for instance, would act, or endeavour to act, as a compass needle, and a varying rate in different azimuths was only to be expected: but, in general it may be asserted that, if a chronometer is free from magnetism, the earth's field will never, of itself, induce sufficient magnetism in the balance to affect its vibrations sensibly.

2. The ship's field. The effect of this is, theoretically, less than that of the earth§, and in consequence is equally incapable of affecting the rate of a chronometer. On the other hand, it is a well-known fact that chronometers almost always exhibit a perceptible change of rate when removed from shore to ship, or *vice versa*, and the magnetism of the hull suggests itself as the first likely cause of this

---

* It is sad to relate that in the few Admiralty chronometers in which this device is still retained, it is not used for its original purpose, but as a means of obtaining small alterations in the rate, which is done by bending the springs of the small weights inwards until the latter no longer touch the rims, and then altering their distance from the balance staff as requisite.

† The earliest experiments were, I believe, those made by the elder Arnold, but the first of which any account was published appear to be some by the Rev. George Fisher, described in the "Philosophical Transactions" for 1820. Subsequently, Barlow, Bond, Arnold and Dent, Airy, Delamarche and Ploix, and many others made investigations on similar lines.

‡ To demagnetise it was found absolutely impossible, but the trouble was completely cured by placing, at a short distance under it, a freely-suspended compass-needle.

§ This is shown by its having less effect upon the compass than the earth's field has.

variation.* Experiments to determine this point were made by MM. Delamarche and Ploix in 1858, but a certain amount of uncertainty attaches to their results, since the experiments were not conducted in the actual magnetic field of a ship, but in that of the compensating magnets which would be used on board to nullify the effects of that field upon a compass. Accordingly, there was a certain amount of artificiality in the results obtained, but they certainly demonstrated that these compensating magnets were incapable of affecting the rate of the chronometers used in the experiment by anything approaching the amount of the average difference between the " ship " and " shore " rates.

3. Local magnetic fields. These fields, if sufficiently powerful, are undoubtedly capable of affecting the going of a chronometer very considerably. Experiments made at Greenwich have demonstrated that a field in which the lines of force are perpendicular to the plane of the balance has practically no effect on the machine's rate, while one in which the lines are at right angles to those of the former field has the maximum effect. It was also found that the effect of such a field varies with the direction of the lines of force, in relation to the XII.-VI. line on the dial, and it was accordingly concluded that practically the whole effect was due to the magnetisation of the steel portions of the balance, that due to the magnetisation of the spring being practically negligible. The alterations in rate showed a maximum acceleration on two bearings 180° apart, a maximum retardation on two bearings midway between these, and four points of no effect midway between the maxima. This agrees with the assumption that the balance alone is affected, since if for simplicity we consider the cross-bar only, the effect of the induced magnetism in it makes it always tend to align itself to the direction of the lines of force. Consequently, if, when at rest, it is already in alignment with them, the time of its vibration will be shortened as the result of the extra magnetic effect assisting the balance to bring it back to the dead-point. Conversely, if its position of rest be at 90° to the lines of force, its time of vibration will be retarded†, while if the position of rest be midway between the former two, the magnetic field will produce no effect on the time of vibration.

The practical conclusion drawn from the experiments, of circuits, compass cards, &c., &c., was that the effect produced by the various local fields upon the rate of a chronometer was slight so long as these were kept at a distance from it equal to not less than half that regarded as being safe for a standard compass.

* This change of rate was, however, noted before the days of iron ships: see, for example, a pamphlet " On the erratic propensities of Chronometers," by Capt. Martin White, R.N., published in 1830. His theory, which may be true to a certain extent, is that, when chronometers are kept for a long period on shore in one fixed position, their balances, having an oscillating motion (and therefore a fixed *mean* position with respect to the magnetic meridian), and subjected to the constant tapping of the escape wheel, acquire, in time, a slight amount of permanent magnetism, in the same way that this is acquired by the hull of a ship while building. When sent to sea, this permanent magnetism causes the observed variations of rate, through the machine's changes of azimuth on different courses.

† Actually, when in this position, no magnetism is induced in it, but this occurs as soon as it moves.

Recapitulating, then—

> If the balance of a chronometer has become permanently magnetised for any reason, the going of the machine will be affected by its position relative to the earth's magnetic field (i.e., to the N. and S. line), and also to the magnetic field of the ship's hull, and to any local fields.
>
> If the balance be free from permanent magnetism, the going of the machine will be unaffected by the earth's field or that of the ship, but it may be affected by relatively stronger local fields caused by permanent magnets or electric currents.

In the early days of chronometers, when the nature of the magnetism of a ship's hull, and its action upon the compass, was not clearly understood, and when, in addition, the process of demagnetising a balance which had become magnetised was a very laborious one (this can now be effected, by the use of the alternating current, in a few seconds), many attempts were made to produce a balance in which steel was eliminated. This necessitated, of course, the adoption of a different metal for the cross-bar, and for the steel portions of the laminæ. John Arnold, working on these lines, produced a balance with a platinum cross-bar, and rims of platinum and brass. His son continued his experiments, in conjunction with E. J. Dent, during the period 1830-1840, and made a large number of experiments. A balance with rims of platinum and silver was found to be the most suitable of the many investigated*, but as compared with the normal balance, it was difficult to make and much less rigid.

Frédéric Houriet, already mentioned as the inventor of a spherical form of balance spring, produced, about 1815, a non-magnetic balance having laminæ of platinum and gold. Ulrich also spent a considerable amount of time and money in similar investigations. He embodied the results of his work in three patents†, covering practically the entire field of the available combinations of metals. The enormous machine shown in Plate XXXI. is fitted with one of his early efforts in this direction, a balance having solid brass arms, moved by the action of a "gridiron" cross-bar consisting of a platinum bar and two brass tubes.

C. A. Paillard, inventor of a palladium alloy extensively employed in balance springs, patented various non-magnetic alloys of the kind for use instead of steel in compensation balances. These have been described in an exhaustive paper read before the Franklin Institute of America, in 1887, by Professor Houston, who stated, in the course of it, that Paillard used rims composed of two different palladium alloys. His English patent, however, specifies the use of his alloy in combination with brass.

* Arnold and Dent also reported to Admiral Beaufort, the Hydrographer, that they found this pattern of balance stood the effect of extreme cold better than any other.

† Nos. 5639 of 1828, 6064 of 1831, and 7350 of 1837.

Balances with rims of brass and nickel, brass and zinc, palladium and aluminium, and various other combinations have also been tried, but in general it has been found that these either involve constructional difficulties, or are too weak to stand rough usage.

It is possible that a final solution of the problem of providing a non-magnetic balance may be obtained from the properties of the nickel-steel alloys, some of which are practically non-magnetic, while it has been found that their susceptibility to magnetism varies with the percentage of nickel in them.

Barometric Error.

This error is the last and the least of those which affect machines fitted with a compensation balance. It is, indeed, only connected with it by the circumstance that balances of this type, as a class, offer much more resistance to the air than a plain circular balance, and that accordingly their motion is to a slight extent affected by variations in the density of the atmosphere.

The amount and nature of the error thus produced has been the subject of several experimental investigations, notably by Harvey in 1824, by Jurgensen about the same time, and, in recent years, by M. Paul Ditisheim and Dr. Ch. Chree. The general result has been to show that most chronometers exhibit a slight change of rate for a variation of barometric pressure, and that these changes are consistent; *i.e.*, a machine which gains slightly at an increased pressure will lose slightly at a reduced one, and *vice versa*, but, on the average, there is no very well marked preponderance of one type of error over the other. This suggests that the effect which, theoretically, ought to be produced—a slight acceleration in decreased pressure—is in many cases masked by imperfect isochronism of the balance spring. For example, if a chronometer be left fast in the short arcs, an increased pressure would, by opposing more resistance to the balance's motion, reduce its arc, and the acceleration produced by this reduction in the arcs might easily overbalance the retardation caused by the increased density of the air. In any case, the error produced by variations of normal amount in the barometric pressure is almost negligible, while in extreme fluctuations it probably does not amount to a second per day.

Variation of Gravity.

It may be worth while, before concluding this chapter, to note briefly a fallacy which, although not so common as it used to be, is still, perhaps, not quite extinct. I refer to the notion that the time of vibration of a balance is affected by the varying force of gravity in different latitudes.

This idea is entirely erroneous. It is perfectly true that the time of vibration of a pendulum of constant length will vary considerably in different latitudes, but this is due to the fact that the time of vibration of such a pendulum depends jointly upon its mass and its weight: or, in other words, upon the relation of the quantity of matter it contains to the pull which the earth exerts upon that matter. And since the latter varies with different latitudes, while the former remains constant for all latitudes, the time of vibration must vary also.

But in a machine fitted with a balance instead of a pendulum, the corresponding elements upon which the time of vibration depends are the mass of the balance and the elasticity of the balance spring. And since neither of these are affected in any way by the force of gravity, it follows that the latter cannot exert any influence upon the time of vibration. The only case in which such influence could possibly be exerted would be that of a balance incorrectly poised, and vibrating in some position other than the horizontal, in which case its motion would, to a slight extent, be affected by a variation of the force of gravity, since it may be regarded as being, in theory, a very badly designed metronome pendulum.*

* In the metronome, and in some patterns of clock, such for example as the "Kee-less" clock made by the company of that name, the pendulum is weighted both above and below its point of suspension, so that its centre of gravity is situated very close to the latter. This greatly increases the time of vibration.

CHAPTER XIII.

MISCELLANEOUS MECHANICAL DEVELOPMENTS

(Chiefly of historical interest only.)

As already explained, by the beginning of the last century a general agreement had been reached as to the essential mechanism required for a marine timekeeper, and the pattern thus evolved remains, in its outline, practically unaltered to-day. It cannot be further simplified with advantage,* and the pressure of competition which brought it into being still operates to reduce to the narrowest limits the refinements which it might otherwise seem desirable to add. ' The survival of the fittest " is as true of mechanism as of animals. A simple mechanism will always drive out a more complicated one of equal efficiency, since it is less likely to be deranged, and also cheaper to manufacture. Furthermore, a simple mechanism will even, in many cases, displace a complicated one of actually greater efficiency, unless the extra efficiency be sufficiently evident to turn the scale in favour of the latter.

Nearly every form of mechanism which is of commercial importance goes through three stages of progress. At first it is simple, being primitive, and for the same reason it is comparatively inefficient. Later, increased efficiency is obtained at the expense of added complication. Finally, a later stage of development is reached, at which a further increase in efficiency is accompanied by a return towards simplicity—but, not, as before, the simplicity of the primitive, but that which comes from a perfect adequacy of the means and a perfect understanding of the ends.

Thus, the bicycle has gone from the early " boneshaker," through complicated types like the " Phantom," " Otto," " Omnicycle," etc., until it has reached its present form : and, similarly, the modern rifle is the son of the complicated and elaborate " wheel-lock " (which embodied a mainspring and a train of wheels), and the grandson of the old and primitive " matchlock."

And in no machine is this process of evolution better exemplified than in the chronometer. The necessity for its maker, if he wishes to remain in business, to produce an efficient machine which shall at the same time be cheap, and therefore must be as simple as possible, has acted as a kind of " Geddes' Axe," sweeping away a number of inessential contrivances, compelling those remaining to establish a clear

* A drastic attempt was made to do this by Restell and Clark, who, in a patent (No. 12154 of 1848) relating to escapements, proposed to dispense with " the detent spring, lifting spring, compensating balance, and occasionally the balance or pendulum spring." However, *plus ça change, plus c'est la même chose,* and chronometers of this Arcadian simplicity are still to seek.

case for their retention, and sternly opposing any further complication unless the increase of efficiency which it brings can be clearly demonstrated, not only by improved timekeeping, but by an even more cogent argument—increased sales and augmented reputation. It is for this reason that the lever watch has superseded the pocket chronometer, that the fusee has all but succumbed to the going barrel, and that the remontoire has made its way into limbo in the company of the enamelled dials, the elaborate engraving and filigree work, and the other expensive luxuries to be found in the chronometers of byegone days. The devices which have established their claim to be added to the equipment of the standard chronometer as Earnshaw left it are few in number, while those which have been tried and discarded, or which have been almost still-born, are very numerous. In the present chapter it is proposed first to describe the former class and then to give some examples of the latter.

The greatest addition which has been made to the chronometer of Earnshaw's day is, of course, auxiliary compensation, which has been dealt with in chapters XI. and XII. It has won its place purely upon its merits, since it is both an added complication and an additional expense. There are, also, at least two other mechanisms, not so important, of which the same can be said. These are the "Up-and-Down" indicator and the make-and-break attachment.

"Up-and-Down" Indicator.

At an early period in the history of the modern chronometer, it was found that it was useful to have some means of knowing how far, at any moment, a machine had run down, without the necessity of opening the case and counting the turns of chain left on the fusee. Naturally, this want was most noticeable in the eight-day chronometer, and, as a matter of fact, such a device makes its first appearance in the earliest eight-day chronometer ever made—Mudge's first machine, completed in 1774. It did not, however, come into general use until later, but by the close of the eighteenth century several plans of the kind had been evolved, and the obvious convenience of the device soon ensured its adoption in all types of chronometer. It is exceptional to meet with a machine of later date than 1820 in which an "Up-and-Down" indicator is not fitted.

The principle upon which the various patterns worked was very simple. The fusee of a chronometer has a reversible motion, amounting to several complete turns and limited by two fixed points—that at which the stop-work comes into action to prevent over-winding, and that at which the chain has so far unwound from the fusee that the pull of the mainspring no longer produces sufficient torque to keep the balance in motion. If, therefore, a pinion carried on the fusee arbor be made to engage with a toothed wheel carrying a pointer, then, provided that the ratio of the gearing is greater than the number of turns made by the fusee in going from the fully wound to the unwound position, the pointer will traverse a sector of a circle during that time, (the radii of the sector corresponding to the "up" and "down" positions) and its position at any intermediate period will be a measure of the amount the chronometer has run down.

The applications of this plan differ but slightly. Mudge, in his first machine, used a pointer traversing an arc of about 150°. This was superseded by a graduated disc, revolving close beneath the dial, its graduations being read through a small aperture. This form appears in fig. 83. The modern plan is to have a pointer, as in Mudge's machine, revolving over an arc of some 350° engraved upon the dial, generally in a position diametrically opposite to the seconds circle.

In addition to being universally fitted in box chronometers, "up-and down" indicators have been fitted to a large number of pocket chronometers. The "chronometer watches," however, issued to H.M. ships (which are, in reality, no longer pocket chronometers, but have lever escapements) are not generally fitted with them.

"Make-and-Break" Attachments.

In special cases, where it is desired to make very accurate observations of the time shown by a chronometer, it has been found an advantage to enable the machine to make and break an electric circuit, the interruptions being recorded upon the revolving drum of a chronograph. Care has, of course, to be taken that the extra work which this imposes on the machine does not affect its timekeeping, and that its steel portions are not rendered liable to be magnetised by the passage of the current.

A method of doing this was devised by Dr. Ad. Hirsch,* in conjunction with MM. Hipp and Dubois, and communicated by him to the "Société des Sciences Naturelles de Neuchatel" in April, 1866. In this arrangement, the make-and-break is effected by means of a separate train and escapement, the latter being unlocked by a secondary escape wheel, mounted on the arbor of the escape wheel proper, once a second.

Charles Frodsham, in 1868, designed a somewhat similar arrangement, operated every 1, 2, 3, or 5 seconds at will.

The modern method, however, which is used, with slight differences, by several makers, is to dispense with the auxiliary train, and to operate the make-and-break by means of a toothed ratchet wheel mounted upon the fourth wheel arbor. The additional work imposed upon the train is very slight, and its amount is practically constant, whether the current be passing or not. Insulated leads are provided, conducting the current to terminals on the outside of the case.

This plan is particularly useful in vessels such as surveying ships, where it is necessary to compare the chronometers frequently by W/T time-signals. To take a chronometer into the wireless-room is undesirable if it can be avoided, and intermediate comparisons by means of a hack watch are clumsy and not extremely accurate. With the make-and-break attachment, the going of a chronometer in the chronometer-room can be recorded upon a chronograph in the wireless room without any difficulty or error.

* For many years Director of the Neuchatel Observatory. He died in 1901, and bequeathed practically the whole of his fortune towards the furtherance of its work.

An extension of this plan, which has been developed by one or two firms of chronometer-makers, notably by Messrs. Thomas Mercer in this country, allows of a master-chronometer controlling a number of receiving dials, fitted with "step-by-step" motion-work, and arranged to show the time of the chronometer in any required part of the ship.

The many devices which, unlike the foregoing, have failed to establish their claim to be considered *real* and *desirable* improvements can be classified roughly as follows:—

1. Those connected with the mechanism of the movement.
2. Those connected with the dial.
3. Those connected with the casing and suspension.

1. Devices Connected with the Mechanism of the Movement.

Abolition of the Fusee.

Although the fusee has held its place in the mechanism of the box chronometer from Harrison's time to the present day, it has been practically supplanted in watches, even of the highest class, by the going barrel, and this fact appears to lend weight to the arguments of those makers who at different times have endeavoured to introduce the going barrel into their box chronometers.

As related in Chapter VI., Le Roy's marine timekeeper had a going barrel, and this was also fitted in several of the timekeepers made by Ferdinand Berthoud and Breguet.

The most persistent advocate of the going barrel, however, both by example and precept, was another French maker, Henri Robert.* Jurgensen also made one or two chronometers so fitted, and there is an example bearing J. R. Arnold's name, and dated 1819, in the museum of the Clockmakers Company.

The respective merits and demerits of the rival plans are briefly as follows. The fusee provides, or can be made to provide, a very perfect adjustment of the varying pull of the mainspring. This renders the force acting at the escape wheel, and the arcs described by the balance, less variable than they would otherwise be, and accordingly makes for good timekeeping. In addition, since the adjustment of the mainspring's pull is effected on correct mechanical principles, and not by the use of what amounts to a frictional brake, the efficiency of the arrangement is higher than that of the going barrel, and accordingly a relatively weaker spring can be used.

On the other hand, it is certainly more complicated than its rival, and thus involves both increased expense and enhanced likelihood of stoppage. It also takes up considerably more space, and it requires the fitting of some form of maintaining power.

---

* See, for example, his pamphlet "Comparaison des Montres Marines au Barillet Denté avec celles à Fusée," Paris, 1839. He also wrote a number of articles on the same subject. It is noteworthy, however, that he advocated the retention of the fusee in *watches*, on the ground that it was difficult to obtain sufficient length of spring for a going barrel giving as good a result.

Plate XXXVI. CHRONOMETER BY BREGUET.

This machine, which is, of course, a very beautiful piece of work, is fitted with a system of four going barrels, and Breguet's " echappement naturelle."

See pp. 243, 321.

The going barrel* is extremely simple, and by the use of a long spring, of which only the centre turns come into action, it is possible to render the torque which it exerts practically the same at any point between the " Up " and " Down " positions. This result is obtained, however, by means of the friction existing between the various coils of the spring—a plan almost as objectionable, in theory, as the old " stackfreed,"† It is cheaper to make than the fusee, and it has the advantage of not requiring any maintaining power.

Against these indisputable advantages must be set the fact that although, in itself, simpler than the fusee, its stop-work and up-and-down indicator have to be of more complicated construction. It is not so efficient, and requires not only a longer but a relatively stronger spring, while, finally, the process of adjusting the spring is laborious, and the permanence of its result less reliable than that of the adjustment obtained by means of the fusee.

It may be noted that in the attempts made by at least one maker of outstanding ability to use the going barrel in box chronometers, an arrangement was employed which was quite as complicated as a fusee. I refer to those made by Breguet, in which two and sometimes four barrels were used, all driving the centre pinion, which floated between them‡. This complicated method of avoiding complication rather suggests spending half-a-crown to save sixpence.

At present, the fusee has held its ground in box chronometers, probably for the simple reason that it is easier to get a good performance from a machine so fitted than from one with a going barrel. In watches, on the other hand, the limited space available has turned the scale very decidedly in favour of the going barrel.

Banking Devices.

Many plans have been tried for the purpose of banking the balance of a chronometer, so as to prevent it from describing more than a full turn in either direction, and so tripping the escapement. It is obvious that the simple method of the early makers—*e.g.*, Harrison and Mudge—in which a pin on the rim of the balance meets a spring standing in its path, is inapplicable with the modern machine, since it restricts the arc of the balance to something less than 180° on either side of the dead point, while in the present-day chronometer this may amount to as much as 270°. Some device is therefore needed which will distinguish between the first and the second times that a point upon the balance passes, or attempts to pass, it while still travelling in the same direction. It is also obvious that while the two semi-vibrations of the balance during one complete swing, which may be distinguished by the names of the " unlocking " and " passing " semi-vibrations, are approximately equal in amount, the banking device need only come into action during one of them, since the limitation of one semi-vibration necessarily connotes a similar reduction of the other.

---

* See p. 48. † See p. 28 *f*.

‡ The machine shown in Plate XXXVI. is of this type.

Practically all of the plans which have been proposed make use of the gradual enlargement of the coils of a helical balance spring when uncoiling, this uncoiling being arranged to coincide with the unlocking semi-vibration.* The earliest attempts appear to have been those made by Hardy and Brockbanks, *circa* 1810.

In Hardy's plan, a small and very light arm is fixed upon the upper turn of the spring (the turn nearest to the balance cock), and plays between two pins fixed in the cock itself. A pin is set in the cross bar of the balance in such a position that for a normal semi-vibration of the balance it just clears the end of the arm carried upon the balance spring. Should the balance be impelled to describe a larger arc, however, the expansion of the upper coil causes the arm to project sufficiently to meet the pin, and so prevent a second unlocking of the escapement.

Brockbank's plan was very similar, but the piece which met the pin carried by the cross-bar was not attached to the spring, but carried upon a separate detent, like the detent of the escapement, and was pushed into contact by means of the expansion of the upper turn of the spring.

In 1826 Mr. J. T. Towson, of Devonport, communicated to the Society of Arts another method of banking, which prevented the balance from describing more than a complete turn in either direction. The fixed end of the balance spring was carried upon a spring stud, which was sufficiently weak to allow the action of the spring, in coiling or uncoiling, to draw it towards or away from the balance staff. Mounted upon the latter was a steel sector, with a turned-up edge, which normally passed through a notch cut in the outer end of the stud. If, however, the balance overturned in either direction, the pull of the spring altered the position of the stud sufficiently to make the edge of the sector come into contact with the end of the stud.

The necessary play of the stud makes this plan objectionable, as it would undoubtedly upset the isochronism of the balance spring. Also, as previously explained, there is no need to bank the balance on both sides of the dead point.

A much simpler form of banking was devised by A. P. Walsh. A thin barrel is mounted on the cross-bar of the balance, and fits closely round the coils of the balance spring. Should the spring be excessively enlarged by an overturn, the coils come into contact with the barrel and exert a pronounced check upon the motion of the balance.

---

* The only other plan which I have come across was most ingenious, but mechanically objectionable. A loose collet, with a small projecting arm, was mounted on the balance staff between the cross-bar and the plate, the arm being thus free to move radially with the balance staff as a centre. Its travel was limited by two pins, one in the plate and the other in the cross-bar, and by this construction the balance could make almost, but not quite, two turns in either direction. Any further movement was arrested by the arm, which was then held at three points—the two pins and the collet.

There are, however, two very serious objections to this plan. The motion of the balance is impeded by the friction of the collet, and when the arm comes into action there is considerable risk of bending or breaking the balance pivots.

A still simpler modification of this plan was evolved by Kullberg. Instead of the barrel, he fitted two upright pins, arising almost vertically from the cross-bar of the balance, and enclosing the coils of the spring. These were inclined inwards, with the result that if the balance overturned the coils of the spring came successively in contact with the pins, and thus exerted a *gradual* check upon the motion of the balance.

In the chronometer of the present day, no banking mechanism is fitted, reliance being placed upon the more generally diffused knowledge of the proper treatment to be accorded to these delicate pieces of mechanism.

BALANCE-LOCKING MECHANISMS.

The need has often been felt of some means of locking the balance of a chronometer during its transport from shore to ship and *vice versa*, or during any period in which it may be exposed to unfair usage. The ordinary plan of securing the balance by means of wedges is liable, as explained in the following chapter, to derange its mechanism seriously.

Ferdinand Berthoud attached great importance to this point, and almost all of his marine timekeepers are fitted with a very simple mechanism of his devising, which provides a very satisfactory solution. He fitted a complete circle of brass around his balance, unconnected with the compensating mechanism, and arranged that a light spring could be brought into contact with this by moving a small nut on the dial, with the result that the balance was at once brought to rest without in any way affecting the operation of the escapement—which remained ready to exercise its normal functions whenever the friction of the spring was removed.*

A still more ingenious plan was designed and executed by Motel, *circa* 1820.

A short pin is planted in the rim of the balance parallel with its axis, and a small detent (fitted, like that of the chronometer escapement, with a passing spring) can be brought at will into the circle described by this pin. Accordingly, if this be done, the balance is brought to rest, and in such a position that on the detent being withdrawn, the chronometer at once starts and continues to go.†

* The machine shown in Plate XXVI. is fitted with this mechanism. Breguet and Louis Berthoud also fitted some of their chronometers with stopping devices of various kinds.

Sir John Ross, the Arctic explorer, in his "Narrative of a Voyage to the Arctic Regions," relates that on one occasion, having to transport a box chronometer for a considerable distance, he allowed it to run down, *in order to avoid damage during transport.* It is difficult to imagine what advantage the gallant explorer expected to derive from this procedure.

† The action of this mechanism is very difficult to understand at first sight, and the manner in which the balance suddenly halts (springing, as it were, to attention) and then steps off smartly as soon as released, is very striking. I recently examined at Greenwich a chronometer made by Motel, having this mechanism, and also the pivoted-detent escapement, conical balance spring, and winding mechanism referred to on pp. 219, 264 and 327 respectively. As a combination of ingenious mechanism and magnificent workmanship it rivals even Mudge's work. (See p. 327 *f*.)

In 1869 considerable attention was devoted to the question by Airy, who consulted various English chronometer makers as to the best manner of locking the balance of a chronometer without the necessity of opening the case. The replies were of varying degrees of merit. H. P. Isaac suggested the use of a pin put through a slot in the cross-bar of the balance, and inserted into a hole in the top-plate. This, however, involved opening the case. Messrs. Dent suggested gripping the balance by springs, but this plan is open to the objection that, although the balance is thereby brought to rest, no longitudinal support is given to it. W. B. Crisp suggested a spring pressing upon the balance, and another acting simultaneously upon the fourth wheel.

The most thorough investigation of the matter was made by Loseby, who pointed out that any successful mechanism must :—

1. Bring the balance to rest, without the possibility of any further motion.

2. Prevent not only the angular motion of the balance but also any longitudinal motion, which would have the effect of burring the points of the pivots.

3. Be operated from the dial, without the necessity of opening the case.

He suggested a plan complying with all these requirements, which involved the use of a circle of fine teeth lying close to the cross-bar of the balance, and raised by a spiral spring (operated by turning a small screw close to the winding hole) so as to press the upper pivot* into its hole, thus bringing the balance to rest by the exertion of a force only slightly greater than its own weight.

This plan met all of Airy's requirements, and accordingly he sought official approval for the payment to Loseby of a small sum, in return for which a model of the invention was to be sent to the Royal Observatory, in order that it might be adopted by other makers and gradually embodied in all chronometers purchased by the Admiralty.† Approval was given for the payment of £30, but Loseby appears to have lost interest in the matter, and there is no record either of the payment or of the model's delivery. However promising the device

---

* It should be explained that throughout this book the terms "upper" and "lower" pivots are used to describe those which are respectively above and below the balance when the chronometer is in its normal position, *i.e.*, suspended horizontally in its gimbals. Amongst chronometer makers, the term "upper pivot" is more often used for that which is uppermost when the machine is on the work-board, dial downwards; *i.e.*, what is here called the "lower" pivot.

† This plan was adopted (in preference to what might seem the more natural one of sending the Government chronometers, by batches, to Loseby for the fitting of this addition) to conform to what has always been the practice of the Observatory—that of regarding the maker of a chronometer as being, generally, the most fitting person to repair or adjust it. The principal exception made to this is when the maker in question has given up business, in which case the machines are generally, but not invariably, entrusted to his successor. Thus, when Arnold and Dent dissolved partnership in 1840, the repair of the chronometers bearing the name of "Arnold and Dent" was divided equally between them, but after Arnold's death in 1843 they were sent wholly to Dent, and not to C. Frodsham, Arnold's successor.

may have appeared from a theoretical point of view, it seems to have been attended by practical disadvantages, for it is a remarkable fact that the only two chronometers (of his own make, too) fitted with Loseby's stopping gear both suffered, when on trial at Greenwich, from a remarkable accidental retardation, suddenly going slow to the extent of some 2 minutes in 24 hours. In any event, whether this occurrence was the cause or not, the question appears, as far as Admiralty chronometers were concerned, to have been dropped, and I have not been able to trace any further devices designed to effect the same purpose.

It may be noted that the frictional brake devised by Harrison, which also acted on the rim of the balance, antedated Berthoud's plan, and that a similar arrangement could easily be made to grip the balance staff, being brought into action by a lever operated from the dial. Loseby's plan, however, appears to be the soundest in theory, as preventing all possible damage to the balance, and it is to be regretted that it was not followed up, and its defects eliminated.

Chronometers Going More than Eight Days.

A period of eight days has been generally taken as the longest for which a chronometer should be designed to go at one winding, and even this is now generally considered to be too long. It is many years since an eight-day chronometer was well placed in the Greenwich trials,* and such machines have been found to yield better results if wound daily, or at the utmost twice a week.

Romilly's watch, going a year at one winding, and Le Roy's first machine, wound every three hours, indicate the limits between which opinion on this point has fluctuated. It is, however, obvious that while there is nothing very objectionable, mechanically speaking, in a weight-driven clock designed to go for a year, the intervals between the windings of a spring-driven timekeeper (in which the varying friction between the coils of the spring may affect the timekeeping) should, if the latter is to be accurate, be kept as short as they conveniently can.† The practical causes modifying this criterion, however, are that if the machine has to be wound more often than once a day, it is almost certain that, when aboard ship, the winding will, occasionally, have to be done by some one not usually entrusted with it. Again, the one-day pattern will only go for about 30 hours, so that if its winding should once be overlooked, it will probably run down before the omission is discovered. The two-day type (going 54 hours or so) is free from this defect, and less expensive than the eight-day, which presents no corresponding advantage. Hence it comes about that the two-day chronometer, wound daily, is the standard type of the present day.

---

* See page 378.

† That is, if it is designed to keep *really accurate time*. For ordinary purposes there is nothing to be said against the spring-driven clock designed to go a fortnight, or even such an extraordinary mechanism as the famous Tompion clock belonging to Lord Mostyn, which strikes the hours and quarters, and, although driven by springs, requires winding but once a year.

One or two attempts have been made to produce chronometers going for more than eight days. E. J. Dent patented, in 1840*, a chronometer with four going barrels, arranged somewhat as in the Breguet pattern referred to on p. 304†, and going for a period which, by varying the design, could be made anything from 8 to 32 days. The barrels were arranged in pairs, each pair driving an intermediate wheel planted between them, and both of the latter driving the centre pinion. The extra long period was thus obtained by the use of an additional wheel in the train, while the increase in power obtained by using several mainsprings compensated for the greater mechanical disadvantage of such a train.

In a plan patented by Poncy in 1840‡, two going barrels are employed in conjunction with a remontoire, the details of the arrangement being curiously reminiscent of Harrison's No. 4. Two models, differing in minor details, are described—one to go three months and the other six weeks.

He also designed a modification of this plan, whereby it could be employed in a clock striking hours and quarters. It may be noted that chronometers, except in fiction§, are not fitted with any form of striking gear¶.

As already explained, there is absolutely no advantage gained by making a chronometer go more than two days between windings, and such machines are inferior both in principle and in detail to the ordinary two-day pattern, although, if well made, they may be found quite satisfactory in use at sea.

WINDING GEAR.

Practically every modern chronometer is wound by the simple and clumsy method of turning it upside down in its gimbals, and pushing a key, normally kept loose in the box, on to the winding square on the fusee arbor.

At first sight it appears amazing that such a plan should be applicable to such a delicate instrument, but it must be admitted that in practice it is, if carefully performed, quite satisfactory, while its simplicity and cheapness, and the influence of tradition, have combined to retain it in favour, in spite of the advantages which, theoretically, are offered by a winding gear which does not involve turning the

---

* Pat. No. 8625 of 1840.

† Breguet's machine went for 8 days only.

‡ Pat. No. 8602 of 1840.

§ Cf. "*The Terror of the Air*," by Wm. Le Queux, London, 1920, p. 100. " . . . at the third stroke of twelve from the ship's chronometer."

¶ Except machines for special purposes. For example, a "chronometer log-watch," designed by Rear-Admiral John W. Tarleton, R.N., and made by Dent, which was tested at Greenwich in 1868, was made to strike a bell at the end of every 14 seconds. It was intended to replace the sand-glass used when heaving the hand-log, but it would have been a waste of time and money for the Admiralty to have adopted it, as the unavoidable errors of the hand-log render such accurate timing both unnecessary and useless.

movement over. It should be added that these advantages are not universally admitted, especially by chronometer makers*, but that they exist is, I think, the general unbiassed opinion.

The earliest marine-timekeeper which had to be reversed for winding was Harrison's No. 4. Owing to its long centre-seconds hand, it would have been difficult to adopt any other method. Kendall followed suit, even in his third machine, whose three small dials would have allowed of the winding square being approached through a hole in the dial without any risk of the key fouling the hands. Mudge, Arnold and Earnshaw did the same, and in this way reversal for winding became, in this country, the standard practice which it has continued ever since.

French chronometer makers, however, took for some time a different view. Le Roy's machine (1765) was wound from the dial, as were practically all of Berthoud's. Louis Berthoud and Breguet adopted the English plan, but Motel and one or two others still declined to sacrifice principle to expediency. Ultimately, however, the cheaper and simpler plan prevailed, even with them†.

The easiest plan to provide for winding from the dial is, of course, that shown in Plate XXVI., in which the winding square is formed on the upper end of the fusee arbor, while a hole is provided in the glass to admit the key. The latter, of course, must not interfere with the motion of the hands, and had better be kept clear of both of them, or, in any case, of the hour hand.

The method used by Motel was to fit, below the winding square, a large bevel wheel, engaging with a bevel pinion situated just above the right hand gimbal pivot. The arbor of the bevel, which was inclined upwards and outwards at an angle of 45° to the vertical, formed the winding square, which was normally covered by a sliding dust-flap. This plan was extremely neat and compact, and there was no possibility of damaging the hands.

A somewhat similar arrangement was used for many years by J. R. Losada, of London. In this the winding arbor, which had considerable end-play, was horizontal, and projected through the side of the case close below the dial, being kept short enough to clear the gimbal ring. It was normally pressed outwards by a spring. On attaching the key and pressing inwards, an intermediate wheel

---

* The reason generally given for not adopting top-winding is that there is a danger of the upper pivot running dry, which is avoided by the daily reversal. The danger is non-existent, and the proposed remedy valueless—in fact, to quote Macaulay, the conjunction of the two "resembles nothing so much as a forged bond with a forged release indorsed on the back of it." The real reasons for retaining the present method—that it is cheap, simple, and not necessarily injurious—are not, as a rule, brought forward.

† In 1833, the official regulations governing the purchase of chronometers for the French Navy contained the proviso that all such machines *must* be wound from the face. It was added, that it would be considered an advantage if the balance of the machine could be readily stopped, for transport, without opening the case. Both these requirements, however, were subsequently abandoned.

engaged with one on the fusee arbor, and after the winding the withdrawal of the key left the spring free to disengage the winding train. This plan exhibited an advantage over Motel's, since no part of the mechanism was in action except at the moment of winding, while in Motel's the bevel wheel and pinion revolved with the fusee while the chronometer was going.

Apart from these neat and effective methods of fitting top-winding gear as an integral part of the movement, several plans have from time to time been put forward of what may be termed "external" winding gear, the internal arrangement of the movement being unaltered. A plan devised by Prest (J. R. Arnold's foreman, who also patented in 1820* a plan for winding, but not setting, the hands of a watch from the pendant) employed a vertical spindle revolving in bearings at the side of the case, and carrying at its upper end the winding square and at the other a pinion engaging with a wheel on the fusee arbor. This was open to the objection that no disconnecting gear was fitted.

Lieut. Langham Rokeby, R.M., designed in 1863 an arrangement on similar lines, but with the vertical spindle mounted on the side of the box instead of being carried on the case. To get the wheel on the fusee arbor into engagement with the pinion, the chronometer had to be locked in its gimbals and the key pressed firmly down. This arrangement was fitted to one or two Admiralty chronometers for trial, but it was found to be clumsy and easily deranged.

A very similar plan was patented† by J. S. Matheson, an optician of Leith, in 1880. The only improvement upon Rokeby's design was that the wheels had no longer to be held in engagement during winding, this being effected by a sliding plate which could be locked either in the engaged or disengaged position.

Probably the best plan of all is that invented by Britten,‡ shown in fig. 82. This is a reversion to Prest's idea, but with the addition of automatic disengaging gear. Not the least of its advantages is that it can be applied to any chronometer.

Here the wheel carried at the lower end of the vertical spindle does not engage directly with that on the fusee arbor, but through an intermediate wheel, mounted on a swinging arm mounted concentrically with the spindle, and extended upwards in the form of a thumb-piece. By pressing on this thumb-piece the intermediate wheel, which is always in mesh with that on the spindle, can also be brought into engagement with that on the fusee arbor, after which rotation of the spindle will wind the chronometer. On the winding being completed, and the pressure on the thumb-piece removed, a spring at once removes the intermediate wheel out of engagement.

---

* Patent No. 4501 of that year.

† Pat. No. 2416 of 1880.

‡ Patented by F. J. Britten in 1887 (Pat. No. 12898). It is better known as "Kendal's winder," having been placed on the market by Messrs. Kendal and Dent.

WINDING KEYS.

These are now invariably of some such pattern as that appearing in Plate XXXVII., consisting of a tubular barrel and a winged head, connected by means of a " tipsy " ratchet* which prevents the fusee from being turned the wrong way (this would strain the maintaining gear badly†. Occasionally old chronometers, especially those by Barraud, may be met with in which the key, either of winged pattern or shaped like a large button with milled edge, is mounted as a fixture on the fusee square. But there is no advantage in this plan, since the chronometer has still to be turned over before it can be wound, and, in addition, it is necessary either for the key to be very flat, or the gimbal ring unusually large.

Pocket chronometers have generally been fitted with key winding, since fusee keyless work presents difficulties‡. The modern " chronometer watch," with going barrel, has, of course, keyless winding work.

SET-HANDS MECHANISM.

This is practically a virgin field for box chronometers, although the hands of a pocket chronometer can readily be set, whether mechanism is provided for that purpose, as in all keyless examples, or not. But for box chronometers it appears, hitherto, to have been thought unnecessary, or dangerous, to provide any special means of altering the indications of the hands, although, as explained in the following chapter, the mechanism of the modern chronometer does not *prohibit*, although it does not facilitate, this operation. As far as I am aware, until the advent of the new Ditisheim chronometer described in the postscript to this chapter, no chronometer maker had followed the lead given, on this point, by Harrison in his No. 5 (see Plate XIII.).

---

* The " tipsy key " or " Breguet key," whose invention is claimed both for Breguet and for Samuel Harlow, of Derby, who patented it in 1789, was a joint, if unconscious, product of the fusee watch and the " three bottle man." Any attempt to force the fusee of an old watch (without maintaining gear) round the wrong way would probably break the click, in which case the watch could not be wound at all. If it were fitted with maintaining gear, the latter would probably jam.

Mention should be made of a very ingenious plan (really a modification of Harrison's maintaining gear) devised by Thomas Moore, a watchmaker of Ipswich, about 1729. Watches so fitted could be wound by turning the key *either way*. The device was described by Thiout in his treatise (1741) and is also illustrated in Britten.

Another plan of winding both ways was patented by Mr. D. A. A. Buck, designer of the original Waterbury watch, in 1880 (American pat. 234236).

† Harrison's form of key, shown in Plate XIV., is really better than the modern pattern, as it enables the winding to be done much more steadily. There is, however, an increased risk of overstrain, and no ratchet is fitted, although that could easily be added.

‡ The winding gear has to be disconnected from the fusee when not in use, as otherwise additional strain is imposed on the mainspring, and any touch on the winding button might stop the watch. Several workable plans for keyless fusee winding have been produced, but none is simple or easy to make. The fact that provision has also to be made for setting the hands from the button introduces an additional element of complication.

Weight-Driven Chronometers.

For the sake of completeness, mention should be made of one or two instances in the last century in which it has been suggested to employ a weight as the prime mover of a chronometer, thus reviving the method previously employed by Arsandeaux, and also by Berthoud in his No. 6 and No. 8 machines.

In 1812 William C. Bond, of Boston, U.S.A., made the first marine chronometer constructed in America. Not being able to obtain a mainspring*, he drove it by means of a falling weight, sliding between three guide bars. In appearance it must have closely resembled Berthoud's machines, having a cylindrical brass case six inches in diameter and a foot deep. It went for thirty hours, and seems to have performed well during a voyage to the East Indies in a vessel belonging to the U.S. Government.

In March of the same year Grimaldi, a London maker, proposed to the Board of Longitude a plan for a new species of chronometer "without mainspring, weight, chain or line," which (I infer) must have been designed to go by its own weight, a plan often employed in the "mysterious timepieces" of the famous N. Grollier de Servières†, and others, but not worth consideration for an accurate marine timekeeper. Maskelyne, however, agreed to receive the machine at Greenwich for trial, but it was not sent, its maker preferring, before constructing it, to solicit the Board for assistance, which he did, unsuccessfully, for over a year.

Another of the same type was described by Thomas Reid, of Edinburgh, in the second edition of his "Treatise on Watch and Clockmaking," published in 1825. It does not appear that the machine was actually constructed. Reid proposed that the movement should slide, remaining horizontal, between three steel rods, the amount of fall allowed being 8 inches, corresponding to a running time of 32 hours.

A very similar machine was proposed by Isabelle, a French maker, and is described in the "Bulletin de la Société d'Encouragement" (No. 52).

A weight-driven chronometer by Gretillat, a Swiss maker resident in France, appears to have attracted some attention about 1860, and

* England was then at war with the United States.

† Nicholas Grollier de Servières (1593-1686). An officer of the French Army, who passed the latter part of his life in devising and constructing a large number of most ingenious mechanisms, chiefly relating to horology. Some account of his work was published by his grandson under the title of "Recueil d'ouvrages curieux de mathématique et de mechanique, on Description du cabinet de Nicholas Grollier de Servières" (Lyon, 1719, 4to.) In this work may be found the original forms of almost all the *outré* clocks which are produced more for amusement than for timekeeping.

An English mechanic, James Cox, also produced, in the eighteenth century, some very remarkable mechanisms of the kind. His *chef d'œuvre* was a "perpetual motion" clock which really lived up to its name—*i.e.*, it never required winding, being driven by the variations of the barometer. There is a description of it in Britten, and a much fuller account in Dircks' "Perpetuum Mobile."

to have been favourably regarded by the French Government, but I have not been able to obtain any details of its mechanism or performance.

However carefully a weight-driven chronometer be made, and however well it may perform in calm weather, it is mechanically unsuited for use at sea. Its sole theoretical advantage is that (in a flat calm) it gives a uniform torque at the great wheel without the necessity of using a fusee. But if the ship be at all lively, the actual variations of this torque will greatly exceed those which might arise from the worst going-barrel ever constructed.*

REVERSED FUSEE.

As mentioned on p.**116**, the usual method of planting the fusee of a chronometer is theoretically incorrect, since the side-pressure upon the pivots of the fusee is the *sum* of the pull of the chain and the resistance to motion offered (on the opposite side of the fusee) by the centre-wheel pinion, while if the pull were exerted on the *same* side of the fusee as the pinion (as it is in the reversed fusee) the pressure on the pivots would only be the *difference* of these two forces. This plan was used by Mudge, and occasionally by later makers, amongst whom may be instanced Barraud and Schoof, but the majority of chronometer makers have, in this as in many other matters, exhibited a typically British indifference to correctness of principle when it is attended by any practical inconvenience†. The firm of Victor Kullberg, however, who have for many years past fitted reversed fusees in all their chronometers, form a praiseworthy exception to this rule.

2. DEVICES CONNECTED WITH THE DIAL AND MOTION WORK.

TWENTY-FOUR HOUR DIALS.

These have often been proposed, and occasionally one meets with a chronometer so fitted, but in practice they are by no means convenient‡. Actually, the dial of a watch or clock is not read by the numbers on the dial, but by the relative position of the two hands,

* It should be noted that Berthoud, who achieved a very considerable measure of success with his weight-drivers, found it necessary to provide a ratchet and click to prevent the weight from moving *up* the guide rods in consequence of the ship's motion.

† Grimthorpe's remarks on this are pointed:

> ". . . I confess I know no reason why the common arrangement should be adhered to, except that it is the common one, which is generally considered reason enough for anything bad."—"*Rudimentary Treatise on Clock and Watchmaking.*"

The practical inconvenience is, that a reversed fusee necessitates either re-planning the movement, or winding the other way. In the latter case, the motion of the hands will be reversed, unless one adopts Mudge's clumsy plan of inserting an extra wheel in the train, which is reminiscent of the early going-barrel watches sold in some manufacturing districts. These had, at first, no sale at all, and their maker discovered that the cause of their unpopularity was that they wound to the right, and not, like a fusee watch, to the left. Nothing daunted, he at once fitted an idle wheel, and so reversed the direction of winding, after which they sold like hot cakes. Truly, *populus vult decipi*.

‡ There is, however, a distinct advantage in having a 24-hour dial for a chronometer showing sidereal time.

and until the use of a 24-hour dial can be made universal for all clocks, watches and chronometers, it is inevitable that, sooner or later, mistakes will occur in reading the dial of a chronometer so fitted.

Using the ordinary hour and minute hands, one of the following plans must be adopted :—

1. The hour hand going twice round the dial in 24 hours, and the minute hand once in an hour, as usual.

2. The hour hand going round once in 24 hours, and the minute hand as before.

3. The hour hand going round once in 24 hours and the minute hand once in two hours.

Of these alternatives, the first has not, as far as I am aware, been employed in a chronometer, although it has sometimes been used in clocks, the two circuits being distinguished either by the use of two rings of figures and an hour hand of variable length, or by a ring of hour numerals, read through apertures in the dial and shifted every twelve hours so as to bring a fresh set of numbers into view.*

In the second plan, the hour numerals are only $2\frac{1}{2}$ minutes apart, instead of 5, and in consequence such a time as 0h. 5m. 45s. may easily be read as 0h. 10m. 45s.

In the third, the " quarter past " and "quarter to " positions of the minute hand will indicate half hours, and the " half past " position a complete hour. Accordingly, it is not at all unlikely that such a time as 12h. 30m. 17s. may be read, in a moment of inattention, as 12h. 15m. 17s.

The second and third plans (both of which necessitate a re-arrangement of the motion-work) have been employed to a certain extent, but neither can be called a really satisfactory arrangement. In addition, any dial showing 24 hours in one circuit looks, even with Arabic numerals†, very crowded.

The number of hours shown on any dial is, strictly speaking, an arbitrary convention, depending upon a tacit assumption that the person reading it is already in possession of some approximate idea of the correct time, accurate to within the largest amount which the dial can indicate. Italian and Japanese clocks, until comparatively recently, showed six hours only. In the case of a chronometer whose accumulated error, allowing the large rate of 10 seconds daily, only amounts to about an hour a year, there would be no inherent diffi-

* A device of this kind was patented by Messrs. Meek and Sturrock, of Edinburgh, in 1885, and a watch on a similar plan was exhibited by R. G. Webster at the Paris Exhibition of 1889. An old chronometer by John Arnold, preserved at Greenwich, has a somewhat similar device, the hours being shown by numerals appearing in a slot cut in the dial, and changing with a jump every hour. Watches have often been made to show both hours and minutes thus, and seconds by an ordinary seconds hand. For a 24-hour chronometer, such a plan might be useful, but as generally executed its mechanism is far from correct in principle.

† Roman figures are obviously not suitable for showing such hours as XVIII. and XXIII.

culty in obtaining G.M.T. accurately from a machine showing minutes and seconds only, provided it were known to within an hour (as is always the case).

By the use of a dial such as those shown in Plates XVI. and XXVI., but with a 24-hour circle for the hour dial, there would be no difficulty in showing 24 hours on a chronometer without the possibility of confusion, but this necessitates a re-planning of the motion-work and other mechanism under the dial.

CHRONOMETERS SHOWING SIDEREAL AND MEAN TIME.

For the purpose of working out the observations taken on board a ship, it is frequently necessary to convert solar into sidereal time, and vice versa. This can be done on paper in a few minutes, but chronometers and pocket watches have sometimes been made in which it is effected mechanically.

George Margetts (1748-1804), already referred to* as the inventor of a form of lever escapement, produced several machines of this kind. They have three dials, showing hours, minutes and seconds, and in the centre of each dial is a smaller one, which gradually rotates backwards, so that the hands indicate, simultaneously, the hour, minute and second of mean solar time on the outer (fixed) rings of figures, and of sidereal time upon the inner (moving) ones. A very large watch fitted with this mechanism is exhibited in the Museum of the Clock-makers' Company, but it is not a chronometer, having a cylinder escapement and no compensation.

Margetts also made several very complicated watches designed to give a certain amount of the information which was normally afforded by astronomical and tidal tables. They showed the tide at various ports, the age and place of the moon, the place and declination of the sun, and the stars visible at any time above an observer's horizon. Also the time in hours and minutes.

One of these watches, and the movement of another, is preserved in the British Museum, and there are also several examples in private collections. The most remarkable of these productions of Margetts, however, is in the possession of Captain Tristan Dannreuther, R.N., to whom I am indebted for the opportunity of examining it. Its dial work exhibits the same complications as that of the watches, but it is much larger, being about the same diameter as a modern chronometer, although considerably thinner. It has a chronometer escapement and a plain brass balance, compensation being effected by a very badly designed compensation curb†. There is no seconds hand. The decoration of the dial, exhibiting the figures of the constellations, is

* See p. 240.

† The curb is quadrantal in shape, like one arm of a balance, and moves an arm, carrying the curb pins, which is not pivoted concentrically with the balance-staff but at a point considerably farther from it than the outer turn of the spring, so that every movement of the pins distorts the latter slightly.

very fine, but the workmanship and engraving of the movement is far from first class—a feature which is characteristic of all Margetts' work. Were it not for this lack of finish, he might have a claim to be regarded as the English Breguet*.

This machine, which is not really a chronometer, but an attempt to produce a mechanical " Nautical Almanac," is, I believe, unique—and certainly for perverted ingenuity it would be difficult to surpass. Putting aside for a moment its enormously increased cost as compared with a chronometer of ordinary pattern, and the extra work imposed upon the mainspring by having to drive such a complicated motion-work, it is open to the fatal objection that its indications would have to be corrected for rate before they could be used, and that this calculation would take at least as long as the time required for looking out the same information in the tables, while the latter method would be far more reliable. In addition, any change of rate on the machine's part (and from its mechanism it is obvious that it would never have been a very reliable timekeeper) would further vitiate the accuracy of its indications.

A design for a somewhat similar machine was submitted to the Board of Longitude in 1795, by two makers named Martin and Jordan, and Maskelyne's very just verdict upon it was as follows :—

> " . . . The Astronomer Royal further reported he had examined Martin and Jordan's Outlines of a Machine for the discovery of the Longitude, which appears to be a combination of Clock Work, which turns a terrestrial Globe upon its Axis, and shows the Year, day of the Month, hour and minute of Time, and the place of the Sun and Moon, and time of high and low Water at London Bridge ; and that it is an Instrument more adapted to the Cabinets of the Curious, and magnificence of great Persons, than for an accurate measure of Time, which alone could render it deserving the attention of the Board."

Breguet, for whom mechanical difficulties hardly existed, also produced one or two watches showing sidereal and mean time, using for this purpose a movement embodying two complete trains, escapements, and balances, and practically constituting two independent watches in one case. One was adjusted to keep mean time, and the other sidereal. The difference in the adjustment of the two balances was not great, a sidereal day being approximately four minutes shorter than a mean solar one.

A pocket watch to indicate mean and sidereal time was also patented quite recently by Messrs. Strömgren and Olsen, of Copenhagen†.

---

* He was, in many ways, a remarkably gifted man. He detected and corrected a large number of errors in the tables of refraction and parallax published by the Board of Longitude, and also produced a large volume of " Horary Tables," a work of enormous labour, designed to provide a graphical method of clearing the lunar distance by inspection. He received from the Board a gratuity of £100 as a reward for this work.

He was for some time chronometer maker to the East India Company, but his circumstances declined, and he died in a lunatic asylum

† Patent No. 2493 of 1915.

All such mechanisms, however well they may be executed, are open to the same fundamental objection—namely, that the results indicated on their dials require correction for rate before they can be used, and are therefore less reliable, and no more readily obtained, than those afforded by the use of a conversion table, or even by ordinary computation.* They are useless and mischievous complications, and the same may be said of the perpetual calendars, tide indicators, astronomical dials, chronograph stop-work, minute repetition work, and other excrescences with which it is customary to overload the average "presentation" watch, which bears about the same relation to a machine designed to measure time accurately that an alderman does to an athlete.†

CHRONOMETERS INDICATING DIFFERENCES OF LONGITUDE.

Of much the same value as the foregoing are the various complicated systems of dialling which have been designed to enable a chronometer to show, by inspection, the time corresponding to any assigned meridian. The utility of this proposal is not very obvious, but it appears to have a perpetual fascination for a certain class of inventor.

Thus, in the minutes of the Board of Longitude for June 3rd, 1797, appears the entry:—

> "A Time-Piece, made by Mr. Martin, was recommended to the Board by Sir Andrew Snape Hammond. The Hands of this Time-Piece, without exhibiting the time, show the longitude by inspection, every day at 12 o'clock, supposing the instant when it is 12 o'clock can be determined at sea."

I imagine, from this description, that two separate hands, connected by motion-work, were arranged to show degrees and minutes of longitude, and that the degree hand revolved once in 24 hours over a dial graduated from 0° to 180° W. clockwise, and from 0° to 180° E. anti-clockwise. *If* the machine could have been arranged to keep exact G.M.T., then the required result would, theoretically, be produced—but the impracticable nature of the proposal was obvious, as appears from the subsequent entry in the minutes:—

> "It was not deemed worthy the attention of the Board."

---

* In addition, all of them, except Breguet's (which requires correction for two separate rates) have inherent errors, arising from the fact that the train of wheels employed does not exactly represent the true proportion between a sidereal and a mean solar day. The train used by Margetts, which included a wheel of 487 teeth, had an error of a second and a half per year, while that of Messrs. Stromgren and Olsen, which is considerably simpler, becomes incorrect to the extent of 57 secs. in that time, or at the rate of about 5 seconds per month.

The following train, however, $\frac{50 \times 182 \times 196}{30 \times 211 \times 281}$ if interposed between two wheels, will cause one to revolve in a mean solar and the other in a sidereal day with an error not exceeding a second in 800 years. See the R.A.S. Monthly Notices for May, 1850.

† It must not be inferred that a complicated watch is necessarily a bad one; on the contrary, such a watch is often an exceedingly fine piece of work, reflecting the highest credit on its maker. But, as is apparent from the Kew trials, where a separate class is reserved for "complicated watches," such a mechanism can never rival or approach, *as a timekeeper*, a machine designed specifically for that purpose.

In 1859 Airy was requested by the Admiralty to report upon a similar machine, in which differences of longitude were indicated by means of a series of shifting metal plates. It was the invention of one Herr Weinbach, of Erbach. Airy's opinion coincided with that previously expressed by the Board of Longitude.

Dials of the kind have been evolved, in quite recent times by Comm. Vincent, of the French Navy; M. Vodopivec, a Bulgarian engineer; and others. But all such plans are open to the fatal objection that they involve a certain amount of additional expense and complication merely for the sake of effecting, mechanically, a short and simple computation which can be done quite as quickly, and with less chance of error, by means of pencil and paper.

ATTACHED THERMOMETERS.

Chronometers may occasionally be met with, although they are not made now-a-days, in which a pointer on the dial shows, in a similar manner to an up-and-down indicator, the temperature of the machine's interior. This involves the use of a metallic thermometer, which practically consists of a spiral compensation curb fitted, like a balance spring, to the arbor of the pointer.*

The device, abstractly considered, is a useful one, especially with a chronometer not fitted with auxiliary compensation, but a loose thermometer of ordinary pattern kept in the chronometer box will give the temperature quite accurately enough without recourse to this comparatively complicated and expensive method.

DEVICES CONNECTED WITH THE CASING AND SUSPENSION OF CHRONOMETERS.

AIR-TIGHT CASES.

To avoid the injury arising from the presence of damp in the inside of a chronometer's case, which causes rust to appear on the balance spring and other (less important) steel portions, and also to prevent the entry of dust (which, of course, accelerates the thickening of the oil) more efficiently than by the usual plan of having a sliding cover over the winding hole, many inventors have been struck with the idea of making the case air-tight, the winding being effected through a stuffiing box or some analogous arrangement, and the interior of the case being rendered a vacuum, or filled either with some inert gas (such as nitrogen) or with perfectly dry air.

As related on p. 42, a marine timekeeper going *in vacuo*, and wound through a stuffing box, was constructed by Jeremy Thacker in 1714, but it seems to have attracted no attention, and the project lay dormant for a century, being then revived by Joseph Manton, a famous London gunmaker. Manton patented, in 1807, a chronometer case very much on Thacker's principle, except that the glass dome over the movement was replaced by a brass box with a glass top, the surface of the glass being ground to fit accurately into a sink turned

* See the remarks on metallic thermometers on p. 261.

in the top edge of the case. The machine was wound by means of a permanently-attached key running through a stuffing-box in the bottom of the case.

From an account of his experiments given by Manton to the Board of Longitude in 1809, it appears that the balance of a chronometer (made by Pennington) in one of these cases did not sensibly alter its arc of vibration in ten months. Air was then admitted, and the machine went 20 seconds per day slower. On restoring the vacuum the chronometer did not return to its former rate, but went some 6 or 7 seconds per day slower than it did at first.

A short unofficial trial of the plan, carried out at Greenwich, gave no very striking results, but a chronometer so fitted was used at sea for two years by Capt. F. Beaufort, R.N. (afterwards Hydrographer), with great success. It must, however, have been difficult, even with the most careful workmanship, to preserve a reasonable degree of exhaustion in the case for more than a short time, and unless the vacuum were frequently renewed (which would undoubtedly alter the rate), it may safely be assumed that a well-fitting case of ordinary pattern would have done almost as well.

Air-tight cases were designed, and in most cases patented, by Dent (1840), Johnson (1858), Plaskett (1860), Dencker (1890), Hammersley and others, all being alike in their general features. The joint between the glass and the bezel was rendered air-tight by packing, and the winding spindle passed through a stuffing-box, the use of the latter not being attended by the difficulties experienced by Manton (and, probably, by Thacker) since no attempt was made to establish any difference of pressure between the inside and outside of the case.

In Dent's patent, the suggestion appears that the case should be filled with an inert gas instead of with air, and this might equally well have been done with any of the other forms.

Perhaps the most ingenious case of the kind is that patented by Herr Nees von Essenbeck, of the Kiel Chronometer Observatory, in 1892. This is an *absolutely hermetic* construction, without any stuffing box or similar device. The joint of the glass is made air-tight by cement or a rubber ring, as before, and the bottom of the case is composed of a thin sheet-metal diaphragm, formed, like those of an aneroid barometer, into annular grooves. This allows its centre considerable freedom of motion in and out, and use is made of this to effect the winding. Fixed to the centre of the diaphragm, on its inner side, is the end of a chain, which runs over a roller and is then wound round a drum mounted on the fusee arbor. This drum is fitted with an internal spring, and has a ratchet and click, so that on pulling the chain the arbor is rotated, while on releasing it the drum is carried round by the spring, and takes up the slack of the chain. A ring is attached to the centre of the diaphragm on its outer side, and by pulling and releasing this ring it is possible to wind the chronometer without the use of any perforation in the diaphragm.

It is, however, still necessary to open the case if it should be desired to lock the balance for transport, although by an extension of the plan this could also, if it were worth while, be done while still keeping the case hermetically sealed.

The provision of an air-tight case for a chronometer, however, is not a point of the first importance,* and it is probably due to this fact that none of the above schemes have ever had any great measure of popularity. In fact, unless pains be taken to ensure the dryness of the enclosed air, an air-tight case may actually tend to assist the formation of rust.

It may be noted that many of the " pedometer-winding " watches made by Breguet (in which the winding is effected by the motion of the wearer, which causes a weighted lever to oscillate up and down, and so wind the spring through the operation of a rack and pinion) have hermetic cases, or nearly so, and can be worn much longer than a watch of the ordinary pattern without requiring to be cleaned. I have not, however, seen many of his pocket chronometers so fitted.

Oil.

In connection with the foregoing, it has been mentioned that the oil used for lubricating the moving parts of chronometers has a tendency to thicken. Airy, in the course of a report made to the Admiralty in 1860, remarked upon this point :—

> " C. Another very serious cause of error was brought out very clearly in this trial : namely, a fault in the oil, which is injured by heat . . . I believe that nearly all the irregularities from week to week . . . are in reality due to the two causes B (defective compensation) and C."

These remarks emphasise the important truth that the time-keeping of any chronometer, even one of perfect design and construction, is at the mercy of its lubricating oil, and that it is accordingly all-important to secure an oil which will not deteriorate in use during a long period.

Many kinds of oil have been tried—mineral oils, such as paraffin ; vegetable oils, such as rape-seed oil, olive oil, and that extracted from various nuts ; and animal oils, such as neatsfoot, porpoise, and sperm oil. Mixtures of all the above have also been used.

The balance of opinion is in favour of an animal oil, and sperm oil appears to fill the requirements of the chronometer maker better than any other. Mineral oil is too thin, and vegetable oils are unstable, and have a tendency to break up and lose all lubricating quality. The sperm oil used has to be of the very finest quality, and is often subjected to additional purifying processes by the chronometer makers, most of whom have recipes of their own.

---

* Alterations in the humidity of the atmosphere have sometimes been suggested as a cause of irregularity in the going of chronometers (*e.g.*, by Dr. Hilficker, of Neuchâtel, in 1889), but the evidence available is not very conclusive. The effect, a slight loss of rate in damp weather, is probably not greater in amount than that caused by variations of barometric pressure. The chronometer maker of the future *may* find it worth while to avoid both by using a vacuum case and electric winding—but this is, to say the least of it, improbable.

It may be added that experiments have been made with various artificial oils prepared by competent chemists, but the results obtained have not been satisfactory.

A plan which has sometimes been successfully employed in clocks, and which dispenses entirely with the use of oil, was suggested for chronometers by L. Herbert,* in 1830. The lubricant employed is plumbago very finely divided. He gave a full account of the elaborate and tedious method employed by him to prepare it, and claimed that if this were followed, and the product employed to charge the holes and pivots, better and more lasting lubrication was obtained than would be possible with oil. *A priori*, the plan appears promising, but I have not come across any record of its practical application in chronometers. By modern chemical methods it would probably not be difficult to obtain much purer and more finely-divided plumbago than was possible in Herbert's time.

JEWELLING.

Connected with the question of oil is that of jewelling. As previously explained, this method of reducing wear and friction is in general use, not only in the chronometer but in all except the cheapest class of watch, for the pivot holes of the more rapidly moving arbors. It might be thought that, if jewelled bearings were an advantage, the mechanical efficiency of a chronometer would be increased by fitting them to every arbor, and, theoretically this is true, but in practice the advantage gained by jewelling the slower moving pivots is so slight in comparison with the expense that this is never done, except perhaps in the case of a presentation watch. In the modern chronometer the pivots of the balance and escape wheel, and the lower pivot of the fourth wheel, are always jewelled. The upper pivot of the fourth wheel is often jewelled, and sometimes those of the third wheel also.

The value of jewelling was not universally admitted at first. Harrison's No. 4 is an example of the lavish use of jewelling, while Le Roy's "montre marine," on the other hand, has no jewels whatever. A later maker, P. P. Barraud, stated† that he had, after mature experiment, *given up jewelling* for his chronometers, reverting to the use of plain brass holes. And J. Bennet, a London watchmaker, in the course of a short pamphlet published in 1830, advocated the use of a metallic alloy of his discovery‡ as giving much better results than jewelling. But in spite of these sporadic efforts to do without jewelling, it is now universally employed in high-class timekeepers, of which the chronometer is, naturally, the leading example.

The friction rollers used by some of the early makers are, of course, long obsolete. They may have been of some slight value in reducing side-friction, but were of no service where end-friction (which, in a box chronometer, kept always horizontal, is far more important) was concerned. The plan of suspension used by Le Roy was, there is no

* In "Gill's Technical Repository," Vol. IV.

† In a letter quoted in "Nicholson's Journal," 1804, p. 208.

‡ Its constituents were: Gold 31%, silver 19%, copper 40%, palladium 10%.

doubt, more effectual even than jewelling for the latter purpose, but although an absolute necessity for his heavy balance it is by no means so for the modern form. In addition, it is bulky and easily damaged.

A curious compromise between rollers and jewelling was occasionally used by Margetts. In some of his chronometers, the end-stone of the lower balance pivot is composed of a flat disc of agate, about an inch in diameter, revolved by a separate train from the great wheel at the rate of a turn in six hours. This arrangement, however, was not primarily intended to reduce the friction between the pivot and the end-stone, but to diminish, by distributing it over a much larger surface, the wear which that friction occasioned.

PLANS FOR KEEPING CHRONOMETERS AT A UNIFORM TEMPERATURE.

A plan much favoured by the smatterers who pestered the Board of Longitude with their half-baked notions was that of keeping chronometers at one uniform temperature, whereby all need for compensation was obviated. This, as previously related,* was put forward by Plank in 1714 and Palmer in 1716. It was also suggested, in 1754, by no less a person than Pierre Le Roy†, and he is remarkable for being, as far as I am aware, the only practical horologist to do so.‡

The plans for keeping a chronometer at a constant temperature put forward by these inventors, and by their successors, Germain (1777)§ and Vancouver (1823) were, theoretically, feasible, but this could not be said of similar schemes advanced by Dumbell (1799), Wilkinson (1820), and Magrath (1822). These inventors were severally inspired with the notion of obtaining a uniform temperature by immersing the chronometer in a vessel of boiling water—a plan which, like the White Knight's similar method of preserving the Menai Bridge from rust, was demonstrably absurd, as no oil would stand such treatment for more than a few minutes.

By using a combination of chronometer-oven and magazine-cooling apparatus, it would undoubtedly be possible, at the expense of a vast amount of time, trouble and material, to keep the chronometers on board a ship at a moderately constant temperature—one not varying, say, more than 1° or 2° in any climate. But even this variation would introduce, if they were left uncompensated, alterations in rate of anything up to 12 seconds per day, while if they were given compensation to correct this, there would obviously be no real necessity for the elaborate heating and cooling arrangements.

As an amusing comment on the foregoing, it may be recalled that some chronometers, specially compensated for extreme low temperatures, were supplied to Sir James Ross's abortive Franklin Relief

* It will be remembered that Le Roy also suggested, as Thacker had done before him, the method of calibrating the machine's going in various temperatures, and obtaining its error by calculation.

† See pp. 39, 41.

‡ See pp. 133, 134.

§ These dates refer to the period at which the scheme was submitted to the Board of Longitude.

Expedition, in 1848-9. On their return to Greenwich, Airy reported that they had been kept *so warm* that no opinion could be formed of the efficiency of the special compensation.

GIMBALS.

These are so simple that there has hardly been any opportunity of improving them. The French makers have used them from the earliest times. In those of Sully and Le Roy, the gimbal ring was square, or nearly so, instead of its present circular shape, while in the chronometers of Berthoud and other makers, which were wound from the top, the ring was, of course, considerably smaller than it would otherwise need to be.

English makers, for some time, lagged behind their French contemporaries in the adoption of gimbals. This may be due to the fact that Harrison had tried and abandoned them. In any case, they were entirely eschewed in the timekeepers made by Kendall* and Mudge, and in the earlier machines constructed by Arnold.

Attempts have sometimes been made to combine spiral suspension springs with the gimbal suspension, so as further to insulate the chronometer from shocks. For small vessels, in which the vibration from the engines is excessive, these may be found of considerable use. They possess the disadvantage, however, of allowing the machine to have a period of vibration which may synchronise with that of the ship's motion, and so produce large swings which affect the timekeeping. To avoid this synchronisation, the centre of gravity is arranged, in the ordinary plan of suspending chronometers, to be only just below the axis of the gimbals, in order that the machine's period of vibration may be as long as possible.

As an example of "how not to do it," an improvement in gimballing proposed by John Lowry, of Belfast, in 1875, may be instanced. To prevent the possibility of chronometers turning over in their gimbals at sea (which, with a well-made instrument, is extremely unlikely to happen, even in the worst weather and the smallest ship), he proposed to extend and enlarge the bottom of the chronometer's box, and to suspend a ball-shaped weight, by a short chain, from the bottom of the brass case. Had the chain been long enough to allow the ball to rest on the bottom of the box, some slight damping effect might have been produced if the chronometer should begin to swing: but as designed by Lowry, the ball hung quite freely, and would never have been still for an instant at sea—nor would the chronometer to which it was attached.

KULLBERG'S ELASTIC SUSPENSION.

An alternative plan, dispensing with the wooden box, was devised by Kullberg about 1885. The chronometer, in its gimbals, is suspended by means of a short rod from the end of a flat spring carried by a stiff central pillar. The plan is of interest, by reason of the proved ability of its inventor, but it argues insufficient knowledge of the conditions under which chronometers are stowed on board ship, and of the shocks to which this Christmas-tree plan would expose them.

* See, however, the footnote on p. 104.

ANTI-MAGNETIC SUSPENSIONS.

William Scoresby, the celebrated Arctic navigator, proposed, in a paper read before the Royal Society of Edinburgh in 1820,* to obviate the effects (which he considerably over-estimated) of the earth's magnetism upon a chronometer, by keeping it always in the same position with regard to the magnetic meridian. His plan, although only applicable to pocket chronometers, was quite feasible, and consisted in mounting the chronometer upon a form of compass card revolving upon a jewelled pivot†, and both counterbalanced and directed by two bar-magnets, placed sufficiently low to bring the centre of gravity of the whole well below the point of suspension, while they were not near enough to the chronometer to induce any magnetism in its balance or balance spring.

The weak point of the plan is that this or any other method of free suspension introduces an element of instability in the chronometer's rate. This was pointed out by Fisher in 1837, and appreciation of the fact led to the gradual disuse of the methods of suspending chronometers in swinging cots or tables which previously had been in considerable use.‡ Later, Lord Kelvin gave the explanation of the fact:§ which is, that the motion of the balance, in a freely suspended chronometer, sets up a corresponding motion of the whole machine. The extent of this motion bears the same proportion to that of the balance as the mass of the latter does to that of the whole machine, and its period is dependent upon the arrangement of the suspension. Kelvin showed that a chronometer suspended from a beam by two cords at diametrically opposite points of the gimbal ring could be made to go faster or slower to the extent of a minute in an hour by altering the distance between the two points at which the cords were attached to the beam. This was due to the fact that if the period of the machine's vibration were shorter than that of the balance, the combined effect of the two motions would be to shorten the time between two successive unlockings of the escapement, since the normal speed at which the balance traversed the requisite arc was increased by that of the machine. Conversely, if the period of the machine exceeded that of the balance, the time of each beat was slightly increased. For the same reason, it follows that if accurate timekeeping be required from a good watch, it is fatal to lay it down upon a smooth polished surface, as it will tend to behave as if suspended, and to gain or lose, depending upon its period of vibration.

---

* Published in the "Transactions" of that body, Vol. IX, 1823, p. 353.

† A similar suspension had been designed, some years previously, by Troughton, the celebrated instrument-maker, but not, apparently, as an anti-magnetic device.

‡ Capt. Barnett, R.N., devised a chronometer-table, with central pivot suspension (to carry four chronometers and a deck-watch) which is free from this objection, and seems to have given satisfaction. There is a description (with drawings) of it in the "Nautical Magazine," Vol. V., 1836, p. 341. It had, however, the disadvantage of exposing the chronometers to considerably increased risk of accidental shock.

§ In a paper read before the Institute of Engineers in Scotland in 1867, reprinted in Vol. II. of his "Popular Lectures and Addresses," London, 1894.

A curious case in point was reported by Admiral Wharton in 1887. A box chronometer was found, while being rated at a chronometer-depôt on shore, to vary its rate very considerably if its gimbals were locked, and tests at Greenwich showed that this was due to an oscillation set up by the going of the machine itself—just as, in the days before " Treasure Cots " were invented, children have been known to acquire the trick of rocking their own cradles. I have not been able to trace another instance of the same kind, but, as the fact in question was previously unsuspected, and its discovery in this particular case probably accidental, it is quite possible that such have, in reality, been by no means uncommon. It follows that when chronometers are rated on shore their gimbals should always be unlocked.

JOHNSON'S MAGNETIC DISPERSER.

Another plan for avoiding the effects of the earth's magnetism was patented by E. D. Johnson in 1856. His scheme provides for a separate one-day movement, entirely independent of the chronometer, installed in a corner of the box. This revolves a large rubber-covered roller, upon which, and upon two other (idle) rollers, the gimbal-ring rests. Owing to the adhesion between the ring and this roller, the former, and with it the whole movement, is caused to rotate slowly around a vertical axis.*

The complication of this arrangement, and its cost, made it a failure from the outset. Its crudity, however, is really its most remarkable point. A much simpler method of securing exactly the same result would be to fit the escapement of the machine with a tourbillon, as was done by Houriet. This would have ensured the rotation of the balance and balance spring, the only parts whose magnetisation could in any way affect the chronometer's going.

POSTSCRIPT.

In closing this chapter, it may be of interest to give a short description of the new type of chronometer recently introduced by the firm of Paul Ditisheim, which contains a number of the devices just described.

The machine, which is shown in Plate XXXVII. has, as will be noticed, a centre-seconds hand, the hours and minutes being shown on a subsidiary dial. The winding is effected by a permanently-attached button at the bottom of the case, and mechanism is provided for setting the hour and minute hands in the same manner as those of a keyless watch. In addition, the balance and escapement are mounted so as to form a complete unit, and can at any time be detached (and if necessary, replaced by duplicates) without disturbing the remainder of the mechanism. The balance is of the " integral " type, with which M. Ditisheim's name has long been associated, and the escapement of

* An account of an earlier form of this invention was published in 1842, under the title of " Johnson's Improvements in Chronometers." It also contains an account of his hermetic chronometer case, previously described. An example of both these inventions is preserved at the British Horological Institute, of which he was one of the founders.

the spring-detent pattern, beating half-seconds (although a lever escapement, beating fifths of a second, can be substituted). The machine has a going-barrel, and runs for 54 hours. Experiments are, I understand, being directed towards providing later models with a barometric compensation, consisting of a moveable cap fitting over the balance.

While, of course, extremely up-to-date, and a very fine example of modern horological development, this design is, in a way, a complete compendium of the chronometer's history. It brings together Harrison's centre-seconds hand and his provision for setting the hands, Kendall's and Cole's* dials, Le Roy's going barrel, Barraud's attached key, Breguet's method of using interchangeable parts, Ulrich's plan of detachable escapement and balance, the escapements of Earnshaw and Mudge and Hutton's auxiliary. It supplies a convincing proof, if any were needed, that the development of the chronometer is by no means finished, and that while utilising to the full the knowledge of the present-day, much may also be gained from a study of the past.

* A dial of very similar design may be seen fitted to a chronometer by J. F. Cole (1840) in the Museum of the Clockmakers' Company.

Plate XXXVII. CHRONOMETER BY PAUL DITISHEIM.
See the description of this machine on p. *343*

CHAPTER XIV.

THE MODERN CHRONOMETER.

Although a comparatively simple piece of mechanism, very little more complicated than an ordinary watch, a chronometer demands, and should receive, a definite minimum of skilled attention and careful treatment. Failing this, it cannot be expected to give results worthy of the skill which its maker has lavished on it, and it is utterly unfair to blame him for defects which are directly traceable, in almost all cases, to the neglect or indifference of the user. No chronometer ever has been, or ever will be, made foolproof, and although the modern chronometer, like the modern motor-car, will stand a very considerable amount of clumsy handling and still go, after a fashion, the fact that it does so is no guarantee that it has not been permanently impaired, or that it will not break down sooner or later—and generally sooner.

Moreover, the amount of attention required is very small, and makes but little demand upon either the time or the mind of the user. I do not suggest that he need be a skilled horologist, or that he should possess the manipulative ability of a friend of mine, who once repaired a broken mainspring in the middle of the Pacific. But he should at least know how to wind a chronometer, how to tighten up the gimbals, and how to take the movement out of the case without doing it damage. More than this is not needed at sea. As Arnold once remarked with reference to his chronometers* :

> " . . . I do not pretend that they may be used as a hammer, or that they may have a fall with impunity: though some have come back into my hands in such a condition that I was surprised they were not totally destroyed. . . . if People indulge an idle curiosity in *looking* at the movement, or let them receive a *blow*, they must run the risk themselves."

In order to provide the definite minimum of information which every chronometer-user should possess, I propose, in this chapter, to give a description of a modern chronometer, such as that shown in Plates XXXVIII. and XXXIX., together with a few notes on the correct method of handling it.

The mechanism of a typical modern chronometer of standard pattern (without auxiliary compensation), is shown in figs. 83 and 84.

For the sake of clearness, the movement (like that of the "Nuremberg Egg," shown in fig. 1, with which it is instructive to compare these figures) has been drawn as if the arbors of the various wheels were all in one plane. Actually, of course, they are arranged in a roughly circular fashion around the centre wheel. For the same reason, the shape of the plates has been made purely conventional, and the top-plate cut away as much as possible, projections being left on it to indicate the method of attaching the stop-work and the spring detent.

* In his "Answer from John Arnold to an Anonymous Letter on the Longitude," London, 1782.

The letters of reference, which are alike in both figures, are as follows :—

FRAMEWORK.

A	The pillar plate.
A′	The top-plate.
B,B	The pillars.

DRIVING POWER.

C	The mainspring barrel.
c	The mainspring barrel arbor, the top-plate end squared to allow of setting-up the mainspring.
r,r′	Ratchet and click.
f	The fusee chain.

FUSEE AND MAINTAINING POWER.

D	The fusee.
d	The fusee arbor, squared at the top-plate end to receive the winding key.
D′,d′	Ratchet wheel and click of the maintaining power.
B′	Stud carrying the stop-work.
S	Stopping-arm.
S′	Stopping-snail.
s	Stopping-arm spring.

TRAIN.

D″	The great wheel.
E	The centre wheel.
e	The centre wheel arbor.
E′	The centre wheel pinion.
G	The third wheel.
g	The third wheel arbor.
G′	The third wheel pinion.
H	The fourth wheel.
h	The fourth wheel arbor.
H′	The fourth wheel pinion.
K	The escape wheel.
k	The escape wheel arbor.
K′	The escape wheel pinion.

UP-AND-DOWN INDICATOR.

P	Pinion mounted on the fusee arbor.
p	Wheel engaging with *P*.

MOTION WORK AND HANDS.

V	The cannon pinion.
V′	The minute wheel.
X	The minute pinion.
X′	The hour wheel.
Y	The minute hand.
Z	The hour hand.

The bulk of the mechanism, particularly the action of the escapement and balance, has already been described in the foregoing chapters, but some notes on points of detail are attached.

FRAMEWORK.

The plates and pillars are of brass. The latter are rivetted into the pillar plate, and have shoulders formed at their upper ends, upon which the top-plate rests, and against which it is held by steel screws. The balance-cock and potence are secured to the top-plate in a similar

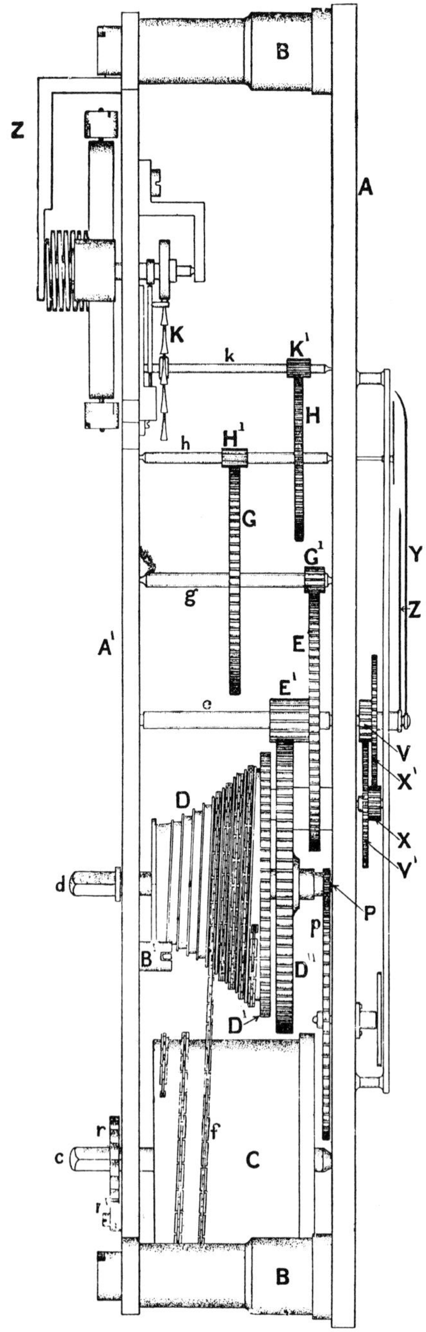

Fig. 83. Modern chronometer movement (elevation).

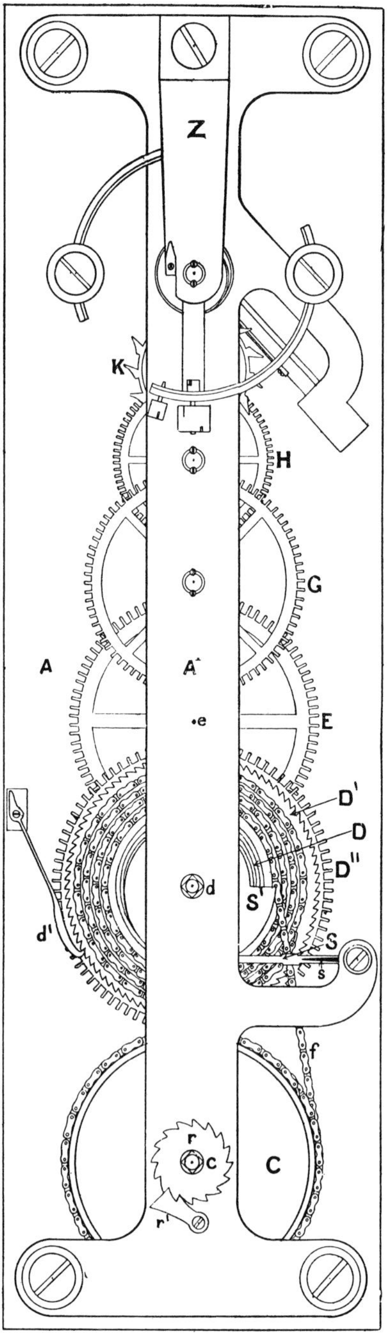

Fig. 84. Modern chronometer movement (plan).

manner by a screw apiece, while to ensure their being in absolutely correct position each is fitted with a pair of "steady-pins"—small pins rigidly fixed into them and entering holes drilled for the purpose in the top-plate.*

Where the pivot holes are jewelled, the jewels are recessed into the plate and held in place by small steel collars and screws. Those holes which are not jewelled have small "sinks," or cups, formed in the plate around the outer ends of the pivots, to retain the oil.†

DRIVING POWER.

The mainspring is, of course, of steel, hardened, tempered, and wound into a spiral. The inner end is secured to a "snailed"‡ hook on the arbor *c*, and the outer to the inner side of the barrel. The method of making the latter attachment varies. In some chronometers a hook is rigidly attached to the spring, and engages with a hole in the barrel: in others, the hole is in the end of the spring, and the hook, or stud, fixed in the barrel.§

The ratchet and click are employed to give the spring its initial tension, after which the fusee provides that the torque on the great wheel due to the further winding of the spring remains practically the same whatever the state of the winding. At first sight it might appear that, if this were the case, and *no* initial tension were applied, this torque would still be zero when the spring was fully wound. This, of course, is not the case. The slope of a correctly-cut fusee is governed by the proportion between the initial and final tensions of the mainspring, and for a spring whose initial tension was nothing the radius of its smaller end would also be nothing, and that of the larger infinity. Theoretically, a fusee should be cut to suit the particular spring used with it, but in practice its shape, and the correct initial tension, are known with quite sufficient accuracy to enable it to be cut to a standard pattern.

The arc described by the balance, of course, depends on the power reaching the escape wheel, and hence upon the initial tension of the spring. Advantage is taken of this fact to test the isochronism of the balance spring by trying the chronometer's going with a normal initial tension, and then with this reduced (by easing back the ratchet wheel) until the arc described by the balance is diminished to, say, three-quarters of a turn.¶

---

* These are universally employed for steadying the cocks, etc., in all classes of chronometers, clocks, and watches.

† Julien Le Roy (father of Pierre) has left it on record that Sully, under whom he studied (see p.144 *f*), devoted considerable attention to providing his machines with "reservoirs," containing a supply of oil sufficient for a long period of going. This idea, however, has not come into general use, principally because it has been found that the oil in the reservoir tends to dry up almost as soon as that in the pivot-holes.

‡ This hook is turned eccentrically with the arbor, so that the first turn of the spring, when fully wound, is not distorted by bearing upon the hook.

§ The latter is now the common form, being more easily fitted. For the other it is claimed, probably with truth, that the coils of the spring lie closer to the barrel, and that it gives a more uniform development of the spring.

¶ This is the method which Maskelyne should have employed (in consultation with Harrison, or Kendall) to test the isochronism of No. 4, instead of reducing the arcs by placing it with the dial vertical, and thus increasing the side-friction of the pivots.

The fusee chain is of steel, one end being hooked into a slot in the barrel, and the other to a similar slot in the large end of the fusee.

The barrel arbor is of steel.

FUSEE AND MAINTAINING POWER.

The fusee is of brass, and contains the maintaining power. The action of this has been already described (see p. 62 and fig. 13). The modern form, while exactly the same as Harrison's in principle, is much simpler, his large spiral spring being replaced by a simple steel split-ring, with ends nearly meeting, lying flat in a sink cut in the larger end of the fusee. One end of this spring is pinned to the great wheel, and the other to the ratchet wheel carried on the fusee. The pull of the fusee chain causes these ends, normally, to approach each other. When the pull of the chain is removed during the winding, the ends spring apart a little, and so urge the great wheel onwards, the ratchet wheel being prevented from turning backwards with the fusee by the click *d'*.

The action of the stop-work is as follows.

The free end of the stopping arm lies, normally, just below the plane of the stopping-snail, being retained in that position by the spring *s*, and in consequence the snail revolves without impediment during the winding. During this process, however, the chain is brought by the grooves of the fusee gradually nearer to the stopping-arm, and during the last turn of the winding the chain bears against it, overcomes the spring *s* (which is very weak), and raises the arm into the path of the snail. The radial face of the latter then meets the stopping-arm, and its further motion is thereby prevented.*

TRAIN.

The wheels are of brass, and the pinions and arbors steel. The numbers of the teeth, as shown in the figures, are as follows :—

Great Wheel	90		
Centre ,,	90	Pinion	14
Third ,,	80	,,	12
Fourth ,,	80	,,	10
Escape ,,	15	,,	10

These numbers are practically standard for all two-day chronometers. Eight-day chronometers have a higher numbered great wheel, generally 144.†

On casting up this train, it will be seen that with the balance making a complete vibration (and the escape wheel therefore advancing one tooth), every half second, the fourth wheel (which carries the second-hand) will revolve once in a minute, the third wheel in eight minutes,

* The date when this form of stop-work was invented is not precisely known, but it is nearly as old as the fusee. It is still fitted whenever the latter is employed. Many other forms have been tried, but none has been found superior.

† They have also a much lighter balance, and a proportionately weaker balance-spring.

Plate XXXVIII. TYPICAL MODERN CHRONOMETER.

The machine, which was taken at random from amongst a number at Greenwich, is a Kullberg, No. 9212.

See p. 235.

and the centre wheel (which carries the minute hand) once an hour. This train, which is the most usual one for chronometers, is known as the "14,400" train, from the balance making that number of vibrations per hour. The train used in pocket chronometers, which beat five times in two seconds, is known, for a similar reason, as the "18,000" train.

Up-and-Down Indicator.

This has already been explained in the preceding chapter.

Motion Work and Hands.

The motion work, which is practically of the same form in chronometers, clocks, and watches alike, provides for the correct relative motion of the hour and minute hands, the second-hand being mounted independently of it on an extension of the fourth-wheel arbor.

The cannon-pinion V fits friction-tight on to the centre-wheel arbor (which revolves once in an hour) and engages with the minute-wheel V', which, together with its pinion X, is mounted, and runs loosely, on a short stud screwed into the top-plate. The centre portion of the cannon-pinion is prolonged in the form of a pipe, and on this pipe there runs loosely a second pipe, to which is rigidly fixed the hour-wheel X'', engaging with the minute-pinion. The hour-hand is attached to a short slotted collet fitting friction-tight on this pipe, while the minute hand fits on to the pipe of the cannon-pinion, which is longer than the other, and projects above it. The proportions of the gearing are such that the hour hand makes one turn for the minute hand's twelve.

It is a generally received notion that it is not feasible to set a chronometer to time by moving the hands, and that this should never be attempted.* From the foregoing description, it is apparent that, as the cannon-pinion is only mounted *friction-tight* on the centre wheel arbor, from which its motion is derived, this idea is incorrect. Actually, the hands can be set in precisely the same manner as those of the old key-winding watches always were—by moving the minute hand, the centre wheel being held by the train, and the cannon-pinion slipping round on its arbor. Attention should, however, be given to the following points :—

1. The hands should always be set forwards, not backwards. The friction of the cannon-pinion on the arbor is intentionally made fairly stiff, and if the hands are turned backwards the escape wheel will tend to do the same, and damage to the detent may result.

---

* As instancing the currency of mistaken ideas of chronometer mechanism, the following experience of my own may be of interest. When undergoing instruction in navigation as a sub-lieutenant, I was solemnly assured by my officer-instructor :—

1. That the hands of a chronometer could not be set, as they were in one piece with the arbor carrying them.

2. That in winding, the key should always be pressed hard down on to the winding square, *as this started the maintaining mechanism.*

2. The turning effect should always be applied to the square formed on the collet by which the hand is mounted on the pipe of the cannon-pinion. In most chronometers, it will be found that the key fits this square. An attempt to turn the hand by pressure on its tip, or at some distance from the collet, will generally result in breaking it before the friction of the cannon-pinion is overcome.

3. For a small alteration (and, theoretically, for one of any amount), it is not necessary to touch the hour hand, since the movement of the minute hand will automatically carry it round the correct distance. If, however, the alteration be a large one (*e.g.*, if it is desired to alter a chronometer five and three-quarter hours slow on Greenwich so as to show G.M.T.), it is obviously better, in order to avoid needless slipping of the cannon-pinion, to advance the hour hand five hours, and then correct the minutes. Owing to its frictional mounting, and the "mechanical disadvantage" of its gearing, the hour hand can be moved either forwards or backwards without risk of damaging the escapement. For the same reason, the minute hand will not follow its motions.

4. No attempt should ever be made to set or to touch the second hand. This *can* be done, by setting it forwards, in the same manner as the minute hand, but there is no necessity for it, and the risk of damaging the escapement is much greater than in the case of the other hands.

It must be emphasised, however, that although there is no mechanical difficulty, if attention be given to these points, in setting the hands of a chronometer, it should be done with caution, and no more force used than is absolutely necessary. Particular attention should be given to seeing that the minute-hand is in its correct position relative to the second-hand, and similarly that the positions of the minute and hour hands agree. The former is the more important, since if with the second hand at *O*, the minute hand is left half way between two divisions, it is obvious that it is impossible to determine, when comparing the chronometer, which minute should be read (or, in the similar case of the hour hand, which hour). To ensure that the setting has been correctly done, careful comparisons should be taken with another chronometer before and afterwards.

GIMBALLING.

Although the chronometer must, of course, hang freely in its gimbals, no play beyond what is absolutely necessary should ever be allowed, and if any be present it should at once be corrected by adjusting the screws provided for that purpose.* Many cases have occurred

* In all modern chronometers the pivots of the gimbals are portions of screwed bolts, secured in place by lock-nuts, generally only finger-tight. After slackening the latter, the end-shake of the pivots can easily be adjusted by screwing them slightly in or out with a screwdriver.

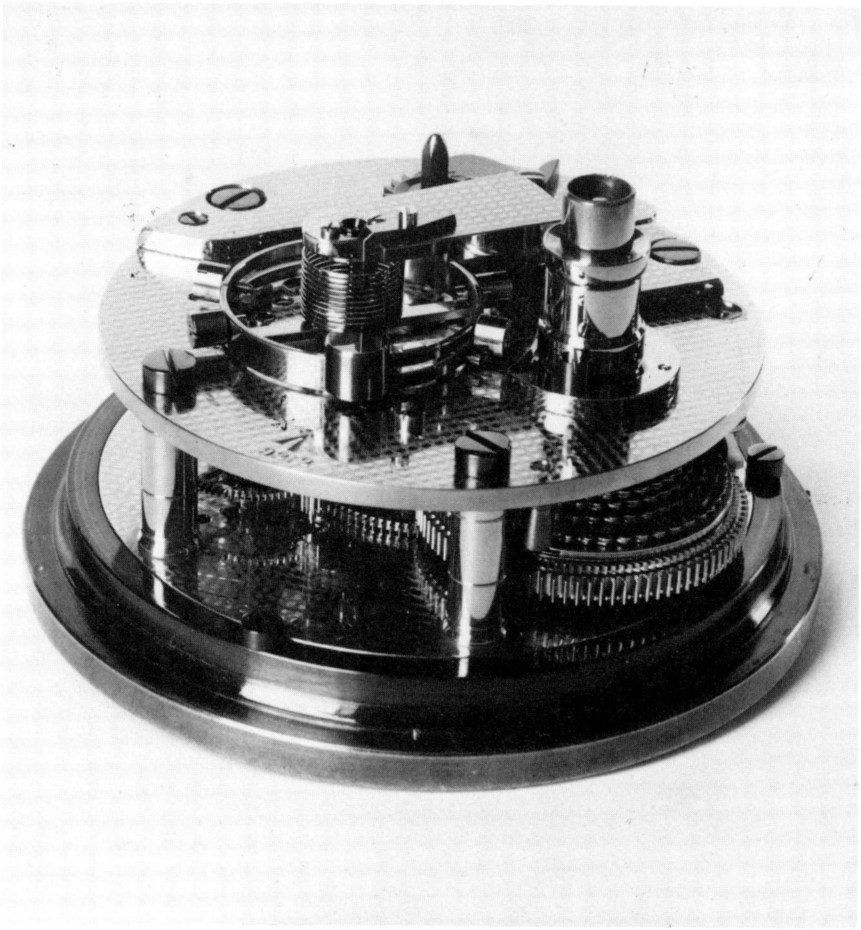

PLATE XXXIX.
Victor Kullberg chronometer No. 9212.
Purchased by the Admiralty May 1918 (£42). Lost in enemy action March 1942.

of chronometers being liable to sudden and mysterious fluctuations of rate, which have been traced to a neglect of this point.

STOWAGE OF CHRONOMETERS.

1. *General Principles.*

The description of a suitable place in which to stow chronometers on board ship is best given in a negative manner. They should *not* be stowed in any place which is

(*a*) Liable to sudden or considerable changes of temperature.
(*b*) Exposed to damp or to dust, such as coal-dust.
(*c*) At or near the ship's bow or stern.
(*d*) In the vicinity of electrical machinery, or of permanent magnets, such as compass magnets. There is no objection to the presence of twin-wire circuits.

Furthermore, they should be stowed in such a manner that, while free to swing in their gimbals, they are protected from any shocks or jars. In addition it is desirable, in order that they may easily be compared with each other, that there should be plenty of light available for reading them, and, for the same reason, that the place of their stowage should be as silent as possible.

2. *Practical Application of these Principles.*

In H.M. Ships, and in many others, the position of the chronometer room is decided, like that of the standard compass, during the building of the ship, and a special chronometer-box is provided in the selected position. In vessels where this is not done, however, the chronometers have generally to be got in where they can, but it is still possible to pay some regard to first principles. Thus a position between decks, with its reduced range of temperature, is obviously more suitable, for reasons *a* and *b*, than the upper deck. Again, by *c* a more or less amidships position is indicated, provided that it is not too near the engines or boilers. The selection of a place avoiding electrical machinery, etc., must, of course, be governed by the circumstances of each case.

As regards a chronometer-box, if none is originally fitted, one must do the best possible in the circumstances. Most chronometer-sellers can supply an outer case, holding one chronometer, which can be screwed down to a shelf. The chronometer-box supplied to H.M. Ships will hold three or more chronometers, and has an outer casing separated by a space of two inches or so from the inner portion (a solid block of wood), which latter supports a tray, divided into compartments, in which the machines are stowed, being held in place by spring packing. The outer casing has two lids, the outer of wood and the inner of glass. It is usual, before stowing the chronometers in this form of chronometer-box, to remove the lids of their own boxes* by unscrewing the hinges.

* Throughout this book, the term " case " is used to describe the inner (brass) case of a chronometer : " box," its outer wooden case ; and " chronometer-box " a special case to hold several chronometers.

This is probably the best plan of stowing chronometers, and the nearer one can get to it the better. On no account should they be stowed in a drawer, or anything else, which has to be moved before gaining access to them: nor, as explained on p. 342, should they be suspended in any way. In default of a proper chronometer-box, a locker, if one can be kept clear for them, provides the best stowage.

WINDING.

Chronometers should always be wound *daily, at one fixed time, and by the same person.* The reason of this is that during the operation of winding the machine's timekeeping is liable to vary slightly from a number of minor causes which then come into play. While face downwards, it probably will not keep exactly the same time as when face upwards; nor, when going under the influence of the maintaining spring will it go at exactly the same rate as when driven by the main-spring: while it must be remembered that however well the fusee be cut and the balance spring isochronised, differences of fractional parts of a second would appear, in the course of a normal 24 hours running, if the time taken to complete each hour were compared with the similar figure for the next hour. All these differences in time-keeping are probably minute—a matter of a small portion of a second per day—but nevertheless they exist. Now, if the winding be done by the *same* person, in the *same* manner, at the *same* time every day, the effect of these errors on a day-to-day comparison will be negligible. If, on the other hand, the chronometer be wound by different people or at different times, this will no longer necessarily be the case; in fact, it may easily happen that the errors of two consecutive days, instead of cancelling each other, produce a very perceptible difference in the daily rate.

For winding, the machine should be turned gently and firmly over by either gimbal, and steadied with the face downwards and *horizontal.* It should be remembered that a chronometer is not usually timed in any position except horizontal*, with dial up, and that while reversing it into the exactly opposite position does not materially affect its timekeeping, holding it at an angle to the horizontal may do so quite seriously. The shutter over the winding hole can now be moved, and the key pushed on to the winding square.

When winding†, always count the turns, but continue to turn on until you feel the key butt, or until you have gone at least a full turn over the number usually required. In normal circumstances, no harm can be done by turning until the stopwork comes into action—that, after all, is its *raison d'être.* It may, possibly, although this is extremely unlikely, fail either through the stopping arm being broken or through it not being lifted quite high enough to meet the stopping-

* An "inclination test" of chronometers for the French Navy was instituted in 1886. The machines were placed with locked gimbals, on a shelf inclined at 25° from the horizontal, and rated with the points XII, VI, III and IX successively lowest.

† It will be remembered that unless the key be turned in the right direction (anti-clockwise) no effect of any kind is produced upon the mechanism.

face of the snail fairly. In such a case, counting the turns affords a safeguard against the key being over-turned far enough to break the fusee-chain.

A one-day (30 hour) chronometer takes about 10 half-turns per day to wind: a two-day (54 hour) one about $7\frac{1}{2}$: and an eight-day about 4, daily. As explained on p. 325, an eight-day chronometer should be wound daily, or at most every four days.

If some precise number of turns be given, without butting the stopwork, one of two things will happen, depending upon whether the fusee turns through slightly more or slightly less than that amount in 24 hours (it is practically impossible for it to do neither, except by a daily miracle). If the former, it follows that the machine is running down, daily, a little more than it is wound up, and as soon as the extra six hours going allowed for by the maker is expended, the chronometer will one day be found stopped just before the time when it should be wound. In the opposite case, where the number of turns given in winding slightly exceeds that required to drive the machine for 24 hours, it will, of course, be wound up every day a little more than it ran down the day before, and sooner or later the stopwork will be found to butt before the usual number of turns has been completed.

When the winding is finished, the chronometer should be gently returned to its normal position, without any jerk, and without being allowed to oscillate. It should be turned back by the same gimbal as was used in reversing it. The result, for example, of turning it over by the inner gimbal, and back by the outer, is to rotate the dial through 180°, so that it ends up with the XII where the VI ought to be. If this happens, it can be returned to correct position by repeating, or reversing, the process.

STARTING.

If a chronometer be accidentally allowed to stop, the instructions generally given for starting it are to lock the gimbals, and give the whole case a quick, but not jerky, turn through about 90°, when the inertia of the balance will allow the escapement to unlock, and at the same time store up energy in the balance spring.*

This is quite a sound plan, but it is clumsy, and the chronometer has to be taken out of its stowage. A better way, which avoids this necessity, is simply to turn the movement over in the inner gimbal until the dial stands vertically, looking to the right or left, and then to rock it slightly, either backwards or forwards, by the outer gimbal.

Whichever plan be adopted, the twist should be made in one direction only, and not "there and back." The latter plan may easily result in a failure to start.

It should be added that if a chronometer which has accidentally been allowed to run down be re-started carefully, soon afterwards, there is no reason why its rate should be materially affected. On the

* Some box-chronometers of obsolete pattern, however, fitted with what would now be thought very light balances, are almost impossible to start in this manner.

other hand, if a machine has been standing idle for some time, it would be unsafe to conclude that it would retain its previous rate, and this should be re-determined before placing any reliance on such a chronometer's going.

TRANSPORTING CHRONOMETERS.

Box chronometers should never be moved about more than is absolutely necessary. It is hopeless to expect that a machine which is frequently brought on deck for comparison with a time-ball, or taken out of the ship for similar purposes, will ever give very consistent results. To avoid the necessity for doing this, all H.M. Ships are provided with a "hack-watch," which is compared both with the chronometer and with the standard of reference. Any chronometer user who is not supplied with such an auxiliary will find that the sum needed for the purchase of a good lever watch in a plain case (or, preferably, in a wooden box with a glass top) is a very sound investment.

The objection to transporting box chronometers, whether going or stopped, is that unless precautions be taken to wedge the balance (which, as described later, involves opening up the movement, and also subsequent re-starting and comparison) the relative positions of the balance and escape-wheel will be affected by any rotary motion given to the machine while carrying it. If it is stopped, this may re-start it; while, if going, it may either be stopped, or made to "trip." Actually, it is not easy, even with intention, to stop a chronometer in this manner;* but it is very easy to make it "trip" and this does not do the escapement any good, while it is fatal to any comparison which may have been taken, since the second-hand may jump forward any amount from half a second upwards.

When carrying a going chronometer from one place to another, the plan generally adopted is to reeve a strap or a handkerchief through the handles of the case, and to carry the machine with one hand, by the loop thus formed, at the full extent of the arm. Carefully done, there is no objection to this plan, but it affords a splendid opportunity for giving the machine, either accidently or through carelessness, a sudden twist, or for knocking it against an obstruction. A much better plan is to use a longer strap passing round the neck, the chronometer being carried in front of the body. In an emergency, this leaves both hands free. In either case, it is hardly necessary to say that one should walk evenly and slowly, and that the gimbals should be locked.

When taking a chronometer in a boat, or by train, the best plan is to put a coat over one's knees and rest the machine on it, steadying it with one hand. In a pulling boat, the recurrent jerk of a powerful stroke, which does the balance pivots no good, is best avoided by giving the order to "pull easy." The unseamanlike plan of pulling broken stroke is not really necessary, and may, in fact, do more harm than good.

* I do not, however, recommend the reader to experiment in this direction unless he possesses an old chronometer which he does not particularly value.

WEDGING THE BALANCE OF A CHRONOMETER.

Full instructions on this subject, which is part of the routine followed in returning Admiralty chronometers to Greenwich, are given in a leaflet issued by the Hydrographic Department. Since, however, this procedure is not often followed except in Admiralty chart depôts, they need not be repeated here *in extenso*. The following hints may, however, be useful to a chronometer user who wishes to pack a chronometer for transport.

The main points to attend to are, first of all, to secure the balance, without doing it any damage, so that it is no longer free to swing ; and, secondly, to take the weight of the movement off the gimbals.

To wedge the balance, the movement must first be taken out of its brass case. To do this, unscrew the glass over the dial, by turning it anti-clockwise, then lock the gimbals, and remove the key. Then, placing the fingers of one hand on the dial, carefully turn the whole box over, bodily, and unless the movement is a tight fit it will slide out into the hand. Ease it out very carefully, taking particular care that no part of the mechanism comes into contact with the edge of the brass case, upright the box again, and put the movement back upside down, so that the dial rests on the rim of the brass case.* If it be laid on a table, there is a risk of damaging either the hands or the balance.

If the movement is a tight fit, and does not slide out, upright the box again, unlock the gimbals, turn the movement partly over, and insert the key on to the winding square. It can then be used to start the movement slightly, after which proceed as before. On no account should any attempt be made to lift the movement out by pulling on the hands.

The balance can now be wedged by inserting two small wedges, preferably of cork, between the top-plate and the cross-bar, in or about the positions shown in fig. 85. The exact position varies in different makes, and the balance need not necessarily be at the dead-point. The following are the essentials :—

1. The positions of the wedges should be symmetrical with regard to the balance staff.
2. They should be as near to the cross-bar as possible, and the strain should be divided between the latter and the rims of the balance, close to their roots.
3. No more force should be used than is absolutely necessary to ensure that the balance is prevented from moving, and that the wedges will stay in position.
4. The wedges should not touch the timing screws, nor should they cause any twisting effect on the rims of the balance.

---

* There is generally a pin in the rim of the dial, which fits into a slot cut in the top edge of the outer case, and prevents the movement from lying flat unless the XII is in the correct position.

The balance once wedged, the movement and glass should be replaced, and the whole taken out of the gimbals, wrapped in paper, and securely packed with paper or dry cloth inside the box so that no movement is possible. Sawdust should not be used, as it may be slightly damp, and may also possibly find its way into the movement. The box should be locked, and packed securely in a hamper, or other yielding outer casing, so that any blows which the latter may receive will be absorbed without reaching the box.

The balance of a hack-watch, or a pocket-chronometer, is generally too small to allow of its being secured in this manner. To prevent it from swinging, which is about all that can be attempted, a long thin strip of dry paper should be rove through it, and secured by snapping the case to.

Comparing Chronometers.

The second-hand of a chronometer moves every half-second, takes a small fraction of a second to travel on to its new position, and waits there for the remainder of the beat. It follows, then, that the time which it indicates is only strictly correct once every half-second, and that unless some definite convention be adopted (the simplest being to regard the instant of the " tick " of each beat as the correct time)* it may be in error by anything up to half a second.

When comparing a chronometer with a standard clock, or with another chronometer, it is customary to read one dial by sight, and the other by sound. There is a slight advantage in keeping the standard times in whole units, and reading the compared chronometer to parts of a second, so that the standard should be the one read by ear. This is done by noting the instant at which it is, say, five seconds off the time selected for the comparison, and then counting the required number of its beats while looking at the chronometer which is being compared.†

As explained in the previous paragraph, the time shown by the standard clock or chronometer is only strictly correct for one instant in each beat, but if the " tick " be taken as the correct moment (and in a series of comparisons it does not in the least matter which moment is assumed, so long as it is always the same one) the chronometer which is being compared can be read to a closer accuracy than half-a-second, by estimating, mentally, the interval between its last beat and the correct moment of comparison. One or two plans have been suggested to assist this, such as beating tenths of a second with the fingers on a table, but after a little practice such artificial assistance generally becomes unnecessary.

---

* The " tick " of a chronometer is caused by the escape-wheel tooth falling upon the locking-stone of the detent. A fainter sound may also be detected upon the return swing, caused by the discharging pallet bending the passing spring.

† To distinguish between the ticks of the two machines, it is best to open the lid of the standard one, and to keep that of the other shut down.

A plan for obtaining a very exact comparison of two chronometers, recommended by the late Captain Lecky, in his deservedly world-famous "Wrinkles in Practical Navigation,"* is to employ, as an intermediary, a chronometer keeping sidereal time. The period between its beats being less than that of one keeping mean time by about $\frac{1}{365}$, the two beats will coincide about once every three minutes. Accordingly, if after comparing them to the nearest half-second, the number of beats to the next coincidence be noted, then, calling this number n, the exact difference between the two beats at the instant of comparison will be

$$\frac{n}{730} \text{ seconds.}$$

In this manner, by comparing two chronometers with a sidereal one, and combining the results, a very exact comparison can be obtained.

In practice, however, it is not very easy to determine the instant when the two beats coincide, since the difference between the sidereal and mean half-seconds is so small†. In fact, the probable error in determining the moment of coincidence is sufficient to render this method little, if at all, more accurate than a direct comparison between the two chronometers.

A modification of this plan, however, used in the "Scientific," or "Vernier" time-signals sent out by the Eiffel Tower W/T installation, provides the navigator within range of these signals with a perfectly satisfactory method of determining the error of a chronometer within $\frac{1}{100}$ second. Briefly, it is as follows:—

At pre-arranged times, the Eiffel Tower sends out a string of 300 dots, the interval between consecutive dots being approximately $\frac{49}{50}$ of a sidereal second. The 60th, 120th, 180th and 240th dots are omitted to facilitate the division of the series. By listening simultaneously to the dots and to the beats of a chronometer, coincidences will be found to occur at approximately every 22 secs. (G.M.T.) The time of each coincidence should be noted.

On the conclusion of the series of dots, the Tower sends out the Greenwich Sidereal Time of the first and last dot. The interval, i, between consecutive dots should then be calculated by dividing the difference by 299‡. The method previously indicated can then be

* I may, perhaps, be pardoned for saying that, personally, I much prefer the editions of "Wrinkles" published in its author's lifetime to those which have appeared subsequently. To my mind, the additions made by other hands are not quite on the same level as the rest of the book, while the chapter relating to the gyro-compass contains several inaccuracies, among them being the extraordinary statement that a bicycle is kept upright by the gyroscopic action of its wheels.

† From the description of the "Vernier" signals given in a later paragraph, it will be apparent that the greater the interval between coincidences the greater the (theoretical) degree of accuracy, but the greater, also, the practical difficulty of determining the moment of coincidence. The gaining rate of one in fifty used in the latter plan is probably the best compromise between theory and practice.

‡ The rate of the "sending" clock, by which the intervals between the dots are controlled, varies slightly from day to day, although it is constant for any particular series.

used for calculating the fractional part of half a second between the chronometer and standard time at the moment of each comparison, the formula now becoming

$$\text{Difference} = \frac{n}{2i} \text{ seconds.}$$

The term "Vernier" signals is derived from the fact that this plan is precisely analogous to the use of a Vernier, as in the sextant, to measure small portions of a unit of length.

The Eiffel Tower, in common with many other W/T stations in all parts of the world, also sends out ordinary W/T time-signals giving hours, minutes and seconds of G.M.T.* This accuracy is sufficient for all ordinary purposes of navigation.

Purchasing a Chronometer.

Broadly speaking, it may be said that if one buys a new chronometer there is very little chance of making a bad bargain. The worst modern chronometer is capable, if carefully treated, of giving results which would greatly astonish the early makers. On the other hand, the amount charged for a good chronometer by a well-known maker is money well spent. Second-hand chronometers, like second-hand sextants, should be avoided, unless the seller can show a register of a good performance, under strenuous conditions of test, made *recently* by an independent authority. In any case, even with a new machine, it is best to obtain this if possible. A good maker, with a reputation to lose, will never send out a badly adjusted instrument. The "shop-tician," on the other hand, is by no means so particular.

I must here take note of a passage in Lecky's "Wrinkles," from which, with all the respect due to one who was an absolute master of his craft, I must totally dissent. In the chapter devoted to the chronometer, which, as a whole, is a most valuable one, appears the following :—

> " . . . Experience has proved that chronometers with the words 'Auxiliary Compensation' engraved upon their face, are not one whit better than those fitted with the ordinary balance. Without this knowledge, a purchaser of one of these instruments might fancy he was getting something 'very special' . . ."

It might just as well be said that because a sounding sextant, whose arc is divided to minutes only, is capable of taking observations with sufficient accuracy for the purposes of navigation, it is therefore a waste of money to get one with a Kew certificate. The auxiliary compensations now fitted in modern chronometers are entirely adequate, in point of strength, for the purpose of withstanding all *fair* usage which they may receive at sea, while of the increased accuracy in timekeeping which they afford there can be no question. It may be pointed out that amongst the chronometers selected annually by the Admiralty from those obtaining a high position in the

* A list of these stations, and also a fuller explanation of the "Vernier" time-signals, will be found in the "Admiralty List of Wireless Signals."

Greenwich trials (which are, in consequence, the pick of the market), there has hardly been, for many years, one which was not fitted with some form of auxiliary compensation.* The subsequent going of these chronometers, as recorded in the chronometer journals of H.M. Ships, affords the best possible proof, if any were needed, of the fact that auxiliary compensations, as a class, are not in any way deficient in robustness. By using Hartnup's method (see p. 297), most excellent results can be obtained with chronometers of ordinary pattern, but the scientific navigator, who is not satisfied with a good instrument when a better is obtainable, will always bear in mind that a chronometer possessing auxiliary compensation (which in itself is the hall-mark of a first-class instrument, since it would be absurd to fit such a device to any other) must always possess, *per se*, an advantage over one not so fitted.

CLEANING.

Chronometers should be cleaned, preferably by the maker, at intervals not exceeding four years. As explained on p. 352, the best oil will, in time, coagulate, and the result of running a chronometer too long without lubrication (for that is what an undue period of service connotes) is that the pivots and jewel-holes wear badly, while the timekeeping of the machine deteriorates noticeably. A chronometer which has run, say, eight years without cleaning may as well be scrapped—the expense of re-pivoting and re-jewelling would be out of all proportion to its future value.

THE FUTURE OF THE CHRONOMETER.

It is sometimes said, and with, at first sight, some show of reason, that the advent of W/T, and W/T time-signals, has sounded the death-knell of the chronometer, as the latter did that of the "lunar." That this is a mistaken impression I hope to show.

As pointed out in the Introduction, the determination of longitude at sea depends upon knowing, simultaneously, the ship's local time (which must, in all cases, be obtained by observations taken on board), and that of some standard meridian. The "lunar" provided a difficult and delicate means of obtaining this by direct astronomical observations. The chronometer gives the same information by carrying on to the ship's present position a standard of time previously obtained when in port. W/T affords a method of obtaining that standard *direct*. The possible error of a small fraction of a second involved in the use of a W/T time-signal is infinitesimal in comparison with the much larger one to which even the best chronometer is liable in the course of a long voyage.

So far, so good. But one important factor in the problem must not be lost sight of. The standard of time afforded by a W/T time-signal is only correct *at the time when that signal is made*. Now, the observations taken on board ship to determine local time must be

* The only exceptions have been a few chronometers fitted with palladium balance-springs.

taken when the conditions are favourable—that is to say, one cannot rely upon making them at the instant when the signal is received—and accordingly some means must be provided of carrying on the time of the signal to that of the observation, or vice versa. In other words, *one must still have a reliable marine timekeeper.*

And so we come back to the old problem which the chronometer has solved—how to keep accurate time at sea. As a *fundamental* method of determining longitudes, there can be no doubt that the chronometer has had its day, and must yield the palm to its younger and more accurate rival. The old method of laboriously transporting a number of chronometers from place to place, and of weighting and balancing their divergent indications,* is obsolete, and must be gathered to the limbo of the three-decker (but not, *pace* Sir Percy Scott, the battleship), fluxions, phlogiston, astrology, the Ptolemaic astronomy, Aristotle's categories, and many other highly-organised systems which have once filled an important place in human progress, but which have been, one by one, discarded for newer, simpler, and better substitutes. A similar fate, one day, is probably in store for the chronometer as a means of finding longitude at sea. When it comes, there need be no repining, for nothing is permanent, and nothing is indispensable. But whenever it comes, and I have given my reasons for thinking that it will not come so long as men go down to the sea in ships, it will close the history of one of the most determined and successful attempts to solve a mechanical difficulty that Man has ever made.

"Let those who have read to the end, pardon a hundred blemishes."

---

* The errors to which the most accurate and laborious determinations of longitude by this plan were liable are well shown in the case of the chain of meridian distances which the "Beagle" carried completely round the world in 1833-7. Although each link in the chain was based upon apparently faultless determinations by a number of chronometers, the total of all of them, which should, of course, have been 24 hours, was no less than 33 seconds in excess. Other excellent instances are afforded by the published results of Tiarks' determination of the longitude of Falmouth (mean of 16 chronometers) in 1823, and Airy's of Valentia (mean of 30 chronometers) in 1844. A full account of the methods in vogue until recently will be found in Admiral Shadwell's "Notes on the Management of Chronometers," published in 1855.

M. Paul Ditisheim has recently performed some wonderful feats in the way of obtaining longitude by transport of his lever watches. A notable example is the Greenwich-Paris difference of longitude, which he determined to a very high degree of accuracy, the watches being carried from Greenwich to Paris, and vice versa, by aeroplane. But such a feat is in the nature of a *tour de force*, and M. Ditisheim himself does not claim that the accuracy obtainable is equal, in general, to that of a W/T determination.

APPENDIX I.

CHRONOMETER TRIALS AT THE ROYAL OBSERVATORY, GREENWICH.

APPENDIX I.

CHRONOMETER TRIALS AT THE ROYAL OBSERVATORY, GREENWICH.

The connection of Greenwich Observatory with chronometers dates from the year 1766, when, as explained in chapter IV., the Board of Longitude sent Harrison's four timekeepers there to be tried under the supervision of the Rev. Nevil Maskelyne, Astronomer-Royal. The precedent thus set has continued to be followed up to the present day.

Many circumstances combined, at the time of this first trial, to make Greenwich by far the most suitable place which the Board could have selected. In order to obtain an accurate standard of time, it was necessary that the trial should be held at an observatory, while it was desirable, in view of the large rewards then on offer to chronometer makers, that the person in charge of the trial should hold an official position—and it was also expedient that he should be a member of the Board. As Maskelyne himself stated,*

> "I acknowledge that I am, from my situation at the Royal Observatory, the proper person to try these timekeepers, and I will add, that I had a hand, as one of the Committee of the Board, who drew up the sketch of particulars, which, through the recommendations of the Board, were afterwards inserted in the Act of the 14th of his present Majesty, in imposing this painful task on myself and my successors in office, for it was not so ordered in the Act of 12th Queen Ann: and that the reasons of the Committee for it, in which I heartily concurred, were to render the trial more accurate and authentic than it could be if conducted by any private person.
>
> "The excellence of the instruments at the Royal Observatory, and the frequent observations of the transits of the heavenly bodies over the meridian, made there in the usual course of business, will always render the rate of going of the Observatory-clock better known than can be expected of the clock in most other places. The astronomer royal is further allowed an assistant by government, and there is always one of them, at least, in attendance upon the observations, and consequently ready to wind up the time-keeper at a stated time every day, and compare it with the transit clock; so that there will never be any occasion to let the watch run down, or leave it in the care of the maker, or any person employed as his agent, which would be making him judge in his own cause. Moreover, the person intrusted by the public with the charge of the Royal Observatory, from his experience in various nice calculations, which arise out of his observations, and must necessarily be made to adapt them to useful purposes, may be presumed better qualified than most other persons to make accurate calculations of the going of the watch, and to draw proper inferences as to its fitness or unfitness to keep time in intervals of long duration."

* "An Answer to a Pamphlet, entitled 'A Narrative of Facts,' lately published by Mr. Thomas Mudge, Junior." London, 1792. (p. iii., iv.).

S

In the main, these remarks are perfectly correct, but it must be pointed out that in the records of the early trials at Greenwich many instances appear of the machines running down through their winding having been forgotten, while with regard to the selection of a method of valuing the results, Maskelyne, with all his presumptive fitness for this, fixed, at the start, upon an extremely bad one, and could not, for many years, be persuaded to discard it.

The earliest trials of Harrison's No. 4 had been made at sea, and, as chronometers are designed for use there, it might at first sight be thought that this was the correct way to try them. The difficulty was, of course, that it involved a vicious circle, since the ship's longitude, when out of sight of land, could only be found by the chronometer, while the error of the latter could not be determined until the longitude was known. Accordingly, a sea voyage could only give the error of the chronometer at a few scattered points, separated by long intervals both of time and space. In order to obtain some idea of the machine's behaviour from day to day, and of the action of its compensation, it was therefore necessary to try it on shore.*

But the result of even a shore trial was only a string of daily comparisons with a standard clock, and at first sight it was not easy to see how best to treat these observations. Should the daily, weekly, or monthly rate be taken? Should the machine be made to afford its own standard of going, by taking a mean of all its errors during the trial? Was a machine whose going gradually accelerated or retarded a better or a worse timekeeper than one which alternately gained and lost? Last, and most important, if a period were to be selected as setting the standard of what the machine's going ought to be for a subsequent period, what proportion should the lengths of the two periods bear to each other?

At the present day, of course, it is easier to answer these questions than it was then. The crux of the whole matter is this:—The best chronometer is that which changes its rate *least* and *slowest*. No machine has ever been made to keep exact time, and no machine ever had an unchanging rate. Its excellence or otherwise as a timekeeper is determined by consideration of how much its rate alters, and how often. To put the matter in the aphoristic and obscure fashion affected by the mediæval schoolmen,† the deciding factor is "rate of change of rate."

Maskelyne decided that he would take as his standard the first month of any machine's going, and obtain the daily rate which it ought to keep in future months by dividing its total error in that first

---

* Chronometers could now be tried at sea without difficulty, daily comparisons with a standard being obtained by W/T time-signals. Halley, shortly before his death in 1742, proposed a somewhat similar plan of putting them in a vessel anchored in the Downs, and obtaining a standard of time by visual signals, from a clock on shore.

† And by modern publicists.

month by the number of days contained in it. Then, at any future time, the difference between the time indicated by the machine and the time which, on this theory, it ought to be showing, was its error.

By this method, of course, no benefit could be derived from any information gained, during the trial, as to what the chronometer's rate was actually doing, and what it might be expected to do. The longer such a trial proceeded, the worse the machine's timekeeping would apparently become, although it might actually have improved considerably.

At this time, and, indeed, much later, there was a good deal of confusion of thought, even amongst men who had studied the subject, as to what was the best method of obtaining a mean daily rate, and how it should be used if obtained.* And thus, while there were many critics ready to point out the defects of "Maskelyne's method," there was none who put forward a better one. For example, Thomas Mudge the younger, in his "Narrative of Facts," proposed that instead of taking the going of the first month in a year's trial as a standard for all subsequent periods of six months, the going of the first six months should be the standard for that of the second. This was open to the obvious objection that the errors of going in the two periods might, and probably would be, pretty considerable, and yet happen to balance each other, also, that a six month's rating-test before each voyage was impracticable from a commercial point of view.

The younger Mudge also proposed two other methods, either to take the mean of the greatest and least daily rates in the course of a year's going as the mean daily rate, or to assume the latter to be the result of dividing the machine's total error in the year by 365. To these proposals, Maskelyne rejoins :—

> " . . . The first method seems preposterous, to take so important an element of the calculation from the two worst goings of all, especially if it be considered that an error of only one second in the assumed daily rate will produce an error of three minutes in the computed going of the watch for six months.
>
> " The last method is very favourable to himself, because let the watch go ever so ill, it will just take off half the error. Both methods are liable to this insuperable objection, that they are impracticable in the case of a sea voyage, because the proposed rate could not be known till the voyage was over, and consequently could be of no use in the voyage."

Mudge's friend and patron, Count Bruhl, also plunged into the fray, and wrote an article entitled "A Short Explanation of the most proper methods of calculating a Mean Daily Rate," which was published as an appendix to Mudge's "Reply to the Answer . . . "† Bruhl endorses the second method proposed by Mudge, but obtains his mean rate by taking the arithmetical mean of either the extreme

* See, for example, the report of the Committee on Mudge's petition for reward (1793).

† See p. 121*f*.

variations of rate, or of all of them combined. He illustrates his proposals with some numerical examples.*

Maskelyne's method was used at Greenwich until the last trial of Earnshaw's chronometers, competing for the £10,000 reward, in 1802. Earnshaw, as related in chap. VIII. stood up for his rights, and succeeded in proving indisputably that Maskelyne's method was too onerous, as in a year's trial it held the machines to their original rates for twelve months, while the Act only prescribed six. He succeeded in inducing the Board to adopt his proposed improvement of judging the going of his chronometers in any period of six months by the standard of their going in the month immediately preceding that period. Some of his comments are amusing :†

> " . . . after the second trial, when I was called to the Board, Sir Joseph Banks informed me that my method would not be allowed by them ! From this I naturally concluded that my timekeepers were to be adjudged by Dr. Maskelyne's method, which the Board had always used, and I altered my timekeepers accordingly. Now after this alteration, in this their last trial, my timekeepers, according to Dr. Maskelyne's method, were within the act, as the greatest error of No. 1, is 3′44″72, and No. 2, 3′7″93 ; both under four minutes. I wrote to the Board to allow this, which was likewise refused.
>
> " If any one asks me what it is these gentlemen want, it is my duty to inform them if possible ; I was informed that a member of the Board said, he thought that timekeepers should be correct enough to be within the limits of the act in every method. *God bless us with patience !* This puts me in mind of a countryman coming from the west, and was angry with his watch because it did not agree with every clock he came to ; just as absurd is it to expect my timekeepers to agree with every method, for there can be but one right method, in course every other must be wrong ; and if the member who made such an expression cannot see this, and the great difficulty, and illegality of holding a watch to its rate for twelve months, instead of for six months, then it is of little use to lay reason before him."

However, the irony of fate decreed that Earnshaw's method, although its advantage over Maskelyne's was admitted,‡ should only be adopted in one instance—and that its use on this one occasion, in preference to its rival, should cost its author £7,000. In later trials, it was superseded by better methods, which will now be described.

---

* Containing numerous errors. Bruhl was apparently cursed with an inability to correct his proofs, and he never succeeded in printing a page of calculations that did not contain numerous mistakes. In a " Table of Errata " printed for use with his " Three registers of a pocket chronometer made by Mr. Thomas (sic) Emery," he remarks " A Report having lately been circulated, intimating that my printed Registers of the Pocket Chronometer were full of gross arithmetical errors . . . I take this method of declaring . . . that the mistakes alluded to in the Registers are, most of them, only the usual and almost unavoidable errors of the press, which, by carefully comparing the printed pages with the original manuscript, I have ascertained . . . " after which he goes on to print upwards of six hundred corrections ! The unconscious humour of this proceeding is only excelled by Pope Sixtus the fifth's famous edition of the Vulgate, which, although swarming with misprints, was prefaced by a Bull excommunicating any printer who altered the text !

† " Longitude," p. 109.

‡ Even by Maskeleyne, who expressly retracted his former views in his reply to Banks' " Protest." (See p. 205.)

The chronometer trials at Greenwich divide naturally into three periods. There is, first of all, that of the early trials, 1766-1802. These were made principally for the Board of Longitude, to test the going of chronometers competing for the great rewards.

Secondly there is the period of the " premium " trials, 1823-1835.

Thirdly, there is the period 1840-1914, during which time annual trials have been carried out at the Observatory in a manner which has remained practically unaltered since their institution.

In the early trials, as previously stated, Maskelyne's method of estimating the accuracy of a chronometer was employed. This was superseded, in the " premium " trials, by the method of obtaining a " Trial Number," based upon the monthly rates. This number, whose amount determined the positions of the machines in order of merit, was found by taking the difference of the greatest and least mean monthly rates, and adding the mean of the extreme variations of daily rate in each month.*

In the last series of trials, a modification of this plan appears,† introduced by Airy, and is still in force. The " trial number is obtained as the result of taking the weekly sums of the daily rates, and evaluating the formula $a + 2b$, where a is the difference between the greatest and least weekly sums, and b is the greatest difference between the sums of two consecutive weeks.

Airy's explanation‡ of the causes which led to the adoption of this particular formula is as follows:

> " . . . This principle has been adopted as well suited to the wants of the royal navy, but may not be so well suited to every other conceivable case.
>
> " Chronometer rates are subject to irregularities of two distinct kinds. One is the irregularity from week to week; this may be supposed to arise from inferior workmanship; it is important in short voyages, but not very important in long voyages except it grows up into the other irregularity. The other is the irregularity in long periods; this will usually arise from defect in compensation, or from change in the state of the oil, combined with want of isochronism; it is injurious in long voyages, and unimportant in short voyages.
>
> " The relative importance of these two classes depends therefore upon the service in which the chronometers are likely to be used. For the general service of the royal navy the different weights are given to the different classes of errors in the proportion . . . described."

In working out trial numbers by means of this formula, the weekly sum of the daily rates is taken as their *algebraical* sum, and accordingly it is possible for a machine which alternately gains and loses to have, apparently, a very small rate. But this is inevitable, and it does not affect the accuracy of the information afforded by this method.

---

* Hence, of course, the smaller the number, the better the chronometer.

† A very complicated formula, devised by Dr. Thomas Young (Author of the undulatory theory of light), who was Secretary to the Board of Longitude from 1822 to its dissolution in 1828, seems to have been used occasionally soon after the " premium " trials were discontinued.

‡ " Horological Journal," vol. V., p. 47.

It may be added that to plot the rate of a chronometer graphically is often an excellent means of forecasting its future performance. This, after all, is the main object of all chronometer-rating, to prophesy, by means of the information which comparison of the machine's going with some standard affords, what that going will be when the standard is no longer available.

In order to bring the results of the early and "premium" trials into line, as far as possible, with those of more modern trials, the recorded going of the machines in these trials, has been re-computed, and $a + 2b$ obtained for each machine. The comparison is still, of course, vitiated to a certain extent by the fact that until 1849 there was no oven-test* (the machines being only tried in natural temperatures), and also by the fact that while the duration of the later trials was uniformly 29 weeks, that of both the earlier series was generally a year and upwards. However, it is thought that the present tabulated results of the three series of trials, giving $(a + 2b)$ for every machine as determined from a period of 29 weeks going, may at least serve to some extent as an indication of how much chronometer-making has progressed during the period 1766-1914.

It may also serve as a corrective to the effects of such brilliant romances as the following account of the Greenwich trials which appeared in "Tit-Bits" a few years ago.

> ". . . On certain occasions there is a complete trial of chronometers open to all makers who have sufficient confidence in their watches.
>
> "During the competition the watches are exposed to every possible variation of temperature. They are baked in furnaces sufficiently hot to cook a joint. In fact, so great is the heat that a badly-made watch has been known to tumble to pieces during the baking test. The moment a watch is taken out of the oven it is plunged into mixtures registering forty degrees of frost.
>
> "To such perfection has the manufacture of chronometers attained that even the most stringent tests fail to cause the slightest variation."

"Maker to the Admiralty."

It may be noted that the purchase by the Admiralty, as the result of a competitive trial or otherwise, of a chronometer or watch is generally regarded as entitling the vendor to assume, if he wishes, the title "Maker to the Admiralty," whether he actually constructed the machine in question or not. This point was amusingly illustrated in a trade dispute over the right to use the name "John Forrest, maker to the Admiralty," tried in the High Court in 1891. In the course of the action, evidence was given to show that Forrest, who died in 1871, had never made a chronometer in his life. Yet such is the persistency of tradition that letters addressed to him are occasionally received at the Admiralty to-day.

---

* Between 1840 and 1848, however, a maker could have his chronometers tried in specially severe temperatures at his own request. After 1848 the oven test (exposure for six weeks to a temperature ranging from 75° to 100° Fahr.) was made compulsory.

A refrigerator for testing chronometers at low temperatures has recently been installed at the Observatory. As with the oven, care is taken that the fabric of the chronometers cannot be injured in any way during their exposure to extremes of temperatures.

The Early Trials.

The trial numbers given in the following table have been computed from the MS. records at Greenwich, the selection of a period of 29 weeks being governed by the circumstances of each case. The period is always a continuous one.

The range of temperature may be taken, except in the case of Harrison's No. 4, as 40°-70° Fahr.

The trial numbers have been calculated from the formula $(a + 2b)$.

Machine	Period of Trial	a	b	Trial No.
Harrison No. 1	7.11.66 to 1.6.67	668·0	235·5	1139·0
Harrison No. 2	4.11.66 to 25.5.67	289·5	200·7	690·9
Harrison No. 3	9.10.66 to 7.1.67	58·5	36·0	130·5
	3.2.67 to 25.5.67	290·8	68·9	428·6
Harrison No. 4	7.7.66 to 22.3.67	59·8	32·3	124·4
Kendall No. 1	3.5.70 to 22.11.70	82·0	28·0	138·0
Kendall No. 2	12.9.72 to 10.3.73	57·0	49·0	155·0
Mudge No. 1	8.4.77 to 29.10.77	5·97	2·88	11·73
Arnold No. 36	29.3.79 to 31.10.79	21·17	11·87	44·91
Mudge "Green"	29.6.89 to 17.1.90	31·46	13·33	58·12
Mudge "Blue"	28.6.89 to 17.1.90	22·87	8·41	39·39
Earnshaw No. 1	27.3.00 to 15.10.00	14·95	5·31	25·57
Earnshaw No. 2	27.3.00 to 15.10.00	17·18	6·62	30·42

NOTES ON THE FOREGOING TABLE.

Harrison's No. 1.

This machine was upwards of thirty years old at the time of the trial, and had been going continuously since its completion. It had suffered a severe fall about six months before the start of the trial, and Harrison had not been given any opportunity of repairing or overhauling it, this being entrusted to Larcum Kendall, who had no special knowledge of its design or construction. In the circumstances, its phenomenally high trial number is not surprising. William Harrison is, however, recorded as having said that it was "by far the most imperfect" of the first three machines made by his father.

The actual length of the trial was 30 weeks. The first has been discarded.

Harrison's No. 2.

This machine, like the previous one, was almost 30 years old at the time of the trial, having been completed in 1739.

The actual length of the trial was one year, of which the first 23 weeks have been discarded.

Harrison's No. 3.

This machine was completed in 1757, having taken about 18 years to con struct. It is impossible to obtain an unbroken period of 29 weeks going, as it stopped half way through its trial (1.10.66 to 25.5.67), and was not re-started until a fortnight later, when it showed a very pronounced acceleration of its daily rate. Two trial numbers have therefore been computed for periods of 13 weeks before, and 16 weeks after, the stoppage.

It should be noted that Nos. 2 and 3 also received rough handling during removal from Harrison's house to the Observatory.

Harrison's No. 4.

The complete trial of this machine lasted for 37 weeks. I have discarded the first week (in which the machine may be presumed to have been settling down after its trials in positions), and the 24th to the 30th inclusive, in which the temperature fell below 40°, a degree of cold which, as Harrison pointed out, its compensation was not designed to encounter.

As pointed out on p. 89*f*, the upper thermometer readings are much below the truth. The range of temperature during the trial was probably 80°

Kendall No. 1.

The length of the complete trial from which this period is taken was 10 months, after which the machine stopped in extreme cold (35° Fahr.) through the detent of the remontoire failing to unlock. K1 was also tried for a month in 1775, prior to being cleaned after its return from Cook's second voyage.

The present period begins one month after the start of the first trial.

Kendall No. 2.

The trial of this machine lasted a year (May, 1772, to May, 1773). The present period commences at the fifth month.

Mudge No. 1

See the remarks at the head of Appendix II.

Arnold No. 36.

As mentioned on p. 177 this was a pocket chronometer, with pivoted detent escapement and compensation balance (all the previous machines were fitted with compensation curbs). The official trial lasted for 13 months, and was extended, unofficially, to eighteen. The present period begins with the second month, at the close of the tests in positions.

No record of the thermometer readings appears to have been preserved.

Mudge "Green" and "Blue."

These periods are simultaneous, and are taken from the last of the three trials of these machines, beginning a week from the start. In the 31st week of the trial both machines were carelessly allowed to stop, and subsequently re-started.

Earnshaw No. 1 *and No.* 2.

Like the preceding, these periods are simultaneous, being taken from the second half of the second trial of these machines for the £10,000 reward. The results may be taken as favourable examples of the going of these two machines.

It may be noted that the standard of performance required to comply with the requirements of the Act sanctioning the payment of the £10,000 reward would, at the present day, correspond, roughly speaking, to a trial number of 16 or thereabouts.

Each of the three trials lasting a year, it is possible, without serious overlapping of the periods, to obtain six trial numbers for each machine, and such were published in the "Horological Journal" for April, 1874. None of them agrees with my figures, those for the two periods given above being respectively 20.4 for No. 1, and 33.5 for No. 2, the period adopted being given as 29 weeks, although actually 28. After careful revision, I am satisfied that the trial numbers now published are correct.

The "Premium" Trials, 1823-1835.

These trials were instituted by the Admiralty with the object of improving the quality of the chronometers purchased for the Navy. With this end in view, premiums of £300, £200 and £100, were offered for the first, second and third machines in a trial of twelve months duration, the order of merit being determined by "trial numbers" calculated as explained below. The first premium was not to be awarded if the winner's trial number exceeded 6 seconds, nor the second, if it exceeded 10. In the seventh and succeeding trials, the total of the premiums (500) remained the same, but it was divided into sums of £200, £170 and £130, the respective trials numbers necessary for their award being 5, 6 and 7½.

The following example shows the calculation of the trial numbers. It is of interest, since the going of the chronometer in question was long regarded as being almost unapproachable, although it corresponds to what would now be thought quite a high trial number (18·0).

1829 Trial. Dent 114 (Winner of first premium).

	Mean Rate.	Extreme Variation.
1829—August	3·43	0·7
September	3·85	1·7
October	3·73	0·8
November	3·87	0·9
December	3·93	1·2
1830—January	3·59	1·4
February	3·59	1·1
March	3·74	1·6
April	3·60	1·1
May	3·58	1·4
June	3·77	0·8
July	3·97	1·6

Greatest difference of mean monthly rates	0·54 sec.
Mean of extreme variations	1·19 „
Add	0·54 „
Trial Number	2·27 sec.

These trials were discontinued in 1835, as no useful purpose appeared likely to be served by continuing them. No marked improvement had been shown, nor any new invention or discovery brought to light. Moreover, it had become apparent that the share taken by various makers in the construction and adjustment of the chronometers which they had entered had been limited to engraving their names on them.* In the 1833 trial the third premium was originally awarded to a chronometer entered, and presumably made by R. Webster, but on the top-plate of which the partly-erased name of "Frodsham" was discovered. In consequence, the premium fell to Molyneux.

To such a pitch, indeed, did matters come, that the Admiralty were compelled to request each entrant to sign the following declaration :—

> "I do hereby declare, to the truth of which I am ready to make oath if required.
>
> "*First*,—I am a chronometer Maker, and carry on at present the business thereof.
>
> "*Secondly*,—I declare that the chronometer, or chronometers' number as prefixed to my signature, is, or are, solely my own property; and that no other maker's name is engraven on any part of the Machine; and I further declare, that I have no concern, either directly or indirectly, with any other Chronometer deposited, or intended to be deposited on the trial now commencing."

At the conclusion of the last trial, that of 1835, the makers of the two first machines both refused to sign this declaration, and the premium accordingly went to the third machine's maker. When discontinuing the "premium" system, the Admiralty, as stated on p. 286, announced that rewards would still be given for further improvements in chronometers, and this was re-affirmed in a circular issued to the trade in 1862, which announced that in future honorary prices would be given by the Admiralty for the first two or first three chronometers in the annual Greenwich trials, provided that a certain standard of merit were obtained. It will be remembered that a similar plan had been adopted in Loseby's case. It has also been tried in France.

With the same end in view, the Clockmakers' Company instituted, in 1880, a series of money prizes for the makers of the first two chronometers in the annual trials.

The trial numbers given in the following table have been calculated from the printed reports of the "premium" trials, the period of 29 weeks comprising the first half of the trial.

The trial numbers have been calculated from the formula $(a + 2b)$.

---

* Or covering up another maker's. Witness the following memorandum, issued from the Observatory on August 10th, 1829.

> "In addition to the Circular of the 1st instant, the Makers are requested to take notice, that no Chronometer will be received in future, on the public trials, excepting the Maker's name is engraven on the Dial-plate itself, and not on a Slip of Brass screwed thereon. And each Maker will be requested to certify that no other Maker's Name is engraven on any other part of the Machine."

Year	Maker and No. of Machine	Prize	a.	b.	a+2b.
1822	* Barraud, 957	£300	24·7	7·7	40·1
1823	§ Murray, 816	£300	8·2	5·3	18·8
1824	† Widenham, 929	£300	13·2	6·0	25·2
1825	‡. French, 20/912	£300	8·5	6·0	20·5
1826	M'Cabe, 167	£300	18·8	7·7	34·2
1827	** Guy, 1410	£300	17·6	9·9	37·4
1828	¶ Dent, 114	£200	7·2	5·4	18·0
1829	‡ Baker, 865	£200	9·8	3·8	17·4
1831	Cottrell, 311	£200	7·8	4·9	17·6
1832	Molyneux, 1038	£200	6·7	2·8	12·3
1833	— Appleton, 145	£170	8·1	4·9	17·9
1834	‖ Carter, 144	£130	9·2	4·4	18·0
1835	‖. Carter, 160	£130	12·4	7·0	26·4

THE ANNUAL TRIALS AT GREENWICH, 1844-1914.

These trials, even at their inception, were practically on the same lines as those of recent years: that is to say, the period of the trial was 29 weeks, and the figure of merit for each machine was obtained by means of the formula $(a+2b)$, previously explained. The only differences were that until 1848 there was no oven-test, and that until permission to enter for the trial had to be obtained from the Hydrographer of the Navy, instead of from the Astronomer-Royal as at present.

* During this trial the machines were sent on a voyage to Madeira and back. The period during which the chronometer was absent from the Royal Observatory has been disregarded.

§ During this trial sixteen of the chronometers, including Murray 816, were transported by sea from Greenwich to Falmouth and back, in connection with the determination of the longitude of that port. The period during which they were absent from the Royal Observatory has been disregarded.

† During this trial, all the chronometers were sent to the Baltic for a fortnight. This period has been disregarded.

‡ These were eight-day chronometers.

. This maker also won the second premium.

** The daily rate of this machine was very large—approximately 15 seconds per day, losing.

¶ In this and subsequent years the premiums were £200, £170 and £130.

— No machine qualified for the first premium, and the first and second were awarded in lieu of the second and third.

‖ No machine qualified for the first or second premiums, and in consequence these were not awarded.

‖. This machine was barely within the limits governing the award of the third premium.

The following table gives the trial numbers, and brief notes of any constructional peculiarities, of the first machines in each year.

It may be noted that until the institution of separate trials of deck-watches, in 1888, the Greenwich trials were open not only to box-chronometers but to pocket ones as well. The last of these to figure in a trial appears to be Reid 2210, entered in 1871, and withdrawn by its maker during the trial.

Another peculiarity of the table is the fact that it does not contain a single eight-day chronometer. One by Frodsham, 3593, was second in 1883, with the excellent trial number of 15·9, and another by the same maker, 3597, was fourth in 1885, but no machine of this type has ever headed the list in the annual trials, although two winners in the " premium " trials were of that pattern.

GREENWICH TRIALS, 1840—1914.

Year.	Maker's Name and No.	Remarks.	*a.*	*b.*	Trial No (*a*—2*b*).
1840	Molyneux & Sons	No details available	11.4	4.3	20.0
1841	Litherland & Davies, 915/18279	No details available	15.5	4.1	23.7
1842	Molyneux, 2166	No details available	10.0	4.6	19.2
1843	Molyneux, 2185	No details available	11.1	5.1	21 3
1844	Appleton, 468	No details available	13.3	5.0	23.3
1845	Poole, 1155	No details available	7.6	6.7	21.0
1846	Hutton, 138	No details available	11.7	7.6	26.9
1847	Massey, 123	No details available	7.2	5.6	18.4
1848	Loseby, 115	No details available	8.7	4.6	17.9
1849	Eiffe, 662	No details available	13.2	10.3	33.8
1850	Loseby, 123	Loseby's mercurial balance	12.7	4.7	22.1
1851	Loseby, 127	Loseby's mercurial balance	16 5	4.4	25.3
1852	Loseby, 125	Loseby's mercurial balance	11.7	9.4	30.5
1853	Lister & Son	Auxiliary compensation	16.4	11.6	39.6
1854	Poole, 1585	Poole's auxiliary	8.6	4.5	17.6
1855	Lawson, 1163	Auxiliary compensation (Poole's)	17.4	6.4	30.2
1856	J. Muirhead, 2119	Poole's auxiliary	23.1	6.8	36.7
1857	Hornby, 1300	Hartnup's balance	23.9	7.3	38.5
1858	Blackie, 497	Auxiliary compensation (unpublished)	14.3	6.2	26.7
1859	Campbell, 837	Ordinary balance with slight alteration	9.6	4.7	19.0
1860	Birchall, 642	Ordinary balance with slight alteration	18.1	3.6	25.3
1861	McGregor, 2776	Poole's auxiliary	14.1	5.2	24.6
1862	Simpson & Roberts, 9/1161	Kullberg's " flat rim " balance	10.9	5.7	22.3
1863	Fletcher, 2690	Auxiliary compensation	6.8	3.6	14.0
1864	Kullberg, 760	Kullberg's " flat-rim " balance	11.2	3.7	18.6
1865	Webb, 5388	Auxiliary compensation	8.7	5.0	18.7
1866	McGregor, 3795	Auxiliary compensation	7.4	5.8	19.0
1867	Sewill, 2263	Auxiliary compensation	9.0	3.6	16.2
1868	Birchall, 1069	Ordinary balance with slight alteration	8.3	4.1	16.5
1869	Fletcher, 2972	Auxiliary compensation	7.9	4.7	17.3
1870	M. F. Dent, 2533	Ordinary balance with extra long rims	5.5	3.8	13.1
1871	Frodsham, 3423	Frodsham's reversed balance	7.8	3.7	15.2
1872	Kullberg, 1799	Kullberg's " flat-rim " balance	10.6	2.8	16.2
1873	Weichert, 2,300	Kullberg's " flat-rim " balance	5.1	3.0	11.1
1874	Sewill, 3084	Auxiliary compensation	9.9	5.7	21.3
1875	Highley, 5435	Auxiliary acting in cold	6.2	3.3	12.8
1876	Graham & Parkes, 1283/21493	Poole's auxiliary	7.0	2.9	12.8
1877	Isaac, 1612	Unpublished auxiliary	9.0	3.5	16.0

GREENWICH TRIALS—*continued.*

Year.	Maker's Name and No.	Remarks.	a.	b.	Trial No. (a—2b).
1878	Pyott, 478	Ordinary balance with slight addition	11.0	5.5	22.0
1879	Keys, 282	Ordinary balance with slight alteration	6.0	2.9	11.8
1880	Cornell, 5658	No details available	16.3	3.7	23.7
1881	Kullberg, 3972	Reversed detent with short spring	8.4	2.3	13.0
1882	Kullberg, 4066	Reversed detent with short spring	5.1	2.0	9.1
1883	Kullberg, 4067	Reversed detent with short spring	8.2	3.4	15.0
1884	Brunner, 3777	No details available	8.0	3.2	14.4
1885	Kullberg, 4139	Reversed detent with short spring	10.3	4.6	19.5
1886	Uhrig, 453	Continuously acting auxiliary	4.0	2.8	9.6
1887	Uhrig, 452	No details available	6.8	3.2	13.2
1888	Kullberg, 4915	Auxiliary: palladium spring: reversed detent	5.3	3.7	12.7
1889	Kullberg, 4739	Auxiliary: palladium spring: reversed detent	3.7	2.7	9.1
1890	Uhrig, 514	Continuously acting auxiliary	8.4	2.6	13.6
1891	Kullberg, 5162	Reversed detent with short spring	8.8	4.7	18.2
1892	Uhrig, 502	Continuously acting auxiliary	10.7	3.6	17.9
1893	Isaac, 1933	Auxiliary compensation	8.5	3.3	15.1
1894	Kullberg, 5433	Auxiliary compensation: reversed detent	3.7	3.4	10.5
1895	Kullberg, 5512	Ordinary balance: palladium balance spring	5.6	3.6	12.8
1896	Kullberg, 6059	Auxiliary compensation: palladium balance-spring	5.1	3.7	12.5
1897	Gardner, 5/4162	Auxiliary compensation: palladium balance-spring	6.0	2.8	11.6
1898	Usher & Cole, 8237	Ordinary balance: palladium balance-spring	6.9	2.5	11.9
1899	Kullberg, 6564	Auxiliary compensation: palladium balance-spring: reversed detent	8.0	3.2	14.4
1900	Kullberg, 6673	Auxiliary compensation: palladium balance-spring: reversed detent	6.7	2.5	11.7
1901	Johannsen & Co., 5219	Auxiliary acting in heat: palladium balance-spring	5.3	2.5	10.3
1902	Johannsen & Co., 5217	Auxiliary acting in heat: palladium balance-spring	7.0	3.2	13.4
1903	Kullberg, 6620	Auxiliary compensation: palladium balance-spring: reversed detent	5.8	3.0	11.8
1904	Kullberg, 7273	Auxiliary compensation: palladium balance-spring	9.0	3.0	15.0
1905	Kullberg, 7583	Auxiliary compensation: palladium balance-spring: reversed detent	8.6	4.6	17.8
1906	Kullberg, 7612	Auxiliary compensation: palladium balance-spring	7.5	3.3	14.1
1907	Johannsen & Co., 6150	Auxiliary acting in heat: palladium balance-spring	14.1	5.5	25.1
1908	Kullberg, 8042	Auxiliary compensation: palladium balance-spring: reversed detent	6.7	4.4	15.5
1909	Kullberg, 8075	Auxiliary compensation: palladium balance-spring	5.0	2.6	10.2
1910	Kullberg, 8159	Auxiliary compensation: palladium balance-spring	6.6	2.3	11.2
1911	T. Mercer, 8306	Mercer's auxiliary: palladium balance-spring	5.0	2.6	10.2
1912	Kullberg, 8361	Auxiliary compensation: palladium balance-spring	5.2	2.4	10.0
1913	Kullberg, 8472	Auxiliary compensation: palladium balance-spring: reversed detent	4.9	2.5	9.9
1914	Kullberg, 8734	Auxiliary compensation: palladium balance-spring	6.2	3.4	13.0

APPENDIX II.

An account of the going of Thomas Mudge's first timekeeper at the Royal Observatory, Greenwich, from April 8th to October 29th, 1777.

NOTE.—This machine was on trial at the Observatory from December 14th, 1774, to March 12th, 1775 (when it stopped with a broken mainspring), and from November 11th, 1776, to February 26th, 1778, when it again stopped from the same cause.

The period for which particulars of its performance are given corresponds in length to that of a modern Greenwich trial (29 weeks). It has been selected so as to give, as far as possible, a correct idea of the machine's capabilities. It eliminates the early portion of the trial, during which the machine exhibited the customary acceleration, and a period, at its close, during which the temperature sank below 40°, and, having thus exceeded the designed range of the compensation, produced a further acceleration.

The trial number, obtained from the formula $(a+2b)$, is the remarkably low one of 11.73. The range of temperature during the 29 weeks was from 41° to 70° Fahr. In those days, of course, there was no oven test. The machine, which is shown in Plate XVIII., was fitted with a very complicated constant force escapement, and with two compensation curbs in lieu of a compensation balance.

The daily rates, which have been accurately transcribed from the original MS. register at Greenwich, were not, of course, directly obtained to the hundredth part of a second. This apparently-suspicious accuracy arises from the fact that the comparisons were subsequently corrected for the rate of the transit-clock, which was very small, and generally obtained by interpolation between observations several days apart.

Number of Week.	Date.		Daily Rate.	Weekly Sum of Daily Rates.	Thermometer.
1	April	8	+3·65	26.11	42°
		9	3·69		44°
		10	3·82		47°
		11	3·67		54°
		12	3·70		52°
		13	3·56		51°
		14	4·02		48°
2		15	3·79	25.35	46°
		16	4·35		44°
		17	3·59		44°
		18	3·86		41°
		19	3·40		42°
		20	3·05		44°
		21	3·31		49°
3		22	3·08	25.05	52°
		23	3·63		53°
		24	3·89		51°
		25	3·68		49°
		26	3·68		49°
		27	3·15		47°
		28	3·94		48°
4		29	3·69	24.50	49°
		30	3·21		50°
	May	1	3·27		54°
		2	3·26		54°
		3	3·36		54°
		4	3·88		54°
		5	3·83		54°
5		6	3·59	24.73	54°
		7	3·57		55°
		8	3·72		54°
		9	3·60		56°
		10	3·51		54°
		11	3·32		51°
		12	3·42		53°
6		13	3·68	24.87	53°
		14	3·54		53°
		15	3·64		53°
		16	3·59		51°
		17	3·65		50°
		18	3·22		52°
		19	3·55		53°

Number of Week.	Date.		Daily Rate.	Weekly Sum of Daily Rates.	Thermo-meter.
7	May	20	+3·57	23.73	51°
		21	3·34		51°
		22	3·43		53°
		23	3·14		55°
		24	3·42		55°
		25	3·09		56°
		26	3·74		56°
8		27	3·03	24.26	57°
		28	3·66		60°
		29	3·66		57°
		30	3·29		60°
		31	3·59		62°
	June	1	3·64		63°
		4*	3·39		66°
9		5	4·09	26.36	63°
		6	3·81		60°
		7	3·87		59°
		8	3·61		59°
		9	3·74		55°
		10	3·79		53°
		11	3·45		52°
10		12	3·93	24.26	53°
		13	3·43		55°
		14	3·56		57°
		15	3·39		57°
		16	3·30		58°
		17	3·12		59°
		18	3·53		58°
11		19	3·55	24.40	57°
		20	3·20		58°
		21	3·34		60°
		22	3·56		60°
		23	3·73		58°
		24	3·25		58°
		25	3·77		58°

* Owing to the cleaning and regulation of the transit clock, there is no recorded rate of the timekeeper for June 2nd, and no rate of the transit clock for either the 2nd or the 3rd. I have accordingly discarded these two days, during which, as far as can be seen, the timekeeper went with its usual regularity.

Number of Week.	Date.		Daily Rate.	Weekly Sum of Daily Rates.	Thermometer.
12	June	26	+3·59	24.88	60°
		27	3·81		59°
		28	3·57		59°
		29	3·53		59°
		30	3·46		60°
	July	1	3·63		58°
		2	3·29		60°
13		3	3·41	23.85	60°
		4	3·34		59°
		5	3·43		58°
		6	3·43		59°
		7	3·45		58°
		8	3·25		57°
		9	3·54		56°
14		10	3·28	23.54	57°
		11	2·88		61°
		12	3·26		64°
		13	3·46		65°
		14	3·71		67°
		15	3·56		67°
		16	3·39		69°
15		17	3·39	26.42	70°
		18	3·86		70°
		19	3·49		68°
		20	4·37		64½°
		21	3·84		62½°
		22	3·83		62°
		23	3·64		64°
16		24	3·48	25.10	63°
		25	3·84		59°
		26	3·66		58°
		27	3·61		59°
		28	3·78		58°
		29	3·30		59°
		30	3·43		60°
17		31	3·65	24.68	60°
	August	1	3·09		61°
		2	3·93		59°
		3	3·58		61°
		4	3·44		61°
		5	3·62		61°
		6	3·37		61°

Number of Week.	Date.	Daily Rate.	Weekly Sum of Daily Rates.	Thermometer.
18	August 7	+3·47	24.44	62°
	8	3·34		66°
	9	3·65		66°
	10	3·77		66°
	11	3·26		65°
	12	3·40		66°
	13	3·55		66°
19	14	4·32	24.84	67°
	15	3·35		68°
	16	3·60		68°
	17	3·25		68°
	18	3·39		67°
	19	3·79		65°
	20	3·14		67°
20	21	3·27	22.94	65°
	22	3·30		63°
	23	3·19		61°
	24	3·46		65°
	25	3·54		65°
	26	3·31		66°
	27	2·87		65°
21	28	3·41	24.51	66°
	29	3·77		65°
	30	3·55		63°
	31	3·19		62°
	September 1	3·58		60°
	2	3·60		60°
	3	3·41		58°
22	4	3·75	23.70	58°
	5	3·42		60°
	6	3·43		62°
	7	3·15		63°
	8	3·39		64°
	9	3·24		65°
	10	3·32		64°
23	11	3·19	25.24	64°
	12	3·54		63°
	13	3·30		62°
	14	3·67		61°
	15	3·85		59
	16	3·90		58°
	17	3·79		59°

Number of Week.	Date.	Daily Rate.	Weekly Sum of Daily Rates.	Thermometer.
24	September 18	+3·69	27.73	62°
	19	3·53		62°
	20	3·58		60°
	21	3·98		58°
	22	4·39		58°
	23	4·49		56°
	24	4·07		56°
25	25	4·23	27.98	59°
	26	4·18		64°
	27	3·87		64°
	28	3·83		66°
	29	4·02		65°
	30	4·18		63°
	October 1	3·67		60°
26	2	4·20	27.10	60°
	3	4·08		58°
	4	3·73		59°
	5	3·96		59°
	6	3·58		59°
	7	3·58		61°
	8	3·97		57°
27	9	3·83	27.66	57°
	10	3·97		57°
	11	3·96		58°
	12	4·39		56
	13	4·30		54°
	14	3·96		54°
	15	3·25		56°
28	16	3·96	28.91	57°
	17	4·14		56°
	18	3·87		55°
	19	4·02		52°
	20	4·07		50°
	21	4·45		47°
	22	4·40		45°
29	23	3·94	28.35	46°
	24	4·03		49°
	25	4·32		50°
	26	3·66		53°
	27	4·03		50°
	28	4·49		48°
	29	3·88		51°

GENERAL INDEX.

NOTE.—The letter *f* after a page number denotes that the information required is contained in a footnote on that page, and not in the text. If common to both, only the page is indexed.

In one or two cases, *e.g.*, 82A, 234B, it will be noticed that extra pages, to contain late information, have been inserted after the numbering of the pages was completed.

(?) after any item indicates that the statement to which it refers is of doubtful accuracy.

In arranging the entries under sub-heads, when such occur, two methods have been followed. In the case of historical characters, such as Harrison, the order of the entries is that of the pages, and hence roughly chronological. In the case of sub-heads such as "Balance spring," where chronological arrangement is less important, the order is alphabetical.

SPECIAL INDEX

to explanations of technical terms.

NOTE.—As stated on p. 18A the explanations given, either in the text or the footnotes, of various technical horological terms are here collected for reference. They may also be found by means of the General Index.